love soup

ALSO BY ANNA THOMAS

The Vegetarian Epicure

The Vegetarian Epicure, Book Two

The New Vegetarian Epicure: Menus for Family and Friends

love soup

160 ALL-NEW VEGETARIAN RECIPES

from the author of *The Vegetarian Epicure*

anna thomas

ILLUSTRATIONS BY ANNIKA HUETT

W. W. NORTON & COMPANY
NEW YORK   LONDON

For information about permission to reproduce selections from this book,
write to Permissions, W. W. Norton & Company, Inc.,
500 Fifth Avenue, New York, NY 10110

For information about special discounts for bulk purchases, please contact
W. W. Norton Special Sales at specialsales@wwnorton.com or 800-233-4830

Manufacturing by Courier Westford
Book design by Studio 421
Production manager: Devon Zahn

Library of Congress Cataloging-in-Publication Data

Thomas, Anna.
Love soup : 160 all-new vegetarian recipes from the author of The Vegetarian Epicure /
Anna Thomas ; illustrations by Annika Huett.
p. cm.
Includes index.
ISBN 978-0-393-06479-7 (hardcover)—ISBN 978-0-393-33257-5 (pbk.)
1. Soups. 2. Vegetarian cookery. I. Title.
TX757.T47 2009
641.5′636—dc22

2009019632

W. W. Norton & Company, Inc.
500 Fifth Avenue, New York, N.Y. 10110
www.wwnorton.com

W. W. Norton & Company Ltd.
Castle House, 75/76 Wells Street, London W1T 3QT

1 2 3 4 5 6 7 8 9 0

To the farmers

And to all the workers who labor
in the fields and the orchards

Thank you! Gracias!

VEGAN-FRIENDLY

To make the book vegan-friendly (and here's a shout-out to my two vegan sons), vegan recipes are indicated with a **V** in the table of contents. This designation includes recipes that are entirely vegan and those that are vegan up to the point of the garnish.

contents

introduction · · · 18

how to shop · · · 28

a word about equipment · · · 33

a few practical notes · · · 36

CHAPTER 1: broths · · · 41

Basic Light Vegetable Broth • **V** · · · 47

Basic Root Vegetable Broth • **V** · · · 49

Basic Dark Vegetable Broth • **V** · · · 50

Vegetable and Ginger Broth • **V** · · · 52

Vegetable Broth with No Onions • **V** · · · 53

Pea Pod Broth • **V** · · · 55

Mushroom Stock • **V** · · · 56

fall and winter soups

CHAPTER 2: beautiful fall soups · · · 61

Menu · · · 64

Potato and Tomato Soup with Sage • **V** · · · 66

Fennel and Onion Soup • **V** · · · 68

Sopa de Poblanos · · · 70

Chard and Yam Soup • **V** · · · 72

Roasted Golden Beet Soup • **V** · · · 74

Old-Fashioned Cream of Mushroom Soup · · · 76

Puree of Carrot and Yam with Citrus and Spices • **V** · · · 78

Creamy Potato and Roasted Garlic Soup · · · 80

CHAPTER 3: green soups . . . 85

Menu . . . 88

Green Soup • **V** . . . 90

Green Soup with Mushrooms • **V** . . . 92

Green Soup with Sweet Potatoes and Sage • **V** . . . 94

Green Soup with Ginger • **V** . . . 96

Arugula and Apple Soup • **V** . . . 98

Kale and Sweet Potato Soup with Cumin and Lemon • **V** . . . 100

Parsley Soup . . . 102

CHAPTER 4: winter squash soups . . . 105

Menu . . . 109

Roasted Kabocha Squash and Celery Root Soup . . . 111

Spicy Butternut Ginger Soup • **V** . . . 114

Roasted Turnip and Winter Squash Soup . . . 116

Red Lentil and Squash Soup • **V** . . . 118

Winter Squash and Yam Soup with Poblano Peppers • **V** . . . 120

Tomatillo, Squash, and Mustard Greens Soup • **V** . . . 122

CHAPTER 5: bean soups . . . 125

Menu . . . 128

White Bean and Garlic Soup with Greens • **V** . . . 130

Fasolia Gigante Soup with Spinach • **V** . . . 132

Green Lentil Soup with Cumin and Lemon • **V** . . . 134

Lima Bean Soup • **V** . . . 136

Menu . . . 138

Black Bean and Squash Soup • **V** . . . 140

Spicy Black Bean Soup with Sweet Peppers • **V** . . . 142

Old-Fashioned Split Pea Soup • **V** . . . 145

Carol's Finnish Pea Soup with Apples • **V** . . . 147

CHAPTER 6: the comfort of soup in deep winter . . . 151

Menu . . . 154
Sopa de Ajo . . . 156
Rustic Leek and Potato Soup . . . 158
Vegetarian Onion Soup Gratin . . . 160
Mushroom-Barley Soup with Cabbage . . . 162
Spicy Indonesian Yam and Peanut Soup • **V** . . . 164
Roasted Root Vegetable Soup • **V** . . . 166
Cauliflower Bisque . . . 169
Neeps and Tatties Soup . . . 172
Caramelized Cabbage Soup . . . 174

CHAPTER 7: big soups and stews . . . 177

Menu . . . 180
The Great Pumpkin Soup • **V** . . . 182
Pickle Soup • **V** . . . 185
Hearty Brown Lentil Soup • **V** . . . 188
Ten-Vegetable Soup with Cranberry Beans • **V** . . . 190
Minestrone for a Crowd • **V** . . . 193
Menu . . . 196
French Lentil Stew with Roasted Carrots and Mint • **V** . . . 198
Stewed Root Vegetables with Moroccan Spices • **V** . . . 200
Kabocha Squash and Cranberry Bean Stew • **V** . . . 203
Farro with Stewed and Roasted Winter Vegetables • **V** . . . 206
Quinoa Stew with Potatoes, Spinach, and Chard . . . 210
Three-Bean and Vegetable Chili • **V** . . . 212

CHAPTER 8: holiday soups . . . 217

Menu . . . 220
Christmas Eve Porcini Soup . . . 222
Beet Soup with Ginger • **V** . . . 226
Persimmon Soup • **V** . . . 228
Sweet Potato Bisque . . . 231
Chestnut Soup . . . 233

spring and summer soups

CHAPTER 9: first tastes of spring . . . 239

Menu . . . 243

Asparagus Bisque with Fresh Dill . . . 245

Sorrel Soup with Mint and Spring Vegetables • **V** . . . 247

Fresh Pea Soup with Mint Cream . . . 249

Purple Cauliflower Soup • **V** . . . 252

Carrot, Orange, and Ginger Soup • **V** . . . 254

Menu . . . 256

Springtime Barley and Mushroom Soup • **V** . . . 258

Fresh Fava Bean and Sweet Pea Soup • **V** . . . 260

Rustic Artichoke and Potato Stew • **V** . . . 262

Creamy Artichoke Soup . . . 266

Curried Spinach and Sorrel Soup . . . 269

CHAPTER 10: green and greener . . . 273

Menu . . . 276

Spring Green Soup • **V** . . . 278

Snap Pea, Asparagus, and Fennel Soup • **V** . . . 280

A Word About Nettles . . . 282

Nettle and Kale Soup • **V** . . . 284

Nettle Soup with Fennel and Leeks • **V** . . . 286

Potage of Baby Spring Greens • **V** . . . 288

Green Soup with Broccoli, Fennel, and Sorrel • **V** . . . 290

CHAPTER 11: sweet summer · · · 293

Menu · · · 298

Butter Bean and Summer Vegetable Soup • **V** · · · 300

Sweet Corn Soup · · · 302

Smoky Eggplant Soup with Mint and Pine Nuts · · · 304

Escarole and Potato Soup • **V** · · · 307

Menu · · · 309

Zucchini and Basil Soup • **V** · · · 311

Zucchini and Potato Soup • **V** · · · 313

Charred Zucchini Soup with Yogurt and Pine Nuts · · · 315

Menu · · · 318

Summer Tomato and Basil Soup • **V** · · · 320

Tomato and Fennel Soup with Blood Orange · · · 322

Cannellini and Golden Tomato Soup • **V** · · · 324

Tomato and Zucchini Soup with Summer Herbs • **V** · · · 326

Pappa al Pomodoro • **V** · · · 328

CHAPTER 12: hearty soups of summer · · · 331

Menu · · · 334

Corn and Cheese Chowder · · · 336

Tortilla Soup · · · 338

Mung Bean Soup with Spinach and Tomatoes • **V** · · · 341

Corn and Pepper Soup • **V** · · · 343

Kale and Tomato Soup • **V** · · · 345

Menu · · · 347

Deconstructed Hummus Soup • **V** · · · 350

Vegetable Soup Pistou • **V** · · · 352

Roasted Eggplant and Garbanzo Bean Soup • **V** · · · 355

Summer Minestrone · · · 358

CHAPTER 13: cold soups . . . 361
    Menu · · · 364
    Gazpacho Andaluz • **V** · · · 366
    Cold Cucumber-Cilantro Soup · · · 368
    Cold Cucumber and Avocado Soup • **V** · · · 369
    Cold Asparagus Soup · · · 371
    Cold Cucumber and Mint Soup with Radishes · · · 373
    Cold Cream of Poblano Peppers with Red Grapes · · · 375
    Cold Cherry-Lemon Soup · · · 377
    Chilled Melon Soup with Mint · · · 379
    Cold Peach and Nectarine Soup with Strawberry Sauce · · · 381

from soup to meal

CHAPTER 14: a few good breads . . . 387
    Three-Grain Bread • **V** · · · 390
    Whole-Wheat Walnut Bread • **V** · · · 392
    Oatmeal Molasses Bread · · · 394
    Grandma's Dinner Rolls · · · 397
    Olive and Rosemary Focaccia • **V** · · · 400
    Potato Pizza · · · 402
    Irish Soda Bread · · · 405
    Fresh Corn and Cheddar Cheese Cornbread · · · 407
    Quick Whole-Wheat Oatmeal Bread · · · 408
    Popovers · · · 409
    Multigrain Scones with Fennel and Orange · · · 411
    Savory Walnut and Herb Biscuits · · · 413
    Crostini • **V** · · · 415
    Parmesan Crostini · · · 417
    Parmesan and Fennel Biscotti · · · 418

CHAPTER 15: hummus and company ... 421

Sprouted Garbanzo Hummus • **V** ... 425

Tapenade with Figs and Citrus • **V** ... 428

Persian Spinach Spread ... 429

Marbled Cannellini Dip with Roasted Tomatoes • **V** ... 431

Lima Bean Spread • **V** ... 433

Eggplant and Roasted Garlic Pesto • **V** ... 434

Simple Basil Pesto • **V** ... 436

Parsley and Walnut Pesto • **V** ... 438

Simple Chipotle Sauce • **V** ... 439

Ancho and Guajillo Chile Puree • **V** ... 440

Table Salsa • **V** ... 442

Harissa • **V** ... 444

Croutons • **V** ... 446

Jeri's Spiced Nuts • **V** ... 448

Grilled Goat Cheese Sandwich ... 450

Sara's Spinach Pie ... 452

Tortilla Española with Charred Red Peppers ... 454

Black Bean Quesadillas ... 456

CHAPTER 16: salads for summer and winter ... 459

Salad of Baby Arugula, Aged Jack Cheese, and Asian Pears ... 462

Barley Salad with Corn and Zucchini • **V** ... 464

Chopped Salad with French Green Lentils ... 466

Cucumber, Rice, and Fresh Herb Salad ... 468

Summer Chopped Salad with Grilled Halloumi ... 470

Heirloom Tomato Salad ... 471

Kale Salad with Cranberries and Walnuts • **V** ... 473

Red Cabbage and Apple Salad • **V** ... 476

Brown Rice and Chinese Cabbage Salad • **V** ... 477

Lentil and Spinach Salad • **V** ... 479

Napa Cabbage Slaw • **V** ... 481

CHAPTER 17: a few easy sweets . . . 485

Butter Cake with Summer Fruits · · · 488
Octavia's Gingerbread · · · 490
Olive Oil and Lemon Cake · · · 492
Angel Cookies · · · 494
Lauren's Badass Trailmix Cookies · · · 495
Bittersweet Chocolate Brownies · · · 497
Farmhouse Apple Crumble · · · 499
Rice Pudding with Dried Cranberries · · · 501
Greek Yogurt with Honey and Walnuts · · · 502
Melons in Orange and Mint Syrup • **V** · · · 503
Tangerine and Strawberry Compote • **V** · · · 505

sincere thanks · · · 506
index · · · 509

love soup

introduction

HOW I LEARNED TO COOK

I grew up in an immigrant family, passing my childhood in a leafy neighborhood in Detroit, Michigan, where all the kids I ran around with in the backyards and streets yelled in English and all the families who came into our house spoke Polish. This felt entirely normal to me.

In the kitchen of the sturdy brick house my father built, cooking was always going on. My mother made stuffed cabbage rolls, mushroom pierogi with beet broth, cucumber salads drenched in sour cream and dill, cottage cheese dumplings, a hunter's stew full of sausage and sauerkraut, thin buttery pancakes—and Old World soups: krupnik, barszcz, and chlodnik, soups that were eaten with slabs of dark bread smeared with more butter. There were many family gatherings, and they were always at home. I don't remember eating in a restaurant until we moved to California, when I was ten, making the great trek across the country in a station wagon and stopping at roadside cafes.

I didn't start cooking until I left home to go to college and had to learn to live on my own. What I didn't realize then was that I had already learned something primal in the kitchen in Michigan. I knew that taking simple, fresh ingredients into a kitchen and turning them into a nourishing meal was part of the natural rhythm of life. I couldn't cook yet, but home cooking was already part of me.

Scraping by on student loans and dreadful jobs, I made food for myself and my college friends and taught myself to be a pretty good home cook. I was moving away from meat then, but the vegetarian culture of that time—the self-denying school—did not appeal to me. I wanted food to be pleasure as well as nourishment, and so I began to develop my own style. And then I wrote a book. What audacity!

The Vegetarian Epicure would change my life. Blithe and fearless as only someone so young can be, I sent off a manuscript to New York, a foreign land, and turned my attention back to my film classes. To my amazement, the book was published—and then sold and sold. It turned out that there were many other people who had stopped eating meat, but had not stopped *eating*.

I had written about the things that I liked: food that drew on tradition but was not bound by it, vegetarian food that tasted real and didn't try to imitate anything else, food that wasn't apologetic but was fresh and delicious. That just seemed sensible to me; I had no idea it was revolutionary.

The revolution for me was that I could quit my job as a waitress and finish my student films. Many years later, when I was at a book-signing party for my third cookbook, a man about my age came up to me and said, "I bought your first book when it was published in the seventies. You helped me get through college, and I want to thank you." I shook his hand and replied, "I want to thank you. You helped *me* get through college, so we're even."

When I left university I worked in film and I traveled; I ate and drank my way through great cities and tiny villages. In Italy I discovered pappa al pomodoro and Tuscan bean soups, and in Greece avgolemono. In Lisbon I ate a bowl of caldo verde, the famous peasant soup of kale and potatoes. I remember it distinctly. Years later it was the influence for my Green Soup. In France I got a Ph.D. in sorrel soups. I married a Mexican American and spent time in Mexico, honing my taste for the pre-Columbian flavors of chiles, chocolate, corn, and black beans.

Cooking was always fun. I never cooked professionally, so I always cooked only what I felt like cooking, for the people I loved. And the more I learned, the more my cooking moved in the direction of simple, vibrant foods made from fresh, local ingredients. Canned and processed foods played a very small part in my kitchen. Farmers' markets drew me like magnets. I wanted food that had history but also a future.

When I had my first baby, a good friend who was already a mom came over with gift-wrapped booties—and a big pot of soup. It was a simple minestrone, with vegetables from her garden, some kidney beans, good olive oil, and chunky pasta. I nearly wept with joy. The era of soup saving my life had begun.

Decades later, when my own mother was old and no longer able to cook and her appetite was gone, I thought, how can I tempt her to eat? I made soup for her, in a leisurely way, in her own kitchen. She watched, contented, as I chopped up vegetables and dropped them in the pot. It was Pickle Soup, the funny name we gave to a hearty soup that had all the remembered flavors of her krupnik and then some. I put the love I felt into that soup kettle with the barley and mushrooms and carrots and potatoes and the finely diced dill pickle that gave the soup its piquant mystery. How happy I was when she ate it and wanted more.

Between those two moments, I faced the question of all mothers: what will children eat? I surrounded my boys with fresh food, and I hoped for the best. I tried to impart to them my sense of the important things: eat real food, cook and have fun with it, share and enjoy.

In that intensely busy time of children and work, soup became my stalwart friend and I learned its true value. Anyone who's been there knows. You're busy, too much to do, time vanishes, the kids are relentless, and everyone is hungry all the time. Something as comforting, delicious, and practical as soup is like gold.

I made easy soups—fresh tomato and rice in the summer, or zucchini soup, because there was never a shortage of zucchini in the garden. Split pea soup in the winter—always one of their favorites—or black bean soup with cornbread. Minestrone anytime. Green Soup came later, when they were teenagers, and it was like a miracle to see them eat it. Along the way, a collection of easy "go-with" foods emerged, special quesadillas that they invented themselves, hummus with pita toasts, dense cornbread—things that turned a bowl of soup into a quick meal between school and soccer.

Soup was the convenience food that fit my philosophy of cooking: start with the best fresh ingredients. It doesn't need to be fancy, but it must be good to begin with or it won't be good in the end. Whenever you can, eat in season and eat local, but don't be rigid—keep having fun.

THE 81-INCH KITCHEN

When the babies grew up and went away to college, my affair with soup entered a new phase: downsize house, upsize soups. For years I had cooked in a spacious old kitchen, a room where a dozen people could cook together with ease. There was even a sofa for kibbitzers. Then I found myself in a kitchen where two people, moving with care, could not avoid bumping butts. It was a temporary kitchen, just for a few months. So I thought.

I had bought a house with lovely views, but it needed to be rebuilt. There was an artist's studio attached to the house, a loftlike industrial space that could be my home during the construction. I gutted it, painted it, and tucked a tiny kitchen under the stairs to the sleeping loft. It was 81 inches from wall to wall.

I packed away all the special pots and pans, the bread machine, pasta maker, and toaster oven, the platters and decanters, and kept only those things I absolutely had to have. I sacrificed a toaster to make room for my *molcahete*, the stone mortar I use to grind spices and salsa. No microwave, but I kept my food processor and my blender. One box of cereal in the pantry, but three or four bottles of good olive oil.

What I really needed was the ability to laugh at my own folly. Two and a half years later, I was still cooking in the 81-inch kitchen. And what was I cooking there? Soup, of course.

Scaling down forced me to rethink what was important to me. I wanted homemade food. I didn't need fancy meals, but I did want relaxed evenings with my friends over good food and a glass of wine. And although I cooked a little of everything in that wee kitchen, more and more I found myself turning to soup.

Here was the first and best comfort food, so easy to make with so little fuss. Real food that was *possible*. It was autumn when I moved into the studio, so I had people over for a bowl of Green Soup. I added a tomato salad with herbs and white beans, and a loaf from the local bakery. I put out a dish of olive oil for dipping. A plate with crumbly blue cheese and walnuts. A good bottle of wine. It was casual, and everyone relaxed. Another bottle of wine was opened. We found some dark chocolates for dessert. It was convivial and easy, and so good.

I found that all my friends, old and new, were delighted to come to the studio and have a soup supper. I would send out e-mails: "The soup kitchen is open." And I discovered the miracle of soup: if you make a pot of wonderful soup, even if every other thing you put on the table was picked up at the deli, you still get credit for a home-cooked meal!

I had many of those easy suppers: a hearty seasonal soup, a bread to go with it, something on the table for people to nibble—olives, hummus, goat cheese, or pesto, any or all. In midsummer, maybe a plate of ripe heirloom tomatoes with basil and garlic. In winter, a slaw of shredded Napa cabbage with brown rice and nuts. People quickly got the hang of it. They'd show up with chutney or home-cured olives. Once my friend Larry Yee came with all the makings of a spectacular roasted beet salad. How much fun it was to see these impromptu soup meals come together.

It was while cooking and sharing those easygoing meals in the studio that I decided to write a soup book. Now I'm moving into the main house. The kitchen island looks like an aircraft carrier to me—such an expanse, so pristine, ready for anything. I look forward to cooking there. But in the 81-inch kitchen I cooked a hundred delicious soups, and they couldn't have been better anywhere else. I learned once more that home cooking is always possible. Soup saved me again.

HOME COOKING, THE VANISHING ART

It seems to me that soup is the last best hope for home cooking.

So many people think they can't cook. They don't have the time, don't have the space or the right equipment, never learned how, fear they'll get it wrong. They watch someone else cook on TV, then order takeout. And so, little by little, the comforting ritual and real bodily nourishment of home cooking slips out of our lives.

Yet we long for it. We want to eat homemade food with our families. And wouldn't it be nice to invite some friends over for a casual meal?

Soup is the way in.

With soup, we can still cook at home, cook from scratch. Even a one-pot kitchen can handle it. Even someone who has never cooked before can fill that pot with bubbling soup. There are soups here with four or five ingredients, like Old-Fashioned Split Pea or Summer Tomato. And for the experienced cook, there are soups of great subtlety. Christmas Eve Porcini Soup has the complexity of a perfume, distilling the earth of ancient forests, the sweetness of winter onions cooked golden brown in butter, and the magic of cognac, all in a clear, delicate broth.

If you are new to the kitchen, these recipes will be your patient and friendly teacher. Start with something really easy. Go ahead—no one is looking. Open that bag of split peas and put them in a pot with water. Boil them a while, then add some cut-up carrots, onion, celery, and a few herbs. Leave that pot to simmer while you read a book or answer your e-mail, then finish it off with salt and pepper—and eat it. You've made Old-Fashioned Split Pea Soup. You're cooking.

Even a luxury soup can be pretty easy to make. Perhaps it is autumn and you have a big butternut squash providing sculptural interest on your counter. Put that squash in the oven to roast. As long as the oven is on, why not roast a few root vegetables, too? Cut up some onions and start them cooking slowly in a bit of olive oil. Stir the onions while you chop some ginger or slice up a pear, or both. By now the house smells like heaven. Anybody who walks in the door will be your willing slave.

When the squash is soft, which you can easily find out by poking it, scoop it out. Then put those vegetables in a pot with some nice broth, simmer it a while, and blast it with the immersion blender. There you are: a beautiful golden puree. Season it with salt and pepper and a little lemon juice. If you want to be fancy, stir in some cream or butter or mascarpone, or just a little more olive oil. Have you noticed that no measurements were mentioned in this little story?

Spicy Butternut and Ginger Soup and Roasted Kabocha Squash and Celery Root Soup are both that easy, and both are gorgeous and delicious. If you follow the recipe, you will have no problem. I write my recipes the way I like to get driving directions: a little extra information can't hurt. And if you are an intuitive cook, measuring with handfuls and dollops, then you will find here a world of seasonal inspiration and wonderful starting points.

WHAT WILL YOU FIND IN THIS BOOK? THE THINGS I LOVE . . .

You will find in these pages a library of soups to take you through the seasons, and a few things to go with those soups. But this is not the public library; it is a personal library, collected by me in my home.

Most of the soups are simple to make, and all of them are made from scratch, from fresh produce. It was a joy to cook my way through the seasons as I was making this book, shopping at the farmers' market. So that you can have the same pleasure wherever you live, I've organized the soups seasonally but very loosely: cold season, warm season.

My soups are vegetarian, and many are vegan. The evolution of my cooking has been away from butter, toward olive oil, and while I love cheese, I generally use it as a garnish.

I like to take familiar vegetables, the plain Janes of the produce stand, and let them be great—zucchini made brilliant with masses of basil and fresh lemon in Zucchini and Basil Soup; rutabagas and turnips roasted until they are succulent, golden nuggets for Roasted Root Vegetable Soup. But I also like to try something new, so you will find Nettle Soup with Fennel and Leeks and Persimmon Soup with Tamari-Toasted Walnuts. Why not?

I love dark leafy greens, fruity olive oil, the flavors of the Mediterranean, the heat of chiles, and fresh herbs in abundance—basil, cilantro, and mint are staples in my kitchen. I have favorite vegetables. Take me to the farm stand in October and I am helpless before the squashes—the butternuts, Tahitians, and gnarly-skinned kabochas, tough on the outside, golden and sweet on the inside. In August, I cannot resist the summer-ripe Purple Cherokee tomatoes. I love red-veined spinach, fresh asparagus, fava beans.

And I confess that I could not live without caramelized onions, soft and brown like a savory marmalade, or the taste of white beans simmered in garlic. I love to roast vegetables—even cabbages—to bring out their secret richness. I love homemade vegetable broths (but I'm a reasonable person and keep a few cans in the pantry for emergencies). I almost always add a touch of lemon juice or cayenne to a soup at the end to bring the flavors into focus, and I love that moment when the soup just comes alive.

I give the finishing touch to soups in the bowl, as they are being served. If you page through the recipes, you will see that many of them ask for a drizzle of fruity olive oil on top of each serving. I don't think of this as a garnish, something optional, a decoration. This use of the olive oil is essential; it completes the soup. I use a minimal amount of oil in cooking the soup and add the rest at the moment of serving; the raw, fresh juice of the olive has an entirely different flavor from oil that has been cooked.

I like to scatter toasted pine nuts across a velvety winter squash soup, or drop a spoonful of brick-red chile salsa into that golden puree. I am addicted to the combination of dark green soup and moist crumbles of feta cheese. Fresh pesto in minestrone. Pumpkin seeds or walnuts roasted with tamari and scattered over persimmon soup. Sour cream on a crimson bowl of sweet-tart cherry soup. Contrasting flavors and textures make the soup exciting: raw and cooked, sweet and salty, soft and crunchy, mild and spicy.

These things are all part of my style, and I hope you like it. But you have your style. It's my recipe in the book, but it's your soup in the pot. Play with it until it is just what you like. Then send me back *your* recipe. That's cooking—it's always about evolution and diffusion of ideas, which is another way of saying it's about sharing. The whole history of cuisines can be seen this way. Let's have a potluck—everyone bring something!

WHAT IS THE GREATEST SOUP?

The greatest soup is the one you learned from your mother when you were knocking around her knees in the kitchen. It's your history and your DNA. Your *Nonna*'s own minestrone. Sopa de ajo, the garlic soup that cures whatever ails you in the bitter Castilian winter. Tortilla soup with chiles and lime, to wake you up at any time of year.

Or Pickle Soup, the barley and vegetable soup that I made for my mom when she wouldn't eat much of anything but would still eat that soup. It was full of our shared history—her Polish traditions, and the way I made them my own.

The greatest soup is the one that is in season. Fresh Pea Soup with Mint Cream in April, Sweet Corn Soup in July. In August, a fresh tomato soup or Deconstructed Hummus, crazy with garlic and perfect with a glass of icy rosé. When the nights get cold, White Bean and Garlic Soup with Greens, and be sure to have big chunks of bread for dipping.

The greatest soup is the one your son, home from college, makes for you, showing off, forgetting that you taught him that soup in the first place.

The greatest soup is the one you make on Saturday with what you find at the farmers' market that morning. You put it together in a relaxed way in your kitchen, and it turns out delicious. So you invite a friend over and have it for lunch, or maybe dinner with a glass of wine and some cheese toast. You know how to cook.

There is a reason that we think of home cooking with nostalgia, that we speak of it in hopeful tones and are thankful when we encounter it. It makes life better. And soup is the food that can get us all cooking again, easily, happily. Anyone can make a good soup, and therefore a home-cooked meal, and therefore a better day.

There is an old Spanish saying, much repeated: "Of love and soup, the second is better." But I say, why choose? Be in love. Eat soup. Love soup!

how to shop

Over the years people have often asked me, "What can I do to improve my cooking?" I always answer, "Improve your shopping."

Here is the foundation of good cooking: use good ingredients. It may seem too obvious, but it is worth repeating. If you start with something good, you will likely finish with something good, perhaps even great. But no amount of skill or fussing can overcome poor ingredients.

Start with the best ingredients you can get, and treat them with respect. Your cooking will improve at once. This is true of even the simplest thing—a pot of soup. Good shopping is the first step in good cooking.

Today I buy most of my produce at my local farmers' market, but when I was in college and writing my first cookbook, there were no weekly farmers' markets. The flourishing movement of local markets that we have all over the country today simply didn't exist. I did my shopping at the supermarket, learning to pick through the vegetables and fruits to find the ones that felt fresh to me. I tried different stores, widening my range, foraging in other neighborhoods until I learned which markets actually cared about their produce, where I could find carrots with the greens attached instead of in a sealed plastic bag, and fruit that smelled like fruit.

I searched out ethnic stores; Asian and Latin American markets were everywhere. I went to the *mercado* in East L.A. and found staggering numbers of chiles, squashes I had not seen before, cilantro, fresh tortillas, and crates of sweet limes for pennies. I prowled the streets around the Orthodox church to find an excellent Greek market, where the olives were a revelation. In the summer, if I could get out of the city, I went to the farm stands that spring up on back roads everywhere, and I took advantage of friends' gardens and backyard fruit.

When the farmers' markets we know today were being started, many supermarket produce sections had one kind of lettuce and two varieties of apples, and the fresh herb selection was parsley. Today's shoppers have experienced the farmers' market and their expectations have changed, so all markets have had to step up. And there are new options all the time. My friend Peter has a microfarm and sells his beautiful seasonal vegetables by subscription. Every week I pick up a bushel basket full of just-picked, very local produce.

Depending on where you live, the good produce in your area might be in a natural foods store, a Chinese grocery, or a roadside stall. Wherever it is, find it. Don't settle for vegetables or fruits that are tired and wilted or that have been grown for longer shelf life rather than for flavor and food value.

SHOP AT THE FARMERS' MARKET!

That's the best piece of advice I can give. If you have a farmers' market near you, it's the single best shopping habit you will form to improve your overall relationship to food. You will shop fresh and shop seasonally. It happens automatically at the farmers' market. And you'll try new things—this is so easy in the convivial atmosphere of a market, where you are often buying directly from the person who grew the food. If you don't know what something is, just ask.

Selecting good produce is no mystery. Greens are firm and glossy. Fruit has fragrance and weight. It looks alive. You can choose produce by looking and smelling, but at the farmers' market you can taste as well. Have a second breakfast of a few mizuna leaves, a snap pea or two, a slice of apricot or melon, some wild arugula, a new or very old variety of tomato.

I love the farmers' market in Ojai, the little town where I live. You can find me there on most Sunday mornings, and I rarely have a list in my hand. I go with my old canvas bag and walk up and down the rows, slowly. Sometimes I buy flowers first, for the sheer pleasure. I chat with my favorite farmers. Getting to know the people who grow your food is one of the gratifying things about shopping at these markets. It has had a profound effect on my own relationship to cooking and eating. Not only is my food better, but I appreciate it more, and I have confidence in its freshness and safety.

I feel the seasons at the farmers' market. In the fall and winter I buy apples or pears in varieties I hadn't heard of a few years ago. I choose big Peter Rabbit cabbages, root vegetables of every kind, frilly purple kale, glossy chard, and gorgeous, sculptural winter squashes—Tahitians so huge they have to be cut in pieces, ghostly blue Hubbards, smooth butternuts, and gray-green kabochas with warty skin that belies their rich golden interior.

I might go home from the market and roast one of those squashes with some onions and green tomatoes, or make a Spicy Butternut Ginger Soup. Or I might make a Green Soup from an abundance of kale and a few shiitake mushrooms. This is how all these soups were first made. They are not fancy recipes, just the easy, fresh food that evolves from shopping at the farmers' market. In December, I really don't want eggplants flown in from Chile. I'd rather have an earthy lentil soup with leeks, or a soup of turnips and rutabagas and carrots, slow-roasted with onions until they are soft and glazed with their caramelized juices.

Around the holidays, pomegranates and persimmons are everywhere, along with fresh crops of walnuts and the first minuscule Pixie tangerines, sweet as candy. Dried fruits, new olive oil, preserves of all kinds, turn up at various stands. I start Christmas shopping.

In the spring I fill my basket with mounds of green peas in their pods and huge, velvety-skinned fava beans. I buy asparagus, blood oranges, sweet new lettuces, fennel, tiny purple artichokes, and maybe, if I get lucky, morels. As spring moves into summer, an air of excitement comes into the market with the first summer fruits. Crowds gather around the earliest cherries, the first crop of apricots. Later, as the weather heats up and tables are piled with peaches and plums and nectarines, the perfume of deep summer is intoxicating. Vendors urge their customers to taste, holding out juicy, dripping slices of fruit.

My market is not very big, but it suits me. I find what I need there, and over the years I've been introduced to many new things. It was at the farmers' market that I first saw Fuyu persimmons, kabocha squashes, mustard greens, fresh lima beans, green garlic, and dozens of other things that are now part of my repertoire. At my market, perfect strangers ask each other, "What do you do with that?" and cooking tips are exchanged on the spot. Sometimes I'm asking, and sometimes I'm telling.

It takes me about half an hour to do my weekly shopping at the farmers' market. I fill my trunk with beautiful seasonal fruits and vegetables, flowers and herbs. But that half-hour gives me much more than a carload of good food and a shot of bluegrass music from the local fiddlers. My approach to food and cooking is re-formed each time. The look, the smells, the tastes, the experience of each season's harvest—this is all immensely satisfying. It's fun, and it starts me thinking about what delicious thing I could make with this Russian kale or that knobby celery root in winter, or with the heirloom tomatoes and colorful eggplants in summer. I'm already cooking. The pleasure of the farmers' market stays with me, and I take it into the kitchen.

THE PANTRY

The basic supplies in your cupboard are the support system for the fresh food you buy. The pantry allows you to be spontaneous at the farmers' market, to bring back what inspires you and start cooking.

My list starts with great extra-virgin olive oil, at least a fruity one and a peppery one. It includes wine vinegar, chipotle chiles, Arborio rice, sea salt, a selection of beans and lentils, pine nuts, dried porcini. I always keep a few cans of a good vegetable broth on the shelf, as well as some excellent dried pasta and barley.

Then there are the exclamation points of my cooking: Lemon! Garlic! Ginger! Mint!

Chiles! These are staples, always in stock. And of course the herbs and spices, the drop of this and pinch of that which can make a dish shine.

Fresh herbs are widely available and always preferred. But occasionally we need to rely on dried herbs. Some of the herbs I use are ones I dry myself. They grow like weeds in my yard—sage, thyme, rosemary, oregano, marjoram, epazote, lavender. The spices that I must have at all times include whole cumin seeds, nutmeg, cinnamon, cayenne, and at least one excellent paprika, currently pimentón de la Vera from Spain.

Your list will reflect your own taste. Search out the finest version of the things you love best and keep them on hand. It is not an extravagance if it encourages you to cook at home more often and to have more fun doing it.

Don't overlook the cheese shop, the bakery, the deli, the wine store. I have favorite haunts where I buy a few special things I love—aged balsamic vinegar, cured olives, pumpkinseed oil, semi-sun-dried tomatoes, superb Belgian chocolate. The simplest things can give the greatest satisfaction. A loaf of hand-shaped, brick-oven-baked bread can transform a meal.

But no matter how elaborate or simple your kitchen may be, seek quality. *Insist* on quality. Do this whether you are buying a loaf of bread and a pound of tomatoes or stocking your wine cellar. This is your food. It's what you will eat, what you will feed your children or share with your friends. It will become part of you, your physical self and your personal culture. So honor yourself and get the best food you can find. Your cooking will improve, your health will improve, and most important, you will have a good time. The chores of shopping and cooking will transform into pleasure.

a word about equipment

What do you need to make soup, anyway? A pot, a sharp knife and a board for chopping, a skillet to sauté onions, a big spoon to stir the soup, a ladle to pour it. Not much.

Measuring cups and spoons are helpful, but you could do without them. Soup is forgiving; you needn't be afraid to eyeball those ingredients.

Of course, plenty of other things are helpful. When you get past the basics, the list can expand with your kitchen ambition. But it's important to remember that with soup, the basics really are basic. Many tasty and nourishing soups can be made with the list above, and they can be made on a single burner in the galley of a boat or over a campfire. Soup is for everyone.

THE BASICS

A 6-quart pot will do for most soups. I have a favorite stainless steel pot, with a thick bottom to prevent scorching, and it holds 8 quarts. Most of my soups fill half of it or less, and that's just right—it's easy to stir or whisk or to use the immersion blender without fear of splashing. So when I say "a large soup pot," that's what I mean: 6 to 8 quarts.

A stockpot is also a good thing to have, especially if you want to make your own vegetable broths. This should be in the 10- to 12-quart range. Smaller pots—a quart or 2 quarts—are very handy for reheating.

Sharp knives are the backbone of any kitchen. Everyone should own at least one great sharp chef's knife. A small paring knife is incredibly handy, and a thin, serrated tomato knife will serve you well with any of the softer vegetables. I also have a special Japanese vegetable cleaver with a razorlike blade. It makes slicing a pleasure.

A solid cutting board, large enough to handle a pile of vegetables, will be in constant use. This can be wood or one of the cheery, colorful plastic or silicone ones. They all get the job done.

A skillet is essential, as many soups (certainly many of mine) require some sautéing. Every kitchen should have a couple of good skillets, smaller and larger; 10 to 12 inches is an ideal size. In my own kitchen, I like at least one of these to be a good nonstick pan, meaning one that does not lose its finish. A sauté pan, meaning a skillet with high, straight sides, is also endlessly useful.

I have a much-loved collection of wooden spoons, but now I also have a set of silicone spoons and spatulas that withstand extremely high temperatures, and I use them daily.

As for ladles, it's amazing how many otherwise well-equipped kitchens do not have a decent ladle. Oh, well. I've been known to grab a teacup and use it to serve soup, and the soup tasted just as good. But why not have a cup-sized stainless steel ladle?

EVERYTHING ELSE

Measuring cups, measuring spoons, and a scale. The scale is the most important! Make sure it weighs in metric as well as our own goofy ounces and pounds, and you will be ready for the future. Many excellent, small, sleek digital scales are available, and they don't cost much.

A good strong blender or a good strong immersion blender, or both. For me, this is essential, as many of my favorite soups are pureed. I love blending several tastes into one new, wonderful flavor, so I use my faithful Oster blender often. It has two speeds, high and low, and that's plenty. The important thing about a blender is that the motor is strong enough, not how many buttons it has. An immersion blender, which lets you puree a soup in the pot, is a very handy tool—it saves steps and saves cleaning. However, some immersion blenders have been known to balk at a piece of vegetable that is al dente.

A colander, a set of sieves, a bowl, a whisk—all these will make your life easier, and you probably already have them.

A mortar or a spice grinder. Perhaps you don't have this, so tell someone you want it for Christmas. There is nothing like the flavor of freshly toasted and ground spices. I use a rough stone *molcahete* that I bought in a village market in Mexico for a few pesos. It has a little pig's head carved on one side and is indestructible. These are available in every Mexican market I've seen in California, and now they are turning up in fancy kitchenware stores. I reduce toasted cumin seeds to a fine meal in moments in my *molcahete*, and I would not do without it. Even when I stripped down my equipment to the minimum for my tiny kitchen, I kept the stone pig.

What else? Pot holders, tea towels, a cheese grater, a panini press, a Felix the Cat clock . . . whatever you want. Just start cooking.

a few practical notes

HERBS, FRESH AND FRESHLY DRIED

I use herbs liberally—basil, thyme, rosemary, sage, mint, cilantro, parsley, marjoram, oregano . . . that's just the starting lineup. These aromatic leaves bring other flavors to life and add excitement to so many foods.

Fresh herbs are always the first choice, and luckily they are now widely available at farmers' markets or in better supermarkets. They're also incredibly easy to grow in the yard or in windowsill pots; most herbs, after all, are considered weeds in their native soil. If you've ever had a patch of mint, you know that the real problem is not how to make it grow but how to make it stop.

But what do you do in winter? Supposing you don't have those windowsill pots and you didn't make it to the farmers' market and it's cold outside and you just want to cook?

In some cases, dried herbs can be used. But dried herbs have a bad rap, because many people use herbs that are not only dried but old, tired, and practically dead. They've been in that cupboard since Nixon was president. Please—throw them out!

There is a solution: dry your own. For me, this good kitchen habit was born out of sheer distraction. I had branches of sage, rosemary, and thyme from the yard, used some for whatever I was cooking at the time, and put the rest down in a basket on a sideboard until I had a moment to get back to them. I meant to pull off the leaves and put them in bags in the refrigerator. When I got back to them, I found dried herbs. *Well*, I thought, *that was easy*. By accident I had started drying my own herbs.

I stripped the leaves off the branches and stuffed them into jars. Now I do this regularly, whenever I have an excess of fresh herbs from the market or from my own unruly bushes. Summer herbs are so wonderful, so potent from the hot sun! I simply spread them in baskets, put them in a dry place, and forget about them for a few days. I don't go out of my way—I only do it when it's pretty effortless.

My home-dried herbs have intense, vibrant flavor, better than what I can get at the store. What's more, they're practically free. And when I do use dried herbs from the store, I try to make sure they aren't ancient.

WATER

H_2O—it's a big part of every soup, and it must be good. As a general rule, the water you enjoy drinking is the water you should use for cooking. If your tap water is sweet and delicious, by all means use it for your soups. But tap water varies tremendously from place to place, so if you buy bottled water for drinking, buy enough for cooking as well.

A soup with a very delicate flavor can be ruined by water with a chlorine aftertaste or some other chemical residue, so in a few instances, such as fruit soups, I specify spring water in a recipe—and filtered water is also fine.

FREEZING SOUPS

One of the winning things about soup is that you can cook once and eat three or four times. Many soups get even better after a day or two in the fridge, and if you want to save some for next week or next month, put it in the freezer. I've yet to meet a soup that didn't freeze well for at least a few months.

Be sure to use good freezer containers, with tight seals. If you are freezing a large quantity of soup, divide it between several smaller containers (I often use pint or quart-sized yogurt tubs). This way you have the flexibility of defrosting only the amount you want. And label those containers: stick a piece of masking tape on the lid, with the name of the soup and the date. You'll be glad you did.

Soups can be defrosted most simply by being left to sit on the kitchen counter for a few hours. You can also pop the frozen block into a pot and warm it *very* gently, on lowest heat, keeping the pot covered so the liquid doesn't evaporate away. If the soup is in a microwave-safe container, then the microwave is another good defrosting option.

DOUBLE THE RECIPE

I admit it: I like a big pot of soup. Half the soup seems to vanish before I have chance to put it away in the refrigerator. I always want to have a bowl right away, and so does anyone else who is around in the kitchen. And then there's the strange, magnetic pull of a pot of soup on the stove. It makes people drop by unexpectedly. Don't ask me to explain this.

What I'm saying is, double the recipe. Many of the soups in this book make enough for about six people. I scaled them down for flexibility, because it feels easier to double a recipe than to cut it in half. But at least sometimes, throw in twice as much of everything, make a big pot, and share. Have a friend over. Freeze some soup. You'll get many happy returns on your hour in the kitchen.

MAKE IT VEGAN

As a matter of preference, I use much more olive oil these days than butter, and I seldom add milk or cream to soups. One outcome of this is that sixty-six of the one hundred soups in this book are vegan, discounting a few garnishes. Other soups are easily adaptable; they might have a spoonful or two of butter, which can easily be switched out for more olive oil.

A number of other recipes, such as hummus, tapenade, and certain breads, salads, and desserts, are also made with no dairy products or eggs.

A NOTE ABOUT MEASUREMENTS

This book is meant to be easily usable by the home cook in an ordinary American kitchen, as well as the home cook anywhere in the great big metric-measuring world. That means that measurements are generally given in a couple of ways.

I try to let common sense be the guide. Sometimes it is enough to know how many large carrots, onions, or apples, and sometimes we need to know more. The precise weight of a hot chipotle chile, down to the gram, can make a difference, while the weight of a green bell pepper is not as significant. And produce varies; I've had heirloom tomatoes the size of walnuts and others that were closer to cantaloupes—so we'd better be using our scales for those beauties.

In cases where exact amounts are important, you may see both volume and weight, and in some cases weight will be given two ways. Take what you need.

CHAPTER 1

broths

Basic Light Vegetable Broth • **V**

Basic Root Vegetable Broth • **V**

Basic Dark Vegetable Broth • **V**

Vegetable and Ginger Broth • **V**

Vegetable Broth with No Onions • **V**

Pea Pod Broth • **V**

Mushroom Stock • **V**

roth: it's what makes a soup a soup. In some soups it is the chorus, in others the star, but you cannot do without it. And making your own broth is both a big deal and not a big deal at all.

It is a big deal because the broth that produces the tastiest soup is the one you make fresh in your own kitchen. Broth provides the subtle flavor base that allows all the other flavors to shine; it adds depth and richness to a soup.

It is not a big deal because making your own broth is one of the simplest things to do. Peel and cut up some vegetables, add water, salt, and a few herbs, and simmer a while. Can you make tea? This is tea with some peeling and slicing added to the process. It's hard to go wrong.

If you think there is no difference between a homemade broth and one from the store, ask yourself if you ever open a can of broth, heat it up, and simply sip it from a cup. No? Me neither. But a hot cup of savory homemade broth, sending up curls of steam full of its earthy and herbal fragrance—that's a delicious drink. If you've never made a vegetable broth, I encourage you to give it a try.

If you don't have time to make a broth, *do not let that stop you from making soup.* You will need some vegetable broth for nearly all the soups in this book, but sometimes it is only a few cups. For most of the soups, especially ones where broth is a smaller component, you can use a good canned broth. I let you know in each recipe when canned broth is an option and when homemade broth is a must.

Many soups make their own broth—at least some of it, sometimes all of it. Dried beans, simmered slowly with sage leaves and whole garlic, make an exquisite broth that is a real argument for never using canned beans. The caramelized onions and dark leafy greens that go into most of the green soups make a perfect starter broth. Tomatoes, if they are one of the juicy varieties, spring an abundance of sweetly acidic liquid and become soup without trying.

In fact, almost any combination of vegetables or legumes simmered in water will release enough flavor to make a very tasty broth, but it might not be enough liquid to give your soup the right consistency; it might need a boost. Then you add some broth. And the better the broth, the better the soup.

Soups with a big mix of ingredients, like any of the minestrones, or the ones with big, bold flavors, like Winter Squash and Yam Soup with Poblano Peppers (p. 120) or Spicy Black Bean Soup with Sweet Peppers (p. 142), can be supplemented with a good commercial broth. But I could not make my Christmas Eve Porcini Soup (p. 222) with canned broth, or the Fresh Pea Soup with Mint Cream (p. 249) that I love in the spring. It just depends on the soup.

MAKING BROTH

The ideal time to make broth is when you are already in the kitchen doing something else. When I come home from my weekly farmers' market, as I sort out the vegetables and put them away I often take a few carrots, a few stalks of celery, an onion or two, the leek tops, the stems from the kale or the chard—whatever is on hand and seems right—clean them up, and throw them in the stockpot with some water.

As I putter around doing other things, the stock simmers. Vegetables are friendly, and they release their essence in less than an hour. By the time I'm ready to head off and do something else, so is the broth. I strain it and put it away in the refrigerator or freezer for future service.

I've made a lot of broth, so I don't measure anymore, but even if you are following a recipe, filling the stockpot is easy. Peeling and slicing is fast, because nothing has to look beautiful. Adding salt and a bay leaf takes seconds. In about 45 minutes, you have an amber-colored and good-tasting broth. Done. If you want a more concentrated broth, simply reduce it by simmering it longer after you've strained it.

You will make a fine broth on your first try by following a recipe. But after you've made three or four of the broths in this chapter, you will be an authority; you will make delicious broths casually, the way you put together a tossed salad. You will know intuitively which herbs can be added in handfuls (parsley and sage and that honorary herb, garlic) and which ones should be used discreetly (fennel greens and mint). You will know that onions and parsnips and fennel add sweetness, turnips and celery root add depth, and lemon juice and cayenne are always available for some kick. You will develop your own taste.

FREEZING BROTH

I like to freeze broth in small containers so I can take out as little or as much as I need. A friend brought me a gift of special containers called food cubes, measured out in half-cups and cups, but any small containers will do, as long as they have tight-fitting lids. I've even recycled yogurt tubs for this purpose. Label your broth and add the date. If you have more than one kind of broth in your freezer, you don't want to be standing there peering at a variety of light brown ice cubes trying to figure out which is which. It only takes a moment to jot down a label.

A vegetable broth will last very well in the freezer for six months. It will probably still be very good for quite a while longer, but like all frozen foods, it will start to lose some of its fresh flavor.

MY BASIC VEGETABLE BROTHS

basic light vegetable broth is the one I make most often and if there is an all-purpose broth, this is it. Its flavor is delicate, slightly herbal, nicely balanced. It is ideal for spring soups; it won't overpower the fresh flavor of asparagus or peas or sorrel. If you are making it particularly for one of these soups, you can customize it by adding a bit of the featured vegetable—some asparagus trimmings or pea pods. However, it is also a fine broth to use year-round, and delicious to sip from a cup.

basic root vegetable broth has a combination of six root vegetables to give it a deep, earthy flavor. It has a natural sweetness from onions and carrots and parsnips and is a good choice for winter soups.

basic dark vegetable broth has the deepest flavor of all my broths. It's a bit more work, because chopped vegetables are first sautéed in olive oil until they are well caramelized, then simmered with other ingredients. But the rich, earthy, slightly sweet, and faintly smoky taste is worth the effort. Use this broth for onion soup, mushroom soups, or on its own with some pasta added.

vegetable and ginger broth uses fresh ginger to give it its distinct flavor and a subtle kick of heat in the finish. It is delightfully gingery and fragrant without being too strong. With an added drop of soy sauce it takes on an Asian character and makes a delicate appetizer soup on its own, with just a few herbs and sliced mushrooms floating in it, or some small edamame and green onions. It is also lovely as the base for an Asian noodle soup, with soba or udon or ramen. This broth can be used, too, in any of the winter squash soups or root vegetable soups, and it can add an intriguing twist to green soups.

vegetable broth with no onions was made for a special purpose, an onionless soup for an allergic friend. However, it turned out so well that I decided to include it here as an option for times when you want a broth that is mellow and gentle in flavor and less sweet than some others.

AND A COUPLE OF CUSTOM BROTHS

pea pod broth is based on fresh pea pods and very little else. Fresh pods are a by-product of fresh pea soup that should not be wasted. This delicate, gold-green broth is also good for asparagus soup and can be used with sorrel and other spring greens.

mushroom stock is an essential ingredient of my Christmas Eve Porcini Soup but benefits any mushroom soup, and adds a whiff of the forest to a root vegetable soup or a hearty winter bean soup.

CHOOSING A CANNED BROTH

Sometimes you don't have a homemade broth ready when you want it. Don't worry—we all use store-bought at times. But choose carefully.

Many organic vegetable broths are available in cans and cartons in my local health food store, and I have diligently tried them. I want to love them, but I must confess that I don't. I find that many of them are overpowered by an excess of carrot or by the acid bite of tomato, neither of which is helpful in most soups. Many also tend to be salty; even the best of them need to be diluted. As for cubes and powders—I detest them. I've never tasted one I'd be willing to use in a soup.

The canned broth that I have found most useful is Swanson's Vegetable Broth, available on the shelves of my local supermarket. In most soups, especially if a recipe calls for only 2 or 3 cups of added broth, this works very well, though I do often dilute it to reduce the salt level. I hope that soon we'll have many excellent commercial vegetable broths easily available. Until then, it's a lucky thing that making your own broth is so easy.

basic light vegetable broth

This is a delicate broth, slightly sweet from fennel and mint, with grassy, herbal notes from leek greens and parsley. It is what I think of as an all-purpose broth—it marries well with a wide range of flavors and can provide a base for many soups. It's also delightful to sip as a hot drink on a cold winter day.

If you want a more concentrated broth, you can reduce this to 10 cups by simmering it longer after you strain it.

And now a word about measurements. I give measurements up, down, and sideways—how many carrots, how many cups when they're sliced, and, for our friends with kitchen scales, how many grams. But folks, there's a lot of latitude here! Medium celery stalks and giant parsnips? No fennel greens on hand today, or fresh out of chard stems? Don't sweat it. Get as close as you can; the broth will be good.

· · · MAKES 11—12 CUPS · · ·

5–6 large leeks, green part, sliced (6 cups; 350 g)
5 large carrots, sliced (3 cups; 450 g)
2 large yellow or white onions, cut up (500 g)
4 large stalks celery, sliced (2 cups; 225 g)
3–4 medium parsnips, sliced (1½ cups; 225 g)
1 cup (60 g) fennel tops
1 bay leaf
1 tsp. fresh or dried thyme

2 tsp. sea salt, plus more to taste
a few peppercorns
5–6 fresh mint leaves, more if very small
6 cloves garlic, peeled
stems from 1 bunch kale or chard, cut up (120 g)
1 cup (40 g) coarsely chopped fresh flat-leaf
   parsley
3½ quarts (3½ liters) water

recipe continues on next page

Combine all the ingredients in an 8-quart stockpot and bring the water to a boil. Lower the heat to a simmer and allow the broth to cook for about 45 minutes. All the vegetables should be very soft, and the broth should have a clear, pale golden color.

Strain the broth through a colander, then through a sieve, and discard the boiled vegetables. Taste, and correct the salt if needed, but be very cautious about this. Vegetable broths almost always reduce further as they cook in a soup, and it is better to keep them somewhat undersalted and adjust the taste of the finished soup.

basic root vegetable broth

In this variation on light vegetable broth, root vegetables provide a mellower and earthier flavor. This broth is excellent for most winter soups, particularly ones that involve root vegetables, as it underscores and deepens their flavor.

This is a good broth for Chard and Yam Soup (p. 72), for Neeps and Tatties Soup (p. 172), and for most winter squash soups. It also pairs very well with cabbage, and belongs in any soup in which the broth remains clear, such as Fennel and Onion Soup (p. 68) and Sopa de Ajo (p. 156).

· · · MAKES 11–12 CUPS · · ·

5 large carrots, sliced (3 cups; 450 g)

2 large yellow or white onions, cut up (500 g)

4 large stalks celery, sliced (2 cups; 225 g)

1 large turnip, diced (1½ cups; 225 g)

1 large rutabaga, diced (1½ cups; 225 g)

3–4 medium parsnips, sliced (1½ cups; 225 g)

½ celery root, diced (1½ cups; 225 g)

2 whole medium Yukon Gold potatoes (225 g)

4 large leeks, green part, sliced (4 cups; 225 g)

1 bay leaf

1 tsp. fresh or dried thyme

1 Tbs. sea salt, plus more to taste

a few peppercorns

6–8 cloves garlic, peeled

stems from 1 bunch kale or chard, cut up (120 g)

1 cup (40 g) coarsely chopped fresh flat-leaf parsley

4 quarts (4 liters) water

Combine all the ingredients in an 8-quart stockpot and bring the water to a boil. Lower the heat and allow the broth to simmer for 45 minutes to an hour. All the vegetables should be soft, and the broth should have an amber color.

Strain the broth through a colander, then through a sieve, and discard the boiled vegetables. Taste, and correct the salt if needed, but be careful: vegetable broths almost always reduce further as they cook in a soup, and it is better to keep them somewhat undersalted and adjust the seasoning in the finished soup.

basic dark vegetable broth

The special flavor of this broth is created by browning some of the vegetables in oil and then slowly simmering them in water. Use this when you want a deep, earthy taste in a soup or stew, as in Vegetarian Onion Soup Gratin (p. 160).

··· MAKES 9—10 CUPS ···

2 medium yellow or white onions (450 g)

8 cloves garlic

5 large carrots (450 g)

4 stalks celery, with leaves (225 g)

4 oz. (120 g) any brown mushrooms

2 Tbs. (30 ml) olive oil

1½ tsp. sea salt, plus more to taste

cayenne

4 large leeks, green part (225 g)

2 medium turnips (350 g)

3–4 medium parsnips (225 g)

1 large potato (180 g)

3 quarts (3 liters) water

⅔ cup (30 g) coarsely chopped fresh flat-leaf parsley

⅔ cup (30 g) coarsely chopped cilantro

1 bay leaf

½ tsp. fresh or dried thyme

1 tsp. peppercorns

Peel and coarsely chop the onions and garlic. Scrape and slice the carrots, and slice the celery and mushrooms. Heat the olive oil in a large sauté pan and add the onions, garlic, carrots, celery, mushrooms, 1 teaspoon salt, and a pinch of cayenne. Stir the vegetables from time to time over a medium-low flame for the next 30 to 45 minutes, until they are well browned. Don't worry about any dark bits that stick to the pan.

While these vegetables are caramelizing, thoroughly wash the leek tops and slice them; you should have about 4 cups. Peel and dice the turnips and parsnips. Scrub the potato and leave it whole.

Transfer the browned vegetables to a stockpot. Swirl a little water around in the pan to deglaze it, scraping up any brown bits, and add it to the pot along with the remaining water, the leek greens, turnips, parsnips, potato, parsley, cilantro, bay leaf, thyme, and peppercorns. Bring the water to a boil, then lower the heat and let it simmer, covered, for about 45 minutes. All the vegetables should be completely soft, and the broth a deep amber brown.

Strain the broth through a colander, then through a fine sieve to eliminate any sediment. Taste, and correct the seasoning with more salt if needed.

vegetable and ginger broth

This delicate, fragrant broth has a distinctive tang from the ginger, which combines well with a touch of soy sauce. If you like, you can add a little hot pepper to bring up the heat.

This broth is ideal to underscore the ginger flavor in Green Soup with Ginger (p. 96), Spicy Butternut Ginger Soup (p. 114), or Red Lentil and Squash Soup (p. 118). It also adds an appealing note of spicy warmth to other winter squash soups, and to Kale and Sweet Potato Soup with Cumin and Lemon (p. 100) and Puree of Carrot and Yam with Citrus and Spices (p. 78).

··· MAKES 11—12 CUPS ···

6 large carrots, peeled and sliced (500 g)

3 stalks celery, with leaves, sliced (175 g)

6 large leeks, green part, sliced (500 g)

1 large yellow or white onion, coarsely chopped (300 g)

3–4 medium parsnips, sliced (225 g)

a small handful of fennel greens

1 ½ cups (60 g) chopped cilantro

¾ cup (30 g) chopped fresh flat-leaf parsley

8 oz. (225 g) fresh ginger, peeled and sliced

5 cloves garlic, peeled

2 tsp. sea salt, plus more to taste

1 Tbs. peppercorns

3 quarts (3 liters) water

1–3 tsp. soy sauce, to taste (optional)

red pepper flakes (optional)

Combine all the ingredients except the soy sauce and red pepper flakes in an 8-quart stockpot and bring the water to a boil. Lower the heat and allow the broth to simmer for 45 minutes. All the vegetables should be soft, and the broth should be somewhat reduced and have a pleasant golden color.

Strain the broth through a colander, then once more through a fine sieve, and discard the boiled vegetables. Taste the broth. If it seems watery, cook it down a little longer before adding the soy sauce and a pinch of red pepper flakes, if you like. Adjust the seasoning with a touch more salt if needed, but be careful: vegetable broths almost always reduce further as they cook in a soup, so it's best to keep them slightly undersalted and adjust the seasoning when finishing the soup.

vegetable broth with no onions

I first made this broth for an onion-allergic friend. The broth became the basis of a creamy garlic soup, enjoyed by all, even onion lovers. Later I found it useful in other soups as well; it is mildly flavorful and, with no onions, less sweet than some other vegetable broths. This is a good choice when you want something unassertive, as with Spring Green Soup (p. 278) or Carrot, Orange, and Ginger Soup (p. 254).

· · · MAKES ABOUT 10 CUPS · · ·

5 or 6 medium carrots, sliced (350 g)

1 large turnip, diced (225 g)

1 cup (60 g) packed fresh flat-leaf parsley

3 large stalks celery, sliced (225 g)

3 medium parsnips, sliced (150 g)

stems from 1 bunch chard, cup up (120 g)

stems from 1 bunch kale, cut up (120 g)

½ head garlic, peeled

1 cup (60 g) chopped fennel greens

1 lb. (450 g) small yellow potatoes, or 1 cup potato peels

1 bay leaf

1 tsp. fresh thyme

1–2 tsp. sea salt, plus more to taste

a few peppercorns

2½–3 quarts (2½–3 liters) water

fresh lemon juice (optional)

cayenne or hot paprika (optional)

Combine all the ingredients except the lemon juice and cayenne in a stockpot; you should have enough water to cover all the vegetables. Bring the water to a boil, lower the heat, and let the broth simmer for about 45 minutes.

Taste the broth and add more salt if it seems needed. If the broth has a pleasant, savory flavor and a pale amber-brown color, it's done. If it seems weak, turn up the heat a bit and leave it to simmer for another 10 minutes. In my experience, no vegetable broth needs more than 45 minutes to an hour.

recipe continues on next page

Strain the broth through a colander, then through a sieve. If you use whole small potatoes, you may want to pluck them out, peel them, and use them in a potato salad—they're tasty.

For a piquant edge, add a little lemon juice or a pinch of cayenne. And as with all broths, this one can be reduced for a stronger flavor. Simply return the strained broth to a clean pot and simmer it until it has the desired strength.

pea pod broth

If you are shelling peas for a fresh pea soup—or for any reason—this is a terrifically simple broth to make. Obviously you want to use this for pea soup, but it is also good for any asparagus soup, or a soup of delicate spring greens.

··· MAKES ABOUT 9 CUPS ···

pods from 3 lbs. (1.3 kg) peas

1 large yellow or white onion, chopped (300 g)

1 large carrot, peeled and sliced (100 g)

2 stalks celery, sliced (100 g)

a few branches of fresh flat-leaf parsley

1 tsp. sea salt, plus more to taste

a few peppercorns

2½ quarts (2½ liters) water

Rinse the pea pods and put them in an 8-quart stockpot or large soup pot with the remaining ingredients. Bring the water to a boil, lower the heat to medium, and let the broth simmer, covered, for about 45 minutes.

Strain the broth and discard the pods and other vegetables. Taste the broth and adjust the salt if needed.

mushroom stock

This is a great stock to use in making mushroom soups, and also for risotto or pilaf.

½ oz. (15 g) dried porcini pieces

2 Tbs. (30 ml) olive oil

1 yellow or white onion, chopped (200 g)

1 clove garlic, chopped

2 large leeks, green part, sliced (120 g)

4 oz. (120 g) fresh mushrooms, sliced

3 medium carrots, peeled and sliced (200 g)

3 medium parsnips, peeled and sliced (200 g)

1 medium turnip, peeled and sliced (150 g)

2 stalks celery, sliced (70 g)

6 big branches of fresh flat-leaf parsley (25 g)

6 big branches of cilantro (35 g)

6–8 fresh sage leaves, or 1 tsp. crumbled dried leaves

a handful of fresh dill

½ tsp. fresh thyme

1 tsp. sea salt, plus more to taste

several peppercorns

2½ quarts (2½ liters) water

Pour boiling water over the dried porcini and leave them to soak for at least half an hour.

Heat the olive oil in a large skillet and cook the onion and garlic in it over medium heat, stirring occasionally, until the onion is golden, about 20 minutes. Add the leek greens, fresh mushrooms, carrots, parsnips, turnip, and celery and cook everything together for another 20 minutes. Transfer the vegetables to an 8-quart stockpot and add the herbs, salt, peppercorns, and water.

Drain the soaking porcini, reserving the water. Wash the mushrooms carefully, getting rid of all the grit. Strain the soaking water through a paper filter. Add both the porcini and the filtered soaking water to the stockpot.

Simmer the stock for about an hour. Strain the stock through a fine-mesh sieve, taste it, and correct the seasoning with more salt if necessary—but as always, be cautious with salt.

Another way . . .

If you have either dark vegetable broth or root vegetable broth already made, you can simply add the soaked and cleaned porcini and the fresh mushrooms to that and simmer it, covered, for half an hour. Strain and use as you would mushroom stock.

fall and winter soups

CHAPTER 2

beautiful fall soups

Potato and Tomato Soup with Sage • **V**

Fennel and Onion Soup • **V**

Sopa de Poblanos

Chard and Yam Soup • **V**

Roasted Golden Beet Soup • **V**

Old-Fashioned Cream of Mushroom Soup

Puree of Carrot and Yam with Citrus and Spices • **V**

Creamy Potato and Roasted Garlic Soup

the farmers' market in the harvest season

Fall comes suddenly where I live. By late September the long summer seems to stretch eternally, pale blue and golden. Then one day we wake up to the cool hush of morning fog, the delight of wearing a sweater while making coffee. Damp air brings the scent of sage and eucalyptus. The evenings draw in.

I love this time of year. Everywhere in the world, the pace picks up—and in the kitchen it slows down. It's soup season.

At the farmers' market, tables that groaned under loads of red tomatoes and heavy, juice-filled melons suddenly are piled with new crops of apples, Asian pears, walnuts, and soon flame-orange persimmons. Albino pumpkins appear like ghosts in the middle of riotous fall color.

The early days of fall are heaven for cooks, as new fruits and vegetables appear almost daily. The hot-weather herbs are still with us: basil, oregano, mint. But cool-weather greens are back in force: spinach, new arugula, every kind of kale and chard.

If you see red-veined spinach at your market, try it. It tastes like spinach with an upgrade, intensely spinachy but somehow sweeter and richer. And sample different kinds of kale. I like them all—curly kale, dinosaur kale (which is another name for cavalo nero or Tuscan kale), and red Russian kale, perhaps my favorite, its flat leaves looking like giant sawtoothed oak leaves. Make your decision based on which one looks freshest, firmest, youngest.

Peppers are stars in this season. We see red and yellow peppers in their myriad varieties, big bell peppers, small lipstick peppers, long, skinny Italian or Hungarian frying peppers. All these are sweet. Fresh chiles are also abundant. Soon they will be hanging on ropes, drying, but in September they are fully ripening and still plump. Poblanos might be found, and jalapeños certainly will be there, turning red by now, and if you live in the

Southwest, there will be many more chiles to choose from. Don't worry too much about the names, because they often change from place to place. Ask the farmer how hot that chile is and how it should be cooked. Try something new.

Coming up behind the showy peppers are the root vegetables, solid, here to stay through the winter. Potatoes, rutabagas, yams, and parsnips are piled in reassuring heaps next to sweet cabbages that have been improved by the first cold nights, and long stalks of Brussel sprouts.

The biggest news at the market in the fall is squash. The hard-shelled winter squashes are here—golden butternuts, kabocha squashes in their gray-green variations, blue Hubbards, gigantic Tahitians, and bright orange pumpkins, all calling to me.

Fall mushrooms are one of the seasonal delights in less arid regions, and if you are the lucky soul who finds field or forest mushrooms in your local farmers' market, take advantage of them. They will bring a woodsy and wild flavor to your mushroom-barley soup that can happen only at this time of year.

There are favorite things that last only a moment—green tomatoes, bushels of them in the week before the tomato field is plowed under, and sometimes an explosion of squash blossoms as the zucchini vines are retired. And there are the things that are in for the long run, like shell beans, just out of their pods, dried and ready to take you through months of good cooking.

Everyone has a favorite moment at the farmers' market, perhaps a moment you wait for or one that takes you by surprise and changes your whole plan. For me, it is the sight of the new-harvest olive oil. The first oil from the new crop of olives has a freshness and a lively intensity of fruit and spice that are all its own. I taste it, I roll it around in my mouth—yes, this is the fresh-squeezed juice of the fruit of the olive tree. As I look around at the abundance of fruits and vegetables, nuts and fungi, I think of the beautiful soups of autumn and the salads and desserts that will go with them, all to be enhanced by a few drops of this green gold.

MENU

chopped salad with french green lentils
-page 466-

. . .

POTATO AND TOMATO SOUP WITH SAGE
-page 66-

sourdough or whole-grain baguettes
fruity or peppery extra virgin olive oil for dipping

. . .

sliced nectarines and plums
with lemon sorbet

The first cool days of autumn are such a wonderful time to cook. You want a pot of something savory bubbling on the stove, but the farmers' market is still overflowing with late-summer produce, with big, intense flavors that have been ripening in the sun for months. This menu crosses the seasons at that ideal moment.

The soup that forms the center of the meal is satisfying and complex. It has the unmistakable earthiness of potatoes and the perfume of sage and onion to balance the sweetness of last-harvest tomatoes.

The chopped salad has raw crunch and a riot of bright flavor: sweet corn and red peppers with crisp fall apples, all mixed into a confetti of every vegetable in the market. Green lentils keep their shape and texture well, so they can hold their own in this salad even if it's made ahead and kept in the refrigerator all day. But the salad is delicious when just made, served slightly warm or at room temperature. And like all chopped salads, it can be adapted as the produce in the market shifts with the season.

Because there is such a range of ingredients in the soup and the salad, I like to eat a very plain bread with this and have an unadulterated olive oil for dipping. For dessert, any fresh fruit would be fine, but I'm suggesting nectarines and plums, the summer fruits that stay late and keep the party going into autumn.

Other ways . . .

I love chopped salads, but they do require some chopping. If you don't already have that lentil salad in the fridge and don't have time to chop, serve a simple mixed green salad with a spoonful of cooked cannellini and a few oil-cured olives scattered over the greens.

Or make it vegan—it's easy. The soup is already vegan; the bread and dessert are as well. Just eliminate the small amount of cheese in the salad recipe, or replace it with a slice of grilled tofu, diced small to match.

potato and tomato soup with sage

Gorgeous tomatoes are abundant in the fall—and here they move away from the brightness of basil and combine with potatoes, slow-cooked onions, and a handful of sage to make a soup with a deep and subtle flavor, perfect for the first cool days.

· · · SERVES 6 GENEROUSLY · · ·

2 red onions (about 1 lb.; 450 g)
2 Tbs. (30 ml) olive oil, plus more for garnish
1½ tsp. sea salt, plus more to taste
1¼ lbs. (570 g) yellow, Yukon Gold, or
   red-skinned potatoes
10 cloves garlic, peeled
2 lbs. (900 g) ripe tomatoes, mixed varieties
½ cup (120 ml) dry white wine
¼ cup (15 g) chopped fresh flat-leaf parsley
2 Tbs. chopped fresh sage leaves or 1 Tbs.
   slightly crumbled dried sage

1 scant tsp. fresh thyme
a small pinch of chopped fresh or dried rosemary
2–3 cups (475–700 ml) basic light vegetable
   broth (p. 47), basic root vegetable broth
   (p. 49), or canned vegetable broth
freshly ground black pepper

· · ·

garnish: fruity green olive oil

Peel and halve the red onions and slice them thinly crosswise. Heat 2 tablespoons olive oil in a large nonstick pan and sauté the onions with a pinch of salt, stirring often on medium heat until they are soft and lightly browned in spots, about half an hour—and don't hurry this.

Meanwhile, scrub and trim the potatoes and cut them into ½-inch dice. In a large soup pot, combine the potatoes and whole garlic cloves with enough water to cover (about 2 cups; 500 ml) and a scant teaspoon of salt. Simmer the potatoes and garlic for about 10 minutes, or until tender but not falling apart.

Peel the tomatoes, either by blanching them and slipping off the skins or by using a serrated peeler, and cut them in pieces, saving all the juice. Add the caramelized onions to the potatoes and garlic, along with the tomatoes and their juice, the wine, and all the herbs.

Simmer the soup, covered, until all the vegetables are soft, about half an hour. Add the vegetable broth; the amount you need will vary with the juiciness of the tomatoes you are using. The soup should pour easily from the ladle, the broth slightly thickened by the potatoes and perfumed with the sage and garlic.

Taste the soup and correct the seasoning with more salt and some freshly ground black pepper. I always drizzle a little fruity green olive oil on each serving of this soup, my favorite finishing touch.

fennel and onion soup

This soup starts with big mounds of sliced fennel and onions, but don't worry—these vegetables will reduce dramatically as they slowly cook down, turning brown and sweet and developing a deep, rich flavor that you will love.

· · · SERVES 6—7 · · ·

3 medium fennel bulbs, trimmed (1 ½ lbs.; 700 g)
4 large yellow onions (2 lbs., 900 g)
4 Tbs. (60 ml) olive oil
1 bay leaf
1 tsp. sea salt, plus more to taste
1 cup (250 ml) dry wine, red or white

6 cups (1 ½ liters) basic light vegetable broth (p. 47) or basic root vegetable broth (p. 49)
freshly ground black pepper

· · ·

optional garnish: cheese croutons

Trim and clean the fennel bulbs, quarter them lengthwise, and slice them thinly crosswise. Peel the onions and do the same, cutting them in quarters lengthwise, then slicing thinly.

Heat 2 tablespoons olive oil in each of two large sauté pans. Add the fennel to one and the onions and bay leaf to the other, each with ½ teaspoon salt. Cook the vegetables slowly over medium-low heat, stirring pretty often, until they are all a gorgeous golden brown. This will take forever—45 minutes to 1 hour—but you can be doing other things as long as you cast an eye on them now and then and give them a stir.

When both the fennel and onions are nicely softened and browned, add the wine to the fennel to deglaze the pan and then add the fennel to the onions. Continue cooking and stirring until the wine has cooked away and the vegetables are sizzling. Combine the caramelized fennel and onions with the broth in a soup pot and use a little of the broth to deglaze the pan, so that all the lovely brown bits go into your soup. Simmer the soup gently, covered, for another 20 minutes to blend all the flavors. Add pepper to taste.

Taste, and correct the seasoning with a little more salt if needed.

Another way . . .

This soup is wonderful with a cheese crouton on each serving, the way traditional onion soup is served. Ladle the soup into ovenproof bowls or individual casseroles, place a piece of toasted French bread on top of each serving, and cover each toast with about 1 ounce grated Parmesan or Gruyère cheese or any sharp, aged cheese that you like. Put the bowls on a baking sheet and slide them under a broiler for a few minutes, just long enough to melt and brown the cheese.

sopa de poblanos

ROASTED POBLANO CHILE SOUP

This is one of the most delicious soups I've eaten. I first made this at Susana Trilling's cooking school when I visited her in Oaxaca, Mexico, and when I returned home I immediately made it in my own kitchen. It's a velvety puree, creamy from goat cheese, slightly spicy but not too hot, and full of the true flavor of fresh poblano chile peppers.

I adapted the recipe to make it vegetarian, and to allow for the fact that we don't have *requeson* here, the fresh white cheese that we got at the open-air market in the village of Etla near Susana's home. I used a creamy young goat cheese with excellent results. Susana garnishes her soup with strips of fried tortillas, but I use toasted pine nuts, which are very tasty with the green chiles.

Fresh poblano chiles are usually only slightly spicier than bell peppers, though like all chiles they can vary and should be tasted. They are available in farmers' markets as well as in Latin American markets and many large supermarkets, beginning in late spring. Epazote is an herb commonly used in Mexican cooking and is available from the same sources.

· · · SERVES 6 · · ·

about 6 fresh poblano chiles (1½ lbs.; 700 g)

1½ tsp. unsalted butter

1 Tbs. (15 ml) olive oil

2 yellow onions, coarsely chopped (1 lb.; 450 g)

1 clove garlic, minced

sea salt

6 cups (1½ liters) basic light vegetable broth
  (p. 47)

½ cup (20 g) chopped cilantro

5 or 6 fresh epazote leaves or 1½ tsp. dried
  crumbled epazote

4 oz. (120 g) creamy white goat cheese

3 Tbs. lightly toasted pine nuts

Roast the chiles under a broiler, in a dry skillet over high heat, or on a charcoal grill, turning them from time to time until the skin is charred and blistered all over. Place them in a paper bag for about 10 minutes to let them sweat and then peel off the skins and remove the stems and seeds. Cut the peeled chiles into strips; you should have about 1 ½ cups of peeled poblano strips.

In a medium nonstick skillet, heat the butter and olive oil and sauté the onions, stirring often, until they are translucent. Add the minced garlic and some salt and cook over low heat, stirring often, until the onions are golden, 20 to 25 minutes.

When the onions and garlic are very soft, combine them in a soup pot with the chile strips, broth, cilantro, and epazote. Cover the pot and simmer everything for about 20 minutes, then puree in a blender, in batches, or with an immersion blender until the soup is perfectly smooth.

Add the goat cheese to the pureed soup, stirring over low heat until the cheese has melted into the soup. Taste, and correct the seasoning with a pinch more salt if needed.

Serve the soup hot, with lightly toasted pine nuts scattered over each bowl. Because of its deep, intense flavor and spicy edge, this soup is best served in smaller portions as a first course—although people may ask for more.

chard and yam soup

Here's a simple and tasty soup that I think of as a "starter soup"—even someone who has never cooked can make this without any trouble. The amounts are pretty flexible, the technique is basic, and the result is delicious.

Like many of my soups, this one really adapts to your taste with its garnishes. Try it with a spoonful of smoky salsa, or some crumbled *queso fresco*, or a plain white goat cheese. A drizzle of fruity olive oil on each serving is great, as are homemade croutons.

· · · SERVES 6 GENEROUSLY · · ·

1 large yellow onion (300 g)

1 Tbs. (15 ml) olive oil

1–2 cloves garlic, chopped

1 large yam (12 oz.; 350 g)

1 bunch chard (12 oz.; 350 g)

6–7 green onions or scallions, white and green
 parts (120 g)

6 cups (1½ liters) any basic vegetable broth
 (pp. 47–50) or 5 cups canned vegetable broth
 diluted with 1 cup water

sea salt, if needed

freshly ground black pepper

fresh lemon juice

· · ·

optional garnishes:

fruity green olive oil

crumbled *queso fresco*, feta cheese, or other
 goat cheese

Simple Chipotle Sauce (p. 439) or other salsa

Chop the onion coarsely and sauté it in the olive oil, over medium heat, stirring often, until it is soft and beginning to color. Add the chopped garlic and keep cooking over low heat, stirring often, until the onion is golden brown, about 15 more minutes.

Meanwhile, peel the yam and cut it into ½-inch dice. Wash the chard, slice the greens off the stems, and cut the leaves into 1- or 2-inch pieces. Thinly slice the chard stems. Wash and trim the green onions and cut them in ½-inch pieces. Combine the yam, chard, green onions, and broth in a soup pot and simmer gently, covered, for about 20 minutes.

Add the sautéed onions to the soup and simmer another 10 minutes, then taste. Add salt if needed, then add pepper and lemon juice to taste.

Ladle the steaming hot soup into deep bowls, drizzle the top of each serving with some fruity green olive oil, drop a few crumbles of cheese on top, and pass a bowl of salsa.

roasted golden beet soup

WITH BEET GREENS

Being Polish, I grew up eating beets, and I never understood people who said they didn't like them. What's not to like? Unless you have only tasted canned beets, which is unfair to beets and to yourself.

Beets come in all colors now, and stripes as well. I make my soup with the deep golden ones for their beauty—I love the bright golden spots among swirls of dark green. But you can use any beets for this soup, or mix them up. Be sure to look for beets with firm, shiny, fresh-looking greens, as the greens are an important part of the soup.

· · · SERVES 6—8 · · ·

1¾ lbs. (800 g) golden beets
1 lb. (500 g) beet greens
2 yellow onions (450 g)
½ small head green cabbage (8 oz.; 225 g)
½ medium celery root, trimmed (5 oz.; 140 g)
4 Tbs. (60 ml) olive oil
1 tsp. sea salt, plus more to taste
6 oz. (175 g) Yukon Gold potatoes

about 4 cups (1 liter) basic light vegetable broth (p. 47) or canned vegetable broth
¼ cup (15 g) chopped fresh dill
3 Tbs. (45 ml) Meyer lemon juice or any fresh lemon juice
hot paprika

· · ·

garnish: crème fraîche, yogurt cheese, or any crumbly white cheese

Preheat the oven to 375°.

Trim the leaves off the beets and reserve them. Scrub the beets, nest them in a large sheet of heavy-duty aluminum foil, and wrap the foil around them to form a packet. Roast the beets for at least an hour, or as long as needed for them to be completely tender. The cooking time will vary with the size of the beets. Rinse the beet greens in several changes of water, remove the stems, and cut the leaves into very thin strips. Reserve the greens; you should have about 8 cups.

Chop the onions and shred or chop the cabbage. Peel the celery root and finely dice the white interior; you should have about 1 cup. Heat 2 tablespoons olive oil in a large nonstick pan and sauté the chopped onion with a generous pinch of salt over medium heat, until it is limp and beginning to color. Add the shredded cabbage and diced celery root and continue cooking, stirring often, until the vegetables are tender and flecked with golden brown.

When the beets are done, slip off their skins, dice them, and set them aside. Scrub and dice the potatoes and combine them in a large soup pot with the vegetable broth, 2 cups water, and 1 teaspoon salt. Bring the liquid to a simmer and cook the potatoes until they are tender, about 10 minutes.

Add the sautéed vegetables, the shredded beet greens, and the diced, roasted beets to the soup pot. Cover and cook the soup for another 20 minutes, adding the chopped dill toward the end of that time. Taste, correct the seasoning with more salt if needed, and add the Meyer lemon juice and a pinch of hot paprika. If you cannot get Meyer lemons, use any lemons but add the juice a bit at a time: it will be more acidic, and you might not need as much.

If the soup seems too thick, add a bit more vegetable broth or water. Shortly before serving, stir in the remaining 2 tablespoons olive oil.

Serve the soup in generous bowls, with a spoonful of crème fraîche or yogurt cheese or some crumbled white cheese sprinkled on the green and gold mosaic.

old-fashioned cream of mushroom soup

This is a traditional creamy mushroom soup, mainly mushrooms and onions, browned in oil and butter and simmered. I made it for my mother when she was older and wanted food to taste the way she remembered it.

In the past this soup would surely have had a lot of cream added, but when I made it this time around, I found that a few tablespoons of light cream were all I needed to get that good old-fashioned flavor. You can certainly add more if you want a richer soup, and you can also use sour cream as a garnish with fresh dill.

· · · SERVES 6 · · ·

1¼ lbs. (570 g) portobello, cremini, or brown button mushrooms

2 medium yellow onions (350 g)

4 cloves garlic

2 stalks celery (150 g)

3 Tbs. (45 ml) olive oil

½ tsp. sea salt, plus more to taste

1 Tbs. unsalted butter

freshly ground black pepper

fresh or dried thyme

2–3 Tbs. (30–45 ml) dry sherry or dry Marsala

6–7 cups (1½ liters) any basic vegetable broth (pp. 47–50) or 5 cups canned vegetable broth diluted with 2 cups water

2½ Tbs. Arborio rice

1 tsp. sweet paprika

3 Tbs. half-and-half or light cream

⅓ cup (20 g) chopped fresh dill or flat-leaf parsley

· · ·

optional garnish: sour cream or crème fraîche

Clean and coarsely chop the mushrooms. Chop the onions; you should have about 3 cups. Mince the garlic and chop the celery to get about ¾ cup.

In a nonstick skillet, heat 2 tablespoons olive oil, add the chopped onions and a pinch of salt, and cook over gentle heat, stirring now and then, until the onions are soft and golden, about 20 minutes.

Meanwhile, in a second skillet, heat the remaining 1 tablespoon oil with the butter and sauté the garlic in it over medium heat for about 2 minutes. Add the mushrooms, ½ teaspoon salt, and black pepper and thyme to taste. Raise the heat to high and sauté the mushrooms, stirring often, until they give up their liquid, sizzle, and begin to turn darker brown, 7 or 8 minutes. Add a splash of sherry or Marsala and stir as it cooks away.

While the mushrooms and onions are sautéing, put the broth, rice, and celery into a soup pot and simmer, covered, for about 15 minutes. (Remember, if you are using canned broth you should dilute it, about 2 parts broth to 1 part water, or it will be too salty.) When the mushrooms and onions are ready, add them to the pot along with the paprika and keep simmering, covered, for another 15 minutes. Remove the soup from the heat and stir in the half-and-half and the fresh dill or parsley. Taste, and correct the seasoning with a pinch more salt if needed.

If you like, drop a spoonful of sour cream or crème fraîche on each serving.

Another way . . .

I like to puree this soup to a semi-rough stage. I add half the fresh dill or parsley to the soup with the half-and-half, then puree it with an immersion blender, using brief pulses, until it is somewhere between smooth and chunky. Then I sprinkle the remaining herbs on top of the soup when I serve it. Of course, you can puree to any degree of smoothness you like. If you do not have an immersion blender, use a regular blender, working in batches. Add a bit more water or broth if the soup seems too thick.

puree of carrot and yam with citrus and spices

This beautiful soup is bright orange and full of subtle, interesting flavors. Parsnips and celery root quietly balance the sweetness of carrots and yams, and a light touch of spices and citrus juices brings out the best in the vegetables without dominating. But for drama in the bowl and on your taste buds, try this with a little spoonful of dark red chile salsa floating on top of each serving. Fantastic!

· · · SERVES 6—7 · · ·

1 large yam (about 1 ¼ lbs.; 570 g)

1 large yellow onion (300 g)

2 Tbs. (30 ml) olive oil

1 tsp. sea salt, plus more to taste

12 oz. (350 g) carrots

6 oz. (170 g) parsnips

4 oz. (120 g) trimmed celery root

1 Tbs. (15 ml) honey or agave nectar

one 1-inch stick cinnamon

½ tsp. coriander seeds, lightly toasted and
    ground

¼ tsp. ground nutmeg

a pinch of hot paprika or cayenne

about 4 cups (1 liter) basic light vegetable broth
    (p. 47) or vegetable and ginger broth (p. 52), or
    3 cups canned vegetable broth diluted with 1
    cup water

grated rind of 1 orange

3 Tbs. (45 ml) fresh orange juice

1 Tbs. (15 ml) fresh lemon juice, plus more to
    taste

1 Tbs. unsalted butter (optional)

· · ·

garnish: fruity green olive oil

optional garnish: Ancho and Guajillo Chile Puree
    (p. 440) or other cooked chile salsa

Preheat the oven to 375°.

Wash the yam, pierce it once or twice with a fork, and roast it until it is completely soft, about 45 minutes (longer if you've got a very large yam). Allow it to cool slightly, then peel.

While the yam is roasting, chop the onion and sauté it in the olive oil with a pinch of salt over medium-low heat, stirring often until it's soft and browned, at least 20 minutes, longer if needed.

Peel and slice the carrots, parsnips, and celery root and combine them in a medium soup pot with about 3 cups water, 1 teaspoon salt, the honey, and the spices. Simmer the vegetables, covered, until they are completely tender, about half an hour. Add the roasted yam and the onion as soon as they are ready, along with the vegetable broth, grated orange rind, and citrus juices.

Puree the soup in a blender, in batches, or with an immersion blender until perfectly smooth. Return it to a clean pot, bring it back to a simmer, and taste it. Correct the seasoning with more salt or a little more lemon juice if needed. Stir in the butter at the end for a richer taste and silky texture—or leave it out if you prefer a vegan soup.

Serve the soup with a drizzle of fresh olive oil on top, and for a really spectacular dish, drop a spoonful of dark red salsa in the center of each bowl. A salsa that is not hot, just mildly spicy and incredibly flavorful, is a splendid finish.

creamy potato and roasted garlic soup

My friend Jane is one of the people who has a standing invitation to come over for a casual bowl of soup and a glass of wine. One evening she called and said that she had met a new friend, an interesting Turkish writer who was visiting our valley on a writer's retreat.

"She's so isolated," said Jane, "up in the hills with no car, and she doesn't know anyone here. Could I bring her with me for a bowl of soup?"

"How about tonight?" I said. "I have a big pot of soup in the refrigerator."

Fifteen minutes later I got an e-mail. The lonely Turkish writer was fiercely allergic to onions, leeks, scallions, shallots, and green onions. Only garlic was all right.

"I can't imagine that any soup you have in the fridge doesn't have one of those in it," wrote Jane, her mournful tone seeping out of my computer screen.

Too true. But I couldn't get that poor woman out of my mind. Was it possible to make a tasty, savory soup with no onions, no leeks, no shallots? The rustic garlic soup I used to eat in Spain came back to me, and I started thinking about garlic in a creamy soup, about roasted garlic and sautéed garlic, about garlic soup served with garlic toasts.

Here is the soup I made for Alev, the lonely, onion-deprived Turkish writer: a creamy purée of roasted garlic with two kinds of potato, and floating in it dark green pieces of kale that had been sautéed with even more garlic.

· · · SERVES 6—7 · · ·

1 large head garlic (50 g)

4 Tbs. (60 ml) olive oil, plus more for roasting the garlic

1 large russet potato (12 oz.; 350 g)

1 large sweet potato (12 oz.; 350 g)

3 large stalks celery (8 oz.; 225 g)

1 tsp. chopped fresh thyme or ½ tsp. dried thyme

1 bay leaf

1 tsp. sea salt, plus more to taste

freshly ground black pepper

red pepper flakes

2 cups (475 ml) whole milk

2–3 cups (475–700 ml) vegetable broth with no onions (p. 53)*

6–7 oz. (200 g) Russian kale, or other kale

1 Tbs. finely chopped garlic

• • •

garnish: Parmesan Crostini (p. 417) or garlic crostini

Preheat the oven to 375°.

Peel the loose outer husk off the head of garlic, slice off a tiny bit of the top, place the garlic on a square of aluminum foil, and drizzle a little olive oil over it. Fold the foil up and crimp to seal it. Roast the garlic for about 40 minutes, or until it gives when pressed. Allow it to cool.

Meanwhile, peel and dice the potatoes, cut the celery into small dice, and combine the vegetables in a soup pot with 3 cups (750 ml) cold water. Add the thyme, bay leaf, 1 teaspoon salt, some black pepper, and a large pinch of red pepper flakes. Bring the water to a boil, lower the heat, and simmer, covered, for 15 minutes or until the vegetables are completely soft.

When the garlic is ready, squeeze the soft roasted cloves out of their skins and add them to the soup. Stir in the milk and puree the soup in a blender, in batches, or with an immersion blender, but

recipe continues on next page

*If you have no problem with onions, basic light or basic root vegetable broth (pp. 47 and 49) serve very well in this soup.

be careful not to overprocess. Stop the moment the vegetables are smooth, or the potatoes could turn gummy.

Return the soup to the pot, and stir in enough vegetable broth to give the soup the consistency you like. Taste, and add salt and pepper if needed.

Trim the kale, slicing away the tough stems, and cut it into 1-inch squares. Heat 1 tablespoon olive oil in a nonstick pan and stir the chopped garlic in it for a minute or two, just until it begins to color. Add the kale and sauté it, stirring constantly at first, then frequently, until it thoroughly wilts. Add a splash of water—just a few tablespoons—then cover the pan and let the kale steam until the water is gone and the kale is tender, 5 to 6 minutes. Stir the kale into the soup.

Drizzle about a teaspoon of the remaining olive oil over each serving and serve with Parmesan or garlic crostini. If reheating, do it gently, and stir the soup from time to time to prevent scorching.

Another way . . .

Add a little cream in place of some of the milk if you want a richer soup, or stir in some creamy goat cheese and let it melt into the soup just before serving.

CHAPTER 3

green soups

Green Soup • **V**

Green Soup with Mushrooms • **V**

Green Soup with Sweet Potatoes and Sage • **V**

Green Soup with Ginger • **V**

Arugula and Apple Soup • **V**

Kale and Sweet Potato Soup with Cumin and Lemon • **V**

Parsley Soup

not so much a soup as a way of life

My passion for green soup began as a post-holiday health plan one cold January. Luckily, I had been to the farmers' market, so my refrigerator was full of hope and leafy greens. I pulled out chard, big shiny leaves. Green onions. Cilantro. A bunch of curly kale. As I washed and chopped, I thought: garlic, onions . . .

I caramelized the onions in a miserly amount of olive oil. I sautéed the garlic, filling the house with the most gladdening aroma. Who could feel downhearted with the smell of sizzling garlic around them? I added a potato because I'm Polish and can't help it, and simmered everything together in some broth. I added a pinch of pepper and a bit of lemon juice and pureed the soup in a blender.

It was so green! I ate a hot bowlful and sat up straighter at once. Vitamins, minerals, and phytochemicals, those mysterious things we don't fully understand yet but we know they're good for us—I could feel them racing through my system. Most important, it was delicious. That's the beauty of a good soup; like a massage, it feels great while it does a body good.

Over the next few days I dipped into the soup often—a snack while working, a bowl for lunch with a bagel, another bowl for dinner with some white cheese crumbled into it. Everyone ate it. Even my son Teddy, who was about twelve then and would rather have eaten snakes than anything green, grudgingly admitted that he liked it.

I hauled home another basket of greens from the market—spinach, leeks, turnip greens—and made another version. I had a plan: more green soup, less of everything else.

One day friends were coming to dinner. The green soup had become my private habit, but why not let it come to a party? I had some mushrooms on hand; I sautéed them with a lavish amount of garlic, and when they were beautifully brown I tossed them into the simmering greens. No potato this time. A dash of rice vinegar instead of lemon juice, and everything pureed to a velvety green cream.

The green soup with mushrooms seemed more important somehow. It had mystery—the earthiness of the hidden mushrooms, the zing of acid. People starting calling for the recipe.

Over the next weeks and months I made many green soups, and not one was the same as the one before. My desk was littered with scrawled green soup formulas. I lost my holiday pounds, but the green soup had become my steady.

I made my soup with yams instead of potatoes. I made it with spinach and nutmeg—it looked like green paint. A friend brought me fresh watercress from her stream, and I put it together with Yukon Gold potatoes: excellent. Once my eye fell upon a kabocha squash as I was preparing the greens. Another time I'd been roasting beets and had all the fresh tops left, so by chance I came up with one of my favorites, beet green soup.

I've probably made forty or fifty different green soups over the past ten years. It's a way of life now. Usually I puree the soup, blending the flavors into one pungent, savory essence of green, but sometimes I leave the individual elements intact—pieces of squash or yam gradually softening and thickening the broth, flecks of browned onion, and always the strips of dark green. Sometimes I garnish the soup with cheese or croutons or even a spicy salsa, and sometimes I eat it in perfect simplicity. Aaaaah . . .

Collected here are half a dozen of my favorite variations on the theme of green.

MENU

sprouted garbanzo hummus
-page 425-

three-grain bread
-page 390-

. . .

ANY GREEN SOUP,
GARNISHED WITH *QUESO FRESCO*

. . .

farmhouse apple crumble
-page 499-

or

sliced fresh apples and walnuts

MENU NOTES

Green soup is your friend: always delicious, very good for you, and it makes a meal so simple. Salad is superfluous, as you're getting a week's worth of dark leafy greens in each bowl, and green soup pairs well with almost any cheese and bread. My favorite is plain *queso fresco* crumbled on top, with a swirl of fresh olive oil, but all cheeses are welcome at the table with this soup.

This exact menu has been my lunch or supper many times: fresh hummus to start, served with a coarse-textured, chewy bread, the green soup of the day, then a crisp Fuji apple and some walnuts to finish. And if you have time to tinker with the fruit, an old-fashioned apple crumble makes the meal more festive.

Another advantage of this menu is that it can travel to a potluck or even an autumn picnic if you have a large thermos.

green soup

This is one of the first green soups I made, and the template for many that followed: loads of greens, some caramelized onion, a potato, and a bit of lemon juice and cayenne to spark the flavors. There are many wonderful soups, but when I'm eating this one I can't think of one I like better.

· · · SERVES 4—6. THIS SOUP CAN EASILY BE DOUBLED—AND SHOULD BE! · · ·

1 bunch chard or spinach, (8 oz.; 225 g)
1 bunch kale, (8 oz.; 225 g)
4–5 green onions, sliced, white and green parts
½ cup (25 g) loosely packed cilantro
1 tsp. sea salt, plus more to taste
1 medium Yukon Gold potato (5 oz.; 140 g)
1 medium yellow onion (225 g)
1½ Tbs. (22 ml) olive oil
Marsala or dry sherry (optional)
1–2 cloves garlic, finely chopped

2½–3 cups (600–750 ml) any basic vegetable broth (pp. 47–50) or canned vegetable broth
freshly ground black pepper
cayenne
1 Tbs. (15 ml) fresh lemon juice, plus more to taste

· · ·

garnish: fruity green olive oil
optional garnishes:
crumbled fresh white cheese
croutons

Wash the greens thoroughly, trim off their stems, and slice the leaves. Combine the chard or spinach, kale, green onions, and cilantro in a large soup pot with 3 cups (750 ml) water and a teaspoon of salt. Peel the potato, or just scrub it well if you prefer, cut it into small pieces, and add it to the pot. Bring the water to a boil, turn down the flame to low, cover the pot, and let the soup simmer for about half an hour.

Meanwhile, chop the onion, heat a tablespoon of olive oil in a skillet, and cook the onion with a small sprinkle of salt over a medium flame until it is golden brown and soft. This will take up to half an hour. Don't hurry; give it a stir once in a while, and let the slow cooking develop the onion's sweetness. If you like, you can deglaze the pan at the end with a bit of Marsala or sherry—not required, but a nice touch.

Add the caramelized onion to the soup. Put the remaining ½ tablespoon oil in the pan and stir the chopped garlic in it for just a couple of minutes, until it sizzles and smells great. Add the garlic to the pot and simmer the soup for 10 minutes more.

Add enough of the broth to make the soup a soup—it should pour easily from a ladle—and puree it in the blender, in batches, or use an immersion blender. Don't overprocess; potatoes can turn gummy if you work them too much.

Return the soup to the pot, bring it back to a simmer, and taste. Add a pinch more salt if needed, grind in a little black pepper, and add a pinch of cayenne and a tablespoon of lemon juice. Stir well and taste again. Now use your taste buds—correct the seasoning to your taste with a drop more lemon juice or another pinch of salt, and then serve big steaming bowls of green soup.

I always finish this soup with my all-time favorite garnish, a thin drizzle of fruity olive oil. This garnish is not a decoration, it is an essential part of the soup. The taste of the fresh, unheated oil is entirely different from the taste of cooked oil, and I deliberately use a modest amount of oil for sautéing so that I can add some fresh oil at the end.

Other garnishes can be added. Crumbled white cheese is a natural; I like Cotija, a dry Mexican white cheese, or feta. Croutons are great, especially if they're made from rye or pumpernickel bread. Garlic croutons are the bomb, as my kids used to say.

Another way . . .

Rice instead of potato: I often eliminate the potato and instead add 3 tablespoons of Arborio rice to the greens when I cook them. That little bit of rice distributes its starch into the water and purees beautifully. No fear of overblending with rice, so you can have a soup of truly velvety texture.

green soup with mushrooms

The deep and rich flavor that sautéed mushrooms impart to this green soup is irresistible. It's one of the soups that I make regularly all winter—a pleasure to eat, and an infusion of vitamins. Wild mushrooms are fabulous in this soup, if you live in an area where you can get them. As with all the green soups, you can either puree this or to leave it in a more rustic chunky form. I like to have all the flavors melded into a velvety puree and see thin loops of golden olive oil shimmering on top.

· · · SERVES 6—7 · · ·

1 bunch chard (8 oz.; 225 g)
1 bunch spinach (8 oz.; 225 g)
3 Tbs. Arborio rice
1½ tsp. sea salt, plus more to taste
3 Tbs. (45 ml) olive oil
2 yellow onions, chopped (450 g)
1 large leek, white and light green parts, sliced
     (4 oz.; 120 g)
8 oz. (225 g) portobello or other brown
     mushrooms
2–3 cloves garlic, minced
¼ tsp. dried thyme
2 Tbs. (30 ml) Marsala or dry sherry

about 4 cups (1 liter) any basic vegetable broth
     (pp. 47–50) or 3 cups canned vegetable broth,
     diluted with 1 cup water
1–2 Tbs. (15–30 ml) fresh lemon juice
freshly ground black pepper
cayenne
                    · · ·

garnish: fruity green olive oil
optional garnishes:
crumbly white cheese
sour cream
croutons

Wash the chard and spinach thoroughly and cut the chard off its thick stems. Coarsely chop the greens. Combine the chard, spinach, and rice in a large soup pot with 4 cups (1 liter) water and a teaspoon of sea salt. Bring the water to a boil, then lower the heat and simmer, covered, for at least 20 minutes.

Meanwhile, heat 2 tablespoons oil in a nonstick pan and add the chopped onions with a big pinch of salt. Cook them over low heat, stirring occasionally, until they soften, about 10 minutes.

Add the leek and continue cooking until the onions and leek are golden brown, about half an hour.

Clean and dice or chop the mushrooms. Heat the remaining 1 tablespoon olive oil in another pan, throw the garlic in, and stir it for a minute or two on high heat, until it starts to turn golden. Turn the heat down slightly, add the mushrooms with a dash of salt and the thyme, and sauté, stirring often, until the mushrooms are sizzling and browning. The time will vary with the moisture in the mushrooms, but figure on at least 15 minutes. Sprinkle the Marsala or sherry over the mushrooms and stir again as it cooks away.

Add the mushrooms to the soup, along with the caramelized onions and leek, deglazing the pans by swirling a little of the broth in them and adding it back to the pot. This gives your soup the benefit of those flavorful, crusty brown bits that like to coat the pans. Simmer the soup for about 10 minutes.

Add the vegetable broth—a little more or less as needed—and puree the soup in a blender, in batches, or with an immersion blender, or leave it as it is. Return the soup to the pot, add a spoonful of lemon juice, and correct the seasoning with more salt if needed, freshly ground black pepper, and a pinch of cayenne. This is the moment when you must taste and adjust the soup to your own palate—and when adding that last bit of salt, remember to wait a few moments before tasting again.

Pour a thin thread of fresh olive oil on every bowl and add crumbles of cheese, sour cream, or croutons, as you like.

Other ways . . .

Chopped green onions, both the white and green parts, can be added to the soup along with the chard and spinach, and cilantro is also very good. Kale can be used instead of chard, and a more pungent soup can be made with the same amount of mustard greens. A medium-sized diced potato can be added to the soup in place of the rice, or you can add neither rice nor potato and thicken the soup purely with the mushrooms.

green soup with sweet potatoes and sage

Onions and sage, a classic pair, give this beautiful soup its subtle character. The sweet potatoes and stewed garlic add a layer of sweetness under the earthy taste of Russian kale, one of my favorite greens—but it is the perfume of sage that brings it all together.

· · · SERVES 5—6. THIS RECIPE CAN EASILY BE DOUBLED · · ·

1 ¼ lbs. (570 g) sweet potatoes

1 ½ tsp. sea salt, plus more to taste

2–3 Tbs. chopped fresh sage leaves or 1–2 Tbs. crumbled dry sage

1 bunch Russian kale (8 oz.; 225 g)

1 bunch green chard (8 oz.; 225 g)

8 cloves garlic, peeled

about 3 cups (700 ml) basic light vegetable broth (p. 47), basic root vegetable broth (p. 49), or canned vegetable broth

2 large yellow onions (500 g)

2 Tbs. (30 ml) olive oil

freshly ground black pepper

fresh lemon juice (optional)

· · ·

garnish: fruity green olive oil

Peel and dice the sweet potatoes, combine them in a large soup pot with 3 ½ cups (800 ml) water, a teaspoon of salt, and the sage, and bring to a boil. Lower the heat and simmer, covered, about 10 minutes.

Wash the kale and chard, trim away the tough stems, and chop the greens coarsely. Add the greens to the soup, along with the garlic cloves and the vegetable broth. Continue simmering gently, covered, for another 20 minutes.

Meanwhile, chop the onions and sauté them gently with a pinch of sea salt in the olive oil over medium-low heat, stirring frequently, until they are soft and golden brown, 30 to 40 minutes. When the onions are ready, add them to the soup and let it cool slightly.

Puree the soup in a blender, in batches, and return it to a clean pot, or use an immersion blender. Add a little more water or broth if the soup is too thick to pour easily from a ladle. Taste, and correct the seasoning with a bit more salt, if needed, and freshly ground black pepper to taste. If you like, add a small amount of fresh lemon juice, but taste as you go—you don't want to overwhelm the lovely flavor of the onions and sage.

When you serve the soup, drizzle a thread of fruity green olive oil on top of each steaming bowl—just a teaspoon or so. This last step is essential, as the taste of the fresh, unheated olive oil is entirely different from that of cooked oil, and it wakes up all the flavors and makes them sing.

green soup with ginger

Here a simple green soup is given a whiff of something more exotic with the addition of fresh ginger. The flavor is not immediately identifiable; the fresh ginger is balanced by the sweet potato and greens, and the result is mysterious and seductive.

For a more distinctly Asian tilt, you could add a small amount of miso or tamari.

· · · SERVES 5—6. THIS RECIPE CAN EASILY BE DOUBLED · · ·

1 large yellow onion (250 g)

2 Tbs. (30 ml) olive oil

1½ tsp. sea salt, plus more to taste

1 large sweet potato (12 oz.; 350 g)

1 large leek, white and light green parts (5 oz.; 140 g)

1 bunch spinach (8 oz.; 225 g)

1 large bunch green chard (12 oz.; 350 g)

3 Tbs. (30 g) chopped fresh ginger, plus more to taste

2 cups (500 ml) basic light vegetable broth (p. 47), vegetable and ginger broth (p. 53), or canned vegetable broth

2–4 tsp. (10–25 ml) fresh lemon juice

freshly ground black pepper

Chop the onion and cook it slowly in the olive oil with a sprinkle of salt, stirring now and then, over low heat until it is soft and golden, about half an hour.

Meanwhile, peel and dice the sweet potato and put it in a large soup pot with 4 cups (1 liter) water and a teaspoon of sea salt. Thoroughly wash the leek, spinach, and chard, chop them coarsely, and add them to the pot, along with the chopped ginger.

Bring the water to a boil, then lower the heat and simmer the soup, covered, for 30 minutes, or until the vegetables are completely tender. Add the caramelized onions when they are ready. When the vegetables are soft, add the vegetable broth and puree the soup in a blender, in batches, or with an immersion blender until it is perfectly smooth.

Return the soup to a clean pot and add 2 teaspoons lemon juice and a few grinds of black pepper. Taste, and correct the seasoning with additional salt or lemon juice.

Other ways . . .

A little miso or tamari can be stirred in at the very end to deepen the flavor, but add it sparingly and taste as you go—you don't want to overpower the greens and ginger.

For a zestier, more assertive soup, use mustard greens instead of chard and slightly increase the amount of lemon juice, adding a teaspoon at a time until your taste buds say *Yes!*

arugula and apple soup

WITH TOASTED WALNUTS

Peppery arugula and tart-sweet apples come together to make a fall soup of surprising delicacy. Arugula loses its sharp bite when it's cooked, but mature arugula will have a more assertive "bitter greens" flavor. It's delicious; don't be afraid of it. Baby arugula will make a delectable but subtler soup.

A few toasted walnuts add a slight crunch and another quintessential taste of fall. Try to get walnuts from the new season's crop, and enjoy their fresh sweetness.

··· SERVES 6—8 ···

1 large yellow onion, chopped (350 g)

1½ Tbs. (22 ml) olive oil

1½ tsp. sea salt, plus more to taste

12 oz. (350 g) Yukon Gold potatoes

2 medium Fuji, Gala, Braeburn, or other apples (400 g)

1 lb. 2 oz. (500 g) arugula

2 cups sliced green onions (3 oz.; 90 g)

½ cup (22 g) coarsely chopped fresh flat-leaf parsley

about 2 cups (500 ml) basic light vegetable broth (p. 47) or canned vegetable broth

2 Tbs. (30 ml) fresh lemon juice, plus more to taste

freshly ground black pepper

cayenne

ground nutmeg

2–3 tsp. (20–30 ml) agave nectar or honey, if needed

½ cup (60 g) chopped walnuts

···

garnish: fruity green olive oil

Sauté the chopped onion in the olive oil with a pinch of salt, stirring often over a medium flame for 25 to 30 minutes, or until the onion is soft and golden brown.

Scrub the potatoes, peel and core the apples, and coarsely chop both. Wash the arugula, and if the branches are large and mature, remove any tough-looking stems. Coarsely chop the leaves.

Combine the potatoes and apples in an ample soup pot with 4 cups (1 liter) water and a teaspoon of sea salt. Bring the water to a boil, then cover the pot and lower the heat to a simmer. After 10 minutes, add the sliced green onions. After 5 more minutes, add the arugula and the parsley. Simmer for another 6 to 8 minutes.

By now your caramelized onions might be ready. If so, add them to the soup, along with 2 cups vegetable broth and a couple tablespoons lemon juice. Grind in plenty of black pepper and add a modest pinch of cayenne and the same amount of nutmeg.

Puree the soup in a blender, in batches, or with an immersion blender, but be sure to stop as soon as you have the feel you like in a soup; cooked potatoes can become viscous if overprocessed. I like to leave this soup at a slightly textured puree, not rough, but not completely smooth either. If the soup feels too thick to you, add a touch more broth.

Taste the soup and correct the seasoning with a bit more lemon juice if needed, or a pinch of salt. If the soup tastes overly tart—this depends on the variety of apples—add a modest spoonful of agave nectar or honey and taste it again.

Toast your chopped walnuts: spread them on a baking sheet and put them in a 300° oven for no more than 10 minutes. As soon as you smell them, they are ready. They will crisp up as they cool.

Drizzle a thread of olive oil on top of each bowl of steaming soup, and sprinkle with a few toasted walnuts.

Another way...

Thick yogurt or crème fraîche, or even a spoonful of heavy cream, can be spooned on top of this soup as a garnish.

kale and sweet potato soup with cumin and lemon

Sturdy kale, leeks, and sweet potatoes keep their distinct textures and flavors in this chopped green soup, and the combination of tart fresh lemon with toasted cumin just shines.

Any kind of kale can be used in this soup. I usually make it with Russian kale, but you can use cavalo nero (dinosaur kale) or curly-leaf kale—or all three. Yams can be used in place of sweet potatoes if that's what you have on hand.

· · · SERVES 6 GENEROUSLY · · ·

2 large leeks, white and light green parts (6 oz.; 170 g)

1 large yellow onion (250 g)

2 Tbs. (30 ml) olive oil

1½ tsp. sea salt, plus more to taste

12 oz. (350 g) sweet potatoes

1 small Yukon Gold or white potato (100 g)

12 oz. (350 g) Russian kale or cavalo nero

4 green onions, sliced

⅔ cup (45 g) chopped cilantro

freshly ground black pepper

2–2½ cups (500 ml) any basic vegetable broth (pp. 47–50), vegetable and ginger broth (p. 52), or canned vegetable broth

1 Tbs. cumin seeds

1–2 Tbs. (15–30 ml) fresh lemon juice

cayenne

· · ·

garnish: fruity green olive oil

optional garnish: crumbled feta cheese

Thoroughly wash and coarsely chop the leeks and chop the onion. Heat the olive oil in a nonstick pan and start sautéing the onion with a sprinkle of salt over a medium flame. When it is translucent and soft, add the leeks and keep cooking, stirring often, until all the vegetables are golden, about 20 minutes.

Meanwhile, peel the sweet potatoes, scrub the Yukon Gold or white potato, and cut them all into ½-inch dice. Trim the thick stems from the kale and cut the greens into 1-inch strips, or chop them very coarsely. Combine both potatoes and kale in a soup pot with 5 cups (1 ¼ liters) cold water and a teaspoon of salt, bring to a boil, then lower the heat and simmer for about 15 minutes.

Add the sautéed leeks and onion to the pot, along with the sliced green onions, cilantro, and a lot of freshly ground black pepper. Add as much of the vegetable broth as you need to give the soup a nice consistency—this is a hearty soup but not a stew, and it should pour easily from a ladle. Simmer the soup gently, covered, for about 10 more minutes.

Lightly toast the cumin seeds in a dry pan just until they are fragrant, and grind them with a mortar or a spice grinder. Stir the cumin and a spoonful of lemon juice into the soup and taste. Add more salt, pepper, or lemon juice as needed, and finish with a pinch of cayenne or any hot red pepper.

Ladle the soup into warm bowls and garnish each bowl with a swirl of fruity olive oil. If you like cheese, a heaping spoonful of tangy crumbled feta dropped on top of each serving is fantastic.

parsley soup

When I first started writing about green soups, I got e-mails from all over. Everyone seemed to have a green soup they'd been making forever and wanted to share. One fellow cook sent me her recipe for a soup in which parsley was used as the main ingredient instead of a flavoring or garnish. I tried it and loved it. Here's my variation on her variation. It's a sort of rustic leek and potato soup that's been taken over by a gang of parsley, but in the nicest way.

I use one of the creamy-textured potatoes, such as Yukon Gold, and I always use flat-leaf parsley, also known as Italian parsley, which has a stronger flavor than curly parsley.

· · · SERVES 6 · · ·

12 oz. (350 g) Yukon Gold or other yellow potatoes

1 tsp. sea salt, plus more to taste

3 bunches fresh flat-leaf parsley (8–9 oz.; 250 g)

3 leeks, white part (8 oz.; 225 g)

2 Tbs. unsalted butter

1 Tbs. (15 ml) olive oil

4 cups (1 liter) basic light vegetable broth (p. 47) or basic root vegetable broth (p. 49), or 3 cups canned vegetable broth diluted with 1 cup water

white pepper

ground nutmeg

½ cup (120 ml) white wine

1–2 Tbs. (15–30 ml) fresh lemon juice

· · ·

garnish: freshly grated Parmigiano-Reggiano cheese

Scrub the potatoes and chop them. Put them in a soup pot with about 3 cups (750 ml) water and a teaspoon of sea salt and simmer them, covered, for about 10 minutes. Meanwhile, rinse and chop the parsley. Most stems are okay here; toss out only the biggest ones. You should wind up with about 4 cups coarsely chopped parsley. Wash and slice the leeks; you should have about 3 cups.

In a large sauté pan, melt a tablespoon of butter with half a tablespoon olive oil and sauté the chopped parsley over medium-high heat, tossing and stirring it until it sizzles in the pan and begins to color, 6 or 7 minutes. Add the parsley to the potatoes.

In the same pan, sauté the leeks over medium heat in the remaining 1 tablespoon butter and ½ tablespoon oil until they are soft and turning gold, about 10 minutes. Add them to the soup, along with the vegetable broth, a generous sprinkle of white pepper, a big pinch of nutmeg, and the white wine. Simmer everything together, covered, for about half an hour. Puree the soup in a blender, in batches, or use an immersion blender. Be careful not to overprocess, as potatoes can become gummy. I like this soup as a rough puree, with plenty of texture.

Return the pureed soup to the pot, bring it to a simmer, and taste. Add more salt if it's needed, stir in a bit of fresh lemon juice for more acidity, and taste again until it's just right. This soup has a pleasingly forward flavor, with a piquant edge from the lemon and pepper, but it should not be sour. The need for lemon juice will depend to some degree on what kind of wine you've added.

Serve the soup hot, garnished with freshly grated Parmigiano-Reggiano cheese.

Another way . . .

A little creamy goat cheese stirred into this soup is delicious, and so is cream. I like it best the way I like all my green soups—with a drizzle of fresh, fruity olive oil on top, and then the cheese passed at the table.

CHAPTER 4

winter squash soups

Roasted Kabocha Squash and Celery Root Soup

Spicy Butternut Ginger Soup • **V**

Roasted Turnip and Winter Squash Soup

Red Lentil and Squash Soup • **V**

Winter Squash and Yam Soup with Poblano Peppers • **V**

Tomatillo, Squash, and Mustard Greens Soup • **V**

all about squash (hardly!)

One of the most exciting things in the fall farmers' market is the great array of winter squashes. Forget about summer now, they seem to say. Look at us, we're beautiful and amazing, and we'll keep in your cellar all winter.

In fact, never mind the cellar. I have often had a perfect white pumpkin on my mantle, or the elegant curves of a long, tawny Tahitian squash decorating my sideboard, for weeks or even months.

But exterior beauty is not a requirement for winter squash. Some of my favorites are the kabochas, with their warty gray-green shells; inside is a brilliant saffron-yellow flesh, sweet and dense and vegetal. Kabocha is a generic name for winter squash grown in Japan, and though there are many types of kabocha, here they are rarely differentiated. A kabocha can be that muddy green and warty one, or it can be smooth and bright orange. It can weigh a pound or 5 pounds.

What does all this mean? When it comes to squash, it's a jungle out there, and I don't just mean the vines. The tangle of varieties and nomenclature can make you crazy. There are dozens, if not hundreds, of squashes. Different varieties sometimes go by the same name, and the same variety can often go by different names. Local usage rules. Moreover, squashes cross and mutate easily, so even the same squash, called by the same name, might be quite different the next time you meet it. Do you think you know what a pumpkin is? I made many pies before I learned that it can be any of the hard-shelled squashes—there's no botanical distinction. And if you've ever made your pumpkin pie from canned pumpkin, you could just as well have called it butternut pie, because that's what's in the can.

Oh, those squashes. They're maddening, but they make the most gorgeous soups you will ever see or eat. Stop worrying about it and enjoy them.

Commonly available where I live and shop are several squashes I can wholeheartedly recommend. The kabochas, of course—their deep yellow or orange flesh has full, rich flavor, natural sweetness, and a dense, fine-grained texture. Butternut squash is also reliably flavorful and sweet; it has a lighter, juicier texture than a kabocha, and the larger butternuts seem to have a more developed flavor. Both of these come in moderate sizes; 2 or 3 pounds is not unusual.

Blue Hubbards are a great old variety. They vary tremendously in size and can weigh up to 50 pounds. Wow! (Of course, most are much smaller.) But in my experience the big Hubbards with the rough, ridged, blue-green skin are the real deal—they have the big flavor. Dainty varieties of many of the old giants are now being bred for the sake of convenience in marketing, but these reduced sizes sometimes have reduced flavor. Too bad, but it's another good reason to shop at the farmers' market, where you can often get a piece sliced to order from a huge squash.

Tahitian squash is another giant. In its long, leisurely maturation it grows to enormous proportions. It looks like a crookneck butternut from the land of Gargantua. But a fine Tahitian has superb flavor, is sweet as honey and silky in texture.

And in October and November pumpkin patches spring up on the roadsides, and there I find good "pie pumpkins," which to me means good soup pumpkins. They change from year to year, and I rely on the farmers to tell me which are best.

choosing, buying, storing

Winter squashes are best in fall and winter—no big surprise there—but they keep extraordinarily well, and if stored in a fairly cool and dry place they actually improve with keeping. In other words, they continue to ripen and develop their flavor while they decorate your sideboard. If you live in a hot or humid place, their sideboard life will be a bit shorter, but at cool room temperature, an intact winter squash will keep for months.

At the market, remember that a hard-skinned winter squash must be hard-skinned.

Press the shell, and if there is any hint of sponginess, the squash is either not yet ready or past its prime. Look also for a thick, strong stem; a skinny or green stem is a sign that the squash is not mature. Vivid color is always a good sign. A pumpkin that is supposed to be orange, golden, or cream-colored should not have greenish areas. A blue-green or gray squash shouldn't be showing pale whitish spots.

If you are buying cut squash, look at the flesh—it should be dense and moist, not fibrous, not dry-looking. And again, look for that saturated, bright color. Cut squash should be refrigerated and used within about a week.

cutting, peeling, cooking

The marvelously hard shell that makes these squashes such good keepers also makes them the very devil to cut and peel. A cleaver is a good tool for this. Otherwise, get out your biggest, strongest chef's knife—and be careful. Knives can slip on that tough skin, but if you use a few simple precautions, you can tame those pumpkins.

First, always put a hard squash on a firm, stable surface, and always, always work with the blade or tip of your knife pointing away from you. The best way to split a squash is to place it on that firm surface and stab it hard with the good chef's knife or whack it with the cleaver. Then take a rolling pin and tap the knife, either on the handle or the point where the blade meets the handle, until you can split the squash in half. You may have to repeat the stab-and-hammer maneuver once or twice for a very large squash.

When the squash is open, scrape out the seeds and strings with a metal spoon. If you are going to roast the squash in the oven, you're done. If you need to peel it, place the halves cut side down on a good cutting board and cut them in thick slices. Lay the slices on their sides and cut away pieces of skin by slicing down toward the board. The blade edge always moves away from you. With this method, you can quickly liberate the squash from its shell and keep all your fingers intact.

MENU

ROASTED KABOCHA SQUASH AND CELERY ROOT SOUP

-page 111-

crusty whole-grain bread

. . .

kale salad with cranberries and pine nuts
-page 473-

. . .

octavia's gingerbread
-page 490-

with yogurt cheese or crème fraîche

see menu notes on next page

Roasted Kabocha Squash and Celery Root Soup is the marriage of a homely squash with a downright scary-looking celery root, which results in a soup of silken, golden beauty and gorgeous flavor.

Soups like these are the payoff for the long maturation of winter squashes. In cooler climates, some stay on the vine for six months before they are ripe, or have to finish ripening in the shed, protected from frost. But when I eat this soup on a cold winter day, I can taste the whole summer and fall in it. It has richness without being heavy, and the deep natural sweetness of the squash is balanced by the assertive taste of the celery root.

Any crusty, chewy whole-grain bread is wonderful with this soup. I've had multigrain sourdough from the excellent local bakery and my own Whole-Wheat Walnut Bread. A simple quesadilla is another perfect match, spiked with a chile salsa to bring a little heat to the party. The taste of chiles is a natural combination with squash soups, and a chile sauce can be used as a garnish as well, a deep brick-red pool in the amber squash puree.

Kale salad brings something very different to this meal. Earthy raw kale is cut in thin shreds, set off by cranberries, pine nuts, and peppery arugula, and lightly marinated in oil and lemon—a complete contrast to the velvet luxury of the golden soup.

For dessert, Octavia's Gingerbread is such a treat, the strong, dark sweetness of molasses and sting of ginger cooled by a spoonful of yogurt cheese or some crème fraîche. But if there's no time to bake gingerbread, have a bowl of creamy Greek-style yogurt with dark wildflower honey poured over it, and a scattering of walnuts—a farmhouse dessert that is fit for a queen.

roasted kabocha squash and celery root soup

WITH MAPLE SYRUP AND BROWNED BUTTER

A rich and lovely soup for the harvest season, this gets its complex flavor from the subtle layering of celery root and turnip under the sweet, golden kabocha squash. The browned butter and maple syrup stirred in at the end turn these simple ingredients into a luxury soup.

If you can't find kabocha squash, you can use butternut squash instead; it is usually available and reliably good.

· · · SERVES 6—7 · · ·

1 kabocha squash (2½ lbs.; 1.1 kg)
3 medium turnips (12 oz.; 350 g)
1 medium celery root (12 oz.; 350 g)
1½ Tbs. (22 ml) olive oil
1½ tsp. sea salt, plus more to taste
2 leeks, white and light green parts (150 g)
1 yellow onion (250 g)
a few rosemary leaves
2–3 cups (475–700 ml) basic light vegetable broth (p. 47), basic root vegetable broth (p. 49), or canned vegetable broth

2–3 Tbs. (30–45 ml) fresh lemon juice, plus more to taste
hot paprika or cayenne
3 Tbs. (45 ml) pure maple syrup, plus more to taste
3 Tbs. unsalted butter

· · ·

garnish: ¾ cup (75 g) chopped pecans, lightly toasted

Preheat the oven to 400°.

Cut the kabocha squash in half with a very sharp knife, scrape out the seeds and strings, and place the halves cut side down on a lightly oiled nonstick baking sheet. Peel the turnips and cut them in wedges. Peel the celery root and cut it into 1-inch pieces. Toss the turnips and celery root

recipe continues on next page

with about half a tablespoon of the olive oil and a pinch of sea salt and spread them on another baking sheet.

Roast all the prepared vegetables in the hot oven for 50 to 60 minutes, or until the squash gives easily when poked with a wooden spoon and the turnips and celery root are tender and flecked with dark brown. When the squash is cool enough to handle, scoop it out of its shell.

While those vegetables are roasting, cut the leeks in half lengthwise, wash them thoroughly, and slice thinly; you should have about 1 ½ cups. Chop the onion and sauté it gently in the remaining 1 tablespoon olive oil, with a dash of salt and the rosemary, stirring now and then over medium heat until it is soft and golden brown.

In a large soup pot, combine the roasted squash, turnips, celery root, leeks, and sautéed onions with 4 cups (1 liter) water and a teaspoon of salt. Simmer the vegetables, covered, about 20 minutes to let them get perfectly soft. Add 2 cups vegetable broth, 2 tablespoons fresh lemon juice, a pinch of hot paprika or cayenne, and the maple syrup.

Allow the soup to cool somewhat, then puree it in a blender, in batches, or in the pot with an immersion blender. The various flavors in this soup are better when blended into one harmonious new flavor, but you can make the texture whatever you like. I prefer this as a silky-smooth soup, but you can stop at a rougher puree if you like. Add a little more vegetable broth if the soup is too thick to pour easily from a ladle. Return the soup to a clean pot and bring it back to a simmer.

In a small saucepan, melt the butter over medium heat. Lower the heat and keep cooking the butter for a few minutes, stirring with a whisk, until it is a light golden brown. Stir the browned butter into the soup.

Taste the soup, and correct the seasoning, whisking in more salt, lemon juice, or maple syrup as needed. This last step is essential, as kabocha squashes vary in sweetness and lemons certainly vary in acidity. As always, when working on the sweet-sour balance you reach a point where only a good pinch of salt will make it right.

Sprinkle each serving of this soup with a spoonful of toasted chopped pecans.

spicy butternut ginger soup

The spiciness in this soup comes entirely from the fresh ginger. It's the soup equivalent of an old-fashioned gingersnap—and no, you can't use powdered ginger from a jar.

I made this soup with Tahitian squash, and it was wonderful. But Tahitian squashes take eleven months to mature, so I imagine they're scarce in Vermont and other places with shorter growing seasons. I've also made it with a good sweet butternut squash, which was delicious, and butternuts are widely available.

· · · SERVES 5—6 · · ·

2½ lbs. (1 kg) butternut or Tahitian squash
2 yellow onions (450 g)
8 oz. (225 g) yellow or red potatoes
1 Tbs. (15 ml) olive oil
1 tsp. sea salt, plus more to taste
about 3 cups (700 ml) basic light vegetable broth
(p. 47), vegetable and ginger broth (p. 52), or
canned vegetable broth
3 Tbs. finely chopped fresh ginger

⅓ cup (20 g) chopped cilantro
2 tsp. (10 ml) rice vinegar
2 Tbs. (30 ml) fresh lemon juice, plus more to
taste
1–2 Tbs. (15–30 ml) honey or agave nectar

· · ·

optional garnish: a little cream or some fresh
cilantro

Preheat the oven to 400°.

Peel and seed the squash. Winter squashes have tough shells, which is why they keep so beautifully for months, but be careful when peeling them, as knives can slip. To peel a winter squash, cut it in half lengthwise, then put it cut side down on a board and slice away pieces of the skin with a very sharp knife, always cutting away from your hand and toward the board. You should have 2 pounds (900 g) of squash after discarding the rind and seeds. Cut it into 2-inch cubes. Peel the onions and cut them in large pieces. Scrub the potatoes and cut them into 1-inch pieces.

Toss the vegetables together with the olive oil and a teaspoon of salt and spread them on 2 baking sheets. Roast the vegetables in the hot oven for half an hour, stir them and turn them over, lower the heat to 375°, and put them back in the oven for another 20 minutes. The vegetables should be soft, and browning on the edges.

Put the roasted vegetables into a large soup pot with 2 cups (500 ml) water and the vegetable broth, fresh ginger, cilantro, and rice vinegar. Simmer everything together for about half an hour, then puree the soup in a blender, in batches, or in the pot with an immersion blender, adding a little more vegetable broth or water if it seems too thick.

Bring the soup back to a simmer and season it with the lemon juice and honey. Adjust the seasoning as needed; squashes can vary enormously in sweetness and lemons in acidity, so you must taste at this point and find the perfect balance. As always, sometimes what is needed is that last pinch of sea salt.

A spoonful of heavy cream or a few sprigs of cilantro—or both—would make a fine garnish for this soup.

roasted turnip and winter squash soup

This soup is a taste of fall. When the weather turns cold and winter squashes appear in the market, the flavors of roasted root vegetables and sage seem just right—and turnips perfectly balance the sweet squash. This is not an overly rich soup, yet it feels luxurious with that little bit of mascarpone whisked in at the end and a scattering of toasted pine nuts on top.

· · · SERVES 6—7 · · ·

1 lb. (450 g) turnips

3 Tbs. (45 ml) olive oil

2 tsp. sea salt, plus more to taste

3 lbs. (1⅓ kg) Tahitian or butternut squash

6 oz. (170 g) potatoes

2 cups (200 g) chopped leeks, white and light
 green parts

1½ Tbs. chopped fresh sage leaves or 2 tsp.
 crumbled dried sage

about 4 cups (1 liter) basic light vegetable broth
 (p. 47), basic root vegetable broth (p. 49), or
 canned vegetable broth

2–3 Tbs. (30–45 ml) fresh lemon juice, plus more
 to taste

freshly ground black pepper

3 Tbs. mascarpone

½ cup (75 g) lightly toasted pine nuts (technique
 on p. 232)

Preheat the oven to 375°.

Peel the turnips and cut them into wedges, toss them with a tablespoon of olive oil and a generous pinch of salt, and spread them on a nonstick baking sheet. Cut the squash in half lengthwise and scrape out the seeds. Place it cut side down on an oiled nonstick baking sheet. If using a portion of a large Tahitian squash, cut it into 2-inch-thick wedges, scrape out the seeds, and arrange the wedges on the oiled baking sheet.

Roast the turnips and squash for at least 40 minutes, or until the squash is completely soft and the turnips are tender and flecked with dark spots. Allow the squash to cool slightly, then scrape it out of its skin and measure; you should have about 4 cups.

Meanwhile, wash and chop the potatoes and combine them with the chopped leeks in a large soup pot with 4 cups (1 liter) water, a teaspoon of salt, and the sage. Bring the water to a boil, reduce the heat, and simmer, covered, for about half an hour, or until the vegetables are tender. Add the roasted squash and turnips and the vegetable broth.

Puree the soup until smooth in a blender, in batches, or use an immersion blender. Return the soup to the pot and bring it back to just under a simmer. Add 2 tablespoons lemon juice, plenty of black pepper, and the mascarpone. Stir and heat gently until the mascarpone has completely melted into the soup. Taste, and correct the salt or lemon juice if needed.

Serve the soup very hot, and garnish each bowl with a generous drizzle of the remaining olive oil and a scattering of toasted pine nuts.

Another way . . .

Toasted pumpkin seeds can be used instead of pine nuts as a garnish. If you want something assertive, a dab of Simple Chipotle Sauce (p. 439) or Ancho and Guajillo Chile Puree (p. 440) floated on top of the creamy soup is truly delicious, and the pine nuts or toasted pumpkin seeds go with it beautifully—scatter them over the two-tone soup.

red lentil and squash soup

Red lentils are actually pink, and turn a rich gold when they are cooked. Here they are combined with a sweet winter squash, spices, and a touch of lemon juice.

This thick, satisfying soup takes well to a number of garnishes, starting with my favorite, a swirl of fruity olive oil. Other great garnishes are a spoonful of medium-hot chile salsa, a drop of sour cream or crème fraîche, and homemade croutons. A few crumbles of any fresh white cheese would also be nice.

· · · SERVES 6—7 · · ·

1 generous cup (200 g) red lentils
1½ tsp. sea salt
1 small butternut squash (1½ lbs; 700 g)
2 medium yellow onions, chopped (450 g)
1½ Tbs. (22 ml) olive oil
1 small yam or sweet potato (5–6 oz.; 150 g)
2 Tbs. minced fresh ginger
1 Tbs. cumin seeds, toasted and ground
1 tsp. turmeric
¼–½ tsp. red pepper flakes, plus more to taste
4–5 cups (1 liter) basic light vegetable broth
    (p. 47) or vegetable and ginger broth
    (p. 52), or 4 cups canned broth diluted with
    1 cup water

2–3 Tbs. (30–45 ml) fresh lemon juice, plus more
    to taste

· · ·

optional garnishes:
fruity green olive oil
chile salsa
sour cream
croutons
fresh white cheese

Preheat the oven to 375°.

Rinse the lentils and combine them in a soup pot with 4 cups (1 liter) water and 1 teaspoon salt. Bring to a boil, lower the heat, and boil gently for about 20 minutes, skimming off any foam that rises to the top.

While the lentils simmer, cut the squash in half, seed it, and put the halves cut side down on a baking sheet. Roast the squash in the hot oven for 45 minutes, or until it is soft. At the same time, sauté the chopped onions in the olive oil with a big pinch of salt over medium heat, stirring often, until they are soft and turning golden brown, 20 to 30 minutes. Peel and dice the yam.

When the lentils are just tender, add the sautéed onions, diced yam, minced ginger, cumin, turmeric, red pepper flakes, and 4 cups vegetable broth. Simmer everything together, covered, for another 25 minutes. As soon as the roasted squash is ready, scoop it out of its skin—you should have about 2½ cups of cooked squash—and add it to the soup. Cook until everything is soft. Add another cup of vegetable broth if the soup seems too thick.

You can stir up the soup and leave it this way, with a rough, rustic texture. Or, if you want a smooth soup, remove it from the heat, let it cool slightly, then purée in a blender, in batches, or with an immersion blender.

Return the soup to the pot and bring it back to a simmer. Stir in the lemon juice a little at a time, tasting as you go. Correct the seasoning with more salt as needed. This is also the time when you might decide to amp up the red pepper a bit, if you like a spicier soup.

winter squash and yam soup with poblano peppers

The rich sweetness of winter squash and yams and the slight spiciness of poblano chile peppers make this an exciting combination. For a milder soup, cut down on the amount of peppers. You can use other chiles, such as Anaheims, in place of poblanos, but try a bit before you add them to the soup, as peppers vary tremendously in their heat.

· · · SERVES 6—7 · · ·

3 lbs. (⅓ kg) kabocha or butternut squash, or a
    combination
1 large yam (12 oz.; 350 g)
3–4 fresh green poblano peppers (10 oz.; 280 g)
2 yellow onions, chopped (500 g)
2 Tbs. (30 ml) olive oil
sea salt
5 cups (1¼ liters) any basic vegetable broth
    (pp. 47–50) or 4 cups canned vegetable broth
    diluted with 1 cup water

½ cup (30 g) roughly chopped cilantro
2–3 Tbs. (30–45 ml) fresh lemon juice
freshly ground black pepper
          · · ·

garnishes:
olive oil or pumpkinseed oil
toasted pumpkin seeds

Preheat the oven to 400°.

Split the squashes lengthwise, scrape out the seeds and strings, and lay them cut side down on a lightly oiled baking sheet. Scrub the yam, pierce its skin with a fork, and put it in a small baking dish. Roast the squashes and yam in the hot oven until they are soft, probably about an hour, then allow them to cool. Scoop out all the soft flesh of the squashes, including any dark, caramelized bits, and peel and slice the yam.

Turn on the broiler. Arrange the whole poblano peppers on another baking sheet and broil them, turning them over as needed, until their skins are charred and blistered. The time will vary with the size of the peppers, but figure on 15 to 20 minutes. When they are charred on all sides, put them immediately in a paper bag and close it tightly to allow them to sweat. After about 5 minutes, take them out and slip off the skins. Remove the stems and seeds, and slice the peppers into thin strips or cut them into small squares.

Meanwhile, slowly sauté the chopped onions in the olive oil with a dash of sea salt, stirring often over medium heat until they are soft and golden brown, 20 to 30 minutes.

In a large soup pot, combine the squash, yam, caramelized onions, 2 cups (500 ml) water, the vegetable broth, and the cilantro. Simmer 20 minutes, then puree the soup in a blender, in batches, or with an immersion blender, until perfectly smooth. Return the soup to the pot and correct the salt to your taste. Stir in a little lemon juice, a little black pepper, and the slices of poblano peppers. If you like to be careful about spicy things, add half the peppers, stir, taste, then add more as you like.

Serve the soup with a thread of olive or pumpkinseed oil swirled on top and a sprinkle of toasted pumpkin seeds.

tomatillo, squash, and mustard greens soup

66 I t's like borscht!" said Teddy's Russian friend, Sveta, when she ate this soup.

I had to laugh. Not like any borscht from Poland or Russia, but I knew what she meant about the combination of sweet, tangy, and peppery vegetables. In this case they were sour tomatillos, mustard greens, and a squash that takes ten months to ripen—things that wouldn't be found in northern Europe. But this soup does capture the essential sweet-tart richness that a good winter borscht should have, so here's a California borscht. Why not?

Ingredient note: Tomatillos look like little green tomatoes with loose, papery husks around them. They are commonly available now in supermarkets, and always in stores that carry Latin American produce.

· · · SERVES 6—7 · · ·

1 small Tahitian squash or medium butternut
   squash (2¼ lbs; 1 kg)
12 oz. (350 g) small tomatillos
2 large yellow onions (700 g)
2 Tbs. (30 ml) olive oil
sea salt
1 bunch curly mustard greens (8–9 oz.; 250 g)
1 cup (about 60 g) chopped cilantro

about 4 cups (1 liter) basic light vegetable broth
   (p. 47) or basic root vegetable broth (p. 49), or
   3 cups canned vegetable broth diluted with
   1 cup water
crushed dried red chiles

· · ·

garnish: fruity green olive oil
optional garnish: crumbled farmer cheese or
   feta cheese

Preheat the oven to 400°.

Cut the squash in half lengthwise, using a very sharp knife or a cleaver, and scrape out all the seeds and strings. Place the squash cut side down on a lightly oiled nonstick baking sheet and roast it until it gives easily when poked with a wooden spoon (and be sure to check this in the thickest part of the squash). Roasting time will vary, but count on about an hour.

Remove the papery husks from the tomatillos, cut them in half unless they are truly tiny, and spread them on a baking pan lined with a piece of foil (tomatillos are messy). Roast the tomatillos in the oven with the squash, but take them out when they look done: soft, juicy, and beginning to color. This should take 20 to 30 minutes, depending on the size of the tomatillos.

Meanwhile, coarsely chop the onions. Heat the olive oil in a large nonstick skillet, add the onions and a big pinch of salt, and cook the onions gently over medium-low heat, stirring often, until they are soft and golden brown, about 30 minutes. Wash the mustard greens, remove and discard the tough stems, and cut the greens into pieces about 1 inch long.

When the squash is done, scrape it out of its skin and chop it roughly. Give the roasted tomatillos a quick chop as well.

In an ample soup pot, combine all the vegetables and the cilantro with 3 cups (750 ml) water, the vegetable broth, and a pinch of crushed red chiles. Simmer the soup, covered, for about half an hour. Taste and correct the seasoning, adding salt if needed, which will depend on the saltiness of the vegetable broth.

Drizzle a little fruity olive oil on top of each serving and sprinkle on a few crumbles of fresh white farmer cheese or feta cheese if you like.

CHAPTER 5

bean soups

White Bean and Garlic Soup with Greens • **V**

Fasolia Gigante Soup with Spinach • **V**

Green Lentil Soup with Cumin and Lemon • **V**

Lima Bean Soup • **V**

Black Bean and Squash Soup • **V**

Spicy Black Bean Soup with Sweet Peppers • **V**

Old-Fashioned Split Pea Soup • **V**

Carol's Finnish Pea Soup with Apples • **V**

beans—buying, cooking, eating

Beans, with their legume cousins lentils and peas, are a great source of protein and fiber. Their virtues in the areas of nutrition and economy are well known, so let's talk about taste. Beans are a great source of deliciousness!

One of my favorite bean recipes is so basic it's startling. Four ingredients: cannellini, sage leaves, garlic cloves, and olive oil. Five if we count the salt. The beans are simmered with sage and garlic, then salt is added when they are tender. Soft and buttery, the white beans swim in a delicate, sage-perfumed broth. A little fresh olive oil is stirred in. Done. With a few chard or spinach leaves added, that rustic Italian dish becomes a soup I could eat all year.

I also have a passion for spicy beans. I love pink lentils blended with Indian spices, black beans in their cloak of ruddy chile puree, or green lentils with fiery harissa.

Humble foods have come back into fashion with their new name—comfort food—and now we can find a dazzling array of heirloom beans in our markets. There are over four hundred varieties of beans. Let's start with cannellini, fasolia Gigante, French green lentils, lima beans, black beans, and green split peas. Here they are, ready to be a sustaining, comforting part of the soup season.

But first, a few practical facts that will make cooking beans much more rewarding.

dried beans still need to be fresh beans

Dried beans will keep almost indefinitely, and this is both a boon and a problem. The question must be asked: how long have those beans been dry? Because beans that have been stored too long become harder to cook. The older the bean, the longer the simmering time before it reaches a pleasant softness, and beans that are too old can be so dry that they don't want to get soft again *ever*.

Buy your beans somewhere that does a brisk business in beans, where you will find beans from the same year's harvest. And once you've bought your beans, don't squirrel them away in the back of your own pantry for an extra year or two before using them.

soaking: not required

Soaking beans before cooking them reduces the cooking time and may result in a slightly more even texture, but it is not required. Some cooks swear by soaking, and others (me) feel that in most cases it can be skipped.

soft water, please

It is essential to use soft water for cooking beans. Spring water is best, or filtered tap water if you have a water softener. Adding a pinch of baking soda will soften water, but can add a chalky taste.

no salt until tender. i mean it.

Do not add salt, or any kind of acid, until your beans are tender. Salt can interfere with the cooking process and keep your beans from achieving a creamy-soft texture. This may be more of a problem with some beans than with others, but I play it safe and add salt later in the cooking process. Lemon, tomato, or any other acid will have a similar effect.

get to know epazote

Epazote is an herb that is widely used in Mexico, most often added to beans as they cook, both for its pleasant flavor and to make the beans more digestible. Long ago I took the advice of my Mexican friends and tried epazote. Now I hardly ever cook beans without it. The leaves have an astringent scent, especially when dried, but develop a lovely, mellow flavor as they cook with beans. You can find fresh or dried epazote in any Latin American market, and in many farmers' markets throughout the summer and fall.

MENU

oil-cured black olives, assorted pecorino cheeses

. . .

WHITE BEAN AND GARLIC SOUP
WITH GREENS
-page 130 -

olive and rosemary focaccia
-page 400 -

. . .

dark chocolate and sweet kishu mandarins

Soups that combine beans or legumes and vegetables make an ideal meal in a bowl. This one is a deeply satisfying combination of slowly simmered white beans infused with sage and garlic and a bounty of dark leafy greens.

The menu built around those flavors is a template for bean soups: something savory to nibble at the start, then the hearty bean soup paired with an excellent bread, and an effortless dessert. It is a rustic meal, but elegant in its simplicity.

However, bean soups can also adapt and expand well into all sorts of more elaborate combinations. A tossed salad of bitter greens would be perfect with this soup, or, in the summer, a plate of ripe tomatoes bathed in olive oil and herbs. That plate of cured olives might be elaborated into a platter with marinated roasted peppers and a caponata, or an assortment of roasted root vegetables, depending on the season.

Dessert can be a flight of fancy—but I defy you to find a more exquisite combination of tastes than an excellent bittersweet chocolate and tiny mandarin oranges. The chocolate might be a truffle, biscotti, a torte, or homemade brownies—or simply a bar of fine chocolate, broken into pieces and passed around with the basket of mandarins.

Kishu mandarins are one of the things I wait for every year, and they arrive in the market, at my friend Jim Churchill's stall, just in time for Christmas. No bigger than walnuts, they explode with juice in your mouth, sweet as candy. When Kishus are not in season, Pixie tangerines or any of the many other varieties of sweet, easy-to-peel tangerines are wonderful here.

Another way . . .

To have a vegan meal, you only need to skip the cheese. Have some spiced or salted almonds with the olives instead. The focaccia is an olive oil bread, and the dessert, dark chocolate and mandarins, is already vegan as well.

white bean and garlic soup with greens

Chard is excellent in this soup, but spinach, kale, or beet greens also work very well. Each one will give its own particular character to the soup. Whichever one you choose, be sure your greens are firm and glossy.

Long ago I learned to simmer white beans with sage leaves, letting the sage impart its perfume to the broth. At some point I began adding peeled garlic cloves as well—more and more of them. Together, the beans, garlic, and sage create a broth that is both delicate and rich-tasting, and that is the basis of this soup. You can add almost anything, or add nothing, and it will be delicious.

· · · SERVES 6 · · ·

8 oz. (225 g) dried white beans, cannellini or
   Great Northerns
2–3 tsp. dried sage or 10 fresh sage leaves
6–7 cloves garlic, peeled
1 tsp. sea salt, plus more to taste
1 large yellow onion, chopped (300 g)
1 Tbs. (15 ml) olive oil
1 bunch young green chard or other greens
   (8 oz.; 225 g)

2–4 cups (500 ml–1 liter) basic light vegetable
   broth (p. 47)
freshly ground black pepper
fresh lemon juice

· · ·

garnish: fruity green olive oil
optional garnishes: Parmigiano-Reggiano cheese or
   croutons

Rinse the beans and put them in a large soup pot with enough cold water to cover them by at least 2 inches. Do not add salt at this point, but add the sage leaves and the peeled whole garlic cloves. Bring the water to a boil and then lower the heat to a simmer. Leave the beans to simmer gently, covered, for as long as it takes them to become tender; this will vary with the age and size of the beans, and can take anywhere from 2 to 4 hours. Add a bit more water if necessary to keep the beans well submerged. When they are almost tender, add salt to taste—at least 1 teaspoon, probably more—and keep simmering until the beans are soft. Ladle out about 1 ½ cups of the beans and reserve.

Cook the chopped onion in a tablespoon of olive oil over medium heat, stirring often, until it is golden brown and tender, 20 to 30 minutes. Wash the chard or other greens thoroughly, cut away any tough stems, and cut into 1-inch strips. If you have tiny spinach leaves, you can leave them whole.

Combine the reserved beans with the caramelized onion and about 2 cups vegetable broth and puree in a blender, or with an immersion blender, until they are smooth and creamy. Add the puree to the beans and their broth in the pot, along with the cut-up greens. Add enough of the vegetable broth to give the soup a good, liquid consistency, so that it pours easily from the soup ladle. Simmer the soup until the greens are tender.

Taste, and correct the seasoning with more salt and some black pepper to taste. Add a discreet squeeze of lemon juice—just enough to clarify the flavor of the soup, not so much that it becomes tart. Serve the soup very hot, with olive oil drizzled on top. If you like, add a generous grating of Parmigiano-Reggiano or a few croutons. I like to serve plain bruschetta with this: slices of baguette brushed with olive oil and grilled.

Even easier . . .

Skip the puree step and simply let all the ingredients simmer together in the bean and vegetable broth at the end.

fasolia gigante soup with spinach

Fasolia Gigante are giant white beans that look like lima beans on steroids. They are huge, and like all dried beans they get bigger as they soak and cook, until some are about the size of a quarter. When they are cooked slowly and long enough, they become beautifully tender yet keep their shape, and at the same time make a lovely broth. If you can't find these giants, use large dried lima beans, which are just as delicious in this soup.

With its lively taste of ripe tomatoes, this is a good summer soup for those times when you want something hearty. It's fine in winter as well; you can use a can of good diced tomatoes instead of fresh ones.

· · · SERVES 6—7 GENEROUSLY · · ·

1¼ cups dried fasolia Gigante or large dried lima
  beans (8 oz.; 225 g)
5 large cloves garlic, peeled
3 Tbs. loosely packed fresh sage leaves (7 g)
1–2 tsp. sea salt, plus more to taste
1 large yellow or red onion (300 g)
2 Tbs. (30 ml) olive oil
fresh or dried thyme
fresh rosemary
8 oz. (225 g) small spinach leaves or chopped
  spinach

12 oz. (350 g) ripe red tomatoes, peeled and
  chopped
freshly ground black pepper
1–2 cups (250–500 ml) basic light vegetable
  broth (p. 47) or canned vegetable broth
· · ·

garnishes:
fruity green olive oil
whole-wheat croutons

In general I don't soak beans overnight, but in the case of these giants it is a useful thing to do; they're just too big to cook evenly to tenderness otherwise. So rinse the beans and soak them in 8 cups (2 liters) of soft or spring water. In the morning, drain and rinse. (If you are using lima beans you can skip this step, but you'll have a shorter cooking time if you do soak the beans.)

Put the soaked beans in a large soup pot with about 7 cups (1 ¾ liters) water, or 9 cups (2 ¼ liters) if using lima beans that have not been soaked. Add the whole garlic cloves and the sage leaves. Bring the water to a boil, then cover, lower the heat, and simmer for a long time—perhaps a couple of hours—until the beans are perfectly tender. The cooking time will vary with the age of the beans. Add more water as needed to keep the beans well covered, and when they are tender, stir in 1 teaspoon salt.

While the beans simmer, chop the onion coarsely and sauté it in the olive oil with a sprinkle of sea salt, stirring it often over a medium-low flame until it's soft and golden, about 20 minutes. Stir in a big pinch of thyme and the same of rosemary and cook for a few more minutes.

Add the onion, spinach, and chopped tomatoes to the beans and their broth, as well as a good amount of freshly ground black pepper, and let the soup simmer another 15 minutes. Taste it, and correct the seasoning with more salt if needed (the beans will have absorbed some of the salt during this time).

If the soup seems thick, add some of the vegetable broth. I like the clear flavors of the broth that this soup makes for itself, starting with the beans and garlic, sweetened by onion and enlivened by the juicy tomatoes, with a piney hint of rosemary, but if it seems more a stew than a soup, I add broth.

Serve the soup in big bowls, with a splash of fruity olive oil and a scattering of croutons on top of each serving. Another nice way to serve this is to place a thick, crisply toasted slice of baguette in the bottom of each bowl and pour the soup over it.

green lentil soup with cumin and lemon

French green lentils, often called Le Puy lentils after the region where they are grown, cook quickly, keep their shape, and taste great. Here they combine deliciously with other greens—leeks, chard, cilantro, and parsley—in a hearty soup. Have an old-fashioned grilled cheese sandwich with this for a completely satisfying meal.

· · · SERVES 6—8 · · ·

1 cup French green lentils (8 oz.; 225 g)
1½ tsp. sea salt, plus more to taste
2 Tbs. (30 ml) olive oil
1 large yellow onion, chopped (250 g)
2 cups (150 g) chopped leeks, white and light
    green parts
1 medium sweet potato, diced (8 oz.; 225 g)
1 large carrot, finely diced (100 g)
1 large stalk celery, finely diced (75 g)
1 bay leaf
1 bunch green chard (8 oz.; 250 g)

2 Tbs. cumin seeds
1 cup (about 60 g) chopped cilantro
¼ cup (20 g) chopped fresh flat-leaf parsley
cayenne
2–3 cups (475–700 ml) basic light vegetable
    broth (p. 47) or canned vegetable broth
1–2 Tbs. (15–30 ml) fresh lemon juice, plus more
    to taste

· · ·

garnish: fruity green olive oil

Rinse the lentils and combine them in a large soup pot with 4 cups (1 liter) water. Bring the water to a boil, then lower the heat and simmer the lentils gently for about 25 minutes, or until tender-firm. After the first 20 minutes, add a teaspoon of sea salt, and when the lentils are ready, remove them from the heat and skim off any foam that may have formed on top.

Meanwhile, heat 2 tablespoons olive oil in a large sauté pan, add the chopped onion and a pinch of sea salt, and cook slowly over medium heat until the onion is soft, 8 to 10 minutes. Add the leeks and continue cooking for another 20 minutes, stirring often, until the leeks and onion are translucent and turning golden.

Add the onion and leeks to the lentils and their broth, along with the diced sweet potato, carrot, celery, another 3 cups water, half a teaspoon of sea salt, and the bay leaf. Simmer the soup gently, covered, for about 20 minutes. Meanwhile, wash the chard, slice away the stems, and coarsely chop the green leaves. Add the chard and simmer the soup another 10 minutes, until the vegetables are all tender.

Lightly toast the cumin seeds in a dry skillet, just until they release their fragrance, about 4 to 5 minutes, then grind them in a mortar or a spice grinder and stir them into the soup. Add the cilantro and parsley, a generous pinch of cayenne, and 2 or 3 cups of light vegetable broth, enough to give the soup the consistency you like. I like my soups to pour easily from the ladle. Heat everything together for a few more minutes, then add lemon juice to taste.

Serve the soup steaming hot in wide bowls and drizzle some olive oil over each serving.

lima bean soup

This is the most basic lima bean soup, perfumed with garlic, rosemary, and red onion.

· · · SERVES 6—8 · · ·

1 lb. (450 g) dried baby lima beans

2–3 sprigs fresh rosemary or 1 Tbs. dried
  rosemary, chopped

1 head garlic (60 g)

1 large red onion (350 g)

1 bay leaf

1½ tsp. sea salt, plus more to taste

2 Tbs. (30 ml) olive oil

1–2 cups (250–500 ml) basic light vegetable
  broth (p. 47) or canned vegetable broth

freshly ground black pepper

· · ·

garnishes:

fruity green olive oil

Herbed Croutons (p. 447)

optional garnish: grated Parmigiano-Reggiano
  cheese

In a large, heavy-bottomed soup pot, combine the lima beans, 8 cups (2 liters) water, and the rosemary. Bring the water to a boil and reduce the heat to low. Peel and coarsely chop the garlic and onion and add them to the pot along with the bay leaf. Simmer the beans gently, covered, for 1½ to 2 hours, or until the beans are soft and much of the water is absorbed. Cooking time will vary with the size and age of the beans. The only way to know when they are ready is to try a few.

Add a teaspoon of salt and the olive oil and simmer the beans gently for another 10 minutes, until the salt is absorbed.

Remove the bay leaf and the rosemary stems and add as much vegetable broth to the bean broth as you need to get a souplike consistency; it should pour easily from a ladle and not spit when simmering. Ladle out a cup or two of the soup and puree it in a blender, then return the puree to the pot; this slightly thickens the broth. Grind in some black pepper, then taste, and correct the seasoning with additional salt if needed. Remember that salt needs a few moments to dissolve and make itself felt, so pause between additions.

Serve hot, drizzled with additional olive oil—essential!—and garnished with herbed croutons, and with Parmigiano-Reggiano cheese if you like.

Some other ways . . .

You can place large croutons, made from whole baguette slices brushed with olive oil and grilled or toasted in the oven, in the bottom of the soup bowls and pour the soup over them.

Or the entire soup can be pureed to a smooth, velvety cream.

Or you can add finely diced carrots, celery, and potatoes to the beans when they are simmering, to make a lima and vegetable soup. Use about 1 cup each of any or all of these vegetables.

MENU

BLACK BEAN AND SQUASH SOUP
-page 140-

oatmeal molasses bread
-page 394-

· · ·

red cabbage and apple salad
-page 476-

· · ·

greek yogurt with honey and walnuts
-page 502-

and roasted persimmons

Every taste in this meal feels like a pure expression of that end-of-fall, beginning-of-winter moment—the day when the cold snaps in or the first snow falls, when you just want to stay in and cook soup and eat it by the fire.

"What's in this black bean soup?" I invariably hear someone say when I serve this soup. The harvest is in it: a beautiful gray-green kabocha squash. That sweet, rich-tasting pumpkin joins with the black beans, an array of vegetables, and a few mild spices for a soup that makes you want winter to last forever.

I like to eat this soup with Oatmeal Molasses Bread, a dense and nourishing loaf with the distinctly seasonal flavor that molasses brings. If you don't bake, stop in at the bakery and ask for squaw bread, anadama bread, or another whole-grain loaf with a touch of sweetness in it.

A bowl of this soup with a thick slice of brown bread is a meal. You could eat a crisp new-crop apple and be done. But a salad makes it an even better meal, so I put that apple together with some red cabbage, enlivened by cider vinegar. The contrast of the smooth, deep-flavored soup and the piquant lift of this tangy salad is always appealing.

Roasted persimmons, another gift of the winter season, are as straightforward as baked apples. Use Fuyu persimmons, which are eaten while still hard, even crisp. They roast beautifully, and a few caramelized wedges on a plate with a dollop of thick Greek yogurt, a few walnuts, and a drizzle of honey is a dessert that is at once extraordinary and simple.

black bean and squash soup

Kabocha squash is pureed with most of the beans to make the thick body of this soup, gives it a slight sweetness and mystery. A touch of jalapeño pepper and some cumin and lemon juice provide a spicy backbone. I love this soup!

1 ¼ cups dried black beans (8 oz.; 225 g)

4–5 cloves garlic, peeled

6 fresh epazote leaves or 1 ½ tsp. crumbled dried epazote

1 ½ tsp. sea salt, plus more to taste

1 small kabocha or butternut squash (1 ¼–1 ½ lbs.; 600–700 g)

1 Tbs. (15 ml) olive oil

1 yellow onion, chopped (225 g)

1 bay leaf

1 medium carrot, finely chopped (80 g)

1 large stalk celery, finely chopped (75 g)

1–2 jalapeño peppers, seeded and finely chopped

1 scant Tbs. cumin seeds, toasted and ground

1 ½ cups (360 ml) any basic vegetable broth (pp. 47–50) or canned vegetable broth

2 Tbs. (30 ml) fresh lemon juice

· · ·

garnishes:

fruity green olive oil

crumbled fresh white cheese, such as *queso fresco*

Rinse the black beans and combine them in a large soup pot with 7 cups (1 ¾ liters) water, the peeled garlic cloves, and the epazote. Bring the water to a boil, then lower the heat and simmer the beans, covered, for at least an hour, or until they are tender. The time will vary with the age of the beans. When they are tender but not mushy, add a teaspoon of salt. Using a slotted spoon, lift out about a cup of the beans and put them aside.

While the beans are cooking, preheat the oven to 400°.

Cut the squash in half, scrape out the seeds, and lay the halves cut side down on a lightly oiled baking pan. Roast the squash for 45 minutes to 1 hour, or until it is soft. Allow it to cool slightly, then scoop out all the soft pulp.

At the same time, heat the olive oil in a skillet. Add the chopped onion, the bay leaf, and a pinch of salt, and gently sauté over medium-low heat, stirring often, for about 25 minutes, or until the onion is soft and golden brown. Remove the bay leaf.

When the beans are tender, add the chopped carrot, celery, and jalapeño peppers to the beans and their broth and simmer for about 10 to 12 more minutes, until the vegetables are tender. Add the roasted squash, the caramelized onion, the cumin, and the vegetable broth.

Allow the soup to cool slightly, then puree it in a blender, in batches, or with an immersion blender, until it is smooth. Return the soup to the pot and add the reserved whole beans and the lemon juice. Taste, and correct the seasoning with more salt if needed.

Serve the soup hot, with a thick drizzle of fruity olive oil and a sprinkle of crumbled white cheese on top of each serving. Fresh corn tortillas or cornbread are sensational with the flavors of this soup.

spicy black bean soup with sweet peppers

This is an exuberant soup, with the savory flavors of black beans, sweet peppers, onions, and carrots spiked with a puree of ancho and guajillo chiles. I like it on the spicy side of the scale, but you can take the heat level down or even eliminate it by adjusting the amount of chile puree.

Ingredient note: I know Mexican cooks who would not think of cooking a pot of beans without throwing in a few epazote leaves. Its flavor complements beans especially well, and it has a reputation for making them a more digestible dish. It can be found in Mexican or Latin American markets, and in farmers' markets during the warmer months.

· · · SERVES 7–8 · · ·

about 1¾ cups dried black beans (12 oz.; 350 g)

8–10 large fresh epazote leaves or 2 Tbs. loosely crumbled dried epazote

2 medium yellow onions (450 g)

6–8 cloves garlic (25 g)

1½ tsp. sea salt, plus more to taste

6 medium carrots (340 g)

2 large stalks celery (175 g)

2 Tbs. (30 ml) olive oil

2 large bell peppers, preferably 1 red and 1 green (450 g)

1 Tbs. cumin seeds

2 Tbs. Ancho and Guajillo Chile Puree (p. 440), plus more to taste

2 cups (500 ml) any basic vegetable broth (pp. 47–50) or canned vegetable broth

1 small bunch cilantro

1 Tbs. (15 ml) fresh lime juice, plus more to taste

· · ·

garnishes:

pumpkinseed oil

cilantro

fresh limes

chile puree

Wash the beans and combine them in a large soup pot with 10 cups (2 ½ liters) water and the epazote. Coarsely chop the onions and garlic and add half of each to the beans in the pot. Bring the water to a boil, then lower the heat and loosely cover the pot. Let the beans simmer until they are tender; this could take anywhere from 1 to 2 hours, depending on the age of the beans. If the water cooks away before they are done, add a little more so the beans stay submerged. When all the beans are soft, add a teaspoon of sea salt.

Meanwhile, peel and slice the carrots; you should have about 1 ½ cups. Trim and slice the celery; you should have about 1 cup. Heat the olive oil in a large skillet and sauté the remaining onion and garlic over medium heat with the carrots, celery, and a big pinch of salt, stirring often, until the vegetables are tender and beginning to brown, about half an hour. Add the vegetables to the cooked beans and their broth. Deglaze the skillet by swirling some of the bean broth in it, then return the liquid to the soup.

Char the bell peppers in a hot oven or under a broiler, turning them a few times until their skins are blistered and blackened on all sides. Put the peppers in a paper bag to sweat for a couple of minutes, then slip off their skins. Core and seed the peppers, cut them into 1-inch pieces, and add them to the soup.

Toast the cumin seeds lightly in a skillet just until they release their fragrance, then grind them in a mortar or a spice grinder and add them to the soup with the chile puree and vegetable broth. Chop half the cilantro and add it to the soup. Tear the remaining cilantro into sprigs and reserve it for the garnish.

Simmer the soup for another 15 to 20 minutes. Add a little lime juice, taste, and correct the seasoning with more salt, chile puree, or lime juice as needed.

recipe continues on next page

Serve the soup in big bowls. Drizzle a little pumpkinseed oil on top of each one (yes, you can substitute olive oil), then drop some fresh cilantro sprigs over it. Pass lime wedges and additional chile puree at the table.

Another way . . .

You can puree part or all of the soup in a blender or with an immersion blender. Add the charred bell pepper pieces after pureeing the soup.

old-fashioned split pea soup

T his is a purist's split pea soup: no fancy fusion experiments, no heavy ham hocks, just the simple and tasty pea soup of childhood memory.

· · · SERVES 6—8 · · ·

1 lb. (450 g) dried green split peas

2–3 stalks celery, chopped (200 g)

3 medium carrots, chopped (225 g)

1 large yellow onion, chopped (300 g)

1 bay leaf

2 tsp. chopped fresh thyme or savory, or 1 tsp. dried thyme

hot paprika

1–1 ½ tsp. sea salt

¼ cup (about 20 g) chopped fresh flat-leaf parsley

about 2 cups (500 ml) basic light vegetable broth (p. 47) or canned vegetable broth

freshly ground black pepper

· · ·

garnish: **croutons**

Combine the rinsed split peas in a large soup pot with 8 cups (2 liters) water and the chopped celery, carrots, and onion, the bay leaf, thyme, and a pinch of paprika. Bring the water to a boil and cook briskly for about 20 minutes. Lower the heat, add 1 teaspoon salt, the parsley, and the vegetable broth, and simmer, covered, for about 40 more minutes. The peas should be completely soft.

Remove the bay leaf. Taste, and add salt if it's needed. Grind in some black pepper. Add a little more vegetable broth if the soup seems too thick, and then puree it in the blender, in batches, or with an immersion blender. I like this soup when it still has a somewhat rough texture, but some like to puree it to a cream and then put it through a sieve. Taste again after pureeing and correct the seasoning if needed.

recipe continues on next page

Split pea soup will thicken quite a lot when it is allowed to cool, but it becomes more liquid again when heated. Nevertheless, it is a thick soup and will be even more so the second time around, so be sure to reheat it carefully, stirring a bit and keeping it covered, and perhaps adding a little more water or vegetable broth.

Pea soup is wonderful with croutons, and the best ones with this soup are made rye bread or from some other dark whole-grain bread.

carol's finnish pea soup with apples

My friend Carol lives in a cold place—Edinburgh—so when she recommends a soup for its "stick-to-the-rib-ishness" I take her at her word. She got this recipe from a place that's even colder. It's a Finnish pea soup made with two kinds of peas, mustard, and apples. When it's done, it has a way of tasting deliciously familiar and exotic all at once.

· · · SERVES 6—7 · · ·

1½ cups dried green split peas (12 oz.; 350 g)

2 large carrots (180 g)

2 medium stalks celery (120 g)

1 tsp. chopped fresh thyme leaves or ½ tsp. dried thyme

1 bay leaf

1 large yellow onion (250 g)

3 Tbs. (45 ml) olive oil

1½ tsp. sea salt, plus more to taste

1 large apple (250 g)

12 oz. (350 g) fresh or frozen green peas

1 tsp. coriander seeds, toasted and ground

¼ teaspoon ground nutmeg

1 Tbs. prepared Dijon-style mustard, plus more to taste

1 Tbs. (15 ml) cider vinegar

2 cups (500 ml) basic light vegetable broth (p. 47), basic root vegetable broth (p. 50), or canned vegetable broth

hot paprika or cayenne

Wash the split peas and put them in a large soup pot with 6 cups (1 ½ liters) water. Peel and finely dice the carrots, wash, trim, and dice the celery, and add both to the pot along with the thyme and bay leaf. Bring the water to a boil, reduce the heat to a simmer, cover, and cook for about half an hour.

Meanwhile, chop the onion and sauté it in 1 tablespoon olive oil with a pinch of salt over medium heat, stirring often. until it is soft and light brown. Peel and core the apple and cut it into small dice. Add the onion and the apple to the soup and simmer for another 15 minutes, then add

recipe continues on next page

the fresh or frozen peas, coriander, nutmeg, mustard, cider vinegar, vegetable broth, a pinch of hot paprika or cayenne, and a scant teaspoon of salt.

Simmer the soup for 15 minutes more to marry the flavors, then taste, and correct the seasoning with additional salt if needed and more paprika or cayenne if you want a spicier soup. Just before serving, stir in the remaining 2 tablespoons olive oil. The soup can be served as it is, or it can be pureed in a blender, in batches, or with an immersion blender (remove the bay leaf first). I like it both ways.

I usually serve this soup with a chewy whole-grain bread—rye is a great match—and a smoked cheese.

CHAPTER 6

the comfort of soup
in deep winter

Sopa de Ajo

Rustic Leek and Potato Soup

Vegetarian Onion Soup Gratin

Mushroom-Barley Soup with Cabbage

Spicy Indonesian Yam and Peanut Soup • V

Roasted Root Vegetable Soup • V

Cauliflower Bisque

Neeps and Tatties Soup

Caramelized Cabbage Soup

the farmers' market in winter

This is the time when cooking feels most important—winter, when the hearth is the home and a pot of soup on the stove is such a comfort.

And what treasures will we find in the market? Things that keep well in a cellar, or grow in the damp dark, or become their best selves only when bitten by frost. Roots, fungus, cabbage . . . it doesn't sound very glamorous. But give these hardy winter edibles slow roasting or leisurely simmering and they transform into the deeply flavored and beautiful soups of the cold season.

Garlic and onions star in their own soups; keep a basket full of them on your counter. Roots are a mainstay, the good friends who come through for you quietly again and again. Turnips and homely rutabagas, wrinkled celery roots, pale parsnips and bright carrots, beets, potatoes of all kinds—old-fashioned slow cooking will transform these common roots into soups and stews of uncommon goodness.

Brassicas are with us all year, but they come into their strength in cold weather. Cabbages, brussel sprouts, broccoli, and cauliflower are all part of this big family. And kale—in my opinion, the best of the brassicas. I find at least three varieties of kale in my market, and I like them all. Red Russian is actually a dark gray-green and looks like very large oak leaves with elaborated edges and reddish purple veining along the stems. Tuscan kale, another favorite, goes by many names: black kale, cavolo nero, and, the funniest moniker, dinosaur kale, for the rippled, puckery texture of its long leaves. Curly kale, the most familiar, is bottle-green or blue-gray in color, exuberantly frilly, and is not just for garnishing plates in diners—it is delicious, and more delicate than Russian or Tuscan kale.

Chard, spinach, collards, and many tasty cabbages do especially well in the cold. The farmers from whom I buy my cabbages at the market explained to me that cabbages lose their sharp bitterness and become sweet, in their own cabbagey way, only after the first frost. When I slice them and roast them in the oven to a soft golden brown, they become downright irresistible.

Mushrooms, the splendid edible fungi, are a reward for what some might consider bad weather. A succession of cool, damp days will bring forth the forest and field mushrooms that cannot be duplicated in cultivation. If you can get your hands on fresh porcini, often available in the drizzly Pacific Northwest, consider that you've won the lottery. And here in California, the February storms sometimes give us improbably huge chantarelles, golden trumpets pushing up from the duff under the coastal live oaks.

The winter market has its share of spectacle, too, in the array of hard-shelled squashes or pumpkins. Flaming red-orange, buttery gold, pale blue, or cream-colored, smooth or warty, tiny or huge, they are a glory of the season. On the subject of winter squashes, you really must have a conversation with the farmer or the greengrocer and ask which of the local varieties are best for eating and which are for decorating.*

There are other splashes of color—brilliant orange persimmons, glowing ruby pomegranates, and, depending on where you live, bins of jewel-like cranberries or ropes of brick-red dried chiles.

This is also the time when we turn to our pantries. Dried beans, barley, rice, and grains that might be less familiar, like quinoa and farro, are all waiting for us. Herbs that were dried in the searing heat of summer are ready to release their flavors.

Winter can be the nicest time in the orange-growing valley where I live. It is the green season; the sky is washed with winter rains, the weather agreeable and cool. But even here we have our share of cold and gray, and we have our ferocious, lashing storms. On such a winter day I stay inside, gather up the best of the winter market and the pantry, and tease out those rich flavors into a superb winter potage.

*Read more about squashes on pp. 106–108.

MENU

a bowl of olives

. . .

SOPA DE AJO
-page 156-

. . .

salad of winter greens

. . .

oranges, dried figs, walnuts

Garlic soup is the definition of comfort in a bowl. It will nourish you, warm you, cure what ails you, and as a bonus keep vampires away for a week.

The soup is made one serving at a time and takes about 10 minutes to put together. Thin slices of day-old bread are softened in the ruddy, garlicky broth, making a bed for the poached egg, and the whole thing is an infusion of your Spanish *abuela*'s love even if you don't have a Spanish *abuela*.

While this robust bowl of soup can be a meal all by itself, I do crave something leafy after all that garlic, and the juicy freshness of citrus. A salad of winter greens is in order—dark green arugula, watercress, young chard, spinach, mizuna, baby kale; any or all of them are so good in the winter. Dress them lightly with oil and lemon juice and perhaps a touch of mustard or honey.

Finish with oranges or tangerines and some dried figs and walnuts—no cooking. This easy meal works as well for a rainy weekday lunch when you're alone in the house as for a convivial party with friends on a cold, snowy evening.

sopa de ajo

GARLIC SOUP

Many years ago I spent a cold autumn and winter on the Castilian plain in Spain, and I ate this hearty, healing soup almost daily. It is every Castilian *abuela*'s remedy for sniffles and aches all winter long. And you don't need your granny, Castilian or other, to tell you that this makes a wonderful cold-weather lunch or supper.

Nothing could be more basic: lots of garlic sautéed in some olive oil, a few thin slices of day-old bread, all of it doused in a paprika-scented broth in which you poach an egg. The most common *sopa de ajo*, the one I learned from Delfina in Segovia so many years ago, makes its own broth from the garlic, olive oil, Spanish paprika, and water. These days I use a light vegetable broth, which deepens the flavor, but if there's no broth handy, I don't hesitate to use water.

This is a soup that is made to order; it takes about 10 minutes once you have your garlic sliced, and you can make one serving or as many as you need.

A note about paprika: it is essential to the flavor of the broth and must be good, so don't reach for that jar that's been in the back of your mother's cupboard for ten years. But good doesn't have to mean fancy; the paprika you buy at the supermarket is fine, as long as it is fresh. I like to mix a sweet paprika about half and half with a spicy one, and my favorite is a Spanish smoked paprika, pimentón de la Vera. You can use any hot paprika for the spicy element, or even just a pinch of cayenne, and you will find the milder or spicier proportion you prefer.

· · · SERVES 1, OR MANY · · ·

for each serving

1 Tbs. (15 ml) olive oil

2–3 cloves garlic

½ tsp. sweet paprika

½ tsp. pimentón de la Vera or other spicy paprika

2 cups (500 ml) any basic vegetable broth
(pp. 47–50), heated

sea salt, if needed

1–1½ oz. (30–45 g) day-old French or sourdough
bread

1 large egg

Have your ingredients ready before you start cooking: peel and thinly slice the garlic, make sure your broth is hot, and have the bread sliced or cubed. I use any kind of French, Italian, or sourdough bread I might have around. If it is a day or two old, slice it thinly or cut it in crouton-sized cubes. If it is very dry, break it up into rough chunks.

If you are making only one serving of soup, make it in a small pot, or you won't be able to poach the egg properly.

Heat the olive oil in a small saucepan or earthenware crock. Sauté the sliced garlic over medium heat, stirring, for about 1½ minutes, or just until it starts to color. Remove from the heat and stir in the paprikas, then add the hot broth. Return the pot to the heat, cover, and simmer gently for 4 to 5 minutes. Taste the broth, and add a pinch of sea salt if it's needed.

Add the dry bread and simmer for 2 more minutes as the bread softens. Break an egg, slide it gently into the soup, and be sure it is fully submerged. If it isn't, ladle some of the simmering broth over it to cook the top. Cook until the white of the egg is opaque but the yolk is still soft, about 3 minutes. Pour the soup into an ample soup bowl and serve at once.

If you are making multiple servings, I suggest that you make no more than 3 in one saucepan, for ease of handling. To serve, use a large spoon to scoop up a poached egg and place it in the soup bowl, then ladle in the hot broth, bread, and garlic.

rustic leek and potato soup

I've been making leek and potato soup for as long as I can remember, and I never get tired of it. Over time, I've changed little things—I've replaced some of the butter with olive oil, and now I use Yukon Gold potatoes and I don't peel them. It's a more rustic version of a soup that feels like an old friend.

· · · SERVES 6—8 · · ·

3–4 large leeks, white and light green parts
  (12 oz. trimmed; 350 g)
2 lbs. (900 g) Yukon Gold potatoes
1 Tbs. (15 ml) olive oil
1 Tbs. unsalted butter
1½ tsp. sea salt, plus more to taste
3 cups (750 ml) basic light vegetable broth
  (p. 47) or canned vegetable broth

3 Tbs. chopped fresh flat-leaf parsley
½ tsp. chopped fresh thyme
freshly ground black pepper
2 tsp. (10 ml) fresh lemon juice
3 Tbs. (45 ml) heavy cream
  · · ·

garnish: chopped parsley or snipped chives

Trim the leeks and wash them well, slice them into quarters lengthwise, then slice thinly crosswise; you should have 3 to 3 ½ cups. Scrub the potatoes and cut them into ½-inch dice.

Heat the olive oil and butter in a skillet, add the leeks and a pinch of salt, and cook the leeks over medium heat, stirring often, until they are soft and just beginning to color, 8 to 10 minutes.

Combine the leeks and potatoes in a large soup pot with 3 cups (750 ml) water, a teaspoon of sea salt, and the vegetable broth and simmer, covered, for about 15 minutes, or until the potatoes are completely tender. Add the parsley and thyme, some black pepper, and the lemon juice. Taste, and correct the seasoning with more salt if needed; potatoes absorb quite a lot of salt, but wait a moment between additions, as salt needs time to dissolve.

Stir in the cream and serve with more fresh parsley or chopped chives sprinkled on top.

Another way . . .

To enjoy a chilled version of this soup, allow it to cool to room temperature and then puree it in a blender, in batches; but be careful not to overprocess, as potatoes can become gummy. Whisk a little cream into the puree, chill it for at least several hours, then taste again when the soup is cold; seasoning sometimes need to be adjusted with a radical change in temperature. Serve the chilled soup with a scattering of snipped chives on top.

And still another way . . .

To make this a vegan soup, use 1 ½ Tbs. (22 ml) olive oil to sauté the leeks and skip the cream at the end.

vegetarian onion soup gratin

It is no secret that traditional French onion soup, the one lovingly described in any literature touching on Les Halles or French bistro cooking, is based on a strong beef broth. Prodigious amounts of onions are cooked down and added to that, and the whole thing is topped with a piece of toasted bread and a pile of Gruyère cheese and then baked until the cheese melts and forms a golden brown crust, dripping over the edges of the individual casserole in which the soup is made. It's a rich, lusty dish.

Making a meatless version of this dish is a challenge that vegetarian onion-lovers continually address. I gave a recipe for onion soup in the first *Vegetarian Epicure* and it was a good one, but it has evolved over time and now it is even better. I customized my basic vegetable broth to get a deeper, more intense flavor, and now I use a mix of red and yellow onions and more olive oil. Here's the ever-evolving onion soup that I'm enjoying right now.

For this soup, use a homemade vegetable stock. Dark Vegetable Broth or Root Vegetable Broth is best. You will need about 8 cups, and if you come up a bit short, it's all right to stretch your broth with canned broth—but don't depend exclusively on the can.

· · · SERVES 6—8 · · ·

3½ lbs. (1.5 kg) red and yellow onions

4 Tbs. (60 ml) olive oil

1 Tbs. unsalted butter

1 tsp. sea salt, plus more to taste

1 tsp. chopped fresh thyme or ½ tsp. dried thyme

2–3 Tbs. (30–45 ml) dry red wine

1 tsp. minced garlic

1 Tbs. tomato paste

4 tsp. (20 ml) aged tamari (soy sauce)

8 cups (2 liters) basic dark vegetable broth (p. 50) or basic root vegetable broth (p. 49)

cayenne

6–8 slices French country bread, toasted

6 oz. (170 g) Gruyère cheese, grated

Peel the onions, halve them lengthwise, and then cut them lengthwise into thin slices. Heat 3 tablespoons olive oil and the butter in your largest sauté pan and add the onions, 1 teaspoon salt, and the thyme. Cook the onions over medium heat, stirring often, until they are soft and golden. This will take at least 45 minutes, perhaps an hour, as the volume of onions slows things down considerably.

Here's my rule of thumb for caramelizing onions: when you think the onions are done, cook them on a low flame for another half-hour. Yes, I mean it! They will be a rich caramel-brown and taste like onion jam. This super-caramelizing is the secret of a good onion soup. At the end, stir in the red wine and let it cook away—it will deglaze the pan and bring all those delicious, sticky dark bits into the soup, where they belong.

In an ample soup pot, heat the remaining tablespoon of olive oil and add the minced garlic, followed a moment later by the tomato paste. Stir this mixture over medium heat for a few minutes, until the tomato paste is sizzling and darkening. Add the tamari, then the vegetable broth and a pinch of cayenne. Bring the broth to a simmer and taste it. It should have a full, deep flavor, but you should not be able to pick out the specific taste of tomato or soy. Correct the salt if needed.

Add the caramelized onions, deglazing the pan again by swirling a little broth around in it. Simmer the soup another 20 minutes or so to marry the flavors.

Preheat the oven to 400°.

Ladle the soup into 6 ovenproof bowls or individual casseroles, or 8 if you want smaller servings. Make sure that each serving has a good proportion of onions in the broth. Place a slice of toasted French bread on top of each serving and sprinkle grated Gruyère cheese over that.

Arrange the bowls on a large baking sheet and put them in the oven for about 2 minutes, or until the cheese has completely melted. At the last minute, slide the soups under the broiler, just until the cheese bubbles and browns.

Serve at once, using pot holders and warning everyone about the hot bowls!

mushroom-barley soup with cabbage

This hearty soup recalls the tastes of my Polish immigrant childhood, but in a more sophisticated version. I deglaze the sautéed mushrooms with sherry, add fresh thyme from the garden and some smoky spicy sweet red pepper, and keep the barley to a delicate minimum so that the brothy quality of the soup is not lost. The soup simmers slowly, filling the house with its inviting fragrance. At dinnertime, ladle up big bowls, sprinkle them with crumbly white farmer cheese or top with a spoonful of sour cream, and have a rustic bread alongside. A dense rye bread or pumpernickel is fantastic with this soup.

A note about paprika: not all are created equal. The paprika that your great-aunt sprinkled on deviled eggs to give them a little color is not what we are looking for here. A good paprika has true, distinctive flavor and will make a difference in your soup. I love pimentón de la Vera from Spain—it is medium-spicy and has a smoky depth to the flavor. I've also used piment d'Espelette, a spicy paprika from the Basque country, and many excellent Hungarian paprikas.

· · · SERVES 6—7 · · ·

¼ cup (50 g) pearl barley

1 tsp. sea salt, plus more to taste

3 medium yellow onions (600 g)

3 Tbs. (45 ml) olive oil

10 oz. (290 g) portobello, cremini, or brown button mushrooms

2 tsp. unsalted butter

2 cloves garlic, minced

freshly ground black pepper

2 tsp. fresh thyme leaves or 1 tsp. dried thyme

3 Tbs. (45 ml) dry sherry

½ small savoy cabbage (12 oz.; 350 g)

4–5 green onions, white and green parts

4 cups (1 liter) any basic vegetable broth (pp. 47–50) or canned vegetable broth

½ cup (30 g) chopped fresh flat-leaf parsley

1 tsp. pimentón de la Vera, piment d'Espelette, or spicy Hungarian paprika

juice of 1 lemon, plus more if needed

· · ·

garnish: farmer cheese, sour cream, or croutons

Combine the barley in a large soup pot with 4 cups (1 liter) water and a teaspoon of sea salt, bring the water to a boil, lower the heat, and simmer, covered, for 30 to 40 minutes as you prepare the vegetables.

Peel the onions, halve them, and slice them thinly. Heat 2 tablespoons olive oil in a large skillet and sauté the onions gently, with a sprinkle of salt on a medium-low flame for at least half an hour. Stir the onions often as they soften and turn golden brown. Don't try to hurry this process.

Meanwhile, clean the mushrooms by wiping them with a damp cloth, trim the dry parts from the stems, and slice them thinly. If they are very large, cut them in half first. Heat the remaining 1 tablespoon oil and the butter in a nonstick pan, stir in the minced garlic for about a minute on high heat, then add the mushrooms and some salt and pepper. Turn the flame down slightly and sauté the mushrooms until they sizzle and turn golden brown, 15 to 20 minutes. Add the thyme and the sherry and stir until the sherry cooks away.

Quarter and slice the cabbage. Trim the green onions and slice them into ½-inch pieces; you should have about 1 cup.

When the onions and mushrooms are nicely browned, add them to the barley in the soup pot, along with the vegetable broth. Use a little of the broth to deglaze the mushroom and onion pans, swirling it around to loosen the sticky dark brown bits. Add the cabbage, green onions, parsley, and paprika. Let the soup simmer, covered, for another half-hour, until all the vegetables are tender. If it gets too thick, add a little water.

Stir in the fresh lemon juice, then taste the soup and correct the seasoning with more salt and pepper if needed. The lemon juice should balance the sweetness of the onions, and the paprika should add just a slight kick of spiciness.

spicy indonesian yam and peanut soup

Yams, parsnips, and carrots, usually mild-mannered, run with a racy crowd in this soup: lots of fresh ginger, some curry, peanut butter, garlic, tamarind, and lemon. It's a *wow!* of flavors, slightly rich, tangy, spicy, and bright.

· · · SERVES 8 · · ·

1 ½ lb. (700 g) yams

12 oz. (350 g) parsnips

12 oz. (350 g) carrots

1 ½ tsp. sea salt, plus more to taste

½ cup grated or chopped fresh ginger
   (5 oz. whole; 140 g)

½ cup (30 g) chopped cilantro

2 large yellow onions (500 g)

2 Tbs. (30 ml) olive oil

3–4 cloves garlic, finely chopped

1 tsp. curry powder

½ tsp. cumin seeds, toasted and ground

1 Tbs. tamarind paste

1–2 Tbs. (15–30 ml) fresh lemon juice

cayenne

⅓ cup (95 g) smooth peanut butter

3–4 cups (1 liter) basic light vegetable broth
   (p. 47), basic root vegetable broth (p. 49),
   vegetable and ginger broth (p. 52), or
   canned vegetable broth

· · ·

garnishes:

additional cilantro leaves

chopped dry-roasted peanuts

optional garnish: Harissa (p. 444)

Peel the yams, parsnips, and carrots, cut them up roughly into pieces no larger than an inch or two, and combine them in a large soup pot with 6 cups (1 ½ liters) water. Add a teaspoon of sea salt, the grated or chopped ginger, and the cilantro leaves. Bring the water to a boil, then lower the heat, cover the pot, and simmer the soup for about half an hour. Test to be sure all the vegetables are tender.

Meanwhile, chop the onions and sauté them in the olive oil, stirring over a medium flame for about 10 minutes. Add the garlic and a pinch of salt and continue cooking for another 15 minutes or so, until onions and garlic are both soft and golden brown. Add the curry powder and cumin, stir for about a minute, and then add the onion mixture to the soup. Deglaze the pan by swirling a bit of the broth around in it and adding it back to the pot.

Stir the tamarind paste, a tablespoon of lemon juice, a pinch of cayenne, and the peanut butter into the soup. Remove the soup from the heat and add 2 cups vegetable broth. Puree the soup in a blender, in batches, or use an immersion blender. Add as much more vegetable broth as you need to get a creamy, souplike texture; the soup should pour easily from a ladle, like a custard sauce.

Taste the soup, and correct the seasoning with more salt or lemon juice if needed. If you don't happen to have tamarind paste, you will want to add a touch more lemon to get the right acid balance.

Serve the soup hot, garnished with cilantro leaves and a few chopped dry-roasted peanuts. Harissa, a mouth-watering condiment for these flavors, can be passed at the table.

roasted root vegetable soup

This is the soup you want when you come inside from a long, cold hike in the damp hills.

I make roasted vegetables at least once a week all winter. It's so pleasant to warm the house, to make it smell good, and then to have that panful of roasted vegetables—winter vegetables that could be boring but now are glazed with olive oil and sherry, sweetly caramelized, dark brown around the edges.

The roasted vegetables are hard to resist right out of the oven, and they're great to add to a salad, to make into an easy risotto, or to wrap in a tortilla with scrambled eggs for the best breakfast burrito. That's why I suggest making double what you need for the soup—it's only about 10 minutes more time peeling vegetables. But if you simply want to make the soup and you promise not to eat a single one when you take them out of the oven, you can cut the amounts for all the vegetables in half.

If possible, use homemade broth for this soup, one that is not too sweet. The roasted vegetables will provide plenty of sweetness.

· · · SERVES 6 · · ·

to make roasted root vegetables

1 lb. (450 g) rutabagas
1 lb. (450 g) turnips
1 lb. (450 g) sweet yams
1 lb. (450 g) fennel
12 oz. (350 g) carrots
2 lbs. (900 g) onions
4 Tbs. (60 ml) olive oil

2 tsp. sea salt
freshly ground black pepper
2 tsp. fresh thyme leaves or 1 tsp. dried thyme
2 tsp. finely chopped fresh sage leaves or 1 tsp.
   crumbled dried sage
3 Tbs. (45 ml) dry sherry

for the soup

⅓ cup (70 g) pearl barley

½–1 tsp. sea salt

5–7 cups (1¼–1¾ liters) any basic vegetable broth (pp. 47–50)

4 cups (600 g) roasted root vegetables

½ cup (30 g) whole leaves fresh flat-leaf parsley

2–3 tsp. (10–15 ml) sherry vinegar

• • •

optional garnish: fruity green olive oil or fresh creamy goat cheese

FIRST, ROAST YOUR VEGETABLES

Preheat the oven to 375°.

Peel and dice all the vegetables to a fairly uniform size, about 1 inch. The onions can be cut in slightly larger pieces, as they are less dense. You should have about 3 cups each of diced rutabagas, turnips, yams, and fennel, 1 ⅔ cups of diced carrots, and 6 cups of cut onions. Mix the vegetables together in a large bowl with the olive oil, salt, pepper to taste, thyme, sage, and sherry. Vary the amounts of herbs to your taste; the amounts given here will add a subtle flavor to the vegetables but won't dominate.

Spread the vegetables over 2 shallow baking pans and roast them for an hour or a little longer, until they are tender and flecked with dark brown spots. Mix and turn the vegetables a few times during the roasting, and about midway through reverse the position of the pans between upper and lower racks in the oven. The vegetables will reduce in volume as they roast, and you should have about 8 cups when they are done.

recipe continues on next page

Combine the barley in a large soup pot with 1 ½ cups (300 ml) water, a dash of salt, and 5 cups vegetable broth. Bring the liquid to a boil, lower the heat, and simmer the barley, covered, for 35 minutes. The barley will swell to two or three times its original size and maintain its distinctive chewy texture.

Add 4 cups of the mixed roasted vegetables (you can coarsely chop them first if the pieces look large to you) and simmer the soup for about 15 minutes to marry the flavors. Taste, and add more salt if it is needed. Add the parsley and sherry vinegar during the last few minutes. If the soup seems too thick, add another cup or so of vegetable broth.

I like to finish this soup with my favorite garnish, a swirl of fruity olive oil, but if you're in the mood for a richer soup, drop a spoonful of soft fresh goat cheese in each steaming bowl as you serve it. Delicious.

Some other ways . . .

This is a soup that can easily be varied. Add sautéed mushrooms, use orzo or fideo noodles in place of the barley, add cilantro or dill instead of the parsley, add a dash of cream if you like. As long as your broth is delicate and savory, you can't go wrong.

cauliflower bisque

WITH BUTTERED BREADCRUMBS

When I was a child we often had cauliflower on the dinner table, and it was a glorious sight. My mother would steam a whole cauliflower and then, in the Polish style, at the last moment she would pour buttery sautéed breadcrumbs over it. The browned butter glistened down the dome of the cauliflower, and the breadcrumbs were so delicious that I've brought them back for a return engagement, scattered across the top of this velvety cauliflower bisque.

· · · SERVES 6—7 · · ·

1 large white cauliflower (2 lbs.; 900 g)

4 cups (1 liter) basic light vegetable broth (p. 47) or basic root vegetable broth (p. 49)

1 lemon, plus more if needed

1½ tsp. sea salt, plus more to taste

2 medium carrots (120 g)

2 medium stalks celery (100 g)

1 large yellow onion (240 g)

3 Tbs. (45 ml) olive oil

5 cloves garlic, chopped

1 tsp. herbes de Provence

2 oz. (60 g) fresh creamy goat cheese or cream cheese

· · ·

garnish: Buttered Breadcrumbs (technique follows)

Trim the cauliflower, cut the florets in small pieces, and put them in a soup pot with 2 cups (500 ml) water and the vegetable broth. Scrub the lemon and slice off a 1-inch-long strip of the zest, making sure you don't have any of the white pith, as that turns bitter. Juice the lemon. Add 2 tablespoons of the juice and the strip of zest to the pot, along with a teaspoon of sea salt. Bring the liquid to a boil, lower the heat, and let it simmer, covered, for 15 minutes. Remove and discard the lemon zest.

Meanwhile, peel, trim, and chop the carrots, celery, and onion. Heat 2 tablespoons olive oil in a skillet and add the chopped vegetables, along with the garlic and half a teaspoon of sea salt. Sauté

recipe continues on next page

the vegetables on a medium flame, stirring often, until they are soft and beginning to color, about 20 minutes. Add the herbes de Provence and keep stirring over medium heat for a few minutes longer.

Add the sautéed vegetables to the cauliflower. Cover the pot again and simmer another 15 minutes, or until the cauliflower is very tender. Remove from the heat and allow the soup to cool slightly.

Puree the soup to a creamy, silky consistency, either in batches in a blender or with an immersion blender. Taste, and add salt or lemon juice if needed. Return the soup to the pot, bring it back to a simmer, and add the cheese and the last tablespoon of olive oil, stirring gently as the cheese melts.

Sprinkle a heaping spoonful of buttered breadcrumbs over each serving of soup at the last minute, just as you are serving it.

Buttered Breadcrumbs

1 cup coarse, soft breadcrumbs
2 Tbs. unsalted butter

You can make big, soft breadcrumbs by cutting up day-old bread into cubes and processing them briefly in a food processor. Alternately, you can crumble any soft bread with your fingers.

Melt the butter in a nonstick skillet, add the breadcrumbs, and stir over medium heat for several minutes. As soon as the breadcrumbs begin to take on a toasty golden color, remove them from the heat. Use them warm from the pan, or spread them in a thin layer on a plate or cookie sheet to cool.

Another way . . .

If you want a vegan soup, omit the cheese and add a little more olive oil at the end. Garnish the soup with breadcrumbs sautéed in olive oil instead of butter.

And if you don't want to make buttered breadcrumbs but you have some good croutons on hand, croutons will be just fine.

neeps and tatties soup

TURNIP AND POTATO SOUP

This is a twist on leek and potato soup. Instead of potatoes alone, I use turnips and potatoes, the "neeps and tatties" beloved in Scotland. These two humble root vegetables taste wonderful together, and turnips are less starchy, so they lighten the texture of the soup. Leeks are melted down in butter to give the soup its rich flavor, and a little bit of cream adds a silky smoothness.

· · · SERVES 6—7 · · ·

2 lbs. (900 g) Yukon Gold potatoes

1 lb. (450 g) turnips

1 tsp. sea salt, plus more to taste

2 large leeks, white and light green parts (300 g)

2 Tbs. unsalted butter

4 cups (1 liter) basic light vegetable broth (p. 47)
    or basic root vegetable broth (p. 49)

freshly ground black pepper

3 Tbs. chopped fresh flat-leaf parsley

3 Tbs. (45 ml) heavy cream

· · ·

garnish: chopped parsley or snipped chives

Scrub the potatoes, trim away any blemishes, and cut them into ½-inch dice. Yukon Gold potatoes have thin skins and do not need to be peeled. Peel and dice the turnips. In an ample soup pot, cover the potatoes and turnips with about 4 cups (1 liter) of cold water, add a teaspoon of salt, and bring the water to a boil. Lower the heat and simmer for at least 20 minutes, or until the vegetables are tender.

Meanwhile, trim and thoroughly wash the leeks and dice only the white and light green parts; you should have 3 to 4 cups leeks, which will look like a lot but will soon be much less. Melt the butter in a skillet and cook the leeks over medium heat, stirring often, until they are soft and beginning to color, 8 to 10 minutes. Add them to the potatoes and turnips and simmer another 10 minutes, then turn off the heat and add the vegetable broth.

Puree the soup in batches in the blender or with an immersion blender, being careful not to overprocess. Return the soup to a clean pot and bring it back to a simmer. Taste, and add more salt if needed. Potatoes can absorb a lot of salt, but add it a little at a time and wait a moment to taste, as salt needs to dissolve and incorporate itself in the soup before you can tell if you've added enough. Grind in plenty of black pepper and add the chopped parsley and the cream.

Bring the soup to a simmer to heat it through just before serving, and garnish each bowl with a sprinkle of parsley or some snipped chives.

Another way . . .

To make a more rustic and assertive version of this soup, skip the cream and do not puree the soup. At the very end, when you add the chopped parsley, also add a couple of tablespoons of chopped fresh dill, half a teaspoon of dill seed, about 2 ounces (60 g) of crumbled feta cheese, and a splash of olive oil. Stir it all up and heat just to a simmer, then serve.

caramelized cabbage soup

For many years a wonderful Hungarian grandma named Juliana had a stall at my farmers' market. She always had spectacular cabbages, and it was during that time that I developed my best cabbage recipes. This soup is one of my favorites. I roast the cabbage before putting it in the soup, a simple technique that develops such a sweet, rich flavor it's hard to believe it comes from an ordinary cabbage.

· · · SERVES 6 · · ·

1 small green cabbage (about 1 lb.; 450 g)
2 Tbs. (30 ml) olive oil
1 tsp. sea salt, plus more to taste
1 yellow onion (8 oz.; 225 g)
1 Tbs. unsalted butter
1½ cups sliced leeks, white part (about 5 oz.;
    140 g)
2 medium carrots (4 oz.; 120 g)
2 medium stalks celery (3½ oz.; 100 g)
1 medium russet potato (8 oz.; 225 g)
5 cups (1¼ liters) basic light vegetable broth
    (p. 47) or basic root vegetable broth (p. 49), or
    4 cups canned vegetable broth diluted with
    1 cup water

1 cup (250 ml) whole milk
2–3 Tbs. chopped fresh dill
freshly ground black pepper, if needed

· · ·

optional garnishes:
sour cream
shredded cheese
rye or pumpernickel croutons

Preheat the oven to 375°.

Cut the cabbage in wedges, remove the core, and slice the wedges thinly crosswise. Toss the sliced cabbage with a tablespoon of olive oil and half a teaspoon of sea salt and spread it on a baking sheet. Roast the cabbage for 30 to 40 minutes; after the first 10 minutes, check it pretty frequently, using a spatula to turn it and move it around. It will turn a lovely, toasty brown all over and shrink to a quarter of its former self.

Chop the onion medium fine. While the cabbage roasts, heat the remaining tablespoon of oil with the butter in a nonstick pan, add the leeks and the onion with a sprinkle of salt, and cook slowly on low heat, stirring now and then, until they are golden brown. This may take as long as 30 to 40 minutes, but it develops a beautiful, sweet flavor in the onions and leeks.

Meanwhile, clean and finely dice the carrots, celery, and potato. I don't peel the potato for this rustic soup; I like the taste and texture of the skin, so I just scrub it and trim off any rough spots. But if you want to peel it, go ahead. Combine the vegetables in a soup pot with the vegetable broth and simmer, covered, for 20 minutes. Add the roasted cabbage and the caramelized leek and onion mixture and simmer the soup, covered, for another 20 minutes. Stir in the milk and the fresh dill, then taste, and add salt and pepper if needed. Let the soup simmer for another few minutes, just until it heats through again.

Serve the soup piping hot, with a dollop of sour cream or a sprinkle of shredded cheese on top, or some crunchy croutons made from rye or pumpernickel bread.

CHAPTER 7

big soups and stews

The Great Pumpkin Soup • **V**

Pickle Soup • **V**

Hearty Brown Lentil Soup • **V**

Ten-Vegetable Soup with Cranberry Beans • **V**

Minestrone for a Crowd • **V**

French Lentil Stew with Roasted Carrots and Mint • **V**

Stewed Root Vegetables with Moroccan Spices • **V**

Kabocha Squash and Cranberry Bean Stew • **V**

Farro with Stewed and Roasted Winter Vegetables • **V**

Quinoa Stew with Potatoes, Spinach, and Chard

Three-Bean and Vegetable Chili • **V**

get out the stockpot

Some soups don't make sense unless they're made in a big pot, in a quantity that can feed your gathered tribe—or your congenial group of pals—and still give you leftovers for lunch the next day.

These are the robust, happy soups that involve many vegetables, legumes, and grains. I suppose you could reduce the fifteen or twenty ingredients in The Great Pumpkin Soup (p. 182), or in my Polish sentimental favorite, Pickle Soup (p. 185), to the tiny quantities that would yield a few modest bowls, but why would you want to? Simmering a quarter cup of dried beans or dicing half a potato and a quarter of an onion seems silly. Like tamales and paella, some foods have bigger ambitions. They want to go to a party.

These soups are not complicated to make—far from it. They simply require a bit more chopping, so they take a little longer, but they pay back grandly in workday lunches and quick suppers, or impromptu dinners when they come out of the freezer weeks later. All of these soups reheat splendidly and freeze perfectly.

These big soups are meant to be the centerpiece of a meal—it's hard to imagine them playing a supporting part. Stews share this sense of importance. They have substance—they *are* the meal. However, except for the Three-Bean and Vegetable Chili (p. 212) and the Kabocha Squash and Cranberry Bean Stew (p. 203), which will feed a crowd, these recipes do not make a huge quantity, though they do sometimes involve more of a process.

Farro with Stewed and Roasted Winter Vegetables (p. 206) is perhaps the most elaborate, and yet it doesn't take much more than an hour's work, and what a rewarding dish it is. Three distinct elements are prepared separately: chewy grains of farro, the stewed vegetables in their broth, and the crisp-roasted garnish vegetables. It's all put together in generous bowls at the moment of serving, preserving the well-developed flavors and textures for a memorable eating experience.

Stewed Root Vegetables with Moroccan Spices (p. 200) are very different. Everything is put together in a Dutch oven for a long, slow simmer, marrying those gentle, wintry root vegetable tastes with the warm spices of a sunny land. This is a stew that I like even better the next day or the next after that; its flavors just keep developing.

In the dark months of the year, when it's damp and cold outside, if you spend some time in the kitchen making a great big soup or a hearty stew—even better, if you cook with friends—I promise that your outlook will improve.

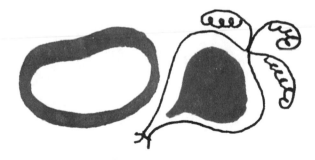

MENU

THE GREAT PUMPKIN SOUP
-page 182-

simple chipotle sauce
-page 439-

fresh corn and cheddar cheese cornbread
-page 407-

• • •

baked apples

MENU NOTES

Soup and bread: it's simple, hearty, plain enough for a kitchen supper, but in this case interesting enough to make a party. Honestly, for me it could be a Thanksgiving dinner. Pumpkin, beans, corn, and chile—what a beautiful harvest.

The pumpkin soup is based on elements that are traditional in Europe, with a combination of white beans and golden squash, leeks, and onion. But it takes a turn into lusty New World flavor with a handful of cilantro, a spoonful of garnet-red salsa dropped into the bowl, and a crunchy scattering of pumpkin seeds.

The cornbread is almost a corn pudding, dense with cheese and chewy with whole corn kernels. In this combination, soup and bread really is dinner.

After this simple but utterly satisfying meal, a baked apple in nothing but its own caramelized juices seems a lovely ending. Although a scoop of vanilla ice cream with that baked apple would not be a bad thing. . . .

The party way . . .

This meal could easily be elaborated and dressed up for company. Add an interesting starter with aperitifs—Persian Spinach Spread (p. 429) with plain crostini, or simply a bowl of spiced nuts. Then have a salad before the soup; it could be the purest version of peppery winter greens tossed with olive oil and a drop of vinegar, or something more unusual, like Red Cabbage and Apple Salad (p. 476). And bring on the ice cream with the baked apples.

the great pumpkin soup

In this excellent, nourishing fall soup, pumpkin is the main ingredient, so it is important to find a good one. That will not be the orange giant you pick out to carve for Halloween. There are many delicious pumpkins, but the huge jack-o'-lantern variety does not make the best eating.

I've had good luck with some smaller varieties; Sweet Mamas, sugar pumpkins, and baby Hubbards come to mind. But pumpkins vary from region to region. You will find different ones at your market from what I will find at mine—and even if we find the same type, it might be using a different name in your neighborhood. Oh, those pumpkins.

The wisest thing to do is simply to ask for a good pie pumpkin. If you're shopping at a farmers' market, ask the growers—they love to share what they know. Even in a supermarket, I frequently see smaller pumpkins labeled as pie pumpkins, and that means they're good soup pumpkins.

As with any winter squash, look for a pumpkin that is hard and has a thick, firm stem and vivid color. If it has been cut open, look for dense, smooth-textured flesh with bright color. And if you can snag a taste, expect a pleasant, vegetal flavor with no bitterness. It will not taste like pie, but it might have a natural edge of sweetness.

And remember, a pumpkin need not be orange, nor even round. Botanically speaking, *pumpkin* is just another word for winter squash. Kabocha, Hubbard, buttercup, delicata, and butternut all qualify if you can't find the sweet round pumpkin of your dreams.

· · · SERVES 10 GENEROUSLY · · ·

¾ cup dried cannellini or other white beans
  (5 oz.; 150 g)

1½ tsp. sea salt, plus more to taste

1 medium pumpkin, about 4 lbs. untrimmed
  (2½ lbs. trimmed; 1.1 kg)

2½ Tbs. (37 ml) olive oil

1 large onion, coarsely chopped (250 g)

8 oz. (225 g) leeks, white and light green parts

12 oz. (350 g) Yukon Gold potatoes

4–5 cups (1–1¼ liters) any basic vegetable broth
  (pp. 47–50)

12 oz. (350 g) green chard

¾ cup (50 g) packed cilantro or fresh flat-leaf
  parsley leaves

2–3 Tbs. (30–45 ml) fresh lemon juice, plus more
  if needed

1–3 Tbs. brown sugar (dark or light)

freshly ground black pepper

nutmeg

• • •

garnishes:

fruity green olive oil

crumbled feta or other fresh white cheese

or:

Simple Chipotle Sauce (p. 439) or Ancho and
  Guajillo Chile Purée (p. 440)

hulled, toasted pumpkin seeds

Put the dried beans in a large soup pot or stockpot with 8 cups (2 liters) water, bring the water to a boil, then lower the heat and simmer the beans, covered, for at least an hour, or until they are tender. This may take up to 2 hours, depending on the age of the beans. Add more water if you need to in order to keep the beans covered. When the beans are soft, add a teaspoon of salt.

While the beans are cooking, prepare the pumpkin: split it in half, scrape out all the seeds and strings, and then cut the pumpkin into wide strips and peel off the hard skin. Do this last part carefully, using a sharp knife and pushing the blade away from you. Cut the trimmed pumpkin into 1½-inch cubes. You should have about 8 cups of cubed pumpkin.

Preheat the oven to 375°.

recipe continues on next page

Toss the pumpkin cubes with a tablespoon of olive oil and a generous sprinkle of salt and spread them on a baking sheet. Roast the pumpkin pieces for about 45 minutes, turning them once or twice, until they are tender and browned in spots.

Heat the remaining 1 ½ tablespoons olive oil in a nonstick skillet and gently sauté the chopped onion in it with a sprinkle of salt, over medium heat, until it softens and begins to color, about 10 minutes. Wash and thinly slice or chop the leeks, add them to the onion, and keep cooking until the leeks are also tender and browning, about another 15 minutes.

Scrub and trim the potatoes and cut them into ½-inch dice. Put the potatoes in a large soup pot with 2 cups (500 ml) water, 4 cups vegetable broth, and a pinch of salt. Bring the water to a boil, lower the heat, and simmer the potatoes for 6 or 7 minutes. Wash the chard, trim off the stems and coarsely chop the leaves, and add the chard to the potatoes.

Add the cooked onion and leeks, the roasted pumpkin, and the cilantro or parsley leaves to the pot and simmer the soup for 15 minutes. The pumpkin will become very soft, and some of it will fall apart, thickening the broth and imparting its lovely orangey gold color.

Add the cooked cannellini with all their broth and taste the soup. Season it with lemon juice, a little brown sugar if the pumpkin is not very sweet, and a bit more sea salt to bring it all together. There should be a subtle sweet-tart balance, and the amount of lemon juice or sugar you need will vary with the type of pumpkin. Grind in a little black pepper and add a pinch of nutmeg.

Serve the soup hot, in deep bowls, with a last-minute drizzle of fruity green olive oil and a sprinkle of crumbled cheese on top of each serving. Another delicious way to finish the soup is with a spoonful of chile sauce and a scattering of toasted pumpkin seeds.

pickle soup

BARLEY, MUSHROOM, AND VEGETABLE SOUP

This is a soup I often made for my mother when she was quite old and her health was failing. She had lost her appetite and was getting so thin. I would go to see her and wonder, What can I do for her? How can I make her feel better?

One day I went into her kitchen and started making this old-fashioned barley and vegetable soup, full of the flavors of her Polish kitchen, the one I grew up in. She enjoyed sitting and watching me cook, and sniffed appreciatively as the air filled with memory and fragrance. We tasted as I worked. I added mushrooms and fresh dill—very good—but when I added the finely diced dill pickles it was fantastic!

My mother ate the soup with relish. She said, "Delicious—so good." No other compliment, no praise from famous chefs, could have meant more. After that, whenever I started cooking for her, she would peer into the pot and ask, "Pickle soup?" I made it over and over, and no one in the family tired of it.

Of course, the pickles are one small part of this soup. They melt into the whole, and if you weren't told about them, you wouldn't necessarily know—you'd just love the tangy, dilly flavor of this great soup.

· · · SERVES 10 · · ·

recipe continues on next page

½ cup (70 g) pearl barley

1½ tsp. sea salt, plus more to taste

2 Tbs. (30 ml) olive oil

1 yellow onion, chopped (250 g)

1½ cups chopped leeks, white and light green
  parts (8 oz.; 225 g)

2 cloves garlic, minced

12 oz. (350 g) portobello, cremini, or other brown
  mushrooms, chopped

thyme

8 oz. (240 g) Yukon Gold potatoes, diced

1 cup (140 g) diced carrots

¾ cup (90 g) diced celery

1 medium turnip, peeled and diced (150 g)

½ bunch green chard (5 oz.; 140 g)

1 wedge Savoy cabbage (5 oz.; 140 g)

1 medium bell pepper, cored and diced, or 1
  large roasted pimiento from a jar (150 g)

½ cup (30 g) chopped fresh dill

¼ cup (15 g) chopped fresh flat-leaf parsley

about 3 cups (750 ml) any basic vegetable broth
  (pp. 47–50) or canned vegetable broth

1 cup (120 g) finely diced dill pickles, plus more
  to taste

freshly ground black pepper

• • •

optional garnish: sour cream, yogurt cheese, or
  farmer cheese

Rinse the barley, put it in a large soup pot with 8 cups (2 liters) water and 1 teaspoon salt, and simmer, covered, for about 30 minutes.

Meanwhile, heat 1 tablespoon olive oil in a skillet and add the chopped onion. Lower the heat to medium and cook the onion, stirring occasionally, for 10 minutes. Add the chopped leeks and continue cooking for another 10 minutes, or until the onion and leeks are soft and beginning to color.

In another skillet, heat the remaining tablespoon of oil and stir the garlic in it over high heat for about a minute. Add the mushrooms, a dash of salt, and a pinch of thyme and sauté the mushrooms until their excess liquid cooks away and they are sizzling, about 10 minutes.

Add the potatoes, carrots, celery, and turnip to the barley, along with another half a teaspoon of salt. You can add a cup or two of water if it is needed to keep everything submerged. Bring the liquid back to a simmer and cook, covered, for 15 more minutes.

While the root vegetables are cooking, wash the chard, remove the tough stems, and chop the leaves coarsely. Shred the wedge of cabbage into ½-inch strips.

Add the sautéed onion and leeks and the sautéed mushrooms to the soup, deglazing the pans with a bit of water. Stir in the chard, cabbage, bell pepper, dill, parsley, and vegetable broth. Simmer for 10 minutes, then add the finely diced pickles and simmer for 10 minutes more.

Taste the soup, and adjust the seasoning with more salt and some freshly ground pepper. The pickles become milder over time, releasing their acidity into the soup as they cook; your soup will have a more subtle flavor after it simmers a little longer.

This is an old-fashioned soup, and tastes great with a spoonful of sour cream or yogurt cheese and equally good with some crumbles of plain white farmer cheese. Rye bread or pumpernickel on the side fits right in.

You'll have a big pot of soup—enough for about 10 meal-sized servings. I like to freeze part of it for another time.

hearty brown lentil soup

A straightforward lentil soup—hearty, familiar, and easy—should be in everyone's soup repertoire. Don't be put off by what looks like a long list of ingredients—half of it is herbs and spices.

I love this basic version, but I frequently add other vegetables to it. You can vary it with tomatoes, spinach or chard, leeks, peppers, squashes, root vegetables—whatever looks good in the garden or the market. Lentils play well with others!

For a spicy soup, stir a spoonful of homemade chile salsa into your bowl—Ancho and Guajillo Chile Puree, Table Salsa, or your personal favorite.

· · · SERVES 10 · · ·

1 lb. brown lentils (450 g)
2½ tsp. sea salt, plus more to taste
4 large carrots (12 oz.; 350 g)
4 medium stalks celery (8 oz.; 225 g)
3–4 small yellow potatoes (12 oz.; 350 g)
1 bay leaf
1 tsp. chopped fresh thyme or ½ tsp. dried thyme
1 large yellow onion (300 g)
4 Tbs. (60 ml) olive oil
1 Tbs. chopped garlic
1½ Tbs. cumin seeds

1 Tbs. (15 ml) fresh lemon juice, plus more to taste
freshly ground black pepper
2 cups (500 ml) any basic vegetable broth (pp. 47–50) or canned vegetable broth
⅔ cup (30 g) chopped cilantro
1 cup (50 g) chopped fresh flat-leaf parsley

· · ·

garnish: fruity green olive oil or ½ cup Table Salsa (p. 442) or Ancho and Guajillo Chile Puree (p. 440)

Rinse the lentils and put them in a large soup pot with 10 cups (2 ½ liters) water and 2 ½ teaspoons salt. Finely dice the carrots, celery, and potatoes and add them to the pot, along with the bay leaf and thyme. Bring the water to a boil, lower the heat, and simmer the soup, loosely covered, for about 1 hour.

Meanwhile, chop the onion medium fine and sauté it in 2 tablespoons olive oil, stirring often over a medium flame until it softens. Add the chopped garlic and keep cooking and stirring until the onion begins to color, about 10 minutes. Add the onion and garlic to the soup as it simmers.

Lightly toast the cumin seeds in a small pan, stirring constantly for a few minutes until they are fragrant. Grind the cumin in a mortar or a spice grinder and add it to the soup, along with 1 tablespoon lemon juice and plenty of black pepper.

Add the vegetable broth and the fresh herbs, bring the soup back to a simmer, and taste. Correct the seasoning with additional salt and a touch more lemon juice if it is needed, and stir in another 2 tablespoons olive oil.

When serving, add a thin drizzle of olive oil on top of each steaming bowl, or put a rounded teaspoon of mild salsa on top of each serving.

ten-vegetable soup with cranberry beans

My friend Pam said this is the soup her grandmother used to make in a huge pot and serve to all the workers on their farm in Michigan.

It's a winter soup, full of familiar cold-season vegetables like carrots, potatoes, turnips, and leeks, and a few summer things from the pantry. Roasted pimiento peppers from a jar and top-quality canned tomatoes are fine here. I like to finish the soup in the bowl with a spoonful of basil pesto from the freezer, a bright flavor that is so welcome in winter.

· · · SERVES 8—10 · · ·

1 cup dried cranberry beans or red kidney beans
 (7 oz.; 200 g)
2½ tsp. sea salt, plus more to taste
1½ yellow onions (350 g)
2 Tbs. (30 ml) olive oil, plus more to taste
5 cloves garlic, minced
2 medium carrots (120 g)
2–3 small Yukon Gold potatoes (180 g)
2 small turnips (180 g)
3 stalks celery (120 g)
1 medium leek, white part (120 g)
½ medium green cabbage (240 g)
½ bunch kale (120 g)
1 red bell pepper (75 g)
3 cups diced tomatoes, with juice (1½ lbs. fresh;
 700 g)

2 bay leaves
½ cup (30 g) coarsely chopped fresh flat-leaf
 parsley
1 tsp. chopped fresh oregano leaves or ½ tsp.
 dried oregano
red pepper flakes
2 cups (500 ml) any basic vegetable broth
 (pp. 47–50) or canned vegetable broth
· · ·

garnishes:
Simple Basil Pesto (p. 436) or any pesto you like
Fruity green olive oil
Parmigiano-Reggiano cheese

Combine the beans in an ample soup pot with 7 cups (1 ¾ liters) water. Bring the water to a boil, then lower the heat, cover, and simmer the beans for 1 to 2 hours, until they are tender. The cooking time will vary with the age of the beans. When the beans are tender, stir in 1 ½ teaspoons salt.

While the beans simmer, chop the onions and sauté them in 2 tablespoons olive oil with a good pinch of salt on a medium flame until they are soft and beginning to color. Add the garlic and keep cooking on a low flame, stirring often, until everything is golden brown, about 15 more minutes.

Peel and slice the carrots, scrub and dice the potatoes, and peel and dice the turnips. Trim and slice the celery and coarsely chop the leek. Cut the cabbage into 1-inch pieces. Cut the kale off its tough stems and chop it coarsely. Trim and quarter the bell pepper and slice the quarters crosswise.

Combine all the prepared vegetables with the sautéed onions and garlic in a large soup pot. Add 4 cups water, a teaspoon of sea salt (less if using canned tomatoes), and the bay leaves. It may seem like you don't have enough water, but just wait; the vegetables make their own broth. Bring the water to a boil, lower the heat; and simmer, covered, for about half an hour.

Add the cooked beans with all their broth, the parsley and oregano, a generous pinch of red pepper flakes, and the vegetable broth. Bring the soup back to a simmer, then taste, and correct the seasoning with a bit more salt if it's needed, or a touch more hot pepper.

Serve the soup steaming hot in deep bowls, and top each serving with a spoonful of basil pesto. If you have no pesto, a drizzle of olive oil and some freshly grated Parmigiano-Reggiano cheese are also delicious.

recipe continues on next page

Another way . . .

½ lb. (250 g) sturdy small pasta such as tubetti, pennette, elbows, or orzo
5–6 cups (1 ¼ liters) additional vegetable broth

Cook the pasta separately in well-salted water until it is al dente, then drain it and add it to the soup, along with a few more cups of vegetable broth. Now you have enough soup for a party—15 or 16 servings. Invite the neighbors. If you have leftovers, be prepared for a thicker soup the next day, as pasta keeps expanding. And for this version, definitely add some grated Parmigiano-Reggiano on top.

minestrone for a crowd

This is a season-crossing soup. With a few adjustments, it's good for fall, winter, spring, or summer. In the fall, you should easily find all the vegetables in the market. In winter or spring, you can use canned tomatoes, but be sure they are top-quality and not overseasoned. Roasted pimientos from a jar are fine, and a spoonful of basil pesto can replace fresh basil leaves.

· · · THIS IS A GREAT BIG POT OF SOUP—ENOUGH TO SERVE 8—10 · · ·

1 cup dried cannellini beans (7 oz.; 200 g)

8–10 cloves garlic, peeled

2 Tbs. chopped fresh sage leaves or 1 Tbs. crumbled dried sage

2 tsp. sea salt, plus more to taste

4 Tbs. (60 ml) olive oil

1 large yellow onion, chopped (300 g)

1 medium fennel bulb (8 oz.; 225 g)

3 medium stalks celery, thinly sliced (120 g)

4 oz. (120 g) kale, spinach, or mustard greens

2 lbs. (900 g) red tomatoes

½ small butternut squash (350 g)

2 red pimiento peppers (125 g)

12 oz. (350 g) zucchini

½ cup (30 g) packed fresh flat-leaf parsley leaves

⅓ cup (20 g) sliced fresh basil leaves

oregano, fresh or dried

freshly ground black pepper

3–4 (750 ml–1 liter) cups any basic vegetable broth (pp. 47–50) or canned vegetable broth

· · ·

garnishes:

fruity green olive oil or pesto

freshly grated Parmigiano-Reggiano cheese

This big batch of minestrone is made in two parts: the dried beans are cooked in one pot, the vegetables in another, and when everything is tender they are combined into a heavenly soup. If they were cooked together from the start, you might wind up with overcooked vegetables by the time

recipe continues on next page

the beans were tender, or the beans might fall apart from too much stirring and bumping. This way everything keeps its texture.

Put the dried cannellini beans in a large pot with 6 cups (1 ½ liters) of water, 6 peeled cloves of garlic, and the sage. Bring the water to a boil, then lower the heat and simmer, covered, for at least an hour, or as long as it takes for the beans to become tender, which will depend on their age. Add water if needed to keep the beans well covered. When the beans are tender, add a teaspoon of salt. (The dried beans can be cooked ahead and kept in the fridge for a day or two with no harm. Keep them in their broth, which becomes part of the soup.)

Meanwhile, heat 2 tablespoons olive oil in a large soup pot. Add the onion and the remaining 2 cloves of garlic, sliced thinly, and stir them occasionally over medium heat for about 10 minutes. Trim the fennel and cut it into ½-inch dice, and add it to the onion along with the celery and 1 teaspoon salt. Cook another 15 minutes, stirring now and then.

Trim the tough stems off the kale and cut the greens into 1-inch strips. Peel the tomatoes and cut them into chunks, keeping all the juice; you should have about 3 cups. Peel and seed the butternut squash and cut it into 1-inch dice; you should have about 2 cups. Seed and coarsely chop the pimientos. Cut the zucchini in half lengthwise and slice them thickly. Add these vegetables to the others in the soup pot, along with 5 cups (1 ¼ liters) water, the parsley and basil, and a generous pinch of oregano. Bring the water to a boil, lower the heat, and let the soup simmer, covered, for 20 minutes.

When the cannellini are ready, add them to the vegetable soup along with all their broth, plenty of freshly ground black pepper, the remaining 2 tablespoons olive oil, and as much of the vegetable broth as you need to give the soup a consistency you like. I like my soups brothy enough to pour easily from the ladle. Simmer the soup a few minutes to marry the flavors, then taste, and adjust with more salt and pepper if needed.

To serve, drizzle a little more fruity green olive oil on top of each steaming bowl, or drop in a teaspoon of pesto, and pass some Parmigiano-Reggiano for those who want it. Put a loaf of crusty bread on the table, or a basket of warm "grandma rolls," and you will feel that all's well with the world.

MENU

green and black cured olives

grilled halloumi slices

. . .

**FRENCH LENTIL STEW WITH
ROASTED CARROTS AND MINT**

-page 198-

baguettes or ciabatta

oil for dipping, harissa

-page 444-

. . .

ripe pears

This uncomplicated but delicious stew derives its flavor from the famous dark green lentils of Le Puy and the earthy sweetness of roasted carrots. But it is the touch of fresh mint and the subtle undercurrent of chile peppers that evoke a Middle Eastern character for me, which plays out in the pungent, salty, and spicy tastes of this menu. I think it's a perfect al fresco lunch for a warm fall day, or an easy supper on a cool night.

Halloumi is a white sheep's-milk cheese from Cyprus that is preserved in brine and that needs to be sliced and briefly grilled to develop its best flavor. It doesn't melt, but just a few minutes in a hot pan, sizzling in its own brine, gives the cheese a golden brown crust and an irresistible salty-toasty flavor.

A bowl of your favorite cured olives and a few slices of warm, freshly grilled halloumi can be an almost effortless starter. Or you can serve everything at once: bread, olive oil for dipping, and harissa for everything—for dropping some extra heat into the stew or for dabbing on baguette slices with halloumi to make amazing little sandwiches.

french lentil stew with roasted carrots and mint

The rich, complex flavor of this stew comes from slow-roasting carrots and onions, simmering earthy lentils, and then adding a touch of sweetness with mint and a subtle bite with chiles. By moderating the amount of vegetable broth you add, you can make this a hearty soup or a real stew.

Be sure to seek out French green lentils, also called Le Puy lentils; they cook to tenderness in less than half an hour but remain firm and distinct. If you don't have harissa or chipotle sauce on hand, you can use another chile salsa or sprinkle in some crushed red peppers (carefully).

· · · SERVES 6 GENEROUSLY · · ·

1½ lbs. (700 g) carrots

1½ lbs. (700 g) yellow onions

4 Tbs. (60 ml) olive oil

1½ tsp. sea salt, plus more to taste

freshly ground black pepper

1 generous cup French green lentils (½ lb., 225 g)

4 cups (1 liter) basic light vegetable broth (p. 47) or 3 cups canned vegetable broth diluted with 1 cup water

1 generous Tbs. chopped fresh mint or 1½ tsp. dried mint

1–2 Tbs. (15–30 ml) fresh lemon juice

1–2 tsp. Harissa (p. 444), or 1½–2 Tbs. Simple Chipotle Sauce (p. 439) or other red chile salsa

· · ·

garnishes:

feta cheese

fruity green olive oil

Preheat the oven to 375°.

Cut the carrots and onions into fairly large pieces, about 1 inch long for the carrots and ½-inch wedges for the onions. Toss the carrots in a bowl with a tablespoon of oil and a sprinkle of salt and pepper, and spread them on a baking sheet. Do the same with the onions. Roast the vegetables for about an hour, or until they are soft and browned, stirring and turning them a few times during the roasting. The onions will need more stirring and will be done sooner than the carrots. When the vegetables are ready, let them cool a little, then turn them out on a board and chop them very coarsely.

Meanwhile, combine the washed green lentils in a large soup pot with 4 cups (1 liter) water and a teaspoon of salt. Bring the water to a boil, turn down the heat, and simmer, covered, for 25 minutes, or until the lentils are tender but still firm. Add the chopped roasted vegetables, vegetable broth, mint, 1 tablespoon lemon juice, and harissa or chipotle sauce to taste. If you are using a different chile sauce, be sure to add it a little at a time, tasting as you go: you're aiming for a subtle undercurrent of spiciness, not a scorcher.

Simmer the stew for about 10 minutes to marry the flavors, then taste, and correct the seasoning with more salt and pepper or a little more lemon juice as needed. If you want a soup rather than a stew, add a bit more broth. Remove the stew from the heat, stir in 2 tablespoons of fruity green olive oil, and serve. Garnish each bowl with a few more drops of olive oil.

Moist chunks of salty feta cheese are delicious as a garnish for this stew, but if you are serving grilled halloumi, the Cypriot cheese suggested in the menu, skip the feta—that's enough salty cheese for one meal.

stewed root vegetables with moroccan spices

Common root vegetables, onions, and winter squash are allowed to simmer gently, perfumed with spices, until they are not common at all but full of delicate flavor, both sweet and earthy.

Green tomatoes are not always available, but I have found that tomatillos make a very good substitute. I reduce the quantity slightly when using tomatillos, as they are more acidic.

To make this into an even more substantial one-dish meal, you can add cooked or sprouted garbanzo beans and serve the stew in generous bowls over couscous.

· · · SERVES 6—7 · · ·

1 lb. (450 g) turnips

8 oz. (225 g) parsnips

8 oz. (225 g) carrots

8 oz. (225 g) yellow potatoes

1 medium butternut or kabocha squash (1½ lbs.; 700 g)

1 large fennel bulb (280 g)

1 lb. (450 g) green tomatoes or 12 oz. (350 g) tomatillos

1 Tbs. cumin seeds

2 large yellow onions (450 g)

3 large cloves garlic

3 Tbs. (45 ml) olive oil

1 tsp. turmeric

1½ tsp. ground cinnamon

1½ tsp. sea salt, plus more to taste

¼ tsp. cayenne

⅔ cup (100 g) raisins

about 3 cups (750 ml) basic light vegetable broth (p. 47), basic root vegetable broth (p. 49), or canned vegetable broth

1 or 2 fresh green chiles, such as jalapeño or serrano, seeded and chopped

2–3 Tbs. (30–45 ml) fresh lemon juice, plus more to taste

1 small bunch cilantro, coarsely chopped

· · ·

garnish: Harissa (p. 444)

Peel the turnips, parsnips, and carrots and scrub the potatoes. Cut the squash in half, scrape out the seeds and strings, and cut away the skin.

Cut all the vegetables into pieces of a similar size—cubes of about 1 inch for the squash and turnips, thick slices or short chunks for the carrots and parsnips. If you have fingerling potatoes, cut each one into 2 or 3 pieces, or leave tiny ones whole. Wash and trim the fennel bulb, quarter it lengthwise, and slice it thickly. Cut the green tomatoes into wedges and cut large wedges in half crosswise. If using tomatillos, peel off their husks and cut them in half, or in quarters if they are large.

Toast the cumin seeds lightly in a pan until they release their fragrance, and grind them roughly in a mortar or a spice grinder.

Coarsely chop the onions and the garlic. Heat the olive oil in a large, deep sauté pan or Dutch oven, add the chopped onions, and stir over medium heat for 10 minutes or until they soften and begin to color. Add the garlic and sauté for a few minutes more. Add the cumin, turmeric, cinnamon, 1 1/2 teaspoons salt, and the cayenne, and stir for another minute, just long enough to warm the spices.

Add all the prepared vegetables and stir them around in the pan over medium heat until they are evenly coated with the spice mixture. Stir in the raisins, vegetable broth, and chopped green chiles.

From this point, the stew can be finished on the stovetop or in the oven. To stay on the stovetop, lower the heat to a simmer and cover the pan. Leave the vegetables simmering for about 45 minutes to an hour, stirring and checking the liquid a few times.

The oven method is even easier: if you're working with a sauté pan, transfer the stew to a large, covered baking dish, such as a Dutch oven or a big casserole, and put it into a 350° oven for 1 to 1 1/2 hours, until the vegetables are tender and the liquid has thickened. If your baking dish is tightly

recipe continues on next page

covered, you don't even need to check and stir; the stew will simmer gently, flavors will marry, and it will be delicious.

When everything is tender, stir in a little lemon juice, taste, and adjust the seasoning with more lemon juice and salt if needed. Add a little more broth or some water if the mixture seems at all dry. There should be a rich broth around the vegetables, lightly thickened with the squash, which begins to soften and come apart at this stage.

Add the cilantro just before serving, and ladle the stew over couscous or rice. Pass the harissa at the table—and warn novices that a small dab might do.

kabocha squash and cranberry bean stew

During a recent December cold spell I had a fire always burning in my fireplace, and kept making big pots of this hearty stew. I never tired of it. Because it involves a bit more process than some other stews, I like to make a big batch and freeze some for another time.

Kabocha squash works well in a stew because its naturally dry, dense texture benefits from some liquid but it holds its shape. Tomatillos add their tart edge, balancing the sweet squash. If you don't have tomatillos, you could substitute green tomatoes and add a dash of fresh lemon juice. The greens can be varied: I always like spinach, but have also used a mix of sliced kale and chard, as well as mustard greens, all with good results.

· · · SERVES 8–10 IN MEAL–SIZED PORTIONS · · ·

2 cups dried cranberry beans (also called
    Borlotti) (12 oz.; 350 g)
8–10 fresh epazote leaves, or 2 Tbs. crumbled
    dried epazote
3 tsp. sea salt
1 medium kabocha squash (4½ lbs.; 2 kg)
3 Tbs. (45 ml) olive oil
12 oz. (350 g) tomatillos
2 large onions, coarsely chopped (600 g)
3 cloves garlic, chopped
2 dried ancho chiles or chiles negro (40 g)

3 large stalks celery (250 g)
1 lb. (450 g) spinach or kale or chard
1 cup (60 g) roughly chopped cilantro, packed
1 Tbs. cumin seeds, toasted and ground
3–4 cups (750 ml–1 liters) any basic vegetable
    broth (pp. 47–50) or canned vegetable broth
red pepper flakes (optional)
1 cup (200 g) dry red quinoa or golden quinoa
    · · ·

garnish: fruity green olive oil

recipe continues on next page

Simmer the beans in 10 cups (2 ½ liters) water, with the epazote, until they are just tender, about an hour. Add 1 ½ teaspoons salt and remove the beans from the heat.

Meanwhile, preheat the oven to 400°.

Cut the squash in half, scrape out the seeds and strings, then peel it and cut it into 1 ½- to 2-inch pieces. Toss the squash pieces with 1 ½ tablespoons olive oil and a scant teaspoon of sea salt and spread them on a baking sheet. Peel the tomatillos and cut them in halves or quarters if they are larger than grape-sized. Spread the tomatillos on a foil-lined baking sheet.

Roast the squash and tomatillos for 50 minutes to an hour, turning and mixing them at least twice during the roasting time. The squash should be tender, with nicely browned spots. The tomatillos should be soft and juicy, and might be slightly charred.

While the vegetables are roasting, heat the remaining 1 ½ tablespoons olive oil in a large non-stick skillet and add the chopped onions and garlic with a big pinch of salt. Cook the onions and garlic over medium heat, stirring often, until they are golden brown and soft, about 30 minutes.

Tear the stems out of the chiles and shake out the seeds. Simmer the chiles in a cup of water for 10 minutes, then leave them to soak until they are soft, about another 20 minutes. Puree the chiles with their liquid in a blender, and strain the puree through a sieve.

Trim and slice the celery. Wash the spinach or other greens, and if the leaves are very large, slice them. Add the chile puree, celery, greens, cilantro, cumin, and the roasted vegetables to the beans, along with enough vegetable broth to give the stew the consistency you like. It should be thick, but not so thick that it will quickly scorch when heated. Simmer the stew gently for another 15 to 20 minutes, then taste it and correct the seasoning with more salt if needed, and a dash of red pepper flakes if you like a spicier dish.

Combine the quinoa in a small pot with 2 cups water and ½ teaspoon salt, bring the water to a boil, then lower the heat, cover the pot, and simmer the quinoa until all the water is absorbed, 15 to 20 minutes. The quinoa should be crunchy-tender.

Serve this stew in big shallow bowls. Place a heaping tablespoon of cooked quinoa in the center of each serving and drizzle some fruity olive oil around it.

This recipe makes enough to feed your family a couple of times, or to put some away in the freezer.

farro with stewed and roasted winter vegetables

Farro is a grain that has become more popular and available in the last few years and now can be found in health-food stores, Italian groceries, and better supermarkets. It is an ancient variety of wheat and is turning up in pastas, bread, and cereals. I love the whole kernels, cooked like rice until they are just tender but still chewy.

For this deeply flavorful stew, winter vegetables are sautéed until they are burnished with a golden brown glaze, then simmered in a rich broth. The finished dish is put together in the bowl: steaming broth and vegetables are ladled over chewy cooked farro, and all of it is garnished with fresh olive oil, a few crisp roasted vegetables, and large gratings of Parmigiano-Reggiano. The farro doesn't get overcooked, and the result is a dish with wonderful texture and layers of flavor. This meal in a bowl makes a great centerpiece for a winter dinner party.

· · · SERVES 6 · · ·

for the stewed vegetables

6 oz. (170 g) Yukon Gold potatoes

6 oz. (170 g) baby turnips

6 oz. (170 g) carrots

6 oz. (170 g) parsnips

½ small kabocha squash (1 lb.; 450 g)

3 stalks celery (120 g)

1 lb. (450 g) yellow onions

3 cloves garlic

6 oz. (170 g) dinosaur kale (also called Tuscan kale)

1 dried guajillo chile

2 Tbs. (30 ml) olive oil

1½ tsp. sea salt, plus more to taste

1 bay leaf

thyme

3 cups (750 ml) basic dark vegetable broth (p. 50)

½ cup (15 g) fresh flat-leaf parsley leaves

3 cups (750 ml) broth from the farro

for the farro

1½ Tbs. (22 ml) olive oil

2 shallots, finely chopped (50 g)

1 dried guajillo chile

1⅓ cups (250 g) uncooked farro

3 Tbs. (45 ml) dry sherry

4 cups (1 liter) basic dark vegetable broth (p. 50)

thyme

1 bay leaf

sea salt, if needed

freshly ground black pepper

for the roasted vegetables

12 oz. (350 g) small parsnips

1 medium red onion (200 g)

½ small kabocha squash (1 lb.; 450 g)

2 Tbs. (30 ml) olive oil

sea salt

• • •

garnishes:

fruity green olive oil

big shavings of Parmigiano-Reggiano

PREPARE THE STEWED VEGETABLES

Scrub the potatoes and cut them into ¾-inch dice. Peel the turnips; if they are very small, cut them in quarters or small wedges, but otherwise dice them like the potatoes. Peel and trim the carrots and parsnips and cut them into ½-inch slices. Peel and seed the kabocha squash and cut half of it into 1-inch cubes.

Trim and slice the celery and coarsely chop or dice the onions. Peel and thinly slice the garlic. Cut away and discard the tough stems of the kale and cut the leaves crosswise into 1-inch strips. Pull the stem out of the guajillo chile, tear the pod into 2 or 3 large pieces, and shake out the seeds; do this with the chile for the farro at the same time.

recipe continues on next page

Warm the olive oil in a large sauté pan, preferably nonstick. Add the sliced garlic and stir it in the hot oil for a minute. Add the onions and about half a teaspoon of salt and sauté over medium-high heat for 5 minutes.

Add all the prepared vegetables except the kale, along with the torn chile pod, bay leaf, a big pinch of thyme, and the remaining teaspoon of salt, and continue cooking over medium heat, stirring often, for about half an hour. Twenty minutes into this time, add the kale. The vegetables should be tender, browned, and beautiful. Remove the chile pod and the bay leaf. Transfer the vegetables to a soup pot, add the vegetable broth and the parsley, and simmer the stew on low heat, covered, for about 15 minutes.

COOK THE FARRO

Put the olive oil in a sauté pan and sauté the chopped shallots in it for 6 or 7 minutes, until they take on a bit of color. Add the stemmed and seeded guajillo chile and the farro, stir over medium heat for about 5 minutes, then add the sherry and let it cook away.

Add the vegetable broth, 2 cups (500 ml) water, a pinch of thyme, the bay leaf, a pinch of salt if the broth is not very salty, and some black pepper. Simmer the farro, covered, for 25 minutes, then taste it; if it is tender but pleasantly chewy, it's ready. Drain the farro, discard the chile pod and the bay leaf, and pour the extra broth into the soup pot with the vegetables; you should have about 3 cups of broth from the farro. Put the drained farro back in the sauté pan and put it aside, covered, until you are ready to serve the stew.

ROAST THE REMAINING VEGETABLES

Preheat the oven to 400°.

Peel the parsnips and cut them into ½-inch-thick spears, 3 or 4 inches long. Cut the red onion into ½-inch wedges. Peel and seed the remaining half of your kabocha squash and cut it into 1-inch dice.

Toss the vegetables with the olive oil and a big pinch of sea salt and spread them on a large baking sheet. Roast the vegetables until they are tender and dark brown in spots, turning them a couple of times as they roast. Crispy edges are perfect. The roasting time will vary with the size of the cut pieces, but count on 30 to 40 minutes. Set aside the roasted vegetables.

PUT IT TOGETHER

When you are ready to serve, bring the stewed vegetables back to a simmer and taste. Correct the seasoning with a pinch more salt if needed. Warm the farro briefly in its pan, stirring it over medium heat for 3 or 4 minutes.

Place a generous half a cup of farro in the bottom of a large soup bowl, then ladle 1 ½ cups of stewed vegetables over it. Place a few of the roasted vegetables on top, drizzle a loop of olive oil over everything, drop a few large shavings of Parmigiano-Reggiano over the top, and serve.

quinoa stew with potatoes, spinach, and chard

This stew is my adaptation of an interesting recipe I once watched cookbook writer Deborah Madison make—something she said she had adapted from a South American cookbook.

Quinoa is a tiny, quick-cooking grain with a pleasant, mild flavor. Most quinoa is amber, but lately I have found red quinoa in my local store, and it's lovely as well as nutritious. Here it's combined with spinach, chard, and two kinds of potatoes for a dish that is hearty without being heavy, just the kind of steaming bowlful of dinner we want in January.

· · · SERVES 6 · · ·

1 cup (250 g) quinoa

1½ tsp. sea salt

8 oz. (225 g) Yukon Gold potatoes

4 oz. (120 g) sweet potatoes

4 oz. (120 g) green onions, white and green parts

6 oz. (170 g) spinach

3½ oz. (100 g) chard

2½ Tbs. (37 ml) olive oil

1 large clove garlic, chopped

2 tsp. ground toasted cumin seeds

1 cup (250 ml) basic light vegetable broth (p. 47) or canned vegetable broth

cayenne

1½ Tbs. (22 ml) fresh lemon juice, plus more to taste

1 cup (60 g) coarsely chopped cilantro

6 oz. (180 g) moist feta cheese, crumbled

· · ·

optional garnishes: Harissa (p. 444) or Table Salsa (p. 442)

Rinse the quinoa thoroughly, running cold water over it in a fine sieve as you stir it with a spoon or with your fingers. This grain has a natural protective coating that is bitter-tasting. Most of it will probably be cleaned off by the time you buy it, but just to be on the safe side, give it a good wash.

Combine the quinoa and 8 cups (2 liters) water in a soup pot with half a teaspoon salt. Bring the water to a boil, then lower the heat and simmer for about 12 minutes. Drain the quinoa and reserve the liquid.

Scrub and dice the Yukon Gold potatoes and peel and dice the sweet potatoes. You should have 2 cups of diced Yukon Golds and 1 cup of diced sweet potatoes. Slice the green onions. Thoroughly wash the spinach and chard and cut both in very thin strips.

Heat the olive oil in a soup pot and stir the garlic in it for about a minute. Add the cumin, potatoes, sweet potatoes, and a teaspoon of salt and stir over medium heat for about 5 minutes.

Add the quinoa liquid to the soup pot, along with the green onions, and simmer for 10 minutes. Add the spinach, chard, vegetable broth, quinoa, and cayenne to taste, and simmer for another 10 minutes, until all the vegetables are tender.

Taste the soup, add salt if needed, and squeeze in some fresh lemon juice. Stir in about half the chopped cilantro.

When you serve the soup, drop a few chunks of the feta cheese into each bowl, then garnish each serving with more cilantro. Alternately, both the feta cheese and the cilantro can be passed at the table and everyone can add more or less, to their own taste. Harissa or Table Salsa can be passed as well, for those with a taste for something spicier.

As with any grain-based dish, be ready for this to thicken when it cools. If you're going to reheat it the next day, you may need to add a bit more vegetable broth.

three-bean and vegetable chili

Agood three-bean chili is a popular meal in a bowl. This one has plenty of vegetables mixed in with the beans, but it's a real chili, made with real chiles. My friend Marie had a recipe she liked, which she had modified. She passed it on to me, I modified it in turn to suit my ideas about chili, and here we go—on to you.

Many people make bean chili with canned beans, but I prefer to cook dried beans. I find them tastier, and the slow simmering, which is no trouble, produces an excellent, flavorful broth to use as the base of the dish.

I also resist packaged chili powders. There are some good ones, but too many people (not you, of course—other people) reach for a can of something that's been sitting in the cupboard for years, wasn't that interesting to start with, and has now died of old age. I like to soak a few dried chile pods in hot water, puree them, and press them through a sieve to get rid of the skins. This easy method gives me a chile puree full of bright, true chile flavor, not just heat. Try this!

· · · SERVES 8—10 GENEROUSLY · · ·

for the beans

1 cup (170 g) dried red kidney beans
1 cup (170 g) dried pinto beans
1 cup (170 g) dried garbanzo beans

20–30 small fresh epazote leaves, or 3 Tbs. dried
    epazote, slightly crumbled
2¼ tsp. sea salt, plus more to taste

for the chile puree

2 oz. (60 g) dried ancho chiles

½ oz. (12 g) dried chipotle chiles

for all the rest

3 Tbs. (45 ml) olive oil

2 yellow onions, chopped (450 g)

4–5 cloves garlic, chopped

sea salt

2 medium carrots, peeled and diced (150 g)

1 large bell pepper, cored and diced (240 g)

1 bunch green chard (8 oz.; 240 g)

4 tsp. cumin seeds

2 Tbs. fresh oregano leaves or 4 tsp. dried oregano

one 28-oz. (800 g) can fire-roasted chopped tomatoes

½ cup chopped cilantro

• • •

garnishes:

crumbled sharp cheddar cheese

cilantro leaves

freshly sliced avocado

lime wedges

You can cook your beans separately, or all together if you are confident that the beans are relatively fresh. I find that garbanzos usually take about 20 minutes longer to get tender than kidney beans or pintos, so I cook mine separately.

Use 4 cups (1 liter) water for each cup of beans and add a third of the epazote leaves to each pot. Bring the water to a boil, then lower the heat, cover the pots, and leave the beans to simmer gently for about an hour. Taste a bean of each type, and cook longer if needed. Cooking time depends on the age of the beans, and you might need another 20 or 30 minutes. The beans should be tender to the bite, with no crunch left, but should not be mushy. Add ¾ teaspoon salt to each pot of beans and allow them to simmer another 5 minutes, then turn off the heat.

While the beans are cooking, prepare the chile puree. Rinse the chile pods and put them in a small saucepan with 2 ½ cups (600 ml) water. Bring the water to a boil, then turn off the heat, cover

recipe continues on next page

the saucepan, and leave the chiles to soak and soften for 40 minutes. If the water does not completely cover the chiles, turn them over after the first 20 minutes.

When the chiles are soft, pull out and discard their stems. Put the chiles and their water into the blender. (I usually throw an old kitchen towel over the lid of the blender to prevent any possible leaking or spraying.) Puree the chiles thoroughly, then press the mixture through a sieve and discard the skins.

Heat the olive oil in a large sauté pan (at least a 5-quart capacity) and cook the chopped onions in it over medium-high heat for a few minutes, until they begin to soften. Add the chopped garlic and a pinch of salt and sauté over medium-low heat, stirring now and then, until the onions are coloring, about 15 minutes. Add the diced carrots and bell pepper and sauté another 10 minutes.

Meanwhile, remove the stems from the chard, cut the greens into 2-inch pieces and set aside. Toast the cumin seeds in a dry pan over medium heat for a few minutes, just until the seeds release their fragrance, then grind them in a mortar or a spice grinder. Add the cumin and the oregano to the sautéed vegetables, stir for a minute, then add the tomatoes, all the beans with their liquid, and half a cup of the chile puree.

Stir, and taste. Add more chile puree, a little at a time, until you feel the heat . . . and remember that the chile flavor is more forward when the puree has just been added; it will mellow as it blends with all the other ingredients.

Everyone has his or her own idea of how spicy a chili should be. I like to add most of the puree, and you may like a milder chili. I can't tell you how many spoonfuls to use, because every chile is a little different. Chiles vary so much in spiciness, even the same variety, that you just have to use your taste buds—which is the great fun of cooking.

What your chili needs now is time. The chili has to simmer very gently as the flavors marry and develop. Turn the heat to low, cover the pan, and just check on it a couple of times over the next hour to make sure it's not getting dry. Halfway into the hour, add the chard and cilantro and taste again for salt and for heat. Adjust if you like.

Serve the chili in ample bowls and pass the garnishes: crumbled sharp cheddar cheese, fresh cilantro leaves, and freshly sliced or cubed avocado. A few wedges of lime are also nice. Cornbread is perfect with this chili.

Chili gets better over the next two or three days if kept in the refrigerator, well covered. It freezes well and reheats like a champ.

CHAPTER 8

holiday soups

Christmas Eve Porcini Soup

Beet Soup with Ginger • V

Persimmon Soup • V

Sweet Potato Bisque

Chestnut Soup

tradition and discovery

In my house the progress of the holidays can be charted by the aromas wafting from the kitchen. As Christmas nears, they build in a winter fugue—forest greenery, spice, wood smoke, sugar and butter, and the culminating perfume of Christmas: wild mushrooms.

In my Polish family, wild mushrooms were always part of the festive Christmas Eve supper. They were cooked down with butter and onions and chopped to a fine-textured filling for the dumplings that went into the clear beet *barszcz*. For a long time my mother could not get fresh porcini, or *prawdziwki*—the real ones—as they were fondly called in Polish. She bought a lavish supply of dried ones instead, and when she plunged those blackened, wrinkled scraps into boiling water to start cooking them, I held my face to the steam and inhaled the irreplaceable essence of true forest mushrooms.

Now I get fresh or flash-frozen porcini and I pay homage to my family tradition with my own once-a-year soup, Christmas Eve Porcini Soup (p. 222)—great slices of sautéed mushrooms and strands of caramelized red onion swimming in a rich, shimmering dark broth.

Some foods seem perfect for the holidays because we've always had them, and others because they're new and exciting. Sweet Potato Bisque (p. 231) and Chestnut Soup (p. 233) are variations on the flavors of American tradition, new ways of enjoying tastes that may have been part of the Christmas menu all your life. You can incorporate them in an elaborate multicourse dinner or use them to bring a special seasonal quality to a casual winter supper.

Perhaps Beet Soup with Ginger (p. 226) is not as familiar, but when I saw the color of this soup, I had to include it with the holiday fare; it is so deeply, vibrantly crimson, so festive in appearance. And then the taste—the snap of ginger against the sweet beets. This is an ideal first course for a sophisticated dinner party some evening in December.

Persimmon Soup (p. 228) is new to me; I first made it while working on this book. It's a discovery that will be part of my late autumn and winter cooking from now on. Persimmons come into the peak of their season between Thanksgiving and Christmas. I learned about roasting persimmons from a neighbor who was writing a book about them and had investigated every possible way of preparing these beautiful flame-orange fruits. From there it was a short leap to the savory-sweet soup with crunchy, salty, tamari walnuts scattered across the top—and to my Thanksgiving table.

Any of these soups can be made anytime through the fall or winter—they will always be delicious—but somehow to me they feel like part of a celebration.

MENU

jeri's spiced nuts
-page 448-

parmesan and fennel biscotti
-page 418-

tapenade with figs and citrus
-page 428-

marbled cannellini dip with roasted tomatoes
-page 431-

. . .

CHRISTMAS EVE PORCINI SOUP
-page 222-

sourdough baguettes

. . .

*salad of baby arugula, aged jack cheese,
and asian pears*
-page 462-

. . .

olive oil and lemon cake
-page 492-

orange and tangerine slices

MENU NOTES

In this meal the traditions of my Polish childhood meet the Mediterranean food culture of my life in California, in a great bowl of wild mushroom soup.

This unusual and festive supper is designed for the dynamics of a party. The first course is an array of finger foods, easy to set out on the coffee table or the sideboard so people can nibble as they mill around, chat, drink a glass of champagne or Prosecco. But these finger foods are extraordinary: spicy caramelized nuts; tapenade with the sweetness of figs winding through the pungent olives; thin, savory biscotti; and a cannellini spread marbled with roasted tomatoes. It feels like a party from the first bite.

Then it's time to sit down at the table, and the elegant porcini soup is served—a profound reduction of forest flavor that calls for your best red wine and your full attention. The soup is followed by its refreshing foil, a salad of pleasing simplicity and seasonal taste. Aged sharp cheese and juicy Asian pears bring back the play of salty and sweet that began the meal.

Dessert is a model of restraint, a beautiful, golden, dense-textured slice of olive oil cake surrounded by orange and tangerine slices.

christmas eve porcini soup

This is the queen of soups, the one I make once a year for Christmas Eve. It is dark, aromatic, and utterly delicious. I feel it's worth the effort of finding the porcini, driving somewhere to pick them up, and then cleaning them. Once that is done, it's quite an easy soup to make.

· · · SERVES 10—12 · · ·

2 lbs. (900 g) fresh porcini or whole frozen
    porcini
9–10 cups (2–2½ liters) mushroom stock
    (recipe follows)
6 oz. (170 g) portobello or Italian brown
    mushrooms
1½ lbs. (700 g) yellow onions
2 Tbs. unsalted butter

2 Tbs. (30 ml) olive oil
3 cloves garlic, chopped
1 tsp. sea salt, plus more to taste
3 Tbs. (45 ml) cognac or good dry sherry
½ cup (120 ml) dry red wine
white pepper
cayenne

If you are using frozen porcini, defrost them slowly in the refrigerator and save any liquid that they give up as they defrost. Frozen porcini are available from produce wholesalers who service better restaurants or at specialty supermarkets.

Prepare the mushroom stock, or if you have dark vegetable broth or root vegetable broth on hand, infuse it with an ounce of dried porcini, as described in the mushroom stock directions that follow.

Thoroughly clean the porcini. Wild mushrooms can be sandy, so wash them carefully; you are going to put them into broth, so water is not an issue. Slice the porcini thinly; if you have very small ones, leave the caps whole. Trim off any woody parts from the stems and slice the stems. If you are using frozen mushrooms, keep the liquid they release, but first strain it through muslin or a paper filter to get rid of any grit. This is essential—a bit of dirt in the bottom of the pot can ruin a glorious soup.

Clean the portobello mushrooms and slice them thinly. Peel the onions, quarter them lengthwise, and then slice them.

Heat a tablespoon of butter and a tablespoon of olive oil in a large sauté pan, preferably a nonstick one, and sauté the garlic in it for 2 minutes, just until it begins to color. Add the sliced portobello mushrooms and toss over medium-high heat, with half a teaspoon of salt, until they soften and give up their excess water, about 8 minutes.

Add the sliced porcini and continue cooking over medium heat, stirring often, until all the mushrooms are much reduced, sizzling in the pan, and nicely browned. This can take up to half an hour, depending on the size of your pan; a bigger pan is better, of course, as it gives you a greater amount of contact with the heat. When the mushrooms are done, add the cognac or sherry and stir another minute or two, until it cooks away. Combine the sautéed mushrooms in a soup pot with the prepared mushroom stock. If you are using frozen porcini, add the liquid they released while defrosting—and be sure you have filtered it.

Meanwhile, in another large sauté pan, heat the remaining 1 tablespoon butter and 1 tablespoon oil and add the sliced onions and half a teaspoon of salt. Cook the onions slowly, stirring them now and then over medium-low heat, until they are meltingly soft and deep golden brown, about 45 minutes. (I remind you about my rule for caramelizing onions: when you think the onions are done, give them at least another 10 minutes, and maybe 20.)

Add the caramelized onions to the soup, along with the red wine; as it is such a modest amount, I like to add half a glass of the great red wine I plan to serve with the meal. Simmer the soup, covered, for 20 to 30 minutes, until the flavors are well developed. Taste the soup, and finish the seasoning with a little more salt if it's needed, a dash of white pepper, and a pinch of cayenne.

Serve this exquisite soup steaming hot, in wide soup bowls.

mushroom stock

This special stock is repeated here for the sake of convenience, as it is an essential ingredient in the Christmas Eve Porcini Soup. It is also an excellent stock to use in making other mushroom soups, risotto, or pilaf.

··· YOU SHOULD HAVE ABOUT 9—10 CUPS OF FLAVORFUL STOCK ···

½ oz. (15 g) dried porcini pieces
2 Tbs. (30 ml) olive oil
1 yellow or white onion, chopped (200 g)
1 clove garlic, chopped
2 large leeks, green part, sliced (200 g)
4 oz. (120 g) fresh mushrooms, sliced
3 medium carrots, peeled and sliced (200 g)
3 medium parsnips, peeled and sliced (200 g)
1 medium turnip, peeled and sliced (150 g)
2 stalks celery, sliced (70 g)

6 big branches of fresh flat-leaf parsley (25 g)
6 big branches of cilantro (35 g)
6–8 fresh sage leaves or 1 tsp. crumbled dried leaves
a handful of fresh dill
½ tsp. fresh thyme
1 tsp. sea salt, plus more to taste
several peppercorns
2½ quarts (2½ liters) water

Pour boiling water over the dried porcini and leave them to soak for at least half an hour.

Heat the olive oil in a large skillet and cook the onion and garlic in it over medium heat, stirring occasionally, until the onion is golden, about 20 minutes. Add the leek greens, fresh mushrooms, carrots, parsnips, turnip, and celery and cook everything together for another 20 minutes. Transfer the vegetables to an 8-quart stockpot and add the herbs, salt, peppercorns, and water.

Drain the soaking porcini, reserving the water. Wash the mushrooms carefully, getting rid of all the grit. Strain the soaking water through a paper filter. Add both the porcini and the filtered soaking water to the stockpot.

Simmer the stock for about an hour. Strain the stock through a fine-mesh sieve, taste it, and correct the seasoning with more salt if necessary—but as always, be cautious with salt.

Another way...

If you have either basic dark vegetable broth (p. 50) or basic root vegetable broth (p. 49) already made, you can simply add the soaked and cleaned porcini and the fresh mushrooms to that and simmer it, covered, for half an hour. Strain and use as you would mushroom stock.

beet soup with ginger

This spectacular magenta soup can be served either hot or cold.

My friend Holly made this for me one winter night, and she said it was based on a summer soup and meant to be served chilled—but we loved it hot, with the added spicy heat of the ginger. I added even more ginger in my own adaptation, and I've had it both ways, hot with a tiny drizzle of cream and well chilled with a big spoonful of thick, slightly sweetened yogurt.

· · · SERVES 6—7 · · ·

12 oz. (350 g) beets
4 oz. (120 g) parsnips
8 oz. (225 g) Napa cabbage
1 fennel bulb (100 g)
1½ cups (150 g) sliced leeks, white part
3 Tbs. (35 g) minced fresh ginger
about 3 cups (750 ml) basic light vegetable broth
   (p. 47), vegetable and ginger broth (p. 52), or
   canned vegetable broth

1 tsp. sea salt
1–2 Tbs. (15–30 ml) fresh lemon juice
· · ·

garnish: plain heavy cream or slightly sweetened
   Greek-style yogurt

Peel and chop the beets and parsnips, and clean and chop the cabbage and fennel. Combine all the vegetables in a soup pot with the ginger, 2 cups (500 ml) water, the vegetable broth, and the salt. Bring the liquid to a boil, then reduce the heat and simmer the soup, covered, for at least half an hour, possibly 45 minutes, until all the vegetables are completely tender.

Allow the soup to cool slightly and puree it in a blender, in batches, until it is perfectly smooth. (My immersion blender left a few chunks of beet behind, so I now prefer to use my good old Oster blender for this soup.) Return the soup to the pot, thin it with a little more vegetable broth if needed, and add lemon juice to taste.

Serve the soup hot, with a swirl of heavy cream in each bowl.

Another way . . .

Serve the soup cold. Prepare the garnish by whisking a tablespoon of sugar into a cup of thick Greek-style yogurt. Allow a couple of minutes for the sugar to dissolve into the yogurt, and place a generous spoonful of the sweetened yogurt on top of each bowl of well-chilled soup.

persimmon soup

WITH TAMARI-TOASTED WALNUTS

Persimmons are the flavor of autumn in California. We eat them plain, in persimmon pudding, in salads, in cookies and breads and muffins, and now in soup.

Fuyu persimmons are a variety that is sweet while still crisp, like apples. Cut into wedges and roasted in the oven, they become a knockout dessert or an unusual, delicious addition to salads. Here, they are the basis for a savory-sweet autumn soup.

Ripe Fuyu persimmons can be very firm or might have a very slight give to them when pressed. By the time they are soft, they are best used for cookies or pudding. Look for vivid orangey gold color, which is a good indication of ripeness.

· · · SERVES 8 GENEROUSLY · · ·

2¾ lbs. (1¼ kg) Fuyu persimmons

3 Tbs. (45 ml) olive oil

sea salt

12 oz. (350 g) parsnips

12 oz. (350 g) white turnips

2 large red onions (500 g)

2½ Tbs. Arborio rice

4 cups (1 liter) basic light vegetable broth
(p. 47) or vegetable and ginger broth (p. 52)

1 Tbs. minced fresh ginger

½ cup (100 g) chopped leeks, white part

1 Tbs. (15 ml) fresh lemon juice

· · ·

garnishes:

heavy cream or half-and-half

chopped Tamari-Toasted Walnuts (technique
follows)

Peel the persimmons, using a sharp potato peeler, and cut out the stems. Cut the persimmons into wedges, and remove any seeds if you are using the seeded variety of Fuyus. Toss the wedges with about half a tablespoon of the olive oil and a pinch of salt and spread them on a nonstick baking sheet.

Preheat the oven to 400°.

Peel the parsnips and turnips. Cut the parsnips into ½-inch sticks and the turnips into wedges, toss them with another ½ tablespoon olive oil and a touch of salt, and spread them on another non-stick baking sheet.

Roast the persimmons and the root vegetables in the hot oven until the persimmons are soft and everything shows dark brownish black spots. Turn the persimmons and the vegetables at least once during the roasting time, which will be around 45 minutes.

Meanwhile, thinly slice or chop the red onions, combine them in a large sauté pan with the remaining 2 tablespoons olive oil and a dash of salt, and cook them over a low flame, stirring often, until they are well caramelized, about half an hour.

At the same time, put the rice in a soup pot with 4 cups (1 liter) water, the vegetable broth, and the minced ginger and leeks. Simmer, covered, for half an hour. Reserve about half of the roasted persimmons and slice them thinly crosswise. Add the rest to the broth, along with the root vegetables and the caramelized onions. Cover and simmer the soup gently for another 20 minutes.

Allow the soup to cool somewhat, then puree it in a blender, in batches, or with an immersion blender, until it is perfectly smooth. Stir in a tablespoon of lemon juice and correct the salt if needed. Stir in the reserved sliced roasted persimmons, and bring the soup back to a gentle simmer just before serving.

Drizzle a tiny bit of cream on top of each bowl and swirl it, then scatter a few tamari-toasted walnuts over the surface.

recipe continues on next page

Tamari-Toasted Walnuts

½ cup coarsely chopped walnuts

1–2 tsp. fine tamari soy sauce

1 tsp. olive oil

Mix the walnuts, tamari, and oil in a bowl until the nuts are all evenly coated. Spread them out on a nonstick baking pan and toast them in a slow oven (about 275°) for 10 to 15 minutes. Scrape them up with a spatula, break them apart if they are sticking together, and toast another 2 or 3 minutes. Allow the nuts to cool.

sweet potato bisque

This gorgeous bisque is perfect as the first course of a winter dinner party, delicately sweet, perfumed with sage and sherry, and topped with toasted pine nuts. The velvety texture is created by the sweet potatoes themselves; with only a touch of cream, the soup tastes rich but not heavy.

· · · SERVES 6—8 · · ·

2 lbs. (900 g) sweet potatoes

1 lb. (450 g) yams

2 small yellow onions (12 oz.; 350 g)

½ medium celery root (5 oz.; 140 g)

1 tsp. sea salt, plus more to taste

1 Tbs. (15 ml) olive oil

1 Tbs. unsalted butter

2 Tbs. chopped fresh sage leaves or 1 Tbs. dried
   sage, slightly crumbled

2–3 Tbs. (30–45 ml) dry sherry

4 cups (1 liter) basic light vegetable broth
   (p. 47) or basic root vegetable broth (p. 49), or
   3 cups canned vegetable broth diluted with
   1 cup water

cayenne

2–3 Tbs. (30–45 ml) heavy cream (optional)

· · ·

garnishes:

fruity green olive oil

⅔ cup (90 g) toasted pine nuts (technique follows)

Preheat the oven to 375°.

Wash the sweet potatoes and yams, arrange them on a baking sheet, and pierce each one with a fork or sharp knife. Roast the potatoes and yams for about an hour, or until they are soft and oozing some syrup. Allow them to cool slightly, then peel them and cut them in big pieces, or, if they are very soft, split them and scoop the flesh out of their skins.

While the potatoes and yams are roasting, chop the onions and peel and finely dice the celery root. Put the celery root in a soup pot with 2 ½ cups (600 ml) water and half a teaspoon of salt and simmer, covered, for about 20 minutes.

recipe continues on next page

Heat the oil and butter in a skillet and sauté the onions with half a teaspoon of salt, over medium heat, until they are soft and turning golden, about 20 minutes. Add the sage, and continue cooking, stirring often, until the onions are caramel-colored, about another 10 minutes. Add the sherry and stir until the sherry has been absorbed.

Add the roasted potatoes and yams and the caramelized onions to the soup pot, along with the vegetable broth and a pinch of cayenne, and simmer the soup on low heat, covered, for another 10 minutes.

Allow the soup to cool slightly, then puree it in a blender in batches, or with an immersion blender, until it is perfectly smooth. Return the soup to the pot, taste it, and correct the seasoning with a pinch more salt or more cayenne as needed. Stir in the cream if you want a richer-tasting soup.

Drizzle a little fruity olive oil on each serving and then sprinkle a spoonful of lightly toasted pine nuts over the top.

Another way . . .

To make this a vegan soup, skip the butter and instead use 2 tablespoons of olive oil to sauté the onion, and omit the cream at the end.

To Toast Pine Nuts

Spread the pine nuts in a dry skillet and stir them over medium-low heat for a couple of minutes, until they begin to give off a fragrance. At this point they can quickly get dark, so watch them carefully and stir constantly. As soon as they are a light golden brown, remove them from the hot pan.

chestnut soup

This is a rich-tasting and distinctive soup for the holidays. You can roast and peel fresh chestnuts for this recipe, or save yourself a lot of time and use either the peeled chestnuts that are available vacuum-packed in jars (from Williams-Sonoma) or the dehydrated ones now available from Italy (from nutsonline.com). I've had good results with both. The dried ones are my favorites; I find them to be more flavorful.

· · · SERVES 8 · · ·

1½ lbs. (700 g) fresh chestnuts in shells, or a 15 oz. (420 g) jar of peeled roasted chestnuts or 9 oz. (250 g) dried chestnuts

2 cups (200 g) coarsely chopped leeks, white part

½ cup (70 g) chopped shallots

1 Tbs. unsalted butter

1 Tbs. (15 ml) olive oil

sea salt

2 Tbs. (30 ml) dry sherry

1 cup peeled and sliced parsnips (120 g)

½ cup chopped celery (60 g)

3–5 cups (¾–1¾ liters) basic light vegetable broth (p. 47) or basic root vegetable broth (p. 49)

½ cup (120 ml) whole milk

freshly ground black pepper

cayenne

2 Tbs. (30 ml) heavy cream, plus more to taste

· · ·

garnish: toasted chopped pecans

optional garnish: heavy cream

If you are using fresh chestnuts, roast them and peel them (technique follows). You should have about 3 cups peeled chestnuts. If you are using dried chestnuts, place them in a medium saucepan with 3 cups (750 ml) water and simmer them, covered, for 40 minutes, or until they are tender. Save all the cooking liquid, which is now a tasty chestnut broth.

recipe continues on next page

In a nonstick soup pot, sauté the chopped leeks and shallots in the butter and olive oil with a dash of salt, stirring often over medium-low heat until they are soft and beginning to turn golden brown, 10 to 15 minutes. Add the sherry and stir over medium heat for another minute.

Add the parsnips, celery, and cooked chestnuts to the leeks and shallots. If you started with dried chestnuts, add the broth from cooking them and about 3 cups vegetable broth. If you are using fresh or vacuum-packed chestnuts, you will need to add about 5 cups vegetable broth. Bring the liquid to a boil, turn the heat down to low, and simmer the soup, covered, for 25 minutes. If the liquid reduces too much and tastes too salty, add a bit of water, a tablespoon at a time. Allow the soup to cool slightly, then stir in the milk and puree the soup in a blender in batches, or with an immersion blender.

Return the soup to the pot and bring it to just under a simmer, then taste. Finish seasoning with a pinch of salt if needed, some freshly ground black pepper, and a pinch of cayenne. Stir in the cream.

Sprinkle a spoonful of toasted chopped pecans over each bowl of soup as a garnish. If you like, drizzle additional cream over the soup before you add the pecans.

To Roast Fresh Chestnuts

Cut an *X* in the flat side of each chestnut, using a very sharp knife and cutting only through the shell. Soak the chestnuts in warm water for about 20 minutes, then drain them and spread them out in a single layer on a cookie sheet. Roast them in a 350° oven for about 15 minutes, or until you see the cut shells beginning to turn up at the corners. Peel the chestnuts while hot, or at least warm, then blanch them in boiling water for a couple of minutes and rub them in a towel to remove the skins.

spring
and
summer
soups

CHAPTER 9

first tastes of spring

Asparagus Bisque with Fresh Dill

Sorrel Soup with Mint and Spring Vegetables • **V**

Fresh Pea Soup with Mint Cream

Purple Cauliflower Soup • **V**

Carrot, Orange, and Ginger Soup • **V**

Springtime Barley and Mushroom Soup • **V**

Fresh Fava Bean and Sweet Pea Soup • **V**

Rustic Artichoke and Potato Stew • **V**

Creamy Artichoke Soup

Curried Spinach and Sorrel Soup

the farmers' market in spring

Spring comes early here in California—strawberries ripen in time for Valentine's Day—but it is a famously unreliable season. I remember one April when Alaskan storms swept down with freezing rain and the mountains that ring our valley were dusted with snow. It looked alpine, except for the oranges down in the groves. Then, overnight, the air softened and filled with perfume.

Spring... whether it comes in March or April or not until the first days of May, it takes our breath away. I take my spring fever straight to the farmers' market, looking for the flavors that sing out, for the giddy, delicious sensation of newness.

Asparagus arrives like a herald, thin stalks and fat ones, announcing the bounty of green things to come. The slender spears are excellent for a sauté, or for roasting until they are golden and almost crisp, like potato chips only so much better. The fat ones are just right for steaming or for slicing very thinly and tossing into salad. Both are wonderful for soup. Freshness is easy to check: the stalks should be firm and the tips tight and clean, with no mushy or broken bits.

Sugar snap peas—just eat one. If you taste the sugar and feel the snap and want to eat another and another, buy them. I love them raw, plain or with a dab of hummus, but even though they are not generally thought of that way, they are marvelous as a soup ingredient. They provide that irreplaceable spring pea essence with a lot less work than shelling peas.

Shelling peas, sometimes called English peas, should also be tasted. Break open a pod and eat a few peas. Sweet? Crunchy? Vibrant with flavor? That's what you want. If the peas are even a little bit dull or starchy, wait for the next batch. Shelling peas are like corn—glorious in their moment, when they have just been picked, but the moment is not long. Look for the crisp, electric-green mint that will go with them, and soft golden-green butter lettuce.

Fennel bulbs will be slim and small in early spring, but their fronds of feathery greens can be luxurious, and both are fine additions to salads and to soups as well. They become mild and sweet with cooking, retaining a mere whisper of their characteristic anise bite.

The new green leaves of the season are everywhere at the spring market: delicate, lemony sorrel, long, spiky dandelion leaves, and pea shoots with their tendrils. Don't forget the peppery wake-up call of mustard in its varying shapes—I love the curly mustard that looks like miniature frisée—and spicy radish greens. And if the radish tops look fresh and green, the radishes to which they're attached will be crisp and gently spicy. Radishes like cool weather, and early spring is their best season.

The greens you've seen all winter are new again, baby versions of themselves. You'll see chard and kale so tiny and delicate that you can toss whole leaves into salad, as well as baby spinach leaves and the tiniest arugula. Look for glossy, perky beet greens and the turnip tops that we find when the rows are thinned in the fields—they're such a treat in a green soup.

And fill your basket with herbs, the little bunches of big flavor that will give your spring soups and salads such verve: marjoram, dill, the many mints, young parsley, and tender new thyme.

All the leafy greens can be judged by their looks. If the leaves are firm and shiny, with bright color, if they show no bruises or frayed edges, you know they are not long out of the field.

Don't touch the nettles! But if you see them, big wild tangles overflowing their bushel baskets, grab them (through a plastic bag, please). Walk on the wild side and enjoy the seasonal pleasure of this stinging plant, so easily tamed into sweetness by a little heat.

In the drama department of the spring market are the fava beans, big, bumpy pods a foot long with fuzzy, suedelike skin and a soft green color. For fava fanatics, these beans define spring. The very young ones only need to be taken out of their pods; later the beans should be blanched and have their little jackets slipped off, but I have always found them worth the effort. During fava season I keep a basket heaped with these overgrown pods on my counter, and friends who drop by can occupy themselves by hulling a few.

Mixed in with all this green is a surprising bouquet of color: the root vegetables. Carrots, small and slender, are almost certain to be good if they are firm and snap when you break one. Look for carrots with their tops attached, as it's a good way to see how fresh they are. Freshly dug new potatoes are full of flavor and not much starch. They come in lovely hues: creamy gold, purple, white, pale brown. White turnips no bigger than golf balls are mild enough to eat raw, and the dainty beets that may be attached to your beet greens are red, pink, gold, and even white.

The beauty contest goes on with the brassicas—unlikely but true. Startling purple cauliflower, small broccoli shoots, and the various new crosses of the two are as eye-catching as anything in the market.

And fruit—the spring fruit that we have been waiting for is juicy, acidic, and piercingly sweet all at once. Blood oranges, streaked with maroon and crimson. Tangerines of all kinds. Brilliant red first-of-season strawberries. And the yellow treasure of springtime, Meyer lemons. Actually, all lemons are treasures, and you should never be without them; lemons are second only to salt as the element that lifts flavor, revealing the life in every food, savory or sweet.

MENU

ASPARAGUS BISQUE WITH FRESH DILL

page 245

grilled goat cheese sandwich

page 450

• • •

salad of baby greens and pea shoots

• • •

chilled orange slices in orange and mint syrup

page 504

see menu notes on next page

Soup and a sandwich—it's been my lunch, and maybe yours, more times than we can count. This soup and sandwich shows yet again that simplicity is sublime when the ingredients are of the highest quality.

The lightly creamy asparagus soup captures all the delicate newness of spring. Pure asparagus flavor, a touch of cream, a bit of fresh dill—it's a standout.

With it, have an exquisitely simple but zesty sandwich. Tangy white goat cheese is layered with a few black olives and a sliver of marinated tomato between two slices of buttered fresh baguette. A few minutes in a hot pan, weighed down with a cast-iron lid, gives the bread a crispy golden finish and melts the cheese. There it is, the best grilled cheese sandwich I've ever had.

A salad is not really a necessity, but it's spring, and time to indulge in those baby greens. Perhaps you have a mesclun, a mix of tender lettuce leaves. Or you might put together your own. Start with a sweet lettuce, like butter lettuce or tiny romaine. Add a little frilly mustard or a few very fresh radish leaves. Throw in sprigs of fennel, whole mint leaves, and the curly, playful-looking tops of the pea vines. Maybe you have nasturtiums in your yard and like to place an edible flower or two on each plate.

While citrus is going strong, a dessert of orange slices chilled in a light syrup is ambrosial. If you live near a citrus-growing region, get blood oranges. They are stunning to look at—some are red right through, others are orange with streaks of maroon. Tangerines are another delicious option; there are numerous varieties that are easy to peel and pull apart. This is pure refreshment.

Another way . . .

This menu is just as wonderful with Sorrel Soup (p. 247) or any of the green soups of springtime.

asparagus bisque with fresh dill

This soup came about from a moment of spring bounty. I was so excited about the asparagus and fresh dill at the farmers' market that I came home with too much of both, and an asparagus festival ensued.

In most of my soups I use onions, but in this one I use only leeks and fennel to support the asparagus, along with some lemon zest and all that fresh dill. It has a pure spring flavor, and although I add only a tiny amount of cream, the texture is velvety and luxurious.

· · · SERVES 6 · · ·

1 ¼ lbs. (570 g) green asparagus

2 medium leeks (7 oz.; 200 g)

1 large fennel bulb (7 oz.; 200 g)

zest and juice of 1 lemon

2 Tbs. unsalted butter (28 g)

3 Tbs. Arborio rice (45 g)

1 ½ tsp. sea salt, plus more to taste

2–2½ cups (500–600 ml) basic light vegetable broth (p. 47), vegetable broth with no onions (p. 53), or pea pod broth (p. 55)

½ cup (22 g) finely chopped fresh dill, plus more to taste

white pepper

cayenne

2–3 Tbs. (30–45 ml) heavy cream (optional)

Using a vegetable peeler or sharp knife, thinly peel the bottom 2 or 3 inches of the asparagus stalks, then snap off the toughest bits at the bottoms (peeling the bottoms first allows you to keep much more of the stalk). Cut the stalks into 1-inch pieces; you should have about 4 cups.

Wash the leeks and chop the white and light green parts only. Trim, wash, and chop the fennel bulb. Grate the zest of the lemon, making sure to get only the yellow and none of the white pith.

Melt the butter in a large skillet or soup pot and cook the leeks over medium heat for 8 to 10 minutes, until they are soft and begin to take on a hint of color. Add the asparagus, fennel, lemon

recipe continues on next page

zest, rice, 1 ½ teaspoons salt, and 3 cups (750 ml) water and bring to a boil. Turn the heat down and simmer, covered, for about half an hour, or until all the vegetables are tender.

Add 2 cups vegetable broth, the dill, and a pinch each of pepper and cayenne. Puree the soup in a blender, in batches, until it is perfectly smooth. Add broth if the soup seems too thick. (With asparagus, which is fibrous, I prefer a container blender to an immersion blender.) Return the pureed soup to a clean pot and stir in a couple of teaspoons of fresh lemon juice, more if you like.

Bring the soup back to a simmer, taste it, and season with tiny amounts of pepper and more salt if needed. Stir in the cream if you wish.

Another way . . .

To make this a vegan soup, replace the unsalted butter with olive oil, and either omit the bit of cream at the end or replace it with a few tablespoons of nondairy creamer.

sorrel soup with mint and spring vegetables

The lemony taste of sorrel sings through this delicious spring soup. I usually add a little lemon juice to my green soups, but sorrel provides all the tart flavor here, and mint adds a balancing sweetness. A few drops of fresh, fruity olive oil glistening on top of each bowl give it the perfect finish.

A word about sorrel: this vibrantly acidic leaf is often used in Europe, where cooks enamored of its lively flavor add it to soups and sauces, but it is underappreciated here. It does turn up regularly at my farmers' market and in my local natural-foods grocery, however. Ask for it at yours. The leaves of cultivated sorrel are long, bright green ovals, and very tender. If you aren't sure—is that sorrel?—just taste it. The characteristic sour taste will tell you at once.

Pretty green sorrel turns khaki green when cooked, so I generally mix it with spinach or other vegetables that hold their green color.

· · · SERVES 6—8 · · ·

3 Tbs. (45 ml) olive oil, divided
2 yellow onions, chopped (400 g)
1½ tsp. sea salt, plus more to taste
1 bunch sorrel (8 oz.; 225 g)
1 small bunch spinach (6 oz.; 170 g)
4 green onions or scallions, white and green
    parts (90 g)
¾ cup (30 g) packed fresh mint leaves
1 large fennel bulb (8 oz.; 225 g)
1 bunch asparagus (8 oz.; 225 g)

3 Tbs. (45 g) Arborio rice
2½ cups (600 ml) basic light vegetable broth
    (p. 47) or canned vegetable broth
freshly ground black pepper

· · ·

garnish: fruity green olive oil
optional garnishes:
crumbled fresh white cheese
toasted pine nuts (technique on p. 232)

recipe continues on next page

Heat 2 tablespoons olive oil in a nonstick pan, add the chopped onions and a pinch of salt, and cook the onions over medium-low heat, stirring now and then, until they are soft and golden brown, 30 to 40 minutes.

Meanwhile, wash and coarsely chop the sorrel, spinach, green onions, and mint leaves. Trim, clean, and thinly slice the fennel bulb. Snap the tough bottoms off the asparagus spears and cut them in pieces. Combine all of the greens except the mint in an ample soup pot with about 4 cups (1 liter) water, a teaspoon of sea salt, and the Arborio rice, and bring to a boil. Lower the heat and simmer, covered, for about 30 minutes.

Add the caramelized onions to the soup, along with the vegetable broth and the mint. Simmer another 5 minutes.

Puree the soup in a blender, in batches, or with an immersion blender, adding a little more broth or water if it seems too thick. Taste, and correct the seasoning with more salt if needed. Grind in a generous amount of black pepper, and stir in the remaining tablespoon of olive oil.

Drizzle a few loops of fruity green olive oil on top of each serving. If you like, scatter a few crumbles of white cheese or some toasted pine nuts over the oil.

fresh pea soup with mint cream

The broth is important to this delicate, fresh-tasting soup, so I start by making an easy broth from the pea pods. Making this customized broth is the easiest thing in the world. You've just shelled the peas and you've got a mound of pods—there they are! Instead of tossing them out, toss them into the stockpot. Add a carrot, an onion, and some celery, cover with water, and simmer. After that, making the soup is a 15-minute job.

If you are buying peas that are already shelled, use Basic Light Vegetable Broth (p. 47). Commercial broths are too oniony or carroty for this soup and will fight with the sweet, pure taste of the spring peas.

· · · SERVES 6 · · ·

for the broth

pods from 3 lbs. (1.3 kg) peas
1 large carrot (100 g)
1 large onion (300 g)
2 stalks celery (100 g)

a few stems of fresh flat-leaf parsley
1 tsp. sea salt, plus more to taste
a few peppercorns

for the soup

1 yellow onion, chopped (300 g)
1 Tbs. (15 ml) olive oil
1 small head butter lettuce, (5 oz.; 150 g)
4 cups shelled peas (1¼ lbs.; 575 g)
6 cups (1.5 liters) pea pod broth
1–2 tsp. lemon juice, plus more to taste

1–2 tsp. sugar
sea salt
freshly ground white pepper

· · ·

garnish: Mint Cream (technique follows)

recipe continues on next page

Give the peas a good rinse while they are still in their pods, then shell them. You should have about 4 cups of shelled peas, even if you try a few while you are shelling—not a bad idea, as you are making sure that they are fresh and sweet.

Set aside the shelled peas and put the pods in a stockpot or a large soup pot. Peel and cut up the carrot, onion, and celery and add them to the pea pods along with the parsley, salt, peppercorns, and 11 cups (2 ½ liters) spring water. Bring the water to a boil, then lower the heat and simmer the broth, loosely covered, for about 40 minutes. Taste it and add a touch of salt if you feel it is needed.

Strain the broth and discard the pods and vegetables. You could have as much as 9 cups of broth, which will leave you some to drink, a bonus of making this soup.

While the broth is simmering, cook the chopped onion in the olive oil in a medium skillet, over moderate heat, until it is translucent and barely beginning to color. Don't let it get brown. Wash the butter lettuce and tear it up.

Combine the cooked onion, peas, and lettuce in a soup pot with 6 cups (1 ½ liters) of the pea pod broth and simmer, covered, for 12 to 15 minutes, or just until the peas are soft.

Allow the soup to cool slightly, then puree it in a blender, in batches, or with an immersion blender, until it is perfectly smooth. Return the soup to the pot, bring it back to a simmer, and taste it. Season with a bit of fresh lemon juice, a teaspoon or so of sugar, some sea salt, and white pepper to your taste. This is a delicate soup, so add seasonings in discreet amounts until you have the right balance of flavor.

Serve the soup hot, with some mint cream dropped or swirled into each bowl. You could also serve this soup with croutons, or sprinkled with chopped dill.

Mint Cream

3–4 Tbs. chopped fresh mint leaves

½ cup (120 ml) heavy cream

Chop the mint finely and immediately beat it into the cream. Beat just until the cream is slightly thickened, but not yet stiff. Keep the cream cold until ready to use.

purple cauliflower soup

A spring or winter soup of strange and subtle beauty, this smooth puree has a dusky lavender color that reminds me of mulberries crushed with cream, but the taste is savory, with gentle potatoes and turnips softening the cauliflower. Its color comes from the bright purple florets, and the other ingredients are all white, so no substitutes, please.

I swirl a little fruity green olive oil on top of each bowl. You could also add cream or scatter crumbled cheese over each serving, if you want a richer soup.

· · · SERVES 6—7 · · ·

1 large yellow onion, chopped (250 g)
2 Tbs. (30 ml) olive oil
¾ tsp. sea salt, plus more to taste
8 oz. (225 g) Yukon Gold potatoes, diced
12 oz. (350 g) young turnips, peeled and diced
8 oz. (225 g) leeks, white and light green parts, sliced

2–3 cups (500–700 ml) basic light vegetable broth (p. 47) or canned vegetable broth
1½ lbs. (700 g) purple cauliflower, cut into florets
freshly ground black or white pepper
fresh lemon juice

· · ·

garnish: fruity green olive oil

Sauté the onion in the olive oil with a pinch of sea salt over medium heat, stirring often, until it is pale golden and soft, 15 or 20 minutes. Meanwhile, combine the diced potatoes and turnips and the sliced leeks in a soup pot with about 3 cups (750 ml) water, 2 cups vegetable broth, and half a teaspoon of salt, and simmer, covered, until the vegetables are just barely tender, about 15 minutes. Add the sautéed onions and the cauliflower and cook another 20 minutes, until the cauliflower is soft.

Allow the soup to cool slightly, then puree it in a blender, in batches, or use an immersion blender, until it is perfectly smooth. Add a touch more broth if the soup seems too thick; it should have some substance but pour smoothly from a spoon. Taste, and correct the seasoning with more salt if needed and a little pepper. If you like lemon as much as I do, add just a little, a teaspoon at a time, tasting as you go. You will see the color of the soup change dramatically, from lavender to bright magenta.

Bring the soup back to a simmer before serving, and swirl a thread of fruity green olive oil over each serving.

carrot, orange, and ginger soup

The ginger in this soup warms up the carrots in a friendly way, but it is not enough to dominate. The orange juice adds both sweetness and a touch of acidity, and the result is a subtle, beautifully balanced, but saturated flavor. If you like spicier food, feel free to add more minced ginger.

· · · SERVES 6—7 · · ·

2 lbs. (900 g) carrots
2 large yellow onions (500 g)
1 stalk celery (45 g)
2 Tbs. unsalted butter or olive oil
2½ cups (600 ml) basic light vegetable broth
    (p. 47), vegetable and ginger broth (p. 52),
    vegetable broth with no onions (p. 53), or
    canned vegetable broth
1½ Tbs. minced fresh ginger, plus more to taste
    (20 g)

¾ tsp. sea salt, plus more to taste
zest and juice of 1 orange
1–2 Tbs. (15–30 ml) fresh lemon juice
1–2 tsp. sugar, if needed
· · ·

garnish:
orange zest
fruity green olive oil
cilantro leaves

Peel and thinly slice the carrots; you should have about 5 cups. Coarsely chop the onions and trim and slice the celery.

Melt the butter or heat the olive oil in a large sauté pan or a skillet with sides and cook the onions in it with a big pinch of salt, stirring often over medium heat until they are golden brown; this will take about half an hour. Add the sliced carrots and celery, 2½ cups (600 ml) water, the vegetable broth, the minced ginger, and half a teaspoon of salt. Cover, lower the heat, and let simmer for 40 to 50 minutes, until all the vegetables are completely soft.

Lightly grate the zest from a clean orange, using a very sharp grater, and then juice the orange; you should have about half a cup of juice. When grating orange peel, remember to use only the orange part and none of the white pith, which can become bitter. Add the orange juice and ¼ teaspoon zest to the soup. Puree the soup in a blender, in batches, or with an immersion blender, until it is perfectly smooth.

Stir a tablespoon of lemon juice into the soup and taste it. Add more lemon juice, a tiny bit at a time, until you like the sweet-tart balance and can still clearly taste carrots and ginger. Correct the seasoning with more salt and a touch of sugar if needed

When you serve the soup, stir a pinch of the grated orange zest into each bowl, then drizzle some olive oil on top and scatter fresh cilantro leaves over it.

MENU

SPRINGTIME BARLEY AND MUSHROOM SOUP

-page 258-

irish soda bread

-page 405-

aged, sharp cheddar cheese

. . .

strawberries

MENU NOTES

When spring hesitates and blustery weather blows in, have this cheering, nourishing meal. The flavor of the soup is all about the freshness of spring, but the barley and the abundance of vegetables give it the stick-to-your-ribs quality of a cold-weather soup—and make it work very well as a one-dish meal.

I always think of Irish soda bread around St. Patrick's Day, and in cooler weather it's pleasant to turn on the oven for a while and let the house fill with the fragrance of baking bread. Soda bread is as fast and easy as a pan of biscuits, and the just-baked sweetness and texture of it pair up perfectly with the thick vegetable soup and a piece of sharp cheddar cheese. A crusty baguette or a whole-grain roll is another good choice.

In early spring, strawberries are the ideal dessert. No one is tired of them yet—they are at their refreshing best. As the soup has a pleasant heft from the barley, I would not recommend a starchy dessert here, but you can dress up the strawberries with cream, ice cream, or a splash of lemon juice and a drizzle of honey. Or they can be perfect in their unadorned, juicy ripeness.

springtime barley and mushroom soup

I love mushroom and barley soups, but they are usually so earthy, full of carrots and turnips and other wintry things—in other words, perfect for winter. In the cool weather of early spring, I want a soup that combines the heft of barley with the fresh flavors of the new season: fennel, asparagus, leeks, and baby dill. This is a soup of delicacy and fresh flavor, yet substantial enough to make a meal.

The vegetable broth you use for this soup should be light and mild-flavored, so that it does not dominate the delicate ingredients. The best choice is a homemade broth.

· · · SERVES 6—7 · · ·

⅔ cup (130 g) pearl barley
8–9 cups (2 liters) basic light vegetable broth
   (p. 47) or pea pod broth (p. 55)
2 Tbs. (30 ml) olive oil
1½ cups chopped leeks, white part (6 oz.; 180 g)
12 oz. (350 g) white button or oyster mushrooms
1 clove garlic, minced
sea salt
8 oz. (225 g) fresh green asparagus

1 large fennel bulb (5 oz.; 150 g)
2 Tbs. chopped fresh dill, plus more to taste
2 Tbs. (30 ml) fresh lemon juice
freshly ground black pepper
· · ·

garnishes:
dill sprigs
crème fraîche

Rinse the barley and combine it in a medium soup pot with 4 cups (1 liter) vegetable broth. Simmer it over very low heat, covered, for about an hour, or until it is tender.

Heat a tablespoon of olive oil in a nonstick sauté pan and cook the leeks over a medium flame until they are just soft, about 10 minutes. Stir the leeks into the barley.

Clean the mushrooms (it's fine to rinse them if you're using them for soup) and slice them thinly, cutting them in halves or quarters first if they are large. Add the remaining tablespoon of oil to the pan and stir the garlic over a medium flame for a minute or two, then add the mushrooms. Salt them lightly and sauté them until they sizzle and begin to color, about 15 minutes.

Meanwhile, trim the asparagus and slice the stalks thinly, at an angle. Cut the trimmed fennel bulb into wedges lengthwise, then slice the wedges thinly crosswise.

Add the mushrooms, asparagus, fennel, and dill to the barley and leeks, along with 4 more cups broth. Simmer the soup, covered, for about 15 minutes, or until all the vegetables are tender but not mushy. Stir in the lemon juice. Add salt and pepper to taste, and a little more of the vegetable broth if you need it to give the soup the consistency you like. I like a soup that pours easily from the ladle.

Garnish the soup with dill sprigs, and for a treat add a spoonful of crème fraîche.

Another way . . .

Try this soup with fresh morels if you can find them. There will be more work in cleaning the wild mushrooms, but the soup will be fantastic.

fresh fava bean and sweet pea soup

When fava beans come into the market in early spring, and especially when they come into my friend Steve's garden, I fall under their strange spell. I usually have a big basket of the oversized, lumpy, velvety-skinned pods on my counter.

They are not just decorative, I explain to guests who drop in. You can eat them—if you're willing to take them out of their pods, blanch the beans, then slip off their little jackets one by one. Yes, it's a bit of work to have fresh fava beans, but it is a spring ritual that's fun to do with a friend while having a cup of coffee, or a glass of wine in the afternoon.

If you are willing to perform the meditative task of shelling favas and sweet peas, you can have this exquisite spring soup. Once the legumes are liberated, it is the easiest soup in the world. The brightly sweet English peas and the slightly richer, starchier favas are wonderful together in a pale green puree flecked with dark bits of mint.

··· SERVES 6—8 ···

2 lbs. (900 g) fava beans in their pods
2 lbs. (900 g) shelling peas in their pods
8 cups (2 liters) pea pod broth (p. 55)
1 Tbs. chopped fresh mint
2 Tbs. (30 ml) fresh lemon juice, plus more to
    taste

cayenne

sea salt

fruity green olive oil

Take the fava beans out of their pods; you should have about 3 cups. Drop the beans into boiling water for a minute or two, then drain them. Slip off their outer skins. Now you should have about 2 cups of peeled, light green beans.

Shell the sweet peas; you should have about 3 cups. Rinse the pods and use them to make pea pod broth.

Combine the peeled fava beans and shelled peas with the broth in a soup pot and bring to a boil, then lower the heat and simmer, covered, for about 20 minutes, or until the favas are perfectly tender. Allow the soup to cool, then puree it until smooth, either in a blender, in batches, or with an immersion blender.

Return the soup to the pot and add the chopped fresh mint, lemon juice, and a pinch of cayenne. Taste, and add salt if the broth does not provide enough, and some lemon juice if needed. Stir in a tablespoon or two of olive oil, and garnish each bowl with another few drops of olive oil at the moment of serving.

rustic artichoke and potato stew

This spring stew is made with tiny artichokes, fennel, and dandelion greens—the half-wild and all-delicious flavors of springtime.

Baby artichokes are the name we give to the tiny ones, but they never actually grow up to be the large globe artichokes, they are simply the smaller flower buds from the lower part of this amazing thistle. They might be from 1 ½ inches to 2 ½ inches long, not counting the stem, and weigh anywhere from an ounce to 2 ½ ounces. You'll have 20 to 30 baby artichokes, which looks like a lot when you are buying them, but when they are trimmed they will be less than half their original weight.

Trimming fresh artichokes takes only a few minutes—about 20 minutes for the big pile of babies you need for this stew—and is well worth the effort for the flavor.

· · · SERVES 6—8 · · ·

2½ lbs. (1.1 kg) baby artichokes

juice of 2 or 3 lemons, and 1 cut lemon

1 large yellow onion (10 oz.; 270 g)

8 large cloves garlic

1 lb. (450 g) small red-skinned or Yukon Gold
potatoes

2 medium fennel bulbs (8 oz.; 250 g)

4 oz. (120 g) carrots

4 oz. (120 g) young dandelion greens

6–7 Tbs. (90–105 ml) olive oil

2 tsp. sea salt, plus more to taste

1 Tbs. fresh thyme, or 1½ tsp. dried

1 bay leaf

a handful of torn or coarsely chopped fennel
greens

6 cups (1.5 liters) basic light vegetable broth
(p. 47) or 3 cups canned broth diluted with
3 cups water

big pinch of fresh or dried marjoram

1½ cups (200 g) shelled peas

freshly ground black pepper

• • •

garnishes:

additional lemon wedges

additional fruity olive oil

First, trim your artichokes. Put 2 ½ quarts (2 ½ liters) water in a bowl with the juice of two or three lemons, and if you don't want your fingers to turn dark, wear rubber gloves.

With a very sharp knife, cut off the top inch or so of the artichoke—almost half of it. Then snap off the tough outer leaves, one at a time, until you get to the tender pale green leaves. If you have purple artichokes, you will see leaves that are yellowy-green at the bottom and lighter purple on top.

With a sharp potato peeler or a small, sharp paring knife, peel the stem and the rough part at the base of the artichoke until it looks smooth and creamy. Trim off the bottom of the stem. The stem itself is good to eat—just like the heart. Cut the trimmed artichoke in half lengthwise, give it a quick rub with a cut lemon, and toss it into the lemon water.

recipe continues on next page

Continue until all the artichokes are trimmed, and leave them in the lemon water until you are ready to use them.

Peel the onion, halve it lengthwise, and cut it in thin wedges. Cut larger garlic cloves in half lengthwise, and leave smaller ones whole. Scrub the potatoes, trim away any dark spots, and cut them in half or in quarters, depending on size. Trim the fennel bulbs and cut them into strips or 1-inch pieces. Peel the carrots and cut into slender 3-inch sticks. Cut the dandelion greens into 2-inch pieces. Strip the fennel greens off of their stems and pull them apart into small bits.

In a very large sauté pan, heat ¼ cup olive oil, add the onions and garlic and a big pinch of salt, and sauté on high heat for 4 to 5 minutes only, stirring often, until the onions are beginning to soften. Add the potatoes, the well-drained artichokes, a teaspoon of salt, the thyme, and the bay leaf. Lower the heat to medium and stir frequently for another 12 to 15 minutes, until all the vegetables have nice dark brown spots.

Add the fennel and carrots and keep sautéing and stirring for another 5 minutes. Add the vegetable broth, and another pinch of salt if needed. Cover, turn the heat down to low, and simmer about 12 minutes. Add the dandelion greens, torn fennel greens, and marjoram, cover and continue simmering until all the vegetables are tender, another 5 to 10 minutes. The total cooking time is about 40 to 50 minutes.

About 2 minutes before serving, add the peas, a tablespoon of lemon juice, and plenty of freshly ground black pepper. Taste, and correct with a touch more salt if needed. Just before serving, stir in 2 to 3 more tablespoons olive oil.

Serve in big, wide bowls, and pass lemon wedges, more olive oil, and sea salt at the table. Have a chewy, rustic bread with this, something that you can dip into the delicious juices around the vegetables.

Another way . . .

Fresh green lima beans or shelled fava beans can be used in place of the peas—both are in season at the same time that artichokes are plentiful. Fresh dill can be used instead of fennel greens, or you can use both. And any kind of mustard greens can be used instead of dandelion greens. All good!

creamy artichoke soup

This creamy soup has delicate yet intense artichoke flavor, and is worth the bit of time it takes to strip down and trim some fresh artichokes. A modest amount of cream gives it its silky texture. I've also made a very tasty vegan version with soymilk and soy cream.

I finish the soup with barely cooked leaves of red-veined spinach, my favorite—it's spinach with an upgrade. The bright leaves floating in the pale soup are beautiful as well as amazingly delicious.

· · · SERVES 6—7 · · ·

8–10 medium globe artichokes, or 20–25 baby artichokes (about 3 lbs.; 1.4 kg, untrimmed, to yield 1 lb.; 450 g, trimmed)

⅓ cup fresh lemon juice, plus more to taste

12 oz. (350 g) Yukon Gold potatoes

1½ tsp. sea salt, plus more to taste

8 whole garlic cloves

2 tsp. fresh marjoram leaves, or 1 tsp. dried marjoram

3 large leeks, white part (10 oz.; 300 g, trimmed)

4 Tbs. olive oil, plus more for garnish

3 cups (750 ml) basic light vegetable broth (p. 47) or lightly diluted canned vegetable broth

1 cup whole milk

2 Tbs. heavy cream, plus more to taste

4 oz. (120 g) small red-veined spinach, whole or cut in wide strips, or any baby spinach leaves

freshly ground black pepper

· · ·

garnish: fruity olive oil

First, trim your artichokes. Put about 2 quarts (2 liters) water in a bowl with the lemon juice. If you don't want your fingers to turn dark, wear rubber gloves.

Snap off the tough outer leaves, pulling them down. They should break cleanly at the tender bottom. Work your way around until you get to the tender, creamy yellow leaves near the inside. With a very sharp knife, cut off the top of the remaining leaves, leaving only about an inch.

Using a small, sharp paring knife, trim away any remaining dark green parts around the base. Cut off about half an inch of the stem, and with a sharp potato peeler or a small, sharp paring knife, peel the stem and the rough part at the base of the artichoke until it looks smooth and creamy. The stem itself is good to eat, like the heart.

Cut the trimmed artichoke in quarters lengthwise, and with the tip of a very sharp knife, cut out the fuzzy choke at the center. (Baby artichokes typically do not have a developed choke in the center, so you can skip the last step with them.) Drop the trimmed artichokes immediately into the lemon water, and leave them there until you are ready to use them. You should have about a pound (450 g) of usable, trimmed artichokes.

Peel and dice the potatoes. Combine them in a soup pot with 3 ½ cups (750 ml) water, 1 teaspoon salt, the peeled garlic cloves, and the marjoram. If you are using larger artichokes, cut them roughly into a few pieces each, and add the artichokes to the pot. Bring the water to a boil, lower the heat and simmer, covered, until the vegetables are very tender, about 20 minutes.

Meanwhile, wash and chop the leeks; you should have about 3 cups. Sauté the leeks in 2 tablespoons of the olive oil, with a pinch of salt, stirring frequently over medium heat for about 10 minutes, until they are soft and turning golden. Add the leeks to the soup, along with the vegetable broth, and continue simmering for another 5 to 10 minutes.

Allow the soup to cool slightly, then puree it in a blender, in batches, or use an immersion blender. Artichokes, even when well trimmed, might have fibrous bits, so a container blender might be more efficient.

Return the pureed soup to the pot and bring it back to a simmer. Add the milk and cream, the spinach leaves, and a good amount of black pepper. Simmer very gently for 4 to 5 minutes, until the spinach is barely tender. Taste and correct the salt if needed.

recipe continues on next page

Lower the heat and carefully stir in a little lemon juice, a few drops at a time, tasting as you go, until the flavor of the soup is beautifully alive and distinct but not yet tart. After this point, the soup must be kept at the faintest simmer, no boiling.

Just before serving, stir in 2 more tablespoons of olive oil, or pour big loops of olive oil on each bowl.

Garlic croutons would be excellent with this, or garlic toast on the side. Or, if you have extra artichoke hearts, dice them, sauté them with lots of garlic and salt, and scatter them on top of the soup. Yes!

Make it vegan . . .

Use unsweetened soymilk instead of milk, and soy creamer instead of cream. I've found that this works beautifully, but be extra careful not to bring the soup to a boil once you have added the soymilk and lemon juice.

curried spinach and sorrel soup

The lemony tang of sorrel is the backbone of this soup, and fresh white goat cheese melts into the soup before it is pureed to give it a rich creaminess. It is a tasty hot soup, and in the summer is equally delicious when served chilled. If you have a jar of roasted and peeled pimiento peppers on hand, dice one and scatter the red morsels across the smooth green soup for a beautiful effect.

· · · SERVES 6—8 · · ·

12 oz. (350 g) fresh spinach leaves
12 oz. (350 g) fresh sorrel leaves
1 small bunch green onions, white and green
    parts (100 g)
1 lb. (450 g) Yukon Gold potatoes
4–5 cups (1–1¼ liters) basic light vegetable
    broth (p. 47), or 4 cups canned vegetable
    broth diluted with 1 cup water
1½ tsp. curry powder

½ tsp. sea salt, plus more to taste
5 oz. (150 g) creamy fresh goat cheese
1 cup (240 ml) whole milk
2 Tbs. (18 g) minced fresh basil leaves
freshly ground black pepper
· · ·

garnish: fruity green olive oil or a swirl of heavy
    cream
optional garnish: diced pimientos

Wash the spinach and sorrel leaves and remove any tough stems. Clean and slice the green onions. Scrub, trim, and dice the potatoes.

Combine the vegetables and the broth in a large soup pot. Add the curry powder and, unless the broth is already very salty, half a teaspoon of salt. Bring the broth to a boil, turn the heat down to medium, and simmer, covered, until the potatoes are completely tender, 20 to 25 minutes.

Remove the soup from the heat, then stir in the cheese and let it melt. Stir in the milk and the basil. Puree the soup until smooth, or leave it lightly textured if you prefer, but be careful not to

recipe continues on next page

overprocess, as that can turn the potatoes gummy. Working in batches with a traditional blender is probably best for this soup; by the time you chase down the last few potato or onion stragglers with an immersion blender, the soup could be viscous. (And a food processor should never be used to puree soups.) Taste, and correct the seasoning with salt and pepper if needed.

To serve the soup hot, bring it just to the point of simmering but do not let it boil. To serve it cold, chill it for several hours or overnight. In either case, finish the soup with a few drops of fruity olive oil on top of each serving or a swirl of heavy cream in the bowl, which is fabulous, though not strictly necessary. Garnish with a scattering of diced red pimientos if you have them.

Another way . . .

Watercress can be used in place of the sorrel in this soup. If using watercress, add 1 to 2 tablespoons of fresh lemon juice at the end to supply the tart edge that sorrel delivers.

CHAPTER 10

green and greener

Spring Green Soup • **V**

Snap Pea, Asparagus, and Fennel Soup • **V**

Nettle and Kale Soup • **V**

Nettle Soup with Fennel and Leeks • **V**

Potage of Baby Spring Greens • **V**

Green Soup with Broccoli, Fennel, and Sorrel • **V**

the green soups of springtime

Winter rains drench our valley, and by spring the hills all around are a green so intense that it shocks the eye. I want to taste that spring green in my bowl of soup.

It's time to leave the rib-sticking soups of winter behind; those deep green soups full of chard and mushrooms now give the stage to light green asparagus, sweet snap peas, the citric tartness of sorrel, the toasty, surprisingly gentle flavor of wild nettles, and all the spring herbs whose flavors explode in your mouth: chives, fennel, sparkling mint, young parsley, chervil, and dill.

The whole meadow is in these next half-dozen green soups: each one is a combination of several ingredients, playing sweet against acidic, combining wild and herbal with flowery and mild.

In Spring Green Soup (p. 278), asparagus, leeks, and few new potatoes mix it up with the first little zucchini, some baby spinach, and a touch of mint. Snap Pea, Asparagus, and Fennel Soup (p. 280) brings in a whole bouquet of herbs. Nettles star in two different soups, one deep and earthy with kale, one bright and fresh with a hint of anise from the fennel bulb. You must try a nettle soup at least once, if only to see the transformation of ordinary, earthly green to a green from another planet.

The Potage of Baby Spring Greens (p. 288) really does look like a bushel of thinnings from the garden—beet greens, turnip greens, fennel greens, and spring onions, a salad made into a soup. In another combination, broccoli gives depth and character to sweet fennel and sour sorrel, and all three are mellowed by one yam, for body and creamy texture.

The flavors are vibrant, bursting with new life, with chlorophyll and sunshine, and all but one are blended. I love to combine the various tastes in just the right balance, then whirl them together into a new flavor, unique to that soup. There's more fun when everyone savors a taste that seems both familiar and elusive. "What's in this?" I hear, again and again.

I've mainly used my good old Oster blender when making these soups, but lately I've been using an immersion blender as well, and I love it. The soup is pureed in the pot; easy soups are even easier. Use whichever tool you prefer, but don't try to puree soup in a food processor; it's built for different tasks and you'll just have a leaky mess on your counter if you pour soup into it.

To give a finishing touch of wide-awake, alive flavor to these spring green soups, a squeeze of lemon juice is almost always added near the end of the cooking time. Tangy goat cheese or garlicky croutons can provide texture and contrast. But the essence of the soup is brought out at the moment of serving with a splash of virgin olive oil, unheated, glistening like a pattern of gold leaf on each delicious bowl of green.

MENU

SPRING GREEN SOUP
-page 278-

. . .

popovers
-page 409-
filled with herbed scrambled eggs

. . .

tangerine and strawberry compote
-page 505-

MENU NOTES

The idea of this little menu is not soup as the center of a menu but rather that a lovely soup in its traditional place as a first course can turn a very simple dish—say, a plate of scrambled eggs—into a delightful meal.

In this version, the eggs are scrambled with a sprinkling of chopped fresh herbs and spooned into crisp, balloonlike popovers just for fun. The eggs could also be mounded on an English muffin or a slice of whole-grain toast, or they might be an omelet.

Here's another way: if you have a little more time, a homemade Potato Pizza (p. 402) makes a knockout combination with the light, vividly green soup. I love the solid, comfort-food quality and the taste of sautéed potatoes and onions on the thick, soft olive oil bread. And that kind of pairing works as well with a slice of quiche, a wrap, a burrito . . .

Start with something hearty and unfussy, add this alluring pool of spring green, and you have an elegant brunch. Finish with bright and juicy spring fruits in a chilled compote. Citrus and berries are macerated in their own juices with a touch of added sugar and slivers of basil and mint.

Any of the green soups of spring are delightful in a menu like this one, as is Sorrel Soup with Mint and Spring Vegetables (p. 247) or Fresh Fava Bean and Sweet Pea Soup (p. 260).

spring green soup

Winter was over, and I could not stop making green soup, so I came up with this simple concoction of easily available spring vegetables and fell in love with it. It became my default soup; for weeks there was always a pot of this in my refrigerator.

Asparagus and the first baby zucchini are layered on a foundation of spinach and leeks and enlivened with some lemon and mint. When the soup is blended, it becomes mysterious. No one can identify everything in it, but it perfectly captures spring.

· · · SERVES 6—7 · · ·

8 oz. (225 g) leeks, white and light green parts
2 Tbs. (30 ml) olive oil
1½ tsp. sea salt, plus more to taste
7 oz. (200 g) Yukon Gold potatoes
8 oz. (225 g) asparagus
12 oz. (350 g) small green zucchini
8 oz. (225 g) baby spinach leaves
2 Tbs. chopped fresh mint leaves or 1 Tbs. dried mint

about 3 cups (750 ml) basic light vegetable broth (p. 47), vegetable broth with no onions (p. 53), or pea pod broth (p. 55)
2–3 Tbs. (30–45 ml) fresh lemon juice
cayenne

· · ·

garnish: fruity green olive oil
optional garnish: crumbled goat cheese, croutons, or sautéed fresh young fava beans

Wash the leeks thoroughly, drain them well, and chop or slice them; you should have about 2 ½ cups. In a large nonstick skillet, cook the leeks in the olive oil with a sprinkle of salt, over medium heat, until they are soft and tender, 8 to 10 minutes.

Meanwhile, scrub and dice the potatoes and put them in a large soup pot with 4 cups (1 liter) water and a teaspoon of sea salt. Simmer the potatoes, covered, for about ten minutes as you slice the asparagus and zucchini and wash the spinach leaves. Add the green vegetables to the pot, along with the cooked leeks. Simmer the soup for about 15 more minutes. Add the mint leaves during the last few minutes.

Remove the soup from the heat, add the vegetable broth, and allow the soup to cool slightly, then puree it until it is smooth, either in a blender, in batches, or with an immersion blender. Return the soup to a clean pot, stir in a little lemon juice and a pinch of cayenne, and taste. Correct the seasoning if needed. If the soup seems too thick, add a little more water or vegetable broth.

Swirl a thread of fruity olive oil over the top of each serving, then garnish as you please with crumbled goat cheese or croutons. For a real treat, sauté a few fresh, peeled fava beans in olive oil and garlic and scatter them across each bowl of soup. Put the chopped garlic in the pan with the hot oil for no more than a minute before adding the favas, then toss over medium heat for 5 or 6 minutes.

A few ways to mix it up . . .

Any spring herbs can be added in small amounts to vary the flavor of this soup—fresh dill, fennel greens, and chives are all good ideas.

Other spring vegetables can be added to the mix as well: a handful of sweet English peas, a small bunch of sorrel instead of the spinach, or green garlic cooked with the leeks.

snap pea, asparagus, and fennel soup

WITH SPRING HERBS

When I first made this soup, I put the whole spring farmers' market in the pot. I couldn't decide between asparagus and dill, or snap peas and mint, so I mixed them all together. The taste is exuberant, both sweet and tart, with bright herbal notes. Spinach, snap peas, and asparagus give the soup its intense green color—the one that was labeled "spring green" in your Crayola box.

Be sure to drizzle a little fruity olive oil on top of each serving. The taste of the fresh juice of the olive brings out these beautiful flavors like a perfect salad dressing.

· · · SERVES 6—8 · · ·

10 oz. (290 g) sugar snap peas

10 oz. (290 g) fennel bulbs

10 oz. (290 g) asparagus

1 bunch green onions, white and green parts
   (4 oz.; 120 g)

6 oz. (170 g) baby spinach leaves

1½ tsp. sea salt, more to taste

3 Tbs. (45 g) Arborio rice

2 large leeks (8 oz.; 225 g)

2 Tbs. (30 ml) olive oil

½ cup (30 g) loosely packed fresh dill

½ cup (15 g) loosely packed fresh mint leaves

3 cups (750 ml) basic light vegetable broth
   (p. 47) or pea pod broth (p. 55)

2–3 Tbs. (30–45 ml) fresh lemon juice, plus more
   to taste

freshly ground black pepper

· · ·

garnish: fruity green olive oil

Wash all the vegetables thoroughly. String and coarsely chop the snap peas. Chop the fennel bulbs; you should have about 2 cups. Slice the asparagus and green onions. Combine these vegetables and the spinach leaves in an ample soup pot with 4 cups (1 liter) water, a teaspoon of salt, and the Arborio rice. Simmer the vegetables, covered, for about 30 minutes.

Meanwhile, chop the white and light green parts of the leeks to yield about 2 cups. Sauté them over medium heat in 2 tablespoons olive oil with a big pinch of salt. Stir the leeks frequently until they are soft and beginning to turn golden, about 20 minutes. Add the cooked leeks to the soup, along with the dill, mint, and broth. (Do not use a strong-flavored vegetable broth for this soup—nothing with tomato in it.)

Allow the soup to simmer for another few minutes, then remove it from the heat and let it cool slightly. Puree the soup in the blender, in batches, or with an immersion blender, until it is smooth. Return it to the pot and add some lemon juice, some freshly ground black pepper, and more sea salt to taste. Remember to stir in the salt a pinch at a time, then wait a moment before tasting.

Bring the soup back to a simmer just before serving, and drizzle a little fruity olive oil on top of each serving.

a word about nettles

The next two soups involve nettles, and you may not yet have made their acquaintance in your kitchen—though if you ever met them in the field or the woods, you know that they sting. Don't hold this against them. They can't help it, and they'll make it up to you in the soup pot. Cooked nettles have a delicate, slightly toasty, almost sweet flavor—and an electric green color!

Stinging nettles are more commonly found in the kitchens of Europe, where nettle soups, broths, teas, and other dishes have been a tasty tradition for millennia. But these sprawling weeds grow all over the United States, too, and are now turning up in a farmers' market near me, and maybe in one near you. They grow on big, bushy stems with many smallish serrated leaves. My farmer friend B. D. Dautch seeds nettles on his meadows and sells them by the handful, his casual unit of measure. A couple of generous handfuls fill a grocery bag and the leaves cook down to a cup or so of nettle puree.

Nettles begin appearing in the market in early spring in California. I've seen them as early as February, and they continue into the summer, although they seem to be most plentiful in March and April.

Nettles do sting when you touch them. Though no permanent harm is done by this, it's best to take some care in handling them, and there are two good ways to get around this nettlesome quality.

The first solution is to wear rubber gloves when cleaning and trimming the nettles. The other way is even simpler. Because nettles are instantly tamed by heat, you need only throw your messy, untrimmed nettle branches into a pot of boiling water, then drain them in a colander. As soon as they are immersed in the boiling water, they lose their sting and you no longer need to fear them. They become the mildest of leaves. You can proceed to strip the leaves off the stems and make your soup.

And your soup will be delicious.

nettle and kale soup

The nutty and sweet taste of nettles and earthy, dark green kale is such a fantastic combination that it had to become a soup. The otherworldly color, a brilliant green, is a bonus.

See the note about handling nettles on p. 282.

··· SERVES 6—8 ···

12 oz. (350 g) nettles
2 medium yellow onions (450 g)
1 Tbs. (15 ml) olive oil
2 tsp. sea salt
12 oz. (350 g) Yukon Gold potatoes
8 oz. (225 g) leeks, white and light green parts
8 oz. (225 g) Russian or Tuscan kale

2 cups (500 ml) basic light vegetable broth
(p. 47) or canned vegetable broth
2–3 Tbs. (30–45 ml) fresh lemon juice
freshly ground black pepper

• • •

garnish: cream, Greek-style yogurt, or crème
fraîche

Wash the nettles. Wearing rubber gloves, pull the nettle leaves off their stems. Alternately, blanch the nettles first and then pull off the leaves.

Coarsely chop the onions. Heat the oil in a skillet, add the onions and a sprinkle of salt, and cook the onions over low heat, stirring often, until they are soft and golden, 25 to 30 minutes.

Scrub and dice the potatoes and wash and chop the leeks. In an ample soup pot, combine the potatoes, leeks, 4 cups (1 liter) water, and the remaining 1 ½ teaspoons salt. Bring the water to a boil, lower the heat, and simmer for about 10 minutes.

Strip the kale from its tough stems, discard the stems, and chop the greens coarsely. Add all the kale and nettle leaves to the soup, along with the sautéed onions, and simmer, covered, for another half-hour, or until the kale is completely tender. Add the vegetable broth, lemon juice, and black pepper to taste, and allow the soup to cool slightly.

Puree the soup in a blender, in batches, or with an immersion blender, being careful not to overprocess. You can make it a smooth puree or leave it slightly textured, as you prefer. Just don't blend it too long, or the potatoes can become gummy. Return the soup to the pot, bring it back to just below a simmer, and taste. Correct the salt, pepper, and lemon juice as needed.

Serve this beautiful deep green soup with a swirl of cream in each bowl or a spoonful of thick Greek-style yogurt or crème fraîche.

nettle soup with fennel and leeks

Because their flavor is subtle, nettles should not be combined with very assertive flavors, or they will be overwhelmed. I tried them with fennel and leeks, two more vegetables that become mild-mannered with cooking, and really liked the combination—flavorful but delicate.

See the note about handling nettles on p. 282.

··· SERVES 6 ···

12 oz. (350 g) nettles
1 medium fennel bulb (150 g)
8 oz. (225 g) leeks, white and light green parts
3 Tbs. (45 g) Arborio rice
1½ tsp. sea salt, plus more to taste
3–4 cups (750 ml–1 liter) basic light vegetable
   broth (p. 47)

2 Tbs. (30 ml) olive oil
1 large yellow onion, chopped (250 g)
cayenne
3–4 Tbs. (45–60 ml) fresh lemon juice
freshly ground black pepper (optional)

···

garnish: crème fraîche or fruity green olive oil

Wearing rubber gloves, give your nettles a good rinse and pull the leaves off the thicker stems. Small, delicate branches are fine to leave. You'll have about 8 cups of nettles, loosely packed. Alternately, dump the untrimmed nettles into a large pot, douse them with boiling water, immediately drain them, and then proceed to strip off the leaves with no gloves and no fear of being stung. You'll have about 2 ½ cups of damp nettle leaves.

Chop the fennel and leek into ¼-inch dice. Combine the fennel, leek, nettle leaves, rice, 1 ½ teaspoons salt, 4 cups (1 liter) water, and 3 cups vegetable broth in an ample soup pot and bring to a boil. Lower the heat and simmer, covered, for about 20 minutes or until the vegetables are tender.

Meanwhile, heat the olive oil in a skillet, add the chopped onion and a pinch of salt, and cook over medium-low heat, stirring often, until the onion is soft and golden brown, 25 to 30 minutes. Add the caramelized onion to the soup and simmer, covered, for another 10 minutes.

Allow the soup to cool slightly, then puree it in a blender, in batches, or with an immersion blender, adding a bit more vegetable broth if it seems too thick. Return the pureed soup to the pot, add a pinch of cayenne, and adjust the salt to taste. Add 3 tablespoons fresh lemon juice, stir, and taste. Isn't it amazing how lemon makes the nettles come alive? Add more lemon juice, a scant teaspoon at a time, until the soup develops the right piquant balance. Finish the seasoning with a few grinds of black pepper if you like.

Garnish each bowl of soup with a spoonful of crème fraîche or a drizzle of fruity olive oil.

potage of baby spring greens

When the first baby beets and turnips and fennel bulbs are coming up in the spring, their tender leaves make a wonderful green soup, fresh and delicate. The beet greens and fennel add a slightly sweet flavor, and new potatoes add creamy body. Only a little fresh lemon juice is needed. Meyer lemons, which are not sour, are ideal for this soup.

· · · SERVES 6—8 · · ·

9 oz. (250 g) fresh baby turnip greens

9 oz. (250 g) firm, glossy baby beet greens

9 oz. (250 g) young spinach leaves

1 small bunch feathery fennel greens (30 g)

4 oz. (120 g) sliced green onions

8 oz. (225 g) new potatoes

2 Tbs. (30 ml) olive oil

2 large yellow onions, chopped (500 g)

1½ tsp. sea salt, plus more to taste

1½ cups (100 g) sliced leeks, white and light green parts

about 4 cups (1 liter) basic light vegetable broth (p. 47) or canned vegetable broth

freshly ground black pepper

1–2 Tbs. (15–30 ml) fresh lemon juice; use Meyer lemons if you can get them

1–2 Tbs. chopped fresh dill

· · ·

garnishes:

fruity green olive oil

lemon wedges

crumbled *queso fresco*, feta cheese, or cheddar cheese

As always, wash all the greens thoroughly, cut away any tough stems (if there are any with these tender young vegetables), and chop all the leaves coarsely. You should have about 3 cups turnip greens and about 4 cups each of beet greens and spinach. Use both the white and green parts of the green onions. Scrub the potatoes and cut them into ½-inch dice.

Heat the olive oil in a nonstick pan, add the chopped onions with half a teaspoon of salt, and cook over low heat, stirring often, until they are soft and translucent, about 20 minutes. Add the leeks and keep cooking until both onions and leeks are very soft and golden brown, another 10 to 15 minutes.

Put the potatoes, green onions, and leafy greens into a soup pot with 3 cups (750 ml) water, 1 teaspoon salt, and 4 cups vegetable broth and bring the liquid to a boil. Lower the heat and let the vegetables simmer, covered, for 10 minutes. Add the caramelized onions and leeks and simmer the soup for another 10 minutes.

Taste, and season with freshly ground black pepper and a little more salt as needed. Then add a little fresh lemon juice, a teaspoon at a time, until the flavors feel heightened; stop before the soup tastes tart. Add the chopped dill, and if the soup seems too thick—more like a stew than a soup—add a little more vegetable broth.

Serve hot, and top each serving with a few drops of fruity green olive oil. Pass lemon wedges at the table for that essential last squeeze of fresh lemon juice, and also a bowl of crumbled *queso fresco*, mild feta, or aged cheddar.

Another way . . .

To make a delicious Cream of Baby Spring Greens, add 2 tablespoons unsalted butter, 2 ½ cups (600 ml) whole milk, a pinch of nutmeg, a pinch of thyme, and a big pinch of spicy paprika after the soup has simmered. Puree the soup in the blender, in batches, or with an immersion blender, until it is smooth, but stop when you have the texture you like, as overprocessing can make potatoes gummy. Taste, and correct the seasoning with more paprika or lemon if needed to balance the milk.

green soup with broccoli, fennel, and sorrel

As with all my green soups, this one was devised from what looked freshest at the market on a particular Sunday morning early in March. It started with a mound of tiny broccoli florets, but any size broccoli will do. This soup captures the moment between winter and spring: the sweet yam and the sour, bright green sorrel mix it up happily with the broccoli.

If you can't find sorrel, use a pound of spinach and add a couple of tablespoons of lemon juice to create that tart edge that sorrel provides.

· · · SERVES 8 · · ·

2 medium yellow onions (450 g)
3 Tbs. (45 ml) olive oil
1½ tsp. sea salt, plus more to taste
12 oz. (350 g) baby broccoli, with leaves, or
    broccoli florets
1 large fennel bulb (6 oz.; 180 g)
8 oz. (225 g) spinach
8 oz. (225 g) sorrel
1 medium yam (6 oz.; 180 g)
3 cups (750 ml) basic light vegetable broth
    (p. 47) or canned vegetable broth

freshly ground black pepper
cayenne
1–2 Tbs. (15–30 ml) fresh lemon juice, as needed

· · ·

garnish: fruity green olive oil
optional garnishes:
crumbled *queso fresco* or cheddar cheese
herbed croutons

Coarsely chop the onions and sauté them gently in 2 tablespoons olive oil with half a teaspoon salt, stirring occasionally over medium heat until they are soft and golden brown. Do not hurry this process; it will take at least half an hour, and when you think the onions are done cook them a little longer—you'll see how the rich, sweet flavor develops.

While the onions cook, thoroughly wash the broccoli, fennel, spinach, and sorrel. Coarsely chop the greens and the fennel bulb. Peel and dice the yam. Combine these vegetables in an ample soup pot with 5 cups (1 ¼ liters) water, the vegetable broth, and 1 teaspoon of salt. This will look like way too much, but it's not: the greens will reduce dramatically the moment you start to cook them. Bring the liquid to a boil, then reduce the heat and simmer the soup, covered, for about 10 minutes.

Add the caramelized onions to the soup and simmer, covered, another 15 minutes. Grind in some black pepper, add a pinch of cayenne, and stir in the remaining 1 tablespoon olive oil. Allow the soup to cool slightly, then puree it until it is smooth, either in a blender, in batches, or with an immersion blender. Taste, and correct the seasoning with more salt if needed. If you are using all spinach instead of a mix of spinach and sorrel, add a little lemon juice now, tasting as you go, until the soup has a delicate, slightly tart edge.

Drizzle a thread of fresh, fruity green olive oil on each serving, and garnish with crumbled cheese or herbed croutons if you like.

CHAPTER 11

sweet summer

Butter Bean and Summer Vegetable Soup • **V**

Sweet Corn Soup

Smoky Eggplant Soup with Mint and Pine Nuts

Escarole and Potato Soup • **V**

Zucchini and Basil Soup • **V**

Zucchini and Potato Soup • **V**

Charred Zucchini Soup with Yogurt and Pine Nuts

Summer Tomato and Basil Soup • **V**

Tomato and Fennel Soup with Blood Orange

Cannellini and Golden Tomato Soup • **V**

Tomato and Zucchini Soup with Summer Herbs • **V**

Pappa al Pomodoro • **V**

the farmers' market in the glory of summer

The market in summer is a delirium of color and scent. Produce is at its voluptuous best. Fruit is like candy, vegetables are explosions of flavor. It's the easiest time to see that good cooking truly consists of choosing the best ingredients and then doing very little to them. The essential tastes of summer call us: tomatoes and basil, sweet corn on the cob, ripe peaches.

There are so many kinds of tomatoes now that it can seem confusing, but I'll help you out: go right for the Purple Cherokees, and then take a few golden Striped Germans and some scarlet Brandywines. Anything else you get is a bonus, but with those varieties, if they are properly ripened, you will have a great tomato experience. From among the heirloom varieties, I have also used Green Zebra and Black Russian, as well as bright yellow Pineapple tomatoes and many different kinds of cherry tomatoes.

Then there are the familiar hybrids that have been in stores and in our gardens forever—Beefsteak, Early Girl, Better Boy, Premium ... I can't begin to name them all. But with tomatoes, so much depends on the right match of variety and place. A tomato that does spectacularly well in my garden might be lackluster in yours. And your farm stand might be offering fabulous tomatoes that I've never heard of. Local success is all that counts, so investigate the stalls at your farmers' market and taste whenever you can. Buy a couple of these and a couple of those and have your own tasting.

When choosing tomatoes, look for smooth, shiny, taut skin. Shapes can be irregular and downright weird, with creases and rough spots, but there should be no wrinkles or puckery areas. However, you should be able to feel the beginning of softness; a firm tomato is all right, but a hard one is unripe. And when you get those tomatoes home, do not put them in the refrigerator! Both flavor and texture begin to deteriorate immediately when you allow tomatoes to get too cold. Why do that to a defenseless tomato that never hurt anybody? Put your tomatoes on a plate or in a shallow basket on your kitchen counter and use them within a few days to a week.

Corn—white, yellow, and variegated—is in the market in exciting, huge mounds. The important thing to know is, when was it picked? The natural sugars in corn that create that can't-stop-eating flavor are perfect when a ripe ear has just been picked but quickly start to turn to starch. If you know the corn was harvested that morning, buy it with confidence. Not sure? Pull back the husk, notch out a kernel with your fingernail, and taste it—it's the foolproof system. And don't worry about the worm-eaten tips; they are a sign of organic farming.

Eggplants are happiest in the heat, and piles of luminous globes flood the stalls during July, August, and September—white, pale violet or deep purple, round or elongated, large eggplants and tiny ones no bigger than a plum. If you see a range of sizes in one variety, choose the smaller ones. But most important, use feel when looking for the young, sweet ones. Eggplants should be plump, firm, and shiny.

It's harder to go wrong with zucchini, but the same rules apply: look for shiny, unblemished skin and a firm feel. Mix green, yellow, white, and pale green summer squashes; it's fun. And accept the zucchini that your neighbors leave on your porch at night. Even a large zucchini is fine for soup if the skin is soft enough to nick easily with your thumbnail, but once the skin has hardened it's a different squash, not the best for summer food. Smaller zucchini are better, in general, with their very soft skin and easy-to-slice shapes.

Peppers are a research project every year. Summer is the time of red bell peppers and scarlet pimientos, Italian frying peppers, and lipstick peppers. It's also the time of hot peppers: jalapeños, serranos, Thai peppers, and countless other kinds. Sample what you find in your market. Luckily, peppers in season tend to be inexpensive, so research is possible. Chat with the grower if you can, or simply take home a variety: invite surprises into your life.

With green beans, yellow wax beans, long beans, and all the other variations of fresh snap beans, look for slender pods without distinct lumps. The lumps indicate that the beans inside are maturing, and the pod has done its job, so it will be tougher now. Haricots verts are thin as threads, the supermodels of the green bean group, perfect for quick steaming. Big flat Romano beans are wonderful simmered in tomatoes and olive oil until they are meltingly soft.

And then there are the shellies. Shelling beans—shellies for short—are available for a fleeting moment. These are the beans that you normally encounter in their hard, dried form, but at harvest time you might find them fresh. They take less time to cook, and have the delicate taste of youth. Where I live we get favas in the spring and fresh, tender limas during the summer, and they are such a treat. When choosing shellies, look for the opposite of the smooth string bean; now you want to see bumpy, well-filled-out pods. Keep shellies in the refrigerator, but only for a few days, as they are perishable.

Cucumbers—Persian or Armenian cucumbers with their thin skins and tiny, soft seeds, tough-skinned cucumbers that need to be peeled and seeded, small pickling cucumbers—are all good now. Look for deep green color and a firm, solid feel; avoid softness, as it is a sign of dryness.

Avocados are still with us, and they are the mate for those cucumbers. Give them a very gentle squeeze. If you feel just a bit of give, you'll have a perfect avocado in a day or two. Too soft means you'll find brown spots inside. Too hard—not a problem, but you'll wait longer before you can use them.

Herbs are strong and flowering. The blossoms of most herbs are delicious in salads, as well as chopped up with the leaves for cooking, but they generally have a much more intense flavor than the leaves. Get big bunches of basil for pesto now; as the summer progresses, plants need to be cut back and the bundles get bigger and bigger. Look for lemon verbena for syrups, mint for everything, and oregano, epazote, garlic, rosemary, sage, thyme—and lavender, which is a delightful addition to herb blends.

Summer fruit cannot be resisted. I walk down the aisles of the market, breathing in the perfume.

Peaches and nectarines are everywhere, golden and blushing, and the white peaches are food for the gods. I never get over the feeling of pure luxury with white peaches; they seem a rare and precious commodity, even though they are plentiful now in my local markets. With all stone fruit, your guide should be perfume, good color, and a nice heft—if a fruit feels too light, it's dry. The juicy ones feel solid and heavy for their size.

Melons are great when they're great, but they can also be tasteless—and that's a big piece of fruit to toss out. To choose a good melon in any of the netted varieties, such as cantaloupe, look at the netting. It should protrude above the skin, giving it true, rough texture, and the color under the netting should be tawny, not green. The place where the stem was attached should be clean, with no withered bit of stem left, and ideally, it should give slightly when pressed. Above all, choose melons with your nose. A mature, vine-ripened melon will have a powerfully sweet, melony fragrance.

When buying berries you are almost guaranteed a taste, and if they look plump and have good color, they are likely to be fine all summer. Look for local strawberries, blackberries, boysenberries, red, black, or golden raspberries, blueberries, and very briefly, mulberries.

And last but most important to me are the dark red or black cherries for Cold Cherry-Lemon Soup (p. 377). When they look plump and shiny, they are ready—and with most cherries, the bigger the better. Taste, experience the burst of juicy summer flavor in your mouth, then go home and cook.

MENU

flatbreads
tapenade with figs and citrus
-page 428-

armenian string cheese

. . .

**BUTTER BEAN AND
SUMMER VEGETABLE SOUP**
-page 300-

. . .

melons in orange and mint syrup
-page 503-

MENU NOTES

The juicy, summery sweetness of the vegetables in this soup and the butteriness of the lima beans conspire to make me want pungent and salty tastes as a counterpoint: olives, string cheese, and herbed flatbread.

The olives are mixed with dried figs and a hint of citrus zest to make the most delicious of tapenades. The Armenian string cheese I like to get is the kind that is wrapped and twisted into a figure-eight bundle; with patience it can be pulled apart into strands a yard long, an entertaining chore. I pile loops and tangles of cheese on a big white platter and serve the basket of flatbreads and the bowl of tapenade alongside, with a cold glass of wine.

The flatbreads might be thin sheets of lavash, or homemade foccaccia, or crispbreads with seeds and herbs. In a pinch, fresh, soft pita bread is always tasty and is widely available.

The melons in orange and mint syrup are a gorgeous dessert. Syrup is usually a sweetener, but ripe melons in the peak of their season are like honey, and this very light syrup is added to provide a zing of citrus and a spike of herbal brightness from mint. Linger over this bowl of cool refreshment as a warm summer evening turns to night.

butter bean and summer vegetable soup

This is a lovely, colorful summer soup—no winter vegetables allowed. No carrots, cabbage, or potatoes. Everything is light and juicy and full of bright flavors, the perfect counterpoint to the creamy texture of the lima beans. It's not for nothing that we affectionately call them butter beans.

··· SERVES 8 GENEROUSLY ···

1 cup dried giant lima beans (7 oz.; 200 g)

2 tsp. sea salt, plus more to taste

2 medium yellow onions (400 g)

2 Tbs. (30 ml) olive oil

1 medium red bell pepper (150 g)

1½ lbs. (700 g) ripe red tomatoes

6 oz. (170 g) green beans

8 oz. (225 g) yellow or green summer squash

6 oz. (170 g) spinach

6 cloves garlic, peeled and chopped

⅓ cup (20 g) chopped fresh basil

1 Tbs. fresh oregano leaves or 1 tsp. dried oregano leaves

1–2 Tbs. (15–30 ml) fresh lemon juice

freshly ground black pepper

···

garnish: fruity green olive oil

Rinse the lima beans, put them in a pot with 7 cups (1 ¾ liters) water over high heat, bring to a boil, and then lower the heat and simmer, covered, for about an hour, or until they are completely tender. This may take longer, depending on the size and age of the beans. Add water if needed to keep the beans covered, and add a teaspoon of salt when they are tender.

Meanwhile, prepare the vegetables. Coarsely chop the onions and sauté them in a tablespoon of olive oil, turning the heat down after the first few minutes and cooking them slowly until they are soft and beginning to color, about 25 minutes.

Char the red pepper under a broiler until the skin blisters, turning it once or twice to get all sides charred. This might take 15 minutes, less if you have a very hot broiler. Put the pepper in a paper bag for 2 minutes to sweat, then slip off the charred skin. Stem and seed the pepper and cut it into ½-inch pieces.

Scald the tomatoes for 45 seconds in a pot of boiling water, drain and rinse with cold water, then slip off their skins and cut them into chunks. Trim the green beans and cut them into 1-inch pieces. Slice or dice the summer squash, depending on the shape. Wash the spinach and chop it coarsely; if the leaves are tiny, you can leave them whole.

In a large soup pot, bring 3 cups (750 ml) water to a simmer and add the green beans and a teaspoon of salt. Let the green beans simmer for 5 minutes, then add the squash, spinach, bell pepper, tomatoes, and sautéed onions. Simmer the vegetables, covered, for 10 minutes.

Add a tablespoon of olive oil to the onion pan and sauté the chopped garlic over medium-high heat for 2 or 3 minutes, until it begins to color. Add the garlic to the vegetables, along with the basil, oregano, and the lima beans with all their broth.

Bring the soup back to a simmer, and taste. Add a little lemon juice, more salt if needed, and some freshly ground black pepper.

This soup can be a meal in a bowl. Serve it in big bowls, with a swirl of fruity green olive oil on top, and some focaccia or Parmesan crostini on the side. Or start with crispy flatbreads and tapenade and a glass of chilled rosé.

sweet corn soup

This is a variation on a creamy corn soup I've made for years. It's made with a light vegetable broth and some milk—no cream at all—so the pure essence of the corn is what you taste. You must have absolutely fresh, very sweet corn for this soup.

· · · SERVES 6—8 · · ·

10 ears sweet white or yellow corn (about 5 lbs.; 2.5 kg)

3½ cups (850 ml) basic light vegetable broth (p. 47)

2 Tbs. unsalted butter

2 medium yellow onions, chopped (450 g)

sea salt

about 2½ cups (600 ml) low-fat milk

white or red pepper

· · ·

garnish: cilantro leaves

Husk the corn, clean away the silk, and slice the kernels off into a bowl with a sharp knife. You should have about 6 cups of corn kernels. Put the corn in a medium soup pot with the vegetable broth and simmer, covered, for about 15 minutes. If you like, you can scoop out a cup or so of the corn kernels and save them to stir into the pureed soup.

Meanwhile, melt the butter in a nonstick skillet and cook the chopped onions in it with a dash of salt over medium heat, until they are soft and golden brown, 25 to 30 minutes. Add the caramelized onions to the corn, along with the milk, and puree the soup in a blender, in batches, until it is as smooth as possible. You can use an immersion blender for this, but corn is fibrous and you'll need to keep blending longer than usual. Have patience, and add a little more milk to thin the soup as needed.

If you like a soup with a rustic texture, you're done. For a silky, creamlike soup, pass it through a sieve: rub the pulp down with a wooden spoon until it is quite dry, then discard the fibrous pulp and return the soup to the pot. Taste it and adjust the seasoning with salt and pepper; you can use white pepper or a pinch of red pepper, whatever you like. If you have reserved some whole corn kernels, add them back in now.

Bring the soup back to a simmer and serve it steaming hot, with a few cilantro leaves floating on top of each serving.

smoky eggplant soup with mint and pine nuts

The deep smokiness that makes this soup so wonderful comes from charred eggplants (roasted over coals or in a very hot oven) and is underscored by a smoky paprika. The spices and fresh mint join the smoky eggplant and yogurt to create a beautiful, faintly exotic flavor, reminiscent of Persian or Turkish salads.

This soup is a revelation when served well chilled, on a hot, languid summer evening. Streak the top of each serving with a thread of olive oil, then drop a spoonful of thick yogurt in the middle, scatter some toasted pine nuts over that, and open the cold Tavel rosé.

But the soup is also delicious hot—and if you want a fiery soup instead of a cooling one, add a touch of harissa, the spicy Moroccan chile paste, as a condiment.

· · · SERVES 6—7 · · ·

2 medium globe eggplants (2¼ lbs.; 1 kg)
2 medium yellow onions (450 g)
3 Tbs. (45 ml) olive oil
sea salt
½ tsp. coriander seeds
1 Tbs. cumin seeds
2 cloves garlic, thinly sliced or chopped
½ tsp. smoked paprika, such as pimentón de la Vera
5 cups (1.2 liters) basic light vegetable broth (p. 47) or canned vegetable broth
½ cup (30 g) chopped fresh mint, plus more to taste

freshly ground black pepper
1–2 Tbs. (15–30 ml) lemon juice
1 cup (240 ml) drained Greek-style yogurt, preferably goat yogurt (technique on p. 317)

· · ·

garnishes:
fruity green olive oil
drained Greek-style yogurt
½ cup (40 g) lightly toasted pine nuts (technique on p. 232)
optional garnish: Harissa (p. 444)

Preheat the oven to 450°.

Select young, firm eggplants, as they will provide the dominant flavor in the soup and must be sweet and fresh. Prick the eggplants in several places with a fork and then roast them on a baking sheet for 45 to 60 minutes, or until they are completely soft and their skin is blistered and blackened in places. This imparts the subtle smoky flavor that will set off the spices and lemon.

Alternately, char the eggplants on a charcoal grill, turning them often. The time needed to achieve a soft, well-cooked eggplant on the grill will depend entirely on the heat of the coals and the size of the eggplants.

While the eggplants are roasting, quarter and thinly slice the onions. Heat 2 tablespoons olive oil in a large nonstick pan and cook the onions slowly with a pinch of sea salt over medium-low heat, stirring often, until the onions are very soft and golden brown, about half an hour.

When the eggplants are well charred and soft to the point of collapse, remove them from the oven or grill and allow them to cool until you can handle them. Split them open and scrape out all the flesh, including the seeds. Remove and discard any seeds that look very dark, as they might be bitter. Chop the eggplant by hand until there are no large pieces left.

In a small skillet, dry-roast the coriander and cumin seeds, stirring them over medium-low heat for a few minutes, just until they release a toasty fragrance. Grind the spices in a mortar or a spice grinder and set aside. Heat the remaining tablespoon of oil in the same small skillet and cook the garlic in it over a very low flame for about 2 minutes

In an ample soup pot, combine the eggplant pulp, the caramelized onions, the freshly ground spice mixture, the fried garlic, and the smoked paprika, along with the vegetable broth, and simmer, covered, for about 10 minutes to marry the flavors. Add the fresh mint, some pepper, a little lemon juice, and more salt if it is needed; this will depend largely on the saltiness of the broth you

recipe continues on next page

are using. Turn off the heat and stir in the yogurt. A large whisk is best for this, as the soup has a rough, rustic texture. Taste the soup, and add a bit more lemon juice if you think it's needed to bring a brighter citric edge to the flavor.

Chill the soup well and serve it with an extra drizzle of olive oil and a spoonful of plain yogurt as well as a scattering of lightly toasted pine nuts. Or serve it hot, with any of the same finishing touches, but reheat the soup carefully to avoid curdling the yogurt; bring it just to a simmer as you stir it. Serve harissa with the soup if you like.

escarole and potato soup

When you're ready for a change from salads every day, put that head of escarole into a soup pot. In this simple combination, escarole and potatoes are enriched first with caramelized onions and fennel, then with a topping of creamy burrata or crème fraîche. The result is a homey soup with a luxurious feel, like an Irish colcannon that got dressed up for a party.

· · · SERVES 6—7 · · ·

2 medium red onions (400 g)
1 medium fennel bulb (200 g)
1 large leek, white and light green parts (200 g)
3 cloves garlic
4 Tbs. (60 ml) olive oil
1½ tsp. sea salt, plus more to taste
1 medium head escarole (about 10 oz.; 300 g)
1 lb. (450 g) Yukon Gold potatoes

3 cups (750 ml) basic light vegetable broth (p. 47) or canned vegetable broth
1–2 Tbs. (15–30 ml) fresh lemon juice
freshly ground black pepper
a small handful of chopped fresh flat-leaf parsley

· · ·

garnish: burrata or crème fraîche

Peel and quarter the onions and slice them thinly. Trim the fennel bulb, cut it in half lengthwise, and slice it very thinly. Trim, clean, and thinly slice the leek, and very thinly slice the garlic cloves.

Heat 2 tablespoons olive oil in a large skillet and add the sliced onions and fennel with a big pinch of salt. Stir them occasionally over medium heat until they wilt, 5 to 7 minutes. Add the sliced leek and garlic and cook the mixture over medium heat, stirring often, until all the vegetables are soft and amber-colored, about half an hour.

recipe continues on next page

Meanwhile, wash the escarole thoroughly and cut it into 1-inch pieces. Scrub and finely dice the potatoes. Combine the escarole and potatoes in an ample soup pot with 3 cups (750 ml) water, a teaspoon of sea salt, and the vegetable broth. Bring the liquid to a boil, then lower the heat and simmer the soup, covered, for about 25 minutes, or until the vegetables are tender.

Stir in the caramelized onion and fennel mixture and add a tablespoon of lemon juice and plenty of black pepper. Taste, and correct the seasoning with more salt and a touch more lemon juice if needed.

Just before serving, bring the soup back to a simmer and stir in the remaining 2 tablespoons of fruity olive oil and the parsley.

Serve the soup hot, and drop a spoonful of burrata or crème fraîche in the middle of each serving.

MENU

ZUCCHINI AND BASIL SOUP
-page 311-

whole-wheat walnut bread
page 392-

· · ·

heirloom tomato salad with fresh mozzarella
-page 471-

· · ·

fresh, ripe peaches

see menu notes on next page

MENU NOTES

One year my basil plants were so happy they grew into huge bushes, with leaves the size of spinach leaves. I started adding more and more basil to everything. Finally I began to use basil as a main ingredient, like spinach with a zingier, peppery flavor. This zucchini and basil soup, the product of overabundance in both areas, became a summer staple.

Because it is not a heavy soup, you can serve this as a first course in a more elaborate meal, but it's also fine as the center of a simple menu. The time of too much basil is also the time of plentiful tomatoes, so an easy salad of sliced red and purple tomatoes, some creamy fresh mozzarella, and a few more fresh basil leaves is the perfect companion. It adds up the best of summer: pungent and sweet, red and green, raw and cooked.

If you aren't having the tomatoes and mozzarella, make your soup heartier: break up some moist feta cheese and garnish each serving with it. It melts slightly into the soup as you eat it—so tasty.

I like Whole-Wheat Walnut Bread (p. 392) with this soup—hearty, crusty, dense with walnuts, it's one of my favorites. Or, have the soup with rich Fresh Corn and Cheddar Cheese Cornbread (p. 407)—another winning combination, and corn is sweet and abundant in the same season. But this is an easygoing soup; a good baguette or a sourdough loaf is also fine.

For dessert, peaches complete a survey of the essential tastes of summer. However, any summer fruit will be welcome, and a cobbler or crisp made with that summer fruit will turn this into a party meal.

zucchini and basil soup

Through years of making zucchini soup every summer, I found I was adding more and more basil. One day, when all the basil plants in the garden had been shooting up and needed to be trimmed, I added an enormous bunch of basil, so much that it became a main ingredient and needed to share top billing with the zucchini.

This is a whole new world of zucchini soup, more peppery and piquant than the usual. It's zucchini soup with the personality of a basil pesto, and it's delicious either hot or chilled.

· · · SERVES 6—8 · · ·

2 lbs. zucchini (900 g)

1 ¼ tsp. sea salt, plus more to taste

3 Tbs. (45 g) Arborio rice (or any white rice)

4–5 Tbs. (60–75 ml) olive oil

2 medium yellow onions, chopped (450 g)

freshly ground black pepper

about 3 cups (750 ml) basic light vegetable broth
   (p. 47) or canned vegetable broth

2 cups packed coarsely chopped fresh basil
   leaves (3 oz.; 90 g)

2–3 Tbs. (30–45 ml) fresh lemon juice

· · ·

garnishes:

creamy goat cheese

fruity green olive oil

optional garnish: grated zest of ½ lemon

Wash, trim, and slice the zucchini and put it in an ample soup pot with 3 ½ cups (850 ml) water, a teaspoon of salt, and the rice. Bring the water to a boil, then lower the heat and let it simmer, covered, for half an hour.

Meanwhile, heat 2 tablespoons olive oil in a pan and add the chopped onions with a pinch of salt. Cook the onions slowly over medium-low heat, stirring often, until they are soft and caramel-colored, about half an hour. When the onions are tender and sweet, add them to the soup pot.

recipe continues on next page

Grind plenty of black pepper into the soup, add the vegetable broth and the fresh basil leaves, and simmer another 2 minutes. Cool slightly. Puree the soup in a blender, in batches, or with an immersion blender. Add a little more broth if the soup seems too thick; it should pour easily from a ladle.

Return the soup to a clean pot and bring it back to a simmer, then stir in 2 tablespoons of lemon juice and at least 2 more tablespoons of fruity green olive oil. Taste the soup, and add pinches of salt and drips of lemon juice until the balance is just right.

To serve, pour the hot soup into a bowl, drop a spoonful of creamy goat cheese on top, then finish it with a little swirl of olive oil and, if you're partial to lemon zest, a few shreds of zest.

zucchini and potato soup

As anyone who has ever grown zucchini knows, you turn your back for ten minutes and when you turn around again you find, under a nearby leaf, a zucchini that is a foot and a half long. I first made this soup from one of those, peeling off the toughest part of the skin.

Since then I've made the soup often, with every size squash. It is my basic zucchini soup, mild-mannered but never bland. It's so simple, and can be varied with the addition of different herbs or cheese. It can even dress itself up for a party: sauté a few freshly picked zucchini blossoms, either whole or chopped, and decorate the pureed version of this soup with them.

· · · SERVES 6—8 · · ·

2¼ lbs. (1 kg) zucchini
2 large yellow onions (500 g)
7 oz. (200 g) Yukon Gold potatoes
2 Tbs. (30 ml) olive oil
1½ tsp. sea salt, plus more to taste
3½ cups (850 ml) basic light vegetable broth
    (p. 47) or canned vegetable broth
½ cup (20 g) chopped fresh basil
¼ cup (10 g) chopped fresh flat-leaf parsley

freshly ground black pepper
2 Tbs. (30 ml) fresh lemon juice, plus more to
    taste

· · ·

optional garnishes:
fruity green olive oil
crumbled feta cheese or *queso fresco*
sautéed zucchini blossoms

Wash and trim the zucchini, halve them lengthwise if they are thick, and slice them or cut them into 1-inch dice. Peel and coarsely chop the onions. Scrub and finely dice the potatoes.

recipe continues on next page

Heat the olive oil in a large sauté pan, add the chopped onions and a pinch of salt, and sauté the onions over medium heat, stirring often, until they are soft and golden brown, 25 to 30 minutes.

Meanwhile, combine 2 cups (500 ml) water, the vegetable broth, the potatoes, and a teaspoon of salt in a large soup pot. Bring the liquid to a boil, reduce the heat, and simmer, covered, for 10 minutes. Add the zucchini and simmer another 10 minutes.

When the onions are ready, add them to the soup pot, along with the chopped basil and parsley. Grind in an ample amount of black pepper and add 2 tablespoons lemon juice. Taste, and add a pinch more salt or a little more lemon juice if needed.

Drizzle 1 teaspoon or so of fruity green olive oil over each bowl of soup just as you serve it, and then garnish to your taste. I like it best with crumbled feta cheese or a spoonful of *queso fresco*. If you're feeling ambitious, sauté those extra squash blossoms.

Another way . . .

The soup can be pureed, either in a blender, in batches, or with an immersion blender (never in a food processor). Be careful not to overprocess, as potatoes tend to become gummy when overworked. Whisk in 1 to 2 tablespoons fruity olive oil just before serving the soup.

I find that the taste of the potatoes becomes more forward in the pureed version of this soup and calls out for more black pepper, so pass the grinder at the table.

charred zucchini soup with yogurt and pine nuts

This soup makes me think of a summer evening on a Greek island. The mint and lemon, the sweet and smoky zucchini and the yogurt—they're all flavors I remember from a wonderful stay on Naxos years ago. It's a simple soup, but very evocative. Have a bowl of salty olives on the table and some sesame bread with olive oil for dipping.

· · · SERVES 6 · · ·

3 lbs. (1.4 kg) slender green zucchini

2 Tbs. (30 ml) olive oil

1 ½ tsp. sea salt, plus more to taste

2 medium red onions (400 g)

about 7 cups (1.7 liters) basic light vegetable broth (p. 47) or 6 cups canned vegetable broth diluted with 1 cup water

3 Tbs. (45 g) Arborio rice

½ cup (15 g) loosely packed fresh mint leaves, chopped

2–3 Tbs. (30–45 ml) fresh lemon juice

freshly ground black pepper

1½ cups (360 ml) drained Greek-style yogurt, preferably goat yogurt (technique follows)

· · ·

garnishes:

fruity green olive oil

½ cup (40 g) lightly toasted pine nuts (technique on p. 232)

Preheat the oven to 375°.

Wash and trim the zucchini and cut it into spears, then toss it with a tablespoon of olive oil and a teaspoon of salt. Spread the zucchini spears on a large baking sheet and roast them in the hot oven for 45 minutes to an hour, turning them once or twice during that time. You want the zucchini to be soft, shrunken, and blackened in spots. The charred flavor of the zucchini makes the flavor of the soup, so don't hesitate to leave it a little longer; it should really look done.

recipe continues on next page

Another option is to grill the zucchini on a charcoal grill. I'm not sure I'd start the coals just for a few pounds of zucchini, but if you are grilling other things, by all means take advantage of the opportunity. Cooking time will depend on the heat of the coals. Spread the zucchini spears evenly over the grill, watch them, and turn them often, until they are soft and tender and well blackened in places.

Either way, when the zucchini is ready it will be reduced to 3 or 4 cups, and its flavor will be concentrated and infused with a smoky depth.

While the zucchini is in the oven or on the grill, peel the onions, cut them in half crosswise, and then cut them into ½-inch wedges. Put the onions in a skillet with a tablespoon of olive oil and a sprinkle of salt and cook slowly over medium heat, stirring often, until the onions are soft and dark brown in places, about half an hour. Now I'll repeat my rule on caramelizing or browning onions: when you think they're done, give them at least another 10 minutes, and maybe more than that. You'll see how the flavor deepens and improves.

In an ample soup pot, combine the vegetable broth and the rice and simmer, covered, for about 20 minutes. Give the charred zucchini a few chops, just enough to have bite-sized pieces, and add it to the broth, along with the browned onion and the chopped mint. Continue simmering for another 5 minutes.

Add a tablespoon of lemon juice, taste, and add more, a teaspoon at a time, until the soup has a faintly tart edge. Grind in some black pepper, and correct the salt if needed. Over low heat, bring the soup back to a simmer.

To serve, put a rounded tablespoon of drained yogurt in the center of each bowl and pour a big ladle of soup over it. Drizzle a thread of fruity olive oil over each serving and scatter toasted pine nuts on top.

If you have leftover soup and heat it up the next day, you may have to add a bit more broth or water, as that tiny bit of rice seems to expand infinitely.

Drained Yogurt

Any plain yogurt that is not thickened with emulsifiers can be drained and thickened naturally in about an hour. It is the same process that is used to make yogurt cheese, but done for a shorter time.

Line a large sieve with a triple layer of cheesecloth, place it over a bowl, and put several cups of yogurt in it. That's all. In about an hour, the bowl will have a cup or so of liquid in it, and the yogurt will be thicker and creamier-tasting. In two hours it will be even more so. If you leave it overnight, you'll have yogurt cheese, which you can spread on bread or crackers like a soft cream cheese.

For this soup you can use the Greek-style yogurt that is now pretty widely available in stores, or you can put about 3 cups of plain goat yogurt into a cheesecloth-lined sieve and allow it to drain until it is reduced by half.

MENU

SUMMER TOMATO AND BASIL SOUP
- page 320 -

olive and rosemary focaccia
- page 400 -

or ciabatta

. . .

mixed garden salad with marinated cannellini

. . .

butter cake with summer fruits
and ice cream
- page 488 -

I fall in love with tomatoes all over again every July, a summer romance that has proved to be a lasting relationship. I've had happy moments standing out in the vegetable garden among the vines, eating a ripe tomato out of hand, still warm from the sun, red juice running down my arm. Aaaah . . .

This soup is concentrated essence of summer tomato with a bit of basil and garlic, a sheen of olive oil. It's a soup to make when the tomato harvest is rolling in and the days are hot, so this is a meal for the porch or the patio, in the cooling evening.

Nothing is better than dipping a piece of fresh focaccia or a crusty chunk of ciabatta into this sweet and tangy red soup. You could stop right there, sitting back with your glass of Chianti, but I like to add a salad, rustic and simple. I start with mixed greens, fresh herbs, perhaps slivers of red bell pepper or avocado, or whatever the garden or the produce stand offers, and add a spoonful of marinated cannellini beans on top for a creamy counterpoint.

Butter cake with summer fruits and ice cream is a favorite dessert of mine for this languid season. You could use a bakery pound cake for the same idea, but this sweet little butter cake mixes up in minutes and bakes in less than an hour. A dusting of powdered sugar makes it elegant. Served slightly warm, with juice-laden peach slices or blackberries around it and a scoop of icy vanilla, it's worth the small extra effort.

A few other ways . . .

The combination of Summer Tomato and Basil Soup with a generous square of Sara's Spinach Pie (p. 452) is a more substantial meal, and a meal to remember.

And of course cornbread! Forget everything I said before. Dense, savory Fresh Corn and Cheddar Cheese Cornbread (p. 407) is such a good match for this soup.

You'll have to have this soup all summer long and try it with these various pairings.

summer tomato and basil soup

This is the simplest of tomato soups—really just an easy tomato sauce with some broth and a little orzo added. But simple does not mean ordinary. This is the pure taste of summer, the sweetness and perfume, the juiciness and tang of real tomatoes, and it should be made only when great, truly vine-ripened tomatoes are in plentiful supply.

You can use your favorite variety of tomatoes or mix them up, which is very rewarding with all the heirloom varieties available now. I like Purple Cherokees for their superb flavor, and the big, golden Striped Germans for their sweet juiciness. However, Early Girls, Premiums, or any of the more widely shipped tomatoes are also fine as long as they are vine-ripened. Taste your tomatoes; if they are good, your soup will be good.

· · · SERVES 6—8 · · ·

3½ lbs. (1.5 kg) vine-ripe tomatoes

2 Tbs. (30 ml) olive oil

½ onion, finely chopped (115 g)

4 cloves garlic, finely chopped

1½ tsp. sea salt, plus more to taste

½ cup (20 g) coarsely chopped or torn fresh
 basil leaves

about 4 cups (1 liter) basic light vegetable broth
 (p. 47) or canned vegetable broth

½ cup (100 g) orzo

freshly ground black pepper

· · ·

garnish: fruity green olive oil

optional garnish: freshly grated Parmigiano-Reggiano

Cut crosses in the tomatoes with a sharp knife and scald them in a pot of boiling water for about 45 seconds, then drain, rinse with cold water, and peel them. Cut them into pieces, or process them briefly in a blender so that they are somewhere between chopped and pureed. Either way, be sure to save all the juice.

Heat 2 tablespoons olive oil in a large, nonstick sauté pan and stir the chopped onion in it over medium heat for 5 to 7 minutes, until it is translucent and soft. Add the garlic and sauté another 2 to 3 minutes.

Add the chopped or pureed tomatoes with their juice, a teaspoon of salt, and the basil. Simmer for about half an hour, until the tomatoes are somewhat reduced and the color is deep.

In a soup pot, combine the cooked tomatoes with the broth and bring the broth to a boil. Add the orzo, lower the heat, and simmer the soup for about 10 minutes, stirring occasionally to be sure the pasta does not clump up or stick to the bottom of the pot. Taste, correct the seasoning with a little more salt if needed, and grind in some black pepper.

Pour a teaspoon of fresh green olive oil on top of each serving of this soup, and sprinkle on some freshly grated Parmigiano-Reggiano if you like.

A word about leftovers . . .

If you have soup left over and reheat it the next day, you will find it thicker. Orzo, like all pasta and rice, expands when it is in a liquid—and just keeps expanding. You will be shocked to see how that little half-cup of orzo tries to take over the whole pot of soup. Just add a little more vegetable broth.

Other ways . . .

The purist version of this soup is made with garlic, a bit of onion, and basil. However, you can add parsley to the basil, or a little fresh marjoram.

For a fancier, less rustic soup, skip the orzo and puree the finished soup in a blender, then stir in some cream and a dash of cognac.

tomato and fennel soup with blood orange

The fennel and blood orange in this soup support the flavor of the tomatoes in both sweetness and acidity, and add their own special taste without taking over. When everything is blended, the result is a tomato flavor with such depth and complexity that everyone will be wondering, what marvelous variety of tomato is that?

· · · SERVES 6 · · ·

2½ lbs. (1.1 kg) ripe tomatoes
1½ Tbs. (22 ml) olive oil
1 medium yellow onion, chopped (200 g)
1 large fennel bulb, chopped (200 g)
1 tsp. sea salt, plus more to taste
freshly ground black pepper
cayenne
1½ cups (360 ml) basic light vegetable broth
　　(p. 47) or canned vegetable broth

¾ cup (170 ml) fresh blood orange juice

· · ·

garnishes:

1 cup (240 ml) drained yogurt or crème fraîche
2 Tbs. sugar
grated zest of 1 blood orange
sprigs of fennel greens

Cut crosses in the tomatoes with a sharp knife and scald them in boiling water for 1 minute, then drain, rinse with cold water, and slip off their skins. Cut the tomatoes into large pieces, saving all the juice. You should have about 5 ½ cups of cut-up tomatoes.

Heat the olive oil in a nonstick skillet. Add the chopped onion and fennel, sprinkled with a big pinch of salt and some pepper. Cook the vegetables over medium heat, stirring often, until they are soft and golden but not brown, about 20 minutes.

Combine the cooked onion and fennel in a soup pot with the tomatoes and their juice, a pinch of cayenne, the vegetable broth, and the blood orange juice. Cover the pot and simmer the soup for about half an hour, or until the fennel is entirely soft and the tomatoes have released their juice and turned dark.

Allow the soup to cool slightly and puree it until it is completely smooth, either in a blender, in batches, or with an immersion blender. Return the soup to the heat, bring it back to a simmer, and taste. Adjust the seasoning with additional salt and pepper if needed, and add a touch more broth if it seems too thick.

Whisk the drained yogurt or crème fraîche with the sugar. Serve the hot soup in shallow bowls and sprinkle a tiny pinch of grated zest over each serving, then drop a big spoonful of the yogurt in the center of the bowl and garnish with sprigs of fennel greens.

cannellini and golden tomato soup

I love all the great heirloom tomatoes that I'm finding now, varieties that were not seen for years or decades. They're in plentiful supply at my farmers' market all summer, and it's exciting to discover their different characters and flavors.

For this soup I usually use Striped Germans, large golden tomatoes that show bright pink streaks when you cut them open. They are extravagantly beautiful, mild, sweet, and juicy. They make a lovely soup with white beans and dark parsley leaves floating in the golden liquid. One time I used Pineapple tomatoes, and you may discover still other golden varieties in your market. Of course, you can use red tomatoes if the golden ones are not available.

Serve this soup with Parmesan crostini made from thin slices of whole-grain bread or with fresh-baked focaccia. Drink a crisp, well-chilled Italian white wine and experience summer heaven.

· · · SERVES 6—7 · · ·

1 cup dried cannellini or other white beans (7 oz.; 200 g)

8–10 cloves garlic, peeled (35 g)

6–8 large fresh sage leaves or 1 Tbs. dried sage, slightly crumbled

2 tsp. sea salt, plus more to taste

2¼ lbs. (1 kg) golden tomatoes

2 Tbs. (30 ml) olive oil

2–3 cloves garlic, chopped

1½ large red onions (500 g)

½ cup (30 g) fresh whole flat-leaf parsley leaves

1–3 Tbs. (15–45 ml) fresh lemon juice

1–2 cups (250–500 ml) basic light vegetable broth (p. 47) or canned vegetable broth, if needed

· · ·

garnish: fruity green olive oil

Put the washed beans in a large soup pot with 7 cups (1 ¾ liters) water, which should be enough to cover them by 2 inches. Add the whole peeled garlic cloves and the sage and bring the water to a boil. Lower the heat, cover the pot, and simmer the beans genty for as long as it takes for them to be buttery-tender. This might be an hour for newly dried cannellini, or double that for older or larger beans. The beans will make a delicate, savory broth that will form the basis of the soup. When the beans are tender, stir a generous teaspoon of salt into the liquid.

Meanwhile, cut crosses in the tomato skins with a sharp knife and scald them in boiling water for 1 minute, then drain, rinse in cold water, and slip off their skins. Cut them into 1-inch pieces; you should have about 4 cups of tomato pieces in their juice. Heat a tablespoon of olive oil and sauté the chopped garlic in it for a minute or two, until it begins to look translucent, then add the tomatoes and half a teaspoon of salt. Simmer the tomatoes about 15 minutes and set aside; they should be very juicy. (If you are using a less juicy variety of tomato, you may have to add more liquid to the soup.)

Peel the onions, cut them in half lengthwise, and then slice them thinly. Heat the remaining 1 tablespoon olive oil in a large nonstick pan and sauté the sliced onions with a sprinkle of salt over medium-low heat until the onions are completely soft and golden brown in spots, 25 to 30 minutes.

When the beans are fully tender, stir in the tomatoes and caramelized onions, as well as the whole parsley leaves. Taste, and correct the salt if needed, then add just a little bit of lemon juice and taste again. Tomatoes vary quite a lot in acidity so go carefully here, adding a teaspoon of juice at a time until you find the acid balance you like.

If the soup seems too thick, add a little vegetable broth. I find that the combination of the broth made by the beans and the juicy golden tomatoes is usually enough and the soup needs no additional broth, but other varieties of tomatoes may be less juicy.

Serve the soup with a last-minute drizzle of fruity olive oil on top, and pass some Parmesan crostini or warm focaccia on the side.

tomato and zucchini soup with summer herbs

For years I made tomato soups and I made zucchini soups—and I don't know why it took me so long to put them together. Now this soup is one of my farm-stand favorites, its sweet summer flavor set off with a clean sparkle of fresh lemon juice and bright herbs at their just-picked best.

· · · SERVES 6—8 · · ·

2 Tbs. (30 ml) olive oil, plus more to taste

2 medium yellow onions, chopped (400 g)

3–4 cloves garlic, finely chopped

1½ tsp. sea salt, plus more to taste

1½ lbs. (700 g) slender zucchini, diced

1½ lbs. (700 g) ripe red tomatoes

4–5 green onions, sliced (90 g)

1 small fennel bulb, finely diced (150 g)

3–4 cups (750 ml–1 liter) basic light vegetable broth (p. 47) or canned vegetable broth

freshly ground black pepper

¾ cup (30 g) loosely packed chopped fresh basil leaves

⅓ cup (15 g) loosely packed chopped fresh mint leaves

3–4 Tbs. (45–60 ml) fresh lemon juice, plus more to taste

· · ·

garnishes:

crumbled feta cheese or *queso fresco*

fruity green olive oil

Heat the olive oil in a large nonstick skillet and sauté the chopped onions and garlic with a teaspoon of salt over medium heat until the onions are golden, about 15 minutes. Add the diced zucchini and keep sautéing until the zucchini is tender and beginning to color in spots, about 20 minutes more.

Meanwhile, peel the tomatoes: cut crosses in their skin with a sharp knife and scald them in boiling water for 1 minute, then drain, rinse with cold water, and slip off their skins. Dice the tomatoes or chop them coarsely, saving all the juice.

In a large soup pot, combine the tomatoes, green onions, diced fennel, 2 cups (500 ml) water, and 3 cups vegetable broth. Add half a teaspoon of salt and a few grinds of black pepper and simmer, covered, for half an hour, or until the vegetables are tender. Add the sautéed onion and zucchini mixture and the chopped fresh herbs and simmer the soup for another 10 minutes or so.

Stir in 3 tablespoons fresh-squeezed lemon juice and taste. Correct the salt if needed, and add more vegetable broth if the soup seems too thick. It should pour easily from a ladle.

Top each serving of this soup with a heaping tablespoon of crumbled feta cheese or *queso fresco* and a drizzle of green olive oil. Lemon wedges can be passed at the table, for those who want another squeeze.

pappa al pomodoro

For this simple, rustic Tuscan dish, you have to have the ripest, most flavorful tomatoes, a good, chewy country loaf, and fruity olive oil. The simplicity of it makes the purity and intensity of the flavors all-important.

· · · SERVES 6 · · ·

3 Tbs. (45 ml) fruity green olive oil

5 cloves garlic, minced

1 yellow onion, finely chopped (225 g)

1½ tsp. sea salt, plus more to taste

3 lbs. (1.3 kg) ripe tomatoes; a juicy variety is best

1 Tbs. finely chopped fresh sage leaves or 1 tsp. crumbled dried sage

½ tsp. finely chopped fresh rosemary

6 oz. (175 g) country bread, a day or two old

freshly ground black pepper

· · ·

garnishes:

fruity green olive oil

freshly grated Parmigiano-Reggiano cheese

Heat a tablespoon of the olive oil in a large nonstick sauté pan and sauté the chopped garlic and onion with a pinch of salt, stirring often over a medium flame until they are soft and golden, about 20 minutes.

Cut crosses in the skins of the tomatoes and scald them in boiling water for 1 minute, then drain, rinse in cold water, and peel them. Chop them finely or give them a quick spin in the food processor or blender; they should not be completely pureed but rather maintain some rough texture. Be sure to save and use all the juice.

Add the herbs and tomatoes to the sautéed onion and garlic, along with a scant teaspoon of salt, and simmer for 10 to 15 minutes only; stop when the tomatoes are a dark red color but before their juice has cooked away.

Meanwhile, cut the bread into small cubes and pulse the cubes in a food processor to make rough, soft crumbs; you should have about 3 cups. Stir the bread into the tomato mixture and pour enough water over it to cover, but no more—about 2 ½ cups to start, a little more if you need it. If your sauté pan is not large enough to hold the soup comfortably, transfer it to a soup pot at this point. Add some salt and freshly ground black pepper. Simmer and stir for another 20 minutes or so, until the texture is somewhere between a soup and a porridge, thick but not stiff.

Before serving, remove the soup from the heat and stir in the remaining 2 tablespoons olive oil. Pass a carafe of the same oil at the table for drizzling over the soup, as well as some freshly grated Parmigiano-Reggiano cheese.

CHAPTER 12

hearty soups of summer

Corn and Cheese Chowder

Tortilla Soup

Mung Bean Soup with Spinach and Tomatoes • V

Corn and Pepper Soup • V

Kale and Tomato Soup • V

Deconstructed Hummus Soup • V

Vegetable Soup Pistou • V

Roasted Eggplant and Garbanzo Bean Soup • V

Summer Minestrone

abundance

Deep summer. Fifty pounds of tomatoes in a bushel basket, corn so sweet that it begs to be eaten raw. Pumpkins begin to swell on the vines, and zucchini has us surrounded.

Perhaps you have a garden. Once, before there were several great farmers' markets nearby, I grew vegetables every summer. I grew tomatoes and basil, sweet peas, runner beans, corn, lettuces, squash, peppers, and eggplants. It was wonderful to go out toward the end of the day, when the sun was low and the air beginning to cool, and to get good and dirty. Standing with a hose, watering freshly turned earth in the early evening, is a sweet pleasure of the season. And what vegetables I had.

Now I get most of my vegetables at the farmers' market, where the abundance of late summer can be overwhelming. I can't stop myself when I see the gorgeous produce spilling from baskets and stalls at the market. And then bags of extra squash or green beans turn up on the doorstep, gifts from gardening neighbors.

Embrace abundance. Make one of the big soups of summer, the ones that gather the whole garden into the pot, like Summer Minestrone (p. 358) or a traditional Vegetable Soup Pistou (p. 352), redolent of garlic, oil, basil, and fennel. Or cut up four kinds of peppers and cook them with sweet corn for a taste you will remember nostalgically in the winter. These soups have the exuberance of summer flavor, with satisfying heft and nourishment.

Corn and Cheese Chowder (p. 336) is an old friend, a beloved favorite of decades, now somewhat trimmed down in butterfat content. Tortilla Soup (p. 338) is an extravaganza of tastes and textures: crisp tortilla strips, creamy avocado, hot chile, all combined in the broth at the last moment, in generous serving bowls. This is a party soup, whether you meant to have a party or not. Mung Bean Soup with Spinach and Tomatoes (p. 341) has a delicately spicy Indian flavor.

If you want to toss all your vegetables into the salad bowl instead of the soup pot, have Deconstructed Hummus Soup (p. 350) with that salad. I often wonder what gave birth to the idea for this soup. Maybe it was impatience—someone didn't want to wait for the garbanzo beans to cool so they could be made into hummus. No matter—it's genius: garbanzos swimming in their savory broth, with raw garlic, olive oil, lemon juice, and herbs added in generous doses to each bowl. The result is stunning, so simple and delicious.

Any of these soups will make a fine summer meal with a good loaf of bread and a glass of wine. They can be expanded with appetizers or salads, and they finish beautifully with platters of summer fruits, the luxury that drops from trees. And many of them can bridge the seasons, taking us into the harvest season of early fall.

MENU

simple basil pesto
-page 436-

plain crostini
-page 415-

· · ·

heirloom tomato salad
-page 471-

· · ·

CORN AND CHEESE CHOWDER
-page 336-

sourdough bread

· · ·

apricots, peaches, plums

MENU NOTES

What is a chowder, anyway? My quick answer would be, a thick soup that involves potatoes and cream. But there are chowders that are tomato-based, and what about vichyssoise? Lots of potatoes and cream, and yet not a chowder.

Whatever it is, this is a great one that I have cooked, eaten, shared with others, and loved for many years. The mild and rich-tasting ingredients are brought to life by a piquant touch of cumin, paprika, and the sharp cheddar cheese.

Enjoy this soup when corn is bountiful and sweet, which is when tomatoes and basil are peaking as well. An heirloom tomato salad, with its juicy sweetness and acidity, is an ideal complement to the creamy chowder. And although the tomato salad has a few basil leaves scattered through it, a whole lot of a good thing is not too much, so have a basil pesto on crostini as a starter. It's one of the spectacular flavors of summer.

Any stone fruit makes a harmonious whole of this meal, and if you happen to have peaches, then you have managed to contain in one meal my four essential flavors of high summer: tomatoes, basil, corn, peaches.

corn and cheese chowder

In my very first cookbook, *The Vegetarian Epicure,* I had a recipe for a corn and cheese chowder. I looked it up recently and saw that it called for . . . 1 ¼ cups of heavy cream! Whoa! Then I laughed and thought, Those were the days. I was a young university student and thin as a rail.

But corn and cheese chowder was one of my favorites, so I made it again and let it evolve with my current style of cooking: less cream, more corn, no flour, plenty of fresh herbs. It's a delicious corn chowder for modern times. (If you're still in school, go ahead, pour in another cup of cream—I don't mind.)

· · · SERVES 5—6 · · ·

1 lb. Yukon Gold potatoes (450 g)

1 bay leaf

5–6 fresh sage leaves, finely chopped, or
   2 tsp. dried, crumbled sage

1½–2 tsp. sea salt, plus more if needed

1 large yellow onion (350 g)

1 Tbs. (15 ml) olive oil

1 Tbs. unsalted butter

1 cup (240 ml) whole milk

1 cup (240 ml) basic light vegetable broth
   (p. 47) or canned vegetable broth

⅓ cup (80 ml) heavy cream or half-and-half

4 cups (600 g) corn kernels, scraped from
   6–7 ears corn

2–3 green onions, white and green parts, sliced
   (50 g)

1 tsp. cumin seeds

½ cup (30 g) chopped fresh flat-leaf parsley

hot paprika

freshly ground black pepper

4–5 Tbs. (75 ml) dry white wine (optional)

4 oz. (120 g) sharp cheddar cheese

Scrub the potatoes, cut them into ½-inch dice, and put them in a large soup pot with 3 cups (750 ml) water, the bay leaf, the sage, and a teaspoon of sea salt. Bring the water to a boil, lower the heat, and simmer for 5 to 6 minutes.

Meanwhile, chop the onion coarsely and sauté it in the oil and butter with a pinch of salt over medium heat, stirring often, until it is translucent and browning in spots, about 15 minutes. Add the onion to the soup, along with the milk, broth, cream, corn, and sliced green onions. Bring the soup back to a simmer and let it bubble for another 6 or 7 minutes.

Toast the cumin seeds for a few moments in a dry skillet, and then grind them coarsely in a mortar or a spice grinder. Add the cumin, parsley, a pinch of hot paprika, and some black pepper to the soup. Taste the soup, and add more salt if needed. Stir in the white wine if you wish.

Keeping the soup at just below the simmer point, slowly stir in the grated cheese, allowing it to melt smoothly into the soup. From this point onward, you cannot let the soup simmer or boil, as that would curdle the cheese. If you need to reheat it, do it carefully, watching and stirring.

I like to serve the soup with thin rye or pumpernickel toasts, or with homemade Oatmeal Molasses Bread (p. 394).

tortilla soup

This soup is like a fiesta, such an exuberant mix of savory and spicy, hot and cool, soft and crunchy. It starts with a chile-infused broth and some vegetables, and then it is put together in the bowl. Fresh slices of avocado, squeezes of lime, barely melting panella cheese, and crisp tortilla strips are all added at the moment of serving.

Panella is a white Mexican cheese that softens with heat but does not melt into strings. If panella cheese is not easily available, try halloumi, which is another cheese that holds its shape when heated. If you want an option for vegans, pass the panella at the table for those who want it, instead of putting it in the bowls.

· · · SERVES 8 · · ·

10 cups (2.5 liters) basic dark vegetable broth
   (p. 50) or basic root vegetable broth (p. 49)
1 dried guajillo chile
1 dried chile negro
8–9 corn tortillas (250 g)
2 cups (500 ml) vegetable oil for frying, or
   2–3 Tbs. olive oil for brushing
1 tsp sea salt, plus more to taste
1 large red onion (250 g)
1 Tbs. (15 ml) olive oil
1 lb. (450 g) ripe tomatoes
½ lb. (225 g) summer squash

½ cup (30 g) chopped cilantro leaves
1–2 Tbs. (15–30 ml) lime juice
8–9 oz. (250 g) panella cheese
2 large ripe avocados (400 g)

· · ·

garnish: fruity green olive oil
at the table:
fresh limes
any good chile salsa or Ancho and Guajillo
   Chile Puree (p. 440)
tortilla strips

First make the broth. You will need a lot of it, and this is not a soup where canned broth can be successfully substituted—it's too important. If you are making the broth especially for this soup, add the guajillo and negro chiles to it. Pull out the stems, tear the pods open, shake out the seeds, and put the chiles in with the rest of the vegetables. If you have broth already made, add the torn chiles to it and simmer the broth, covered, for 20 minutes, then strain out the chiles and discard them.

While the broth is simmering, make the *tostaditos,* the crisp little tortilla strips that give this soup its name. The traditional method is to deep-fry them. Cut the tortillas in half, then crosswise into ½-inch strips. Heat the vegetable oil in a large sauté pan, and when the oil is hot enough to make a drop of water jump and sizzle, drop in a handful of the strips. Move them around a little so that they don't stick to each other, and after about 1 ½ minutes they should be crisp and golden brown. Scoop them out with a slotted spoon and drain them on paper towels as you drop in the next handful, and so on until you're finished. It takes only a few minutes.

Alternately, you can brush the tortillas on both sides with a little olive oil, then cut them into strips, spread them on a cookie sheet in one layer, salt them lightly, and bake them in a 400° oven for about 10 minutes or until they are crisp and golden brown. I prefer this method, but don't let me stop the traditionalists. The important thing is not to eat them all before you serve the soup.

Cut the red onion in half and slice it thinly. Sauté the onion over medium heat in the olive oil with a sprinkle of salt until it is soft and light brown, at least 20 to 25 minutes. Meanwhile, peel and roughly dice the tomatoes and thinly slice the summer squash.

Heat the strained broth in a soup pot, add the cooked onion, the tomatoes, and the squash, and let the soup simmer, covered, for about 15 minutes, or until all the vegetables are tender. Taste, and correct the seasoning with more salt if it's needed. Stir in the cilantro and add 1 to 2 tablespoons fresh lime juice.

recipe continues on next page

Shortly before serving the soup, cut the panella cheese into ½-inch dice. Peel the avocados and slice them or cut them into cubes.

Put a heaping spoonful of panella into the bottom of each deep bowl and ladle steaming hot soup over it, then place a few pieces of avocado and a swirl of olive oil in each one and top with a small handful of crisp tortilla strips.

At the table, pass lime halves, salsa, and additional tortilla strips.

mung bean soup with spinach and tomatoes

A mixture of ginger, garlic, and cumin, stir-fried briefly in oil, gives this soup its intriguing, spicy flavor. Serve it with chapatis or with flour tortillas, the Mexican cousin of the chapati. A Middle Eastern flatbread is another good choice, and a bit of your favorite chutney on the chapatis or the flatbread would go beautifully with this.

Mung beans are much favored in Indian cooking. These small green or yellow beans cook easily, have a delicate flavor, and are very high in protein—no wonder they're popular. They are commonly available in health-food stores as well as in any store that sells Indian spices and products.

· · · SERVES 6—8 · · ·

¾ cup (175 g) dried mung beans
1½ tsp. sea salt, plus more to taste
12 oz. (350 g) fresh spinach leaves
1½ lbs. (700 g) ripe red tomatoes
1 small green or red bell pepper (150 g)
about 2 cups (500 ml) basic light vegetable broth (p. 47), vegetable and ginger broth (p. 52), or canned vegetable broth
1½ Tbs. (10 g) cumin seeds
2 Tbs. (30 ml) sesame or canola oil (do not use toasted sesame oil)
2 Tbs. minced fresh ginger

3 cloves garlic, minced
red pepper flakes
2 Tbs. (30 ml) fresh lemon juice, plus more to taste
½ cup (15 g) chopped fresh mint
½ cup (30 g) chopped fresh cilantro

· · ·

garnish:
chopped fresh mint
chopped fresh cilantro
optional garnish: Greek-style yogurt or yogurt cheese

recipe continues on next page

In an ample soup pot, combine the rinsed mung beans with 6 cups (1 ½ liters) water and bring to a boil. Boil hard for about 5 minutes, skimming off any foam that forms at the top. Reduce the heat to a simmer and cook until the beans are tender, probably about an hour or a bit more. Skim off the foam again toward the end of the cooking time.

Mung beans are funny—they explode as they cook, and partly disintegrate. The result is a broth that is somewhat thickened but still has an interesting texture, although I can never find an actual whole bean in it. Add 1 ½ teaspoons salt at the end of the cooking time, when the beans are tender.

Meanwhile, wash the spinach well in several changes of water. If the leaves are small, leave them whole. If they are large, cut them into 1-inch strips, and don't worry about stems unless they are quite thick. Peel and dice the tomatoes; you should have about 3 cups. Trim and dice the bell pepper. Add the spinach, tomatoes, bell pepper, and vegetable broth to the beans and simmer the soup for at least another 20 minutes.

Toast the cumin seeds in a dry pan over medium heat for a couple of minutes, just until they release their fragrance, then grind them in a mortar or a spice grinder. In a small nonstick skillet, heat the oil, add the minced ginger and garlic, and stir-fry for 3 or 4 minutes, until both are beginning to color. Remove from the heat and stir in the toasted cumin, then add the mixture to the soup.

Sprinkle in a few red pepper flakes and stir in the lemon juice, as well as 2 tablespoons each of chopped mint and cilantro. Taste the soup, and correct the seasoning with more salt or lemon juice if needed.

When you serve the soup, pass the remaining chopped mint and cilantro at the table to sprinkle on top of each serving. A heaping spoonful of thick drained yogurt is wonderful in this soup, as is a spoonful of yogurt cheese.

corn and pepper soup

Sweet corn and a variety of savory peppers make the flavor base of this delicious summer soup, and a few potatoes give it body that is very satisfying. When you are slicing the corn kernels off the cobs, be sure to taste them, and use only sweet, good-flavored corn, none that has gone starchy.

··· SERVES 8—10 ···

3 medium fresh poblano chiles (12 oz.; 350 g)

1 large red bell pepper (200 g)

1 large green bell pepper (200 g)

1 lb. (450 g) Yukon Gold or red-skinned potatoes

2 celery stalks (70 g)

2 yellow onions, chopped (400 g)

2 Tbs. (30 ml) olive oil

1½ tsp. sea salt, plus more to taste

about 5 cups (1.2 liters) basic light vegetable broth (p. 47) or canned vegetable broth

4 cups (675 g) corn kernels scraped from 5 ears of corn

½ cup (25 g) chopped cilantro

1 fresh green jalapeño pepper, minced

juice of 1 lemon, plus more to taste

• • •

garnish: fruity green olive oil

optional garnishes:

chopped cilantro

chopped or sliced fresh jalapeño

Roast the poblano chiles on all sides in a hot oven or under a broiler, or grill them over charcoal, until they are blistered all over. Put them in a paper bag for a few minutes to sweat, then slip off the charred skins. Seed the peppers and cut them into 1-inch pieces.

Trim and seed the bell peppers and cut them into ½-inch dice. Scrub and trim the unpeeled potatoes and cut them into ½-inch dice. If you are using tiny potatoes, the ones that are the size of a walnut, cut them in halves or quarters. Trim and dice the celery; you should have ½ cup.

recipe continues on next page

Sauté the chopped onions in the olive oil with a bit of sea salt, stirring often on medium heat until they soften and begin to take on a nice golden color, about 20 minutes.

Meanwhile, combine the potatoes and the diced celery in a large soup pot with 3 cups (750 ml) water and a teaspoon of salt. Bring the water to a boil, then lower the heat and simmer, covered, for about 10 minutes, or until the potatoes are tender.

Add the vegetable broth, the cooked onions, the bell peppers, and the poblanos and simmer for about 5 minutes. Add the corn kernels, cilantro, and jalapeño and simmer for 5 minutes longer. If the soup seems too thick—more like a stew—add a little more vegetable broth. Season with the juice of 1 lemon, or more if the lemon is very sweet. Adjust the salt to taste.

Serve this hearty soup in large bowls and drizzle additional fruity olive oil on top of each serving. If you wish, add chopped cilantro to taste, and pass a small bowl of chopped or sliced jalapeños for those who want a spicier soup.

kale and tomato soup

Here's a truly season-crossing tomato soup. Flavors from summer and winter meet beautifully in early fall, when tomatoes are still at their best, but this soup also was a treat during a late, cool spring in California, when I used greenhouse tomatoes and it's fine in midsummer. Potatoes and kale give it substance, and tomatoes add sweetness and a bit of acidity for a bold, hearty soup.

These flavors beg for cheese toasts made with Parmigiano-Reggiano, and the soup can be varied by adding cooked cannellini or garnishing with a spoonful of pesto.

· · · SERVES 6—8 · · ·

8 oz. (225 g) Russian kale, or any kale

12 oz. (350 g) Yukon Gold potatoes

1 ½ lbs. (700 g) red tomatoes

1 stalk celery (50 g)

8 oz. (225 g) leeks

1 ½ tsp. sea salt, plus more to taste

2 Tbs. (30 ml) olive oil

1 red onion, chopped (250 g)

5 cloves garlic, finely chopped

¼ cup (15 g) chopped fresh basil leaves

¼ cup (15 g) chopped fresh flat-leaf parsley

½ tsp. red pepper flakes, plus more to taste

3 cups (750 ml) basic light vegetable broth (p. 47) or canned vegetable broth

· · ·

garnish: fruity green olive oil or Simple Basil Pesto (p. 436)

Wash the kale and trim away the hard stems. Cut the leaves into 1-inch strips, and if the strips are long, cut them in half. Scrub the potatoes, trim away any blemishes, and cut them into ½-inch dice. Peel the tomatoes and chop them coarsely, and thinly slice the celery. Trim the leeks, cut them in half lengthwise, wash them thoroughly, and then slice them, using only the white and palest green parts. You should have about 1 ½ cups.

recipe continues on next page

In a large soup pot, combine the kale, potatoes, tomatoes, celery, about 3 ½ cups (850 ml) water, and a teaspoon of sea salt. This will look like too much kale, but it will soon shrink remarkably. Bring the water to a boil, lower the heat, and simmer, covered, for about half an hour, or until the vegetables are tender.

Meanwhile, heat a tablespoon of oil in a sauté pan and cook the chopped red onion in it over medium heat until it softens, about 5 minutes. Add half the chopped garlic and ½ teaspoon salt and continue cooking, stirring often, until the onion is beginning to color, about 20 minutes. Add the leeks to the pan and keep cooking until the leeks are soft, then add the mixture to the soup, along with the basil and parsley.

In a small sauté pan, heat the remaining 1 tablespoon olive oil. Add the remaining chopped garlic and stir for a minute or two, just to let it lose its raw edge. Add the red pepper flakes and stir over medium heat for another minute or so, but no longer than it takes for the garlic to turn golden. Immediately pour this mixture into the soup, deglazing the pan by pouring a ladle of the broth into it, swirling it around, then adding it back to the soup. This last bit of freshly sautéed garlic and red pepper thrown on the gentler flavors of the soup charges it with a delicious intensity.

Add the vegetable broth, correct the seasoning with a bit more salt and red pepper to taste, and gently simmer the soup for another few minutes to marry the flavors.

Drizzle a little fruity olive oil over each bowl, or add a spoonful of green pesto. And don't forget the cheese toasts.

Another way . . .

For an even more substantial soup, add about 2 cups cooked cannellini or other white beans when you add the vegetable broth, and pass a bowl of grated Parmigiano-Reggiano at the table.

MENU

cucumber, rice, and fresh herb salad
-page 468-

black oil-cured olives

sliced tomatoes

• • •

DECONSTRUCTED HUMMUS SOUP
-page 350-

crusty focaccia or pita breads

• • •

fresh melon slices

see menu notes on next page

I visited Jerusalem on a research trip once. We had very little time and a lot of work to do, but my colleagues said, You must see the old city, if only for a few hours. So I was taken into the heart of the ancient quarter, and there, in one of the narrow lanes of the bazaar, with Arabic and Hebrew mixing in my ears, smells of spices and coffee in the air, we stopped in a restaurant so tiny that the five of us nearly filled it.

I couldn't read the Arabic menu, but no matter. It was all hummus, served six different ways, passed through a small window from the postage-stamp kitchen—the freshest, most amazing, rich and irresistible hummus, served with high stacks of fluffy pita bread and, if you were fancy, a salad of quickly cut-up cucumbers and tomatoes.

I finally understood hummus. It's a meal! It can take center stage.

Which brings me to this fantastic soup, in which all the ingredients of hummus are presented as a hot soup, the raw and the cooked combining in a wildly delicious way. Freshly cooked garbanzo beans swim in their own savory broth, spiked at the last moment with liberal amounts of chopped raw garlic, olive oil, lemon juice, and handfuls of chopped parsley. Bring on the pita bread, the focaccia, or a big, chewy boule. Divine.

Raw cucumbers and ripe tomatoes are wonderful with hummus, and they are perfect as well with this steaming soup.

In this menu, the tomatoes are sliced, perfectly plain, with a bowl of salty, oil-cured olives alongside. The cucumber and rice salad is another whiff of the Middle East: cilantro and mint and lightly toasted cumin seeds add sparkle and depth to a mixture of cucumbers, sweet onions, walnuts, and rice, bound together with tangy yogurt. It is the ideal cooling companion for the soup, and a salad that can be made well in advance.

Cooling refreshment comes back for dessert, with sweet slices of juicy, summer-ripe melon.

Another way . . .

I am a huge fan of the cucumber and rice salad, but if you don't have time to make it, serve a platter of sliced raw vegetables—those ripe tomatoes, some cucumber slices, and red or green bell peppers, with chopped fresh herbs, sea salt, and olive oil for dipping. Or open a jar of marinated semi-sun-dried tomatoes and arrange them on a plate, and put a few dolmades from the deli on another.

deconstructed hummus soup

Afriend sent me this recipe, with the following note: *Here is a soup recipe that is wildly easy and remarkably good.* I have found it exactly so.

Have all the elements ready: garbanzo beans in their broth, chopped garlic, parsley, and lemon juice. Put it all together in big soup bowls and serve with a chilled rosé or white wine and large chunks of rustic bread.

· · · SERVES 6—8 · · ·

1 lb. (450 g) dried garbanzo beans
1 dried guajillo chile
2 tsp. sea salt, plus more to taste
3–4 cups (750 ml–1 liter) basic light vegetable
    broth (p. 47) or canned vegetable broth
1 head garlic, peeled and finely chopped
1 cup (60 g) coarsely chopped fresh flat-leaf
    parsley

1 cup (240 ml) fresh lemon juice
¾ cup (180 ml) olive oil, plus more to taste
freshly ground black pepper

· · ·

at the table:
fruity green olive oil
lemon wedges

Soak the dried garbanzos overnight in a large pot of spring water (tap water can be used if you have a water softener). In the morning, drain them, discard the water, and rinse the beans. (You can skip this step and simply allow a longer cooking time, but this is one time when I like to presoak the beans—they're the whole show, and I want them to cook as evenly as possible.) Tear the stem out of the guajillo chile and scrape out and discard all the seeds.

Put the beans back in the pot with 12 cups (3 liters) water and the chile pod and simmer the beans until they are tender, probably about 1 hour. Skim off any foam that forms on top, and add 2 teaspoons salt when the beans are done. After a few minutes, taste the bean broth and add more salt if needed. Discard the chile and add a few cups of vegetable broth; you want the beans to be swimming in a generous amount of broth.

Put a rounded teaspoon of chopped garlic in each soup bowl. Seems like too much? It's not. When the hot broth hits the garlic, the garlic softens considerably, and this is not the time to worry about breath.

Ladle on a big scoop of beans and at least a cup of the steaming broth. Then toss in a rounded tablespoon or more of chopped parsley, 1 or 2 tablespoons fresh lemon juice, and the same amount of fruity green olive oil. Don't skimp! Grind on some black pepper. Serve.

You may want to drizzle on even more olive oil or add another squeeze of lemon juice, so have the olive oil bottle and the lemon wedges on the table. Serve a crusty, chewy bread and perhaps some olives. In hot weather, an icy rosé; in cold weather, a Rhone wine. Heaven.

vegetable soup pistou

Pistou is a one of the soups that has traditionally been a meal in a bowl. I remember going to a dinner party long ago, when I was a student and just learning to cook, and finding that the menu consisted of appetizers followed by a big bowl of pistou served with a rustic, chewy bread. It was a great menu then and it's a great menu now.

There are many versions of this soup, all having in common the *pistou* itself, the French cousin of pesto, a sauce of basil, pine nuts, olive oil, and garlic that infuses each bowl of soup with a fresh, pungent fragrance.

Pistou is best in summer or fall, but it's almost a seasonless soup. Zucchini, tomatoes, and basil are the essential summer ingredients; at another time of year you might substitute tomatoes from a can or skip them (they're a supporting player), use winter squash, and open up one of those jars of pesto you put up in August.

Although this is a traditional French Mediterranean dish, I've added a few nontraditonal leaves of epazote to the beans as they cook, to make them more digestible. You will find epazote in any market that stocks Latin American products.

· · · THIS IS A BIG POT OF SOUP—IT SERVES 8—10 · · ·

1 cup (200 g) dried cannellini beans

4–5 epazote leaves, fresh or dried

12 medium fresh sage leaves

8 cloves garlic, peeled

2 tsp. sea salt, plus more to taste

1½ medium yellow onions (350 g)

3 oz. (90 g) leek, white part

3 Tbs. (45 ml) olive oil

1 small fennel bulb (150 g)

8 oz. (225 g) zucchini

4 oz. (120 g) green beans

3 oz. (90 g) kale or spinach

12 oz. (350 g) tomatoes or (in winter only) canned tomatoes with their juice

4 oz. (120 g) carrots

2 stalks celery (120 g)

1 very small dried hot pepper or 1 tsp. minced fresh jalapeño

3 Tbs. fresh flat-leaf parsley chopped

2 bay leaves

a few rosemary leaves

a sprig of thyme

fennel seeds

1–2 cups (250–500 ml) basic light vegetable broth (p. 47) or canned vegetable broth, if needed

for the pistou

2 cloves garlic

¼ cup (45 g) toasted pine nuts (technique on p. 232)

⅓ cup (80 ml) olive oil

1 cup (45 g) packed fresh whole basil leaves

½ tsp. sea salt

Rinse the beans and put them in a large soup pot with 8 cups (2 liters) water, the epazote and sage leaves, and all but one of the peeled garlic cloves. Bring the water to a boil, then lower the heat to a simmer and leave the beans to cook gently, covered, until they are tender. This may be only an hour or it may take as long as 2 hours; start checking after the first 50 minutes. Add water if it's needed to keep the beans covered. When the beans are soft, add a teaspoon of salt and simmer another 5 minutes.

recipe continues on next page

Chop the onions, thinly slice the leek, and mince the remaining clove of garlic. Heat the olive oil in a nonstick pan and sauté the onions, leek, and minced garlic with a sprinkle of salt, stirring often over medium heat until the vegetables are soft and coloring, 20 to 25 minutes. Set them aside.

Prepare all the vegetables:

Trim, quarter, and thinly slice the fennel. Cut the zucchini in half lengthwise, then cut into ½-inch slices. Trim the green beans and cut them in pieces. Trim the tough stems off the kale and cut the greens into 2-inch pieces. Peel and dice the tomatoes. Peel and thinly slice the carrots. Trim and slice the celery stalks. Trim and finely chop the hot pepper.

In a large soup pot, combine the fennel, green beans, kale, and carrots with 4 cups (1 liter) water. Add a teaspoon of sea salt and bring the water to a boil. Lower the heat and simmer the vegetables gently for 10 minutes. Add the zucchini, tomatoes, celery, hot pepper, all the fresh herbs, and a pinch of fennel seeds and simmer another 10 minutes. Add the sautéed onions and leek.

When the cannellini are tender, add them to the vegetables along with all their broth. Taste the soup, and add a pinch more salt if needed. This soup makes its own broth and there should be plenty of it, but if it seems too thick, add a little vegetable broth.

MAKE THE *PISTOU*

Combine the garlic and pine nuts in a food processor and pulse briefly. Add a little olive oil, process again, then add all the basil, the salt, and a little more oil, continuing to process until it is all well blended.

Serve the soup in large bowls and float a teaspoonful of *pistou* on the top of each serving.

roasted eggplant and garbanzo bean soup

The deep yet lively flavor of this soup comes from the combination of slow-simmered beans with oven-roasted vegetables, finished with a bright touch of hot pepper, some mint, and lemon juice. It's a delicious soup for late summer or for fall, when the weather suddenly turns cool but there is still a plentiful harvest of eggplants and peppers on hand.

Serve this hearty soup in big bowls, and make it the center of the meal.

A word about hot peppers: this soup is meant to be subtly spicy, not searing. Hot peppers can be so different, even within the same variety, so it's helpful to taste a hot pepper before adding the whole thing. You can always add more.

· · · SERVES 6—8 AS AN ENTRÉE · · ·

1 cup (200 g) dried garbanzo beans

2 tsp. sea salt, plus more to taste

1 large globe eggplant (1¼ lbs.; 500 g)

2 red or green bell peppers (400 g)

3 Tbs. (45 ml) olive oil

2 medium yellow onions, chopped (400 g)

4 ripe red tomatoes, peeled and chopped (500 g)

1 small hot pepper, finely chopped, or a big pinch of red pepper flakes

4 cloves garlic, peeled and minced

about 2 cups (500 ml) basic light vegetable broth (p. 47) or canned vegetable broth

2 Tbs. chopped fresh mint leaves

a few chopped fresh oregano leaves or a pinch of dried oregano

2 Tbs. (30 ml) fresh lemon juice, plus more to taste

· · ·

garnish:

fruity green olive oil

garlic or Parmesan crostini or large croutons

recipe continues on next page

Soak the garbanzo beans in about 8 cups (2 liters) water for 5 to 6 hours or overnight. (I generally do not presoak beans, but garbanzos can be tough little customers and this helps them cook evenly.) Drain and rinse the beans and put them in a large soup pot with 6 cups water, which should be enough to cover them by a couple of inches. Bring the water to a boil for 5 minutes and skim off any foam that rises to the top. Turn down the heat and simmer the beans, loosely covered, for about an hour, or however long it takes for them to be completely tender. As always with beans, cooking time will be determined by the age of the beans. Add a teaspoon of salt and simmer another 10 minutes as the salt absorbs.

If you decide to cook the garbanzo beans without soaking them first, use 8 cups of water instead of 6 and be prepared for a longer cooking time, perhaps up to 2 hours.

While the beans are cooking, preheat the oven to 400°.

Pierce the eggplant in a few places with a fork, place it on a baking pan, and roast it until it is soft, probably 50 to 60 minutes. At the same time, roast the peppers on a separate baking sheet, turning them as their skins char, 15 to 20 minutes. When the peppers are soft and well blistered, put them in a paper bag for a few minutes to sweat, then slip off their skins, remove the stems and seeds, and cut them into ½-inch pieces.

The eggplant is ready when it gives easily when poked with a wooden spoon and is somewhat collapsed and wrinkled. Remove it from the oven and allow it to cool slightly, then slice it open and scoop out the soft flesh. If the seeds are dark, scrape them out and discard them. Chop the eggplant flesh coarsely.

While the vegetables are roasting, heat 1 ½ tablespoons olive oil in a medium skillet and sauté the chopped onions with a pinch of salt over medium-low heat, until they are soft and golden brown, 25 to 30 minutes.

Add the eggplant, peppers, caramelized onions, chopped tomatoes (you should have about 2 cups), and hot pepper to the garbanzo beans and their broth. Add the remaining 1 ½ tablespoons olive oil to the onion pan and sauté the minced garlic in it for 2 to 3 minutes, just until it barely begins to color. Add the garlic to the soup pot as well, along with the vegetable broth. The broth from the beans and the juice from the tomatoes should provide most of the liquid that the soup needs, but if it looks too thick—more like a stew—add a little more vegetable broth.

Simmer the soup, covered, for another 15 minutes, until all the vegetables are tender. Stir in the mint, oregano, and lemon juice, taste, and add salt and more lemon juice if needed.

Put one garlic or Parmesan crostino or a few croutons in the center of each bowl, then ladle the soup on top and drizzle with a bit of olive oil.

summer minestrone

Bursting with green beans, tomatoes, zucchini, and sweet red peppers, this is a minestrone for late summer, when markets are overflowing with voluptuous ripe produce. The garbanzo beans make a lovely broth on their own and give body to a soup that is entirely satisfying yet not heavy.

To make this soup a meal, serve it with Fresh Corn and Cheddar Cheese Cornbread (p. 407), another perfect thing to make in late summer.

··· THIS IS A BIG SOUP, ENOUGH FOR 10—12 SERVINGS ···

1 cup (200 g) dried garbanzo beans
2–3 tsp. sea salt, plus more to taste
1 large yellow onion (300 g)
2 Tbs. (30 ml) olive oil
1 Tbs. chopped garlic
½ cup (75 g) diced carrots
½ cup (50 g) thinly sliced celery
1 cup (150 g) diced red bell pepper
2½ cups (160 g) green beans cut in 1-inch pieces
3 cups (900 g) peeled and diced tomatoes

5 cups (700 g) diced or sliced green and yellow zucchini
5–6 cups (1¼ liters) basic light vegetable broth (p. 47) or canned vegetable broth
a piece of Parmigiano-Reggiano cheese rind, about 2-inches square
1 cup (30 g) whole fresh flat-leaf parsley leaves
½ cup (15 g) fresh basil leaves torn or cut in strips
red pepper flakes

···

garnish: fruity green olive oil

I've found that garbanzo beans cook a little more evenly (and quickly, of course) if they are presoaked. This step is not necessary, but if you like, you can soak the beans in about 6 cups (1 ½ liters) water for a few hours or overnight, then drain and proceed. Cooking time for the beans will now be about an hour.

Rinse the garbanzo beans and combine them in a large soup pot with 12 cups (3 liters) water. Bring the water to a boil, lower the heat, and simmer the beans gently until they are completely tender; this may take up to 2 hours, depending on the age of the beans. When the beans are tender, add 1 ½ teaspoons salt and simmer another 15 minutes.

Coarsely chop the onion and sauté it in the olive oil with a sprinkle of salt over medium heat until it is just translucent. Add the garlic and stir over medium heat for another 2 or 3 minutes.

Add the sautéed onion and garlic to the beans and their broth, along with the carrots, celery, red bell pepper, green beans, tomatoes, zucchini, 5 cups vegetable broth, and the cheese rinds and simmer, covered, for 20 minutes. Add the parsley, basil, and a pinch of red pepper flakes. If the soup seems too thick, add a bit more vegetable broth. Cover and simmer another 10 to 15 minutes, then taste, and correct the seasoning with a pinch more salt if needed.

Drizzle a little fruity olive oil on top of each steaming bowl.

Another way . . .

If you don't want to take the time to cook garbanzo beans, you can drain and rinse a can of garbanzos and use them instead. I prefer to cook the dried beans because they taste so much better and make a beautiful broth to start the soup. But it's not a tragedy if you use canned beans here; just start the soup with 4 cups water and 6 cups vegetable broth, and add a little more broth at the end if the soup seems too thick.

Make it vegan . . .

If you are vegan, only a rind of Parmigiano stands between you and this soup. Toss it, my friend, and pour on the olive oil.

cold soups

Gazpacho Andaluz • **V**

Cold Cucumber-Cilantro Soup

Cold Cucumber and Avocado Soup • **V**

Cold Asparagus Soup

Cold Cucumber and Mint Soup with Radishes

Cold Cream of Poblano Peppers with Red Grapes

Cold Cherry-Lemon Soup

Chilled Melon Soup with Mint

Cold Peach and Nectarine Soup with Strawberry Sauce

refreshment

Cold soups are one of the rewards of a hot summer.

It was on a sultry day in August that I came up with my favorite cucumber soup. I had a bowl full of Persian cucumbers from my farmer neighbor, Peter, and some excellent goat yogurt in the fridge. From there to the blender was a quick step. I added handfuls of cilantro and mint, and a little toasted cumin seed to evoke the Indian raitas I love. A splash of lemon juice and some salt, a few pulses in the blender, and that was it. The ease of it was astounding.

Dipping my spoon into that icy cold cucumber soup, creamy and light, flecked with dark green, was the culinary equivalent of jumping in the pool.

Many cold soups are just that easy—they're first cousins to the blender smoothie. Others, like Cold Asparagus Soup (p. 371) and the amazing Cold Cream of Poblano Peppers with Red Grapes (p. 375), take some cooking, but they can be simmered in the cool hours of the morning, then put away to chill. At lunch or dinnertime, you have a ready, reviving treat.

Cold soups can be made from a remarkable variety of ingredients. They can be appetizers or desserts. Fruit soups are seductively lovely, perfumed with summer ripeness and showing off their colors. A bowl of chilled peach and nectarine soup with a swirl of cream in it, or a deep magenta cherry soup, can elevate the simplest meal to elegance. And the savory soups, pungent with garlic, oil, vinegar, and spices, are salad in a bowl but better—they're colder!

Gazpacho (p. 366), the mother of all cold soups, the elixir from Andalucia, is a summer staple. Mine is the familiar combination of tomatoes, peppers, cucumbers, and onions, all run through a blender and enhanced with virgin olive oil, wine vinegar, garlic, and a bit of bread. But the Spanish make gazpacho from everything. I've seen recipes for a white gazpacho made with almonds and pine nuts, another made with fava beans, and a green one made with fresh cilantro and parsley. Elizabeth David put black olives into hers, and garnished it with chopped hard-cooked eggs.

I learned about the marvelous fruit soups of eastern Europe while traveling in Hungary many years ago. In a garden restaurant, we sat under a canopy of trees and ate a cold cherry soup. It was a moment of epiphany. I still think there is no greater soup than the Cold Cherry-Lemon Soup (p. 377) that I make each July, adapted from the Hungarian original I ate in Budapest. It takes some work, but it's worth every minute.

If I only have ten minutes, though, I make an exquisite blender soup. My favorite of these is the one I make with peaches and nectarines. The ripe fruit is peeled, sliced, then blended to a silky smoothness with yogurt, honey, lemon juice, a hint of nutty Marsala, and cinnamon. It is chilled well—even put in the freezer for a bit—and served with fresh strawberry sauce swirled into each bowl: beautiful and mouthwatering.

Spicy, salty, fruity, sweet—pour a bowl of any one of these fine cold soups and awake from the torpor of summer.

MENU

a bowl of cured black olives

• • •

GAZPACHO ANDALUZ
-page 366-

• • •

tortilla española with charred red peppers
-page 454-

crusty baguette with olive oil for dipping

• • •

summer fruits with angel cookies
-page 494-

Gazpacho paired with tortilla española is one of those perfect meals for me, a combination I ate at least a hundred times in Spain. The Spanish have carried on a love affair with both these dishes since time immemorial, and when you eat them together in this simple menu, you will know why.

All summer long, gazpacho is the liquid salad that can be ready in your refrigerator, ice-cold, tangy, slightly spicy, and wholly delectable. A classic Spanish tortilla is a thick, flat, round omelet made from eggs, potatoes, onions, and great olive oil, cooked to a golden brown on both sides. It is savory and rich-tasting, good at any temperature but best a few hours after it is made. There are countless variations on this great rustic dish, and the simple one I include here has roasted sweet red peppers added to the potatoes and onions.

Because this is such quintessentially Spanish food, we must have olives, and more olive oil for dipping a chunk of bread. But nothing else is needed.

Nothing except dessert, that is. In Spain you might have flan, or a piece of *turron*, the famous almond and honey nougat. At home I recall that flavor with angel cookies, a version of easy almond macaroons.

Have a picnic . . .

This quick, delicious summer meal is ideal for a picnic. Put the gazpacho in a container in the cooler; bury it in the ice with the cold drinks. The tortilla travels on its plate, as it is best eaten at room temperature, or it can go in the cooler if you're in hot, humid weather. Tortilla española is such a good traveler that for many years it was my default potluck dish.

gazpacho andaluz

There are as many variations of gazpacho as there are restaurants in Andalucia. Actually more, because every home cook also has a version of this classic cold soup of Spain. Mine is a pretty simple one: a few summer vegetables, some good extra-virgin olive oil, some tasty sherry vinegar. It's a salad put into a blender, then chilled to refreshing iciness.

I use more tomatoes than some do, but I never use canned tomatoes. I also pull back from the lavish amounts of oil called for in traditional Spanish recipes. I like to put a carafe of my best fruity olive oil on the table and let everyone add more to their own taste.

As with all simple recipes, the quality of the ingredients makes or breaks the dish. If you swoon with delight at the sweetness of your tomatoes, then you will do the same with the soup. If your tomatoes leave you indifferent—well, they won't get better by being chopped, so wait for the worthy ones to come into the market. But if you start with good vegetables and great olive oil, this could become your favorite soup of the summer.

· · · SERVES 6 · · ·

2½ lbs. (1.1 kg) vine-ripe tomatoes

12 oz. (350 g) bell peppers

1 lb. (450 g) cucumbers

¼–½ cup (40–75 g) diced sweet onion

2 oz. (60 g) French bread with crusts removed

2–3 tsp. chopped garlic

½ cup (120 ml) fruity green olive oil, plus more to taste

5 Tbs. (75 ml) sherry vinegar or red wine vinegar, plus more to taste

3–3½ tsp. sea salt

freshly ground black pepper

1 tsp. sugar, if needed

1 cup (250 ml) spring water, if needed

· · ·

garnishes:

1½ cups (200 g) finely diced bell peppers (all colors)

1 cup (125 g) finely diced cucumber

1 cup (175 g) red and yellow cherry tomatoes, halved

fruity green olive oil

Cut crosses in the skins of the tomatoes with a sharp knife, scald them in boiling water for a minute or less, drain them, and plunge them in cold water. Peel and core them and chop them coarsely. You should have 4 ½ cups, and be sure to save all the juice. Core, seed, and chop the bell peppers (2 cups). Peel and seed the cucumbers, taste the ends to check for any bitterness, then slice or dice them (3 cups).

Taste the onion. There is a tremendous variation in onions, and even the same variety can taste radically different depending on the season. If you have a sweet onion, such as a Vidalia or Maui, you may want to use ½ cup. If tasting it raw makes you gasp for water, only use a tiny amount, perhaps 2 tablespoons.

Cut the bread into cubes and soak it in water until it is softened, 5 to 10 minutes, then squeeze out the excess.

Mix all the vegetables with the bread, garlic, olive oil, sherry vinegar, 3 teaspoons sea salt, and some pepper in a large bowl. Puree the mixture in a blender, in batches, or with a strong immersion blender, until it has the texture you like. Gazpacho can be rough and chunky or perfectly smooth. I like to puree it until it is fairly homogenous, then garnish with chopped vegetables for an interesting contrast. If the soup seems too thick, add a small amount of water, about ¼ cup at a time, until you like the consistency.

When the soup is blended, taste it, and adjust the seasoning by adding salt, vinegar, and perhaps a pinch of sugar. Keep stirring, tasting, and adding a sprinkle of salt and a drop of sherry vinegar until the flavors are full, piquant, and well balanced. This is a vivacious soup!

Chill the soup thoroughly in the refrigerator for at least 4 hours. I like to finish by putting it in the freezer for half an hour or so just before serving.

Serve in chilled bowls, and pass the various garnishes as well as extra olive oil.

cold cucumber-cilantro soup

WITH GOAT YOGURT

Cilantro, mint, and toasted cumin seeds join together to perfume this refreshing summer soup, and a subversive bit of jalapeño adds a streak of heat under the cooling yogurt, just as in my favorite Indian raitas.

Thin-skinned Persian cucumbers can be used for this, but I prefer the type that needs peeling. If you can't find a good goat yogurt, use plain cow's-milk yogurt instead.

· · · SERVES 6 · · ·

1½ lbs. (700 g) cucumbers

¾ tsp. sea salt, plus more to taste

3 cups (750 ml) whole goat yogurt

½ cup (30 g) packed cilantro leaves

½ cup (20 g) packed fresh mint leaves

2 tsp. cumin seeds, toasted and ground

1 tsp. minced fresh jalapeño

2 Tbs. (30 ml) fresh lemon juice, plus more to taste

½ cup (120 ml) water

· · ·

optional garnish: chopped unsalted pistachio nuts

Peel the cucumbers, quarter them lengthwise, cut out the seeds, and slice or dice them. You should have about 4 cups. Toss the cucumbers with the salt and leave them in a bowl for 15 minutes or so. Do not drain.

Add the yogurt to the cucumbers and their liquid, stir in the cilantro, mint, and cumin, and pulse everything in a blender a few times, in batches, or use an immersion blender. I prefer a chunkier texture for this soup, sort of half blended, but you can make it as smooth as you like. Add the minced jalapeño.

Season the soup with the lemon juice and a bit more salt if you like, and then stir in enough water to make a souplike consistency; the soup should not be watery but should pour easily from a ladle. Chill the soup for several hours, and serve in chilled bowls.

Sprinkle a few chopped pistachios on top of each serving if you like.

cold cucumber and avocado soup

This lovely and refreshing cold soup earns raves in the hot days of late summer. Serve it in small bowls, each cool green pool scattered with drops of olive oil, bright red cubes of tomato, and a few crisp croutons.

Long, soft-skinned cucumbers, called English, Armenian, or Persian cucumbers, are best for this soup because they can be used with skin and seeds. If they are very large, check for mature seeds and remove them, but a slender cucumber of this type generally has tiny, soft seeds that puree perfectly.

Watercress adds a little bite to the mild cucumber and avocado. Arugula can be used instead, or a bunch of cilantro, but choose one—don't mix the flavors.

This recipe is based on proportions for one large avocado and can easily be doubled.

· · · SERVES 5 · · ·

2 lbs. (900 g) soft-skinned cucumbers
6 oz. (170 g) watercress
¾ cup (180 ml) fresh lemon juice
2 cloves garlic, peeled
1 small jalapeño pepper (use more if it's
   very mild)
1 large Haas avocado (7 oz.; 200 g)

1–2 tsp. sea salt

· · ·

garnishes:
fruity green olive oil
1 ripe red tomato, finely diced
homemade croutons (p. 446)

Trim the ends off the cucumbers, taste each end, and trim off any bitter part. Cut the cucumbers into cubes. Wash the watercress, remove any heavy stems, and chop it roughly. You should have about 2 cups.

recipe continues on next page

Combine half the cucumbers and most of the lemon juice in the container of a blender and puree. The cucumbers will soon be a liquid, and you can then easily add the remaining cucumbers, the watercress, garlic, and jalapeño. Puree until everything is smooth, working in batches if you need to. (I find that my immersion blender does not work well with this raw soup.)

Cut the avocado in half, remove the pit, peel the avocado, and cut the flesh into cubes; you should have not quite 1 cup of diced avocado. Add the avocado to the cucumber puree, along with a teaspoon of sea salt, and process again. The mixture will become thicker and creamier. Stir everything together in a bowl and taste. Add more lemon juice and more salt, a bit at a time and stirring thoroughly each time, until the balance feels right to you. I like to feel the citrus edge against the creaminess of the avocado, and while I don't want a distinctly salty taste, the various flavors become clear only when the right amount of salt is added. Use your taste buds—it's fun.

Chill the soup well. Serve it in small bowls, and drizzle each serving with a little fresh fruity olive oil, then scatter a few tomato cubes and croutons on top.

cold asparagus soup

The first time I made this luxurious soup, I couldn't believe how easy it was. After you simmer the asparagus in the vegetable broth, there's not much more to it. Once I had steamed asparagus left over from a dinner party, so I tossed it in the blender with the broth and a bit of goat cheese, then stirred in the lemon juice and dill. The result was worthy of a party of its own.

· · · SERVES 5—6 · · ·

1½ lbs. (700 g) fresh untrimmed asparagus or
   3 cups (500 g) cooked asparagus pieces
3 cups (750 ml) basic light vegetable broth
   (p. 47) or pea pod broth (p. 55)
3 Tbs. (45 ml) heavy cream
¼ cup (15 g) chopped fresh dill
3 Tbs. (45 ml) fresh lemon juice, plus more
   to taste
⅛ tsp. cayenne, plus more to taste

2 oz. (60 g) creamy white goat cheese
1 Tbs. (15 ml) olive oil
sea salt to taste
freshly ground white pepper to taste

· · ·

garnishes:
fresh sprigs of dill
crème fraîche, sour cream, or yogurt cheese

Break off and discard the tough bottoms of the asparagus stalks, then thinly peel the lower parts of the remaining stalks. You want as few of the strings as possible. Cut the asparagus in pieces and simmer it in the vegetable broth until it is tender, about 10 minutes. Allow the mixture to cool.

Alternately, if you already have cooked asparagus, cut it up and measure 3 cups or 500 grams.

recipe continues on next page

Combine all the ingredients and puree them in a blender, working in batches. (An immersion blender may not work well for the fibrous asparagus, unless it is an industrial-strength model.) Press the asparagus puree through a medium sieve and discard the dry, fibrous pulp. Taste the soup, and correct the seasoning with additional salt, pepper, lemon juice, and cayenne.

Chill the soup in the refrigerator for several hours. Serve very cold, garnished with dill sprigs and crème fraîche.

cold cucumber and mint soup with radishes

This is the soup for the dog days, when it's too hot to cook and almost too hot to eat. The pale green color with darker green flecks of mint, the soothing creaminess of fresh yogurt, and the icy temperature—it's the cure for summer doldrums.

Lovely thin slices of breakfast radishes float on top to provide a pleasant crunch. These are slender, long radishes that are not too hot, but any mild radishes that look fresh and good in your market can be used.

Serve this soup very, very cold. I like to put it in the freezer for the last half-hour before serving—and I leave myself a note so I don't forget about it there.

· · · SERVES 6 · · ·

1 ½ lbs. (600 g) Persian cucumbers
1 ½ tsp. sea salt
4–5 Tbs. (60–75 ml) fresh lemon juice
⅔ cup (30 g) packed fresh mint leaves
3 cups (700 ml) nonfat yogurt
1–2 tsp. sugar

1–3 Tbs. (15–45 ml) heavy cream, to taste

· · ·

garnishes:
1 small bunch French breakfast radishes or any
   mild radishes (120 g)
fresh mint sprigs

Wash the cucumbers but do not peel them; Persian cucumbers are the type with soft skin and small, soft seeds, so you can use the whole thing. Trim off the ends, tasting both ends to make sure there is no bitterness, and cut the cucumbers into ½-inch dice. You should have about 4 cups.

Combine the cucumbers, salt, 4 tablespoons lemon juice, the mint leaves, yogurt, and 1 teaspoon of sugar in a bowl. Working in batches, puree this mixture in a blender until it is smooth, or use a strong immersion blender. Stir in 1 tablespoon cream and taste the soup, then refine the

recipe continues on next page

sweet-tart balance by adding a little more lemon juice if it seems bland or a touch more sugar if it's too tart. Add more cream to your taste. Sometimes I like a very light version of this soup, almost nonfat, but other times a creamier version appeals.

Chill the soup well, at least an hour in the refrigerator. Just before serving, wash, trim, and thinly slice the radishes. Ladle the cold soup into bowls and scatter some thin radish slices over each serving. Garnish with the mint sprigs.

cold cream of poblano peppers
with red grapes

This chilled soup made with roasted poblano peppers is spicy and cooling at the same time, and the sautéed red grapes are crazy good with the fresh green chiles. Cold and hot and sweet all at once, it's a real party in your mouth.

This is not a main-course soup—it's too creamy for that—but a brilliant starter for a dinner party.

Poblano peppers are large dark-green pods and are available fresh from early summer through fall. If you order chiles rellenos in a Mexican restaurant, they are very likely made with these chiles. Poblanos are quite mild as chiles go but like all chiles, they vary.

· · · SERVES 6 AS A FIRST COURSE · · ·

1 lb. 2 oz. (500 g) fresh green poblano peppers

2 Tbs. (30 g) unsalted butter

1 large yellow onion, sliced (300 g)

½ tsp. sea salt, plus more to taste

1½ cups (360 ml) drained or Greek-style low-fat yogurt

1½ cups (360 ml) basic light vegetable broth (p. 47) or canned vegetable broth

1 cup (240 ml) whole milk

1½ cups (225 g) red seedless grapes

· · ·

optional garnish: ⅓ cup (80 ml) heavy cream

Char the poblano peppers, turning them occasionally under a broiler until the skins blister and blacken all over, probably about 15 minutes, but this depends on your broiler. Put the chiles in a paper bag for a few minutes to sweat, then slip off their skins, remove the stems, and scoop out the seeds.

Melt 1 ½ tablespoons butter in a nonstick pan and gently cook the sliced onion, with a big pinch of salt over medium-low heat until it is soft and golden, at least 20 minutes.

recipe continues on next page

Whisk together the yogurt, broth, and milk in a deep bowl, stir in the roasted chiles and sautéed onion, and puree it all in a blender, in batches, until it is smooth, or use an immersion blender. Taste, and correct the seasoning with a bit more salt if needed. Chill the puree well.

Melt the remaining ½ tablespoon butter in a nonstick pan and sauté the grapes gently over medium-low heat, stirring often, for about 8 to 10 minutes. The grapes should be softened and slightly caramelized, amber in color and glazed with their own juices. Cover the pan and set the grapes aside until you are ready to serve the soup.

Serve the soup very cold, and just before serving scatter some of the grapes across the top of each bowl. Add a drizzle of heavy cream if you want an even more luxurious soup.

cold cherry-lemon soup

This is the queen of summer fruit soups. Sweet dark-red cherries are electrified by the intensity of fresh lemon, and the flavors sing out.

I used to thicken this soup with egg yolks, but lately I've made this lighter version. It is an elegant first course for a summer dinner party, and can also be a dessert soup if you make it just a touch sweeter.

· · · SERVES 6 · · ·

2 lbs. (900 g) sweet dark-red cherries, such as Bing

3–4 large lemons with good thick rinds

⅔ cup (140 g) sugar, plus more to taste

sea salt

1¼ cups (300 ml) spring water or filtered water

1 cup (240 ml) fruity white wine, such as Johannesberg Riesling or pinot grigio

1 Tbs. cornstarch

1 cup (240 ml) crème fraîche, sour cream, or yogurt cheese

2–3 Tbs. superfine sugar or powdered sugar

Wash the cherries, stem them, and pit them. Select about 12 of the best-looking cherries and set them aside.

Wash and dry 3 lemons and finely grate their yellow zest until you have 3 teaspoons of zest. Do this delicately, so that you do not get any of the white pith, as it only adds bitterness. Juice the lemons and strain the juice; you should have a little over 1 cup. Use the fourth lemon if you need more zest or juice.

In a stainless steel or enameled soup pot, combine all but the reserved cherries, the lemon zest, 1 cup of the lemon juice, ⅔ cup sugar, a tiny pinch of salt, the water, and the wine. Stir over medium heat as the sugar dissolves and the liquid comes to a boil. Lower the heat and simmer gently, covered, for about 15 minutes.

recipe continues on next page

Dissolve the cornstarch in ¼ cup (60 ml) water and stir it into the simmering soup. Raise the heat enough to get a boil, and stir constantly for about 4 minutes, or until you see the cloudiness of the cornstarch fade and the glossy liquid thicken slightly.

Remove the soup from the heat and allow it to cool. Puree the soup in a blender, in batches, or use an immersion blender. When the soup looks completely smooth, press the puree through a medium-fine sieve. Taste, and correct the sweet-tart balance with a bit more lemon juice or a tiny bit more sugar. The soup should be noticeably tart, with strong, luscious cherry flavor and a hint of sweetness.

Sweeten the crème fraîche, sour cream, or yogurt cheese with 2 tablespoons superfine or powdered sugar, mixing until the sugar is completely dissolved. Add more sugar if needed. Cut the reserved cherries in half.

Serve the soup ice-cold in shallow bowls, with a spoonful of sweetened cream in the center of each one and a few cherry halves decoratively placed as a garnish.

chilled melon soup with mint

This light and elegant soup is an ideal start for a summer dinner party. It can be made with honeydew, Persian, Sharlyn, Saticoy, or any of the juicy, dense-fleshed varieties of melon. The seductive flavor of an excellent field-ripened melon is what this is all about, so be sure your melon is sweet and intensely flavorful.

Use a dry wine, but one that has a distinct fruitiness, such as a pinot grigio, a drier riesling, or a flowery sauvignon blanc.

· · · SERVES 8 · · ·

1 cup (200 g) sugar, plus more to taste

3 cups (750 ml) spring water or filtered water

1 large, ripe melon (6 lbs.; 2½ kg)

2 cups (500 ml) dry white wine, such as riesling, pinot grigio, or sauvignon blanc

½ cup (120 ml) strained fresh lemon juice

sea salt

4–6 Tbs. finely chopped fresh mint

1 cup (240 ml) heavy cream

Combine 1 cup sugar in a saucepan with 3 cups (750 ml) spring water and bring it to a simmer, washing down any crystals from the sides of the pan with a brush. When the sugar is completely dissolved, simmer the syrup for another five minutes, then allow it to cool completely.

Seed the melon, cut it into wedges, and slice away the rind. Cut the soft, ripe flesh in pieces and puree the melon in a blender. You should have about 5 cups of puree.

Stir the wine into the melon puree. Add the sugar syrup gradually, starting with half a cup and tasting as you go, then adding even smaller amounts as the sweetness becomes pronounced. You might use 1 ½ cups of syrup, maybe a bit more, but you won't know until you do the final balancing act of sugar syrup to lemon juice.

recipe continues on next page

When the sweetness begins to assert itself, add 2 tablespoons of the strained lemon juice and a pinch of sea salt. Taste again. Now add a tablespoon of lemon juice or a tablespoon of sugar syrup, tasting each time, until you achieve just the right tart-sweet balance without overwhelming the melon flavor. Stir in 2 tablespoons of chopped fresh mint.

Remember, every melon is different, every lemon is different, every wine is different. Your own taste buds are the most important piece of equipment in your kitchen, and the most fun to use.

Chill the soup in the refrigerator for at least 3 hours. I like to put it in the freezer for the last half-hour or so before I serve it.

Just before serving, add 2 tablespoons chopped fresh mint to the cream, along with a little sugar if you like, and beat the cream with a whisk until it just begins to thicken. Taste, and add more mint if you like.

Serve this beautiful soup very cold, in chilled bowls, with a spoonful of the soft mint cream in the center of each serving.

Another way . . .

If heavy cream is too rich for you, you can make a lighter mint cream with ½ cup heavy cream, whisked until it is slightly thickened, mixed with ½ cup nonfat Greek-style yogurt. Sweeten this mixture to taste and stir in the chopped mint.

cold peach and nectarine soup
with strawberry sauce

This is one of those marvelous cold soups that requires no cooking. It's made in the blender, then chilled a few hours in the refrigerator and served like a blessing of cool refreshment in the long, hot days of summer. With a little less honey and a little more lemon juice, it becomes an appetizer soup. With a touch more honey and less lemon juice, it's a lovely dessert soup.

· · · SERVES 6—8 · · ·

2¼ lbs. (1 kg) white or yellow peaches
2¼ lbs. (1 kg) white or yellow nectarines
3 cups (700 ml) plain low-fat yogurt
4–6 Tbs. (80–120 g) honey

2–4 Tbs. (30–60 ml) fresh lemon juice
2 Tbs. (30 ml) sherry (optional)
½ tsp. ground cinnamon

for the strawberry sauce

1 pint sweet strawberries (12 oz.; 350 g)
1 Tbs. sugar
1 Tbs. (15 ml) lemon juice
1 tsp. chopped fresh mint

1 tsp. chopped fresh basil

· · ·

optional garnish: mint sprigs

Use fully ripe, juicy peaches and nectarines. Peel and slice all the fruit, saving the juice. Stir in the yogurt and as much honey and lemon juice as you want, which depends on whether you will serve the soup as an appetizer or a dessert. Add the sherry, if you like, and the cinnamon. Puree this in a blender, in batches, or use an immersion blender. Chill the mixture well.

recipe continues on next page

Hull and wash the strawberries and puree them with the sugar, lemon juice, mint, and basil. Strain the strawberry puree if you want it perfectly smooth, and chill it well.

Ladle the soup into shallow bowls and drizzle a spoonful of strawberry sauce in the center of each serving. You can paint pictures on your soup and make it as beautiful or amusing as you want. Once for a lunch party I made the initials of the guests in their soup with strawberry sauce. You don't have to stop playing with your food just because you're out of kindergarten.

from soup to meal

CHAPTER 14

a few good breads

Three-Grain Bread • V

Whole-Wheat Walnut Bread • V

Oatmeal Molasses Bread

Grandma's Dinner Rolls

Olive and Rosemary Focaccia • V

Potato Pizza

Irish Soda Bread

Fresh Corn and Cheddar Cheese Cornbread

Quick Whole-Wheat Oatmeal Bread

Popovers

Multigrain Scones with Fennel and Orange

Savory Walnut and Herb Biscuits

Crostini • V

Parmesan Crostini

Parmesan and Fennel Biscotti

a word about yeast breads: easy

Here's some good news for anyone who likes a great, crusty loaf of bread. You can bake it yourself, even if you are a busy person. I'm talking about yeast-leavened bread with a truly crusty crust. Not that I have anything against quick breads—I love them—but in this case I'm talking about the real thing.

The secret is the wet-dough method. It turns out that if you make a dough with enough moisture in it—more than the traditional bread dough has—you can get an excellent loaf of bread with no kneading. The work time is minimal. And here's a bonus: you can make a big batch of this dough and store it in the refrigerator for days. Then, when you want fresh bread, cut off a chunk of that dough, put it on a baking sheet, let it rest a bit, and bake it.

I did not invent this wonderfully easy way to make excellent bread. I discovered it when my friend Lisa called me in excitement: "I have a book called *Artisan Bread in Five Minutes a Day*—don't laugh—I'm bringing it over."

She brought it over, and I read about the high-moisture, stored-dough method of bread baking that Jeff Hertzberg and Zoë François had worked out. We started baking bread every day, and I loved the fact that I could have a bowl of ready dough in the refrigerator for a week and bake whenever the mood struck.

This is not the only book that describes a wet-dough, no-knead method of making yeast breads. In *My Bread*, Jim Lahey, of Sullivan Street Bakery fame, gives detailed instructions on his own method, which produces bread with a crackling crust and moist, chewy body.

Lahey's method requires utterly simple ingredients and almost no labor, but it takes a bit more planning—the first rise of the dough lasts 12 to 18 hours! That long, slow rise gives the bread its deep flavor, but the amazing crust comes from a true stroke of genius—

the bread is baked in a very hot oven, in a preheated, covered pot. The pot acts as an oven within the oven, trapping steam from the wet dough to make that amazing crust.

Baking bread is fun, and having fresh bread in the house is a treat. And now, with these wet-dough methods, it's so simple. If you like to bake, go out and get these books for your cookbook shelf—you'll be glad you did. Meanwhile, the first three breads in this chapter are recipes I worked out using a wet-dough method to make the dense whole-grain bread that I love—and that goes so well with soup.

AND A WORD ABOUT QUICK BREADS: EVEN EASIER

Quick breads are indeed quick, but do not discount them—they can be as nutritious, complex, and varied as yeast breads, just crumblier. The world of quick breads is huge. I've scratched its surface here with an Irish soda bread, a dense cornbread, biscuits, scones, and popovers, just to make a start.

Quick breads are just that: a good start, a perfect way for beginners in the kitchen to try their hand at baking. No kneading, no waiting: stir up a dough, put it in a pan, and bake it. There it is—immediate gratification. But these breads are a boon to all of us, newbies and old hands alike, when we want something fresh-baked, warm and fragrant from the oven, but we want it in a hurry.

three-grain bread

This great-tasting, dense, peasant-style loaf is easy, easy, easy to make. It's based on the wet-dough, no-knead method. You have to allow a few hours for rising, but the work is a snap.

A little bit of rye flour gives a slightly sour taste, and the cornmeal and honey add a touch of sweetness. Together they make a richly textured, not quite pumpernickel but more than whole-wheat experience. It's the perfect bread to serve with many soups, and fine for sandwiches.

· · · MAKES 1 LARGE LOAF · · ·

3 cups (420 g) stone-ground whole-wheat flour

½ cup (60 g) rye flour

2 Tbs. (20–30 g) cornmeal, plus more for the
    baking sheet

1½ cups (360 ml) warm water

¼ cup (60 ml) honey or agave nectar

1 Tbs. (10 g) active dry yeast

2 tsp. sea salt

2 Tbs. (30 ml) canola oil

Mix together the whole-wheat flour, rye flour, and 2 tablespoons cornmeal. These do not have to be sifted together; a quick whisking will combine them well enough.

In a large bowl, combine the warm water, honey, yeast, and salt. The water should feel hot to the touch but not scalding, like hot bathwater. Stir and let the yeast dissolve.

Whisk in half the flour mixture and the canola oil. Then, using a wooden spoon or some other strong, large spoon, stir in the rest of the flour. You will have a sticky dough, stiff enough to form a ball but somewhat softer than you might expect a bread dough to be. Pat it into a ball and put it back in its bowl.

Cover the bowl with a lid (not airtight) and leave the dough to rise for 3 to 4 hours; it will rise until it collapses. At this point you can shape your loaf and bake your bread. Or you can form your dough into a ball, put it in a smaller bowl or a plastic container, and put it away in the refrigerator for up to 5 days. This way you can bake a loaf of bread anytime you want; you only need a few minutes to shape the loaf and dust it with flour. Be sure the bowl or container is covered but not sealed airtight. I usually put a pot lid of appropriate size over a kitchen bowl.

When you want to bake your bread, prepare a baking sheet by sprinkling a layer of cornmeal over an area somewhat larger than the loaf. This will prevent the loaf from sticking and will form a wonderful, crunchy bottom crust.

To form the loaf, wet your hands with water, pick up the dough, and quickly shape it into a fairly smooth ball, pulling the sides down and pinching them together on the bottom. Flatten the ball slightly and place the loaf pinched side down on the cornmeal-coated baking sheet. Leave the loaf to rise for about 45 minutes. If you have just taken the dough out of the refrigerator, add an hour to allow the cold dough to come to room temperature.

While the loaf is rising, preheat the oven to 375°. Put a broiler pan or shallow roasting pan on a lower rack, where it will not be in the way of the bread.

When the loaf has swelled to about 1 ½ times its starting size, sprinkle it lightly with whole-wheat flour and cut a shallow cross in the top by pulling a sharp knife gently across it. Put the loaf in the middle of the hot oven, then pour 1 cup of hot tap water into the broiler pan. Quickly close the door. The steam created when this water hits the hot pan will help give your bread a lovely crisp crust.

Bake the bread for 55 minutes, or until a toothpick inserted near the center comes out clean. Let it cool on a rack. The bread will slice much more obediently once it is cool.

To make a big batch . . .

This can easily be doubled or even tripled. The method is exactly the same, but be sure you have a really large bowl for that initial rising. If you double the recipe, you will have enough dough for 2 large loaves or 3 smaller loaves. Mix once, bake bread all week!

whole-wheat walnut bread

This flavorful whole-grain bread is so delicious you will want to bake a loaf every day. Use the very best walnuts you can find for this. If you don't have walnut oil, use 2 tablespoons olive oil instead. Most importantly, use fresh whole-wheat flour, meaning flour that is less than a year old. Whole-grain flour that has been kept in a cupboard too long can start to become bitter. (If you don't bake frequently, think about keeping your flour in your freezer.)

· · · MAKES 1 LARGE LOAF · · ·

1½ cups (360 ml) warm water

¼ cup (60 ml) honey or agave nectar

1 Tbs. (10 g) active dry yeast

2 tsp. sea salt

3½ cups (500 g) whole-wheat flour

1 Tbs. (15 ml) walnut oil

1 Tbs. (15 ml) olive oil

1 cup (110 g) coarsely chopped walnuts

cornmeal for the baking sheet

In a large bowl, combine the warm water, honey, yeast, and salt. The water should feel hot to the touch but not scalding, like hot bathwater. Stir and let the yeast dissolve.

Whisk in half the flour, the walnut oil and olive oil, and half the walnuts. Then, using a wooden spoon or some other strong, large spoon, stir in the rest of the flour and walnuts. You will have a sticky dough, stiff enough to form a ball but somewhat softer than the usual bread dough. Pat it into a ball and put it back in its bowl.

Cover the bowl with a lid (not airtight) and leave the dough to rise for 3 to 4 hours; it will rise until it collapses. At this point you can shape your loaf and bake your bread. Or you can re-form the ball of dough, put it in a smaller bowl or a plastic container, and put it away in the refrigerator for up to 5 days. Now you can bake a loaf of bread whenever you like; you only need a few minutes to shape the loaf and dust it with flour. If you are storing the dough, be sure the bowl or container is covered but not sealed airtight. I generally put a pot lid of appropriate size over a ceramic kitchen bowl.

When you want to bake your bread, prepare a baking sheet by sprinkling a layer of cornmeal over an area somewhat larger than the loaf. This will prevent the loaf from sticking and will form a wonderful, crunchy bottom crust.

To form the loaf, wet your hands with water, pick up the dough, and quickly shape it into a fairly smooth ball, pulling the sides down and pinching them together on the bottom. Flatten the ball slightly and place the loaf pinched side down on the cornmeal-coated baking sheet. Leave the loaf to rise for about 45 minutes. While the bread is rising, preheat the oven to 375°. If the dough has been refrigerated, add an hour to allow the cold dough to come to room temperature, and turn on the oven after that. Put a broiler pan or shallow roasting pan on a lower rack of your oven, where it will not be in the way of the bread.

When the loaf has swelled to about 1 ½ times its starting size, sprinkle it lightly with whole-wheat flour and cut a shallow cross or three slashes in the top by pulling a sharp knife gently across the dough. Put the loaf in the middle of the hot oven, then pour 1 cup of hot tap water into the broiler pan. Quickly close the door. The steam created when this water hits the hot pan will give your bread a crisp crust.

Bake the bread for 55 minutes, or until a toothpick inserted near the center comes out clean. Let it cool on a rack, and try not to slice it until it is at least somewhat cool.

To make a big batch . . .

Like the previous recipe, this one can be doubled or tripled with no problem. The method is the same, and you simply have to have a larger bowl for the initial rising. If you double this recipe, you will have enough dough for 2 large loaves or 3 smaller ones.

oatmeal molasses bread

Here is one more yeast bread based on the wet-dough, no-knead method. The combination of oats, whole-wheat flour, and a touch of cornmeal, sweetened with dark molasses, makes a rich-tasting loaf that is wonderful with many winter soups, almost essential for split pea soup, and also makes fine sandwiches.

I've found that if I make a double batch of this dough and bake one loaf immediately and the second one a few days later, there is an interesting difference in the taste of the bread. The first loaf is a bit sweeter. The next one, after the yeast has a chance to work slowly for a few days, has a very subtle leaning toward sourdough. Both are marvelous, and it's fun to see how the dough keeps developing.

· · · MAKES 1 LARGE LOAF · · ·

¾ cup (180 ml) hot water

¾ cup (180 ml) whole milk

¼ cup (60 ml) dark molasses

4 tsp. active dry yeast (½ oz.; 14 g)

2 tsp. sea salt

2½ cups (350 g) unbleached white flour

¾ cup (105 g) whole-wheat flour

1 cup (100 g) rolled oats, plus more for the top
  of the loaf

2 Tbs. (25 g) cornmeal, plus more for the baking
  pan

2 Tbs. (30 ml) canola oil

In a large bowl, combine the hot water, milk, molasses, yeast, and salt. The liquid should feel hot to the touch but not scalding, like hot bathwater. Stir and let the yeast dissolve.

Mix together the white and whole-wheat flours, the rolled oats, and 2 tablespoons cornmeal. Whisk half the flour mixture and the canola oil into the yeast mixture. Then, using a wooden spoon or some other strong, large spoon, stir in the rest of the flour. You will have a sticky dough, stiff enough to form a ball but somewhat softer than you might expect a bread dough to be. Pat it into a ball and put it back in its bowl.

Cover the bowl with a lid (not airtight) and leave the dough to rise for 3 to 4 hours; it will rise until it collapses. At this point you can shape your loaf and bake your bread. Or you can form the dough into a ball again, put it in a smaller bowl or a plastic container, and put it away in the refrigerator for up to 5 days. This way you can bake a loaf of bread whenever you like; you only need a few minutes to shape the loaf and dust it with flour. If you are storing the dough, be sure the bowl or container is covered but not sealed airtight. I usually put a pot lid over a kitchen bowl.

When you want to bake your bread, prepare a baking sheet by sprinkling a layer of cornmeal over an area somewhat larger than the loaf. This will prevent the loaf from sticking and will form a wonderful, crunchy bottom crust.

To form the loaf, wet your hands with water, pick up the dough, and quickly shape it into a fairly smooth ball, pulling the sides down and pinching them together on the bottom. Flatten the ball slightly and place the loaf pinched side down on the cornmeal-coated baking sheet. Sprinkle the top of the loaf with some rolled oats and pat them down gently.

Leave the loaf to rise for about 45 minutes. If you have just taken the dough out of the refrigerator, add an hour to allow the cold dough to come to room temperature.

While the loaf is rising, preheat the oven to 375°. Put a broiler pan or shallow roasting pan on a lower rack, where it will not be in the way of the bread.

When the loaf has swelled to about 1 ½ times its starting size, sprinkle it lightly with whole-wheat flour and cut a shallow cross in the top by pulling a sharp knife gently across it. Put the loaf in the middle of the hot oven. Pour 1 cup of hot tap water into the broiler pan and quickly close the door. The steam created when this water hits the hot pan will give your bread a crunchier crust.

Bake the bread for 55 minutes, or until a toothpick inserted near the center comes out clean. Let it cool on a rack. The bread will slice well once it is cool.

recipe continues on next page

To make a big batch . . .

This recipe can easily be doubled or even tripled. The method is exactly the same, but be sure you have a really large bowl for that initial rising. If you double the recipe, you will have enough dough for 2 large loaves or 3 smaller loaves.

grandma's dinner rolls

My mother often made these rolls of feathery lightness and delicate, buttery flavor. As far back as I can remember, she made them for every company dinner, every special visit. When I came home from college during winter break, pans of cooling rolls, just baked, were waiting on the kitchen counter. Later, when my children were small and my mother came to visit, she baked them in my kitchen, and that's when they got their name: Grandma rolls.

These are tender, melt-in-your mouth rolls that are best eaten the same day they are baked. If you are making them for a dinner party or if there are going to be kids around, you should probably double the recipe, because these tend to vanish as they come out of the oven.

· · · MAKES 20 SMALL ROLLS · · ·

1 Tbs. (10 g) active dry yeast	1 tsp. sea salt
¼ cup (60 ml) warm water	¾ cup (180 ml) warm whole milk
¼ cup (60 g) sugar	3½–4 cups (500–560 g) unbleached white flour
1 large egg, plus 1 egg yolk	6 Tbs. (85 g) unsalted butter, softened

Dissolve the yeast in the warm water with a pinch of the sugar. In a large bowl, beat the whole egg with the salt until the egg looks slightly foamy. Beat in the remaining sugar, the warm milk, and the yeast mixture. Add about half the flour and stir until well combined. Beat in 4 tablespoons (½ stick) of softened butter . This can be done the old-fashioned way, by vigorously slapping the dough up against the side of the bowl with a wooden spoon, or by using an appliance with a dough hook. You will have a sticky, glossy batter.

recipe continues on next page

Add most of the remaining flour, a little at a time, until the dough is hard to stir with the spoon. Then turn it out on a floured board and knead it gently for 3 to 4 minutes only. Do not work in more flour than necessary to keep the dough from sticking. You want it to feel smooth, tender, and pliable, but not as firm and springy as a bread dough. If you have flour left over, don't worry about it; the amount you use can vary, and you must go by the feel of the dough.

Form the dough into a smooth ball and put it in a large, buttered bowl, turning it over once to coat it. Cover the bowl with a kitchen towel and leave it in a warm spot for the dough to rise to double its size, probably about 1 hour. Punch it down and let it rise again, about 45 minutes. Punch it down once more.

Cut the dough into 2 equal parts. Melt the remaining 2 tablespoons butter. On a floured board, roll out half of the dough into a rectangle about 18 inches by 6 inches. Brush it with butter and fold it over once lengthwise. You should now have a strip of dough about 3 inches wide and 18 inches long. Cut it crosswise into 10 equal pieces.

Take one piece of dough at a time and gently pull it out to a length of 6 or 8 inches. Hold it by its two ends and twist them in opposite directions a few turns. Now you have in your hands something that looks like a piece of rope. To form the roll, tie this ropelike strand of dough into a loose knot—any kind of knot—and tuck one or both ends up through the middle.

Place the rolls on buttered baking sheets, about 2 inches apart. Continue the same way with the other half of the dough.

Once you have shaped the first few rolls, you will quickly acquire the knack and find that it is not at all difficult. In fact, it's a lot of fun, and it all takes less time to do than it does to describe. Also remember that whatever the shape of your rolls when you form them, they'll look just fine when they've risen again and are baked.

Cover the rolls on their baking sheets with kitchen towels and leave them to rise again in the warm kitchen for about half an hour, or until they look puffed up and soft; they will not quite double in size.

Preheat the oven to 400°.

Beat the egg yolk in a cup with a teaspoon of water and brush the risen rolls lightly with this egg wash. Bake the rolls for about 10 minutes, until they are golden brown.

This makes 20 small rolls, which is not very many. I always double this recipe, as half the rolls usually are eaten before dinner can be served.

If you are not going to consume these rolls within a few hours of baking, allow them to cool on racks and then put them in an airtight container. If you want to keep them longer than a day, freeze them and defrost them shortly before serving. Two or 3 minutes in a hot oven will bring back their just-baked softness and fragrance.

olive and rosemary focaccia

Olive and rosemary focaccia is a classic, but I often vary it by adding other herbs. Lately I've been adding lavender and thyme, which give it a floral, herbal quality that I find delightful. However, if you don't have lavender on hand, please don't let that stop you. Either way, this is a wonderful, easy bread. Serve it with hummus or pesto, or with almost any soup.

· · · MAKES 1 LOAF · · ·

2½ tsp. active dry yeast (¼ oz.; 7 g)

1¼ cups (300 ml) warm water

½ tsp. sugar

1 tsp. sea salt

3–3½ cups (425–500 g) unbleached white flour

3 Tbs. (45 ml) olive oil

1½ Tbs. chopped fresh rosemary

1 tsp. chopped fresh thyme

1 tsp. chopped fresh or dried lavender

¼ cup (40 g) slivered Kalamata olives

cornmeal for the baking pan

coarse salt (optional)

Dissolve the yeast in the warm water with the sugar, and if you have any doubt about the age or "liveness" of the yeast, leave it for 10 minutes, until it starts to foam. Stir in the salt, 1 cup flour, 2 tablespoons olive oil, the herbs, and the olives. Then start adding in the remaining flour, one scoop at a time, until the dough is too stiff to stir with a spoon.

Turn the dough out on a well-floured board, sprinkle more flour on top of it, and knead it gently for 7 to 8 minutes, working in only as much more flour as you need to keep it from sticking. When the dough is smooth and elastic, form it into a ball and put it into a large, oiled bowl, turning it once to coat it. Cover the bowl with a kitchen towel or a loose lid and leave the dough in a warm place to rise for 45 minutes to an hour, until it has approximately doubled in volume.

Sprinkle a baking sheet with cornmeal. Punch the dough down and form it into a smooth ball, then roll out the ball into an oval about 12 inches by 16 inches and transfer it to the baking sheet.

You can leave your focaccia plain, dimple it with your fingertips, or cut shallow crisscross slashes in the top with a sharp knife. If your baking sheet is large, you can make several short cross-wise cuts right through the loaf and then gently pull it apart to make slight gaps where you have cut. Brush the loaf lightly with the remaining tablespoon of olive oil and, if you like, sprinkle it with coarse salt. Cover it with a dry kitchen towel and let it rise again in a warm spot for 20 to 30 minutes, until it begins to look puffed and soft.

While the focaccia is rising, preheat the oven to 425°.

Bake the focaccia for 25 to 30 minutes, or until it is golden on top and sounds hollow when the bottom is tapped. Serve it warm if you can—it's fabulous when it's fresh out of the oven. It can be cut in squares to serve, but I like to lay a whole focaccia directly on the tablecloth or on a large bread board and let everyone tear pieces off.

Another way . . .

You can replace 1 cup white flour with whole-wheat flour for a delicious whole-wheat focaccia.

An even better way . . .

Double this recipe and save half the dough for the next day: at the point when you are going to roll out the focaccia, divide the dough in two and put half away in an oiled, covered bowl in the refrigerator. The next day, take it out and leave it on the counter long enough to return to room temperature, then roll and bake.

potato pizza

This mouthwatering dish came about one cold day during a winter rainstorm, when I was in the mood for potatoes but also had a hankering to bake pizza. The great thing about being the cook in your own kitchen is that you're the boss and you really can have whatever you want. So, potato pizza: hearty, hunger-killing, with a thick savory topping of potatoes, onions, melting white cheese, and pungent olives.

This pizza adapts well to variations. The basic combination of potatoes with a creamy fresh cheese can make a foundation for plenty of other flavors. Try it with sautéed spinach and garlic, or with sautéed portobello mushroom slices, as suggested below.

· · · SERVES 6—8 · · ·

for the pizza dough

½ cup (120 ml) whole milk

¾ cup (180 ml) hot water

1 Tbs. (10 g) active dry yeast

1 tsp. sugar

1 tsp. sea salt

3½ cups (500 g) unbleached white flour

1 Tbs. (10 g) rye flour (optional)

2–3 Tbs. (30–45 ml) olive oil

a little cornmeal

for the toppings

2½ lbs. (1 kg) red-skinned or Yukon Gold potatoes

2 large yellow onions (500 g)

3 Tbs. (45 ml) olive oil

2 tsp. sea salt, plus more to taste

freshly ground black pepper

fresh or dried thyme, chopped or crumbled

12 oz. (350 g) *queso fresco* or white farmer cheese

1½ cups (180 g) drained marinated artichoke hearts

20–24 Kalamata olives, sliced off the pits

½ cup (50 g) grated provolone cheese

In a large mixing bowl, combine the milk and the hot water. Add the yeast to this lukewarm liquid, along with the sugar and salt. Wait for a few minutes to make sure that it begins to froth, then stir in about 2 ½ cups white flour, the tablespoon of rye flour if you like, and 2 tablespoons olive oil. Stir until a thick dough forms.

Sprinkle the rest of the flour on a board and turn the dough out on it in a mound. Knead the dough for about 10 minutes, working in as much more of the flour as is needed to make it smooth and elastic. Form the dough into a ball and put it in a lightly oiled bowl, turning it over once, then cover the bowl with a kitchen towel and leave it in a warm place to rise for 45 to 50 minutes.

While the dough is rising, prepare the toppings.

Scrub and trim the potatoes, then cut them into ½-inch dice. Chop the onions. Heat the olive oil in a large nonstick pan and add the potatoes, onions, 2 teaspoons salt, pepper to taste, and a big pinch of thyme. Cook this over medium heat, stirring often, for about 10 minutes, until the potatoes and onions begin to color slightly. Cover the pan, lower the heat, and continue cooking for another 15 to 20 minutes, stirring occasionally. Don't be afraid to scrape up the brown bits and stir them in.

Crumble the *queso fresco* or farmer cheese. Drain the artichoke hearts well, trim away any tough leaves, and cut the hearts into quarters or wedges.

When the pizza dough has more or less doubled in size, punch it down, divide it into 2 equal-sized pieces, and form each piece into a smooth ball. Take one ball at a time and pat it, roll it, pull it, until it is the shape you want and about ¼-inch thick. (I don't have special pizza equipment, so I roll my dough into a rough rectangle and use a large cookie sheet.) If the dough is very springy, cover it with a slightly damp towel and let it rest for about 10 minutes. It will relax and become easier to stretch.

recipe continues on next page

Prepare 2 large baking sheets or pizza pans by lightly oiling them with the remaining 1 tablespoon olive oil and sprinkling them evenly with cornmeal. Lay the rolled-out pizza dough on the baking sheets or pizza pans.

Preheat your oven to 550° (or as hot as you can get it).

Divide the toppings equally between your pizzas: First dot the dough as evenly as possible with the potato mixture, then sprinkle the crumbled white cheese among the potatoes. Next lay pieces of artichoke heart and sliced black olives here and there, and finish by sprinkling on a little grated provolone cheese.

Bake the pizzas for about 6 minutes, then reverse their positions between upper and lower racks and bake for about another 5 to 6 minutes. Check the pizzas toward the end of this time; they can get overdone fast at these temperatures. The crust should be lightly browning on the edges, and the cheeses should be soft and bubbly.

Eat the pizzas hot from the oven, with a glass of red wine.

This makes 2 medium pizzas or 4 to 6 generous individual pizzas. If the pizza is joining a soup or is being served with other foods in a more elaborate menu, then it's enough to serve 6 to 8.

Some other ways . . .

greek pizza: Substitute feta cheese for part of the *queso fresco* and sprinkle on some chopped fresh oregano. Add slices of marinated sun-dried tomatoes.

mushroom pizza: Eliminate the olives and artichoke hearts and add a cup or so of thinly sliced marinated or sautéed mushrooms instead.

green pizza: Chop a pound or two of fresh spinach and sauté it in olive oil with a spoonful of chopped garlic until it is wilted and has given up its excess moisture. Mix it in with the potatoes and onions, or layer it on top of them.

irish soda bread

WITH FENNEL AND ORANGE

I love soda bread. It tastes so good, with the nuttiness of whole-wheat flour, the very slight sweetness of oats, and that pinch of sugar. This is the perfect little quick bread for any occasion when you want something hot and freshly made in very little time. You can have fresh bread in under an hour.

I've made many soda breads over the years, and every time I feel I've got the recipe I want to use forever, I think of something else I'd like to try. Recently I made this version, which I'm sure will not be found in Ireland. I used fennel seed and freshly grated orange zest to flavor it, a combination that happens to be available in my backyard. My son Toddy once said, "This is the queen of bread."

· · · MAKES 2 SMALL LOAVES · · ·

1¾ cups (420 ml) buttermilk

1 large egg

2 Tbs. (28 g) unsalted butter, melted

2 tsp. whole fennel seeds

grated zest of 1 orange

2 Tbs. turbinado sugar or any sugar

½ cup (75 g) raisins

2 cups (280 g) whole-wheat flour

1½ cups (200 g) unbleached white flour, plus
   more for the board

1¼ tsp. baking soda

1 Tbs. baking powder

1¼ tsp. salt

1 cup (90 g) rolled oats

Preheat the oven to 375°. Line a large baking sheet with parchment.

Beat together the buttermilk, egg, and butter. Toast the fennel seeds in a small skillet for a minute or two, just until they are fragrant. Add the toasted fennel seeds, orange zest, sugar, and raisins to the buttermilk mixture and stir well.

Sift together the flours, baking soda, baking powder, and salt. Stir in the rolled oats and then the buttermilk mixture. The dough may be sticky. *recipe continues on next page*

Turn the dough out on a well-floured board. It should be stiff but moist, so dust the top of it with flour and then push and fold it gently, dusting with more flour to keep it from sticking, just until it holds together and can be shaped. This is not a bread you want to knead—it will be more tender if you do not overwork it.

Divide the dough into 2 parts and form each part into a smooth ball, pulling down the sides and pinching them together in one place. Place the balls pinched side down on the baking sheet, press down slightly, and cut a shallow cross in the top of each one with a sharp knife.

Bake the loaves for 35 to 40 minutes, until they are puffed up and browned on top and a toothpick inserted in the center comes out clean. Allow the loaves to cool slightly on a rack before cutting them.

Another way . . .

Instead of using a combination of whole-wheat and white flour, you can use 3 ½ cups of the white whole-wheat flour made by King Arthur Flour. It is lighter in texture than most whole-grain flour and makes a very nice loaf without the addition of any refined white flour.

fresh corn and cheddar cheese cornbread

This moist, dense cornbread is almost like a corn pudding, and it turns a soup into a meal. Full of eggs, buttermilk, fresh corn, and cheese, it provides plenty of nourishment with its comforting chewiness and flavor. All this, and it takes minutes to make.

You can use any cornmeal, but stone-ground cornmeal tastes best and gives you real crunch in the texture.

··· SERVES 6—8 ···

1¼ cups (170 g) unbleached white flour
½ tsp. baking soda
1 Tbs. baking powder
1 tsp. sea salt
1½ cups (275 g) cornmeal, stone-ground if possible
2 Tbs. sugar
1 cup (250 ml) buttermilk

2 cups (225 g) fresh or frozen corn kernels
3 large eggs
1 cup (80 g) sliced green onions, green and white parts
2½ oz. (70 g) grated sharp cheddar cheese
½ tsp. chopped fresh thyme
2 Tbs. (30 g) unsalted butter, melted

Preheat the oven to 375°. Prepare an 8-inch square baking dish by buttering it and lining the bottom with buttered parchment.

Sift together the flour, baking soda, baking powder, and salt. Mix in the cornmeal and sugar.

Combine the buttermilk and half the corn kernels in a blender and process until you have a rough puree. Beat the eggs lightly, then add the buttermilk mixture, the remaining 1 cup whole corn kernels, and the sliced green onions, grated cheese, and thyme.

Stir the wet ingredients into the dry ones, mixing everything together thoroughly, and stir in the melted butter. Pour the thick batter into the prepared pan, spreading it evenly. Bake the cornbread for about 40 minutes, or until a toothpick inserted near the center comes out clean. The top should be slightly puffed and lightly browned.

Allow the cornbread to cool just a bit before cutting it into squares to serve.

quick whole-wheat oatmeal bread

This dense, faintly sweet oatmeal bread is ready in about an hour, and the only problem is waiting for it to cool before slicing it. The loaf is crumbly at first but becomes less so as it cools down. I love this bread with sharp cheddar cheese.

· · · MAKES 2 MEDIUM LOAVES · · ·

2 cups (300 g) whole-wheat flour

2 cups (300 g) unbleached white flour

4 tsp. baking powder

1 tsp. baking soda

1½ tsp. sea salt

⅓ cup (60 g) light brown sugar or raw sugar

1 cup (100 g) rolled oats

1 large egg

3½ Tbs. (50 g) unsalted butter, melted and cooled

1¾ cups (420 ml) buttermilk

Preheat the oven to 375°. Prepare 2 medium loaf pans: butter the pans, line the bottoms with rectangles of parchment paper, and butter the paper.

In a mixing bowl, sift together the whole-wheat flour, white flour, baking powder, baking soda, and salt. Whisk in the brown sugar and the rolled oats.

In another bowl, lightly beat or whisk together the egg, melted butter, and buttermilk. Add the wet mixture to the dry one and stir together with a wooden spoon (or any big, strong spoon) until everything is just combined into a thick dough.

Cut the dough in half. Wet your hands and quickly form half the dough into a rough oblong. Drop the loaf into a prepared pan, then repeat with the other half of the dough. Alternately, you can scoop dough into a pan with a spoon and pat down the top.

Bake the bread for 45 to 50 minutes, or until a toothpick inserted in the center of a loaf comes out clean.

Allow the bread to cool in the pan for 5 minutes, then remove it and let it cool completely on a rack.

popovers

Hardly anything in the bread and muffin world is as much fun and as easy as popovers. The batter for popovers can be mixed up in minutes and baked in a little over half an hour, and they can be watched through the window of the oven for entertainment. Seeing them balloon up into their odd mushroom shapes is a kick. And then you get to eat them.

This recipe is a basic formula that I have used for years and that always works, but now I use half whole-wheat flour and half all-purpose flour, and I like to add a pinch of thyme. It's just enough to add a faint, savory undertone to the flavor.

· · · SERVES 6 · · ·

3 large eggs
1 cup (240 ml) whole milk
2 Tbs. (28 g) unsalted butter, melted, plus more
   for the pan

½ teaspoon sea salt
½ teaspoon finely chopped fresh or dried thyme
½ cup (75 g) whole-wheat flour
½ cup (75 g) unbleached white flour

Preheat the oven to 425°.

Beat the eggs with the milk, 2 tablespoons melted butter, salt, and thyme. Beat in the flours until the batter is perfectly smooth.

Brush 12 nonstick three-inch muffin cups lightly with butter. Distribute the popover batter evenly between them, filling the cups about halfway.

Bake the popovers for 15 minutes, then reduce the temperature to 350° and bake for 20 minutes more. The popovers will balloon up high over the rim of the muffin cups and turn a deep golden brown.

recipe continues on next page

As soon as you take the popovers out of the oven, loosen them gently by sliding a knife around their edges and tilt them sideways in their cups. This will prevent steam from collecting underneath and making them soggy.

I think the popovers are best if served immediately out of the oven. They can be allowed to cool for a while, but they should be eaten within an hour or two of being baked if possible, as popovers will soften and deflate if held too long after baking.

Twelve popovers should serve 6 people, but if we're going to be truthful, it's probably just about enough for 4.

multigrain scones with fennel and orange

These scones can be eaten with butter and jam for breakfast or with a wedge of crumbly cheddar cheese and a bowl of soup or a salad for supper. The nutty taste of buckwheat flour is underscored by the walnuts, and the fennel seeds and orange rind add a faint, exotic spiciness.

If you don't have any buckwheat flour on hand, you can add another ¼ cup whole-wheat flour instead. The scones will still be tasty.

· · · MAKES 16 SCONES · · ·

1½ cups (210 g) unbleached white flour, plus
   more for the board
1¼ cups (175 g) whole-wheat flour
¼ cup (40 g) buckwheat flour
1 Tbs. baking powder
1 tsp. baking soda
1¼ tsp. sea salt
3 Tbs. sugar

4 Tbs. (55 g) cold unsalted butter
1 cup (100 g) rolled oats
1 tsp. fennel seeds
⅔ cup (75 g) chopped walnuts
⅔ cup (100 g) raisins
1½ cups (360 ml) buttermilk
1 large egg
grated zest of 1 large orange

Combine the flours, baking powder, baking soda, salt, and sugar in the container of a food processor and give the dry ingredients one quick spin. Add the cold butter, cut into slices, and pulse briefly, just until the mixture resembles coarse meal.

Transfer the dry mixture to an ample mixing bowl and stir in the rolled oats, fennel seeds, walnuts, and raisins. In another bowl, lightly beat together the buttermilk, egg, and grated orange zest, and stir this into the dry mixture as well.

recipe continues on next page

Turn the dough out onto a floured board and knead it a few turns, dusting with more flour to keep it from sticking, but stop as soon as the dough is holding together and has no large pockets of flour. The tenderness of the scones depends on not overworking the dough.

Preheat the oven to 375°. Line 2 baking sheets with parchment paper, or butter them.

Divide the dough into 2 parts and form each into a thick disk about 7 inches across. Using a large, very sharp knife, cut the disks cleanly into quarters and then eighths, making neat wedges. Arrange the wedges on the baking sheets and bake them for about 25 minutes, or until puffed up and beginning to turn golden brown. Reverse the positions of the sheets in the oven about midway through the baking time. When the scones are done, a toothpick inserted in the center of a scone should come out clean.

Allow the scones to cool slightly on a rack, then serve warm or at room temperature.

savory walnut and herb biscuits

I love walnut bread, those big, chewy loaves with shiny crusts and the rich taste of walnuts and whole grains, which are so good with cheese and wine. But I love biscuits, too. These mix up and bake in minutes and have the earthy flavor of walnuts combined with delicate fresh herbs. Tarragon brings a note of sweetness, marjoram is like a polite oregano, and chives supply the onion flavor without going overboard. Try other herbs; sage, rosemary, and thyme would be lovely.

Eat these warm if possible! They are delicious with sharp cheddar cheese and apple slices, wonderful with nettle soup, with scrambled eggs, with a salad of sweet lettuce, mint and goat cheese. . . . They are tasty with just about everything.

··· MAKES 10 12 BISCUITS ···

1 cup (140 g) whole-wheat flour, pastry flour if
   possible
1 cup (140 g) unbleached white flour, plus more
   for the board
1 Tbs. baking powder
¾ tsp. sea salt

6 Tbs. (85 g) cold unsalted butter
½ cup (50 g) chopped walnuts
1 tsp. chopped fresh tarragon
1 tsp. chopped fresh sweet marjoram
1 Tbs. chopped fresh chives
¾ cup (180 ml) buttermilk

Preheat the oven to 425°. Line a baking sheet with parchment paper, or butter it.

Combine the flours, baking powder, and salt in the bowl of a food processor and pulse once to combine. Add the cold butter, cut in pieces, and pulse briefly, until the mixture has the texture of coarse meal. Transfer it to a mixing bowl.

recipe continues on next page

Stir in the chopped walnuts and herbs, then add the buttermilk and stir with a fork until the mixture just holds together. Put the dough out on a lightly floured board and very gently knead it for a few turns, just until it can be rolled out. The less you work the dough, the more tender the biscuits.

Roll the dough out ¾-inch thick and cut out biscuits with a 2-inch round cutter. Arrange the biscuits on the baking sheet and bake them for 12 to 14 minutes, or until they are puffed and golden brown.

Serve the biscuits hot or warm.

crostini

I am sure that crostini were first made when some intelligent Italian housewife said, "What are we going to do with this day-old bread? We can't eat stale bread—we're Italian, we have standards. But we're not wasteful, either." She cut that bread up in thin slices, brushed it with good olive oil, dropped a few grains of salt here and there, and toasted it in the oven (while other things were cooking, because she was thrifty).

You can do the same. Once you get in the habit of making crostini, you will always have these delicious, crunchy, crackerlike toasts to bring out with the cheese or hummus or soup. Your crostini will vary, because you have various breads in your kitchen, so you won't get bored. Your homemade crostini will be superior to the crackers you can buy in the store. And they'll be free! Only a spoonful of olive oil and a few minutes of your time are added to the bread you might toss out, and there you are.

Crostini are a good habit, not a recipe. Here is the basic technique for plain crostini.

· · · MAKES ABOUT 40—60 CROSTINI · · ·

1 baguette, or part of one
3–4 Tbs. (45–60 ml) olive oil

flaky sea salt or granulated salt

Preheat the oven to 375°.

Cut the baguette in thin slices, about ¼-inch thick at the most, and lay the slices in a single layer on a baking sheet or sheets. Spray the slices with olive oil, or brush them lightly, using a pastry brush. Sprinkle a little sea salt over the oiled bread slices.

Bake the crostini for 10 to 20 minutes; take a peek after the first 10 minutes. Baking time will vary with the density of the bread and the thickness of the slices. The crostini should be golden brown around the edges, but not deep brown.

recipe continues on next page

Remove the crostini from the oven and allow them to cool on the baking sheets. They will crisp up as they cool off. Store the crostini in a tin, a plastic container, or a sealable plastic bag.

Other ways . . .

Crostini can be made from any bread, as long as it can be thinly sliced. Very crumbly breads and sweet breads are not appropriate, but big round sourdough loaves, whole-grain peasant loaves, ciabatta—all of these will make good crostini. It can be difficult to cut thin slices evenly from very large loaves, so cut a large loaf in half lengthwise, then slice thinly crosswise. Brush or spray with olive oil and bake as above. And remember that a dense whole-grain bread can take longer to crisp up in the oven. Check after 10 minutes and adjust the baking time to the needs of the bread.

To make crostini with herbs, sprinkle a little chopped thyme, minced rosemary, or chopped marjoram over the crostini after they are brushed with olive oil and salted.

parmesan crostini

These cheese-dusted crostini are tasty with a glass of wine, alone, or with pesto or any bean-based spread. They also can elevate the idea of soup and crackers to a whole new level.

Like anything in the crostini and crouton family, this is a technique more than a recipe. The amount you make probably depends on how much day-old bread you have on hand.

· · · MAKES ½ POUND CROSTINI · · ·

as an example

about ½ lb. (225 g) plain or sourdough baguette
about 2 Tbs. (30 ml) olive oil

about 3–4 Tbs. (25 g) freshly grated Parmesan cheese

Preheat the oven to 350°.

Cut the bread in thin slices—no more than ¼-inch thick. Arrange the slices in a single layer on a baking sheet, or 2 sheets if you are making a bigger batch.

Brush or spray the bread slices with the olive oil. Spraying allows a lighter touch, but a pastry brush also works very well. Sprinkle the grated Parmesan cheese over the lightly oiled bread.

Bake the crostini until they are crisp and golden brown. Baking time will vary with the density of the bread and the thickness of the slices, but count on at least 10 minutes, and up to 25. Watch them closely at the end, as they can be almost done, almost done, and then suddenly overdone.

Transfer the crostini to a rack and allow them to cool. They will finish crisping up as they cool off.

parmesan and fennel biscotti

Biscotti do not always have to be sweet! These thin, crunchy, savory biscotti are a delectable treat with a glass of wine, an ideal nibble to have on hand when guests drop by. The tang of Parmesan cheese, the snap of pepper—what a wonderful surprise.

· · · MAKES ABOUT 5 DOZEN BISCOTTI · · ·

2 cups (300 g) unbleached white flour, plus more
    for the board
¼ cup (45 g) coarse-ground yellow cornmeal
1½ tsp. sea salt
1¼ tsp. baking powder
½ tsp. baking soda
1 tsp. freshly ground black pepper

cayenne
2½ oz. (75 g) freshly grated Parmesan cheese
2 tsp. fennel seeds
½ cup (40 g) coarsely chopped pine nuts
2 large eggs, beaten
½ cup (120 ml) buttermilk

Combine the flour, cornmeal, salt, baking powder, baking soda, black pepper, and a pinch of cayenne in a medium bowl and whisk them all together. Stir in the grated cheese (you should have about ¾ cup), fennel seeds, and chopped pine nuts.

In a small bowl, beat together the eggs and buttermilk. Pour the wet mixture into the dry one and stir together with a fork until a crumbly dough forms. Turn the dough out onto a lightly floured board and knead it a few turns, just until it is smooth. It may still be slightly sticky, but don't worry. Form the dough into a ball, wrap it in plastic wrap, and let it rest about 15 minutes.

Preheat the oven to 375°. Line a baking sheet with parchment paper.

Divide the dough into 3 equal parts. Take one part at a time, keeping the rest of the dough wrapped, and gently roll and shape it into a 1-inch-diameter log. It will look too skinny, like a rope, but don't worry. Put the 3 logs on the baking sheet, spacing them 2 inches apart, and flatten them slightly with the palm of your hand.

Bake the logs for 20 minutes, until they are golden. The tops may split as they bake; once again, don't worry. Let them cool on their baking sheet for a few minutes, then carefully transfer them to a rack and let them cool at least 20 minutes more. These loaves must be cool in order to slice well, so don't try to cheat on the time. Meanwhile, lower the oven temperature to 225° and line 2 baking sheets with fresh parchment paper.

Using a very sharp, thin, serrated knife, slice the logs on the diagonal about ¼-inch thick. Arrange the slices on the baking sheets and bake them for 35 to 45 minutes. Flip the biscotti over and bake for another 35 minutes, or until they are dry and crisp. Let the biscotti cool completely on racks.

If you pack these biscotti in airtight tins, they will keep well for several weeks, but only if no one knows where they are.

CHAPTER 15

hummus and company

Sprouted Garbanzo Hummus • **V**

Tapenade with Figs and Citrus • **V**

Persian Spinach Spread

Marbled Cannellini Dip with Roasted Tomatoes • **V**

Lima Bean Spread • **V**

Eggplant and Roasted Garlic Pesto • **V**

Simple Basil Pesto • **V**

Parsley and Walnut Pesto • **V**

Simple Chipotle Sauce • **V**

Ancho and Guajillo Chile Puree • **V**

Table Salsa • **V**

Harissa • **V**

Croutons • **V**

Jeri's Spiced Nuts • **V**

Grilled Goat Cheese Sandwich

Sara's Spinach Pie

Tortilla Española with Charred Red Peppers

Black Bean Quesadillas

starters, condiments, and soup companions

Hummus is a favorite appetizer at my house, and a frequent companion of soup. A generous bowl of hummus served with crostini, pita triangles, or a baguette, along with a bowl of olives and a bottle of wine, can take care of everyone until that bowl of soup is ladled up.

Sprouted garbanzo bean hummus rules the world of spreadable legumes, but it has many close cousins that are also delectable, dips and spreads that pack big flavor and sustenance into a few spoonfuls smeared on breads or crackers or served with crisp vegetables at the start of a meal. These include my favorite tapenade, made of salty olives and sweet figs; spreads made of cannellini, of roasted eggplant, of spinach and yogurt; and a supremely simple concoction of mashed lima beans. All of them can be made ahead, just like soup. They are ready at a moment's notice to transform that soup into an interesting meal.

And what about those hungrier times? For those moments, I've included a handful of items in the hearty eating list. How can we have a book about soup and not provide at least one spectacular grilled cheese sandwich? Or a killer quesadilla? Tortilla Española with Charred Red Peppers (p. 454) and Sara's Spinach Pie (p. 452) had to be included simply because I love them so much. Then I had to control myself and remember that after all, this is a soup book. But I hope these few examples of the sturdy soup companions will lead the way to many variations of your own.

the essential condiments and garnishes . . .

Here also are the savory and spicy condiments that I could not live without—the finishing touches, the flashes of savory intensity. Simple pesto, smoky salsa, or a dab of fiery harissa can transform a dish. With a dip of a spoon, something very good becomes extraordinary.

My soups like accessories. Croutons, shavings of cheese, loops of glistening olive oil, a pool of brick-colored chile puree in a golden squash soup, a drop of harissa in the lentils . . . something raw on a slow-cooked soup, or a surprising crunch on a creamy puree. . . . Contrast enlivens your eating experience.

Condiments are a good way to vary favorite soups. I made a Spring Green Soup (p. 278) and served it one day with a spoonful of thickened yogurt and chopped fresh herbs, another day with croutons and olive oil. And when I had fresh fava beans on hand, I served that soup with sautéed favas, fruity olive oil, and croutons. Too much? No! It was terrific.

Winter squash soups are rich and slightly sweet, so they call out for tangy, moist pieces of feta cheese and sprigs of fresh cilantro, or a drop of your favorite chile sauce. And yes, I've done all three of those at once. A minestrone is so much livelier with a spoonful of fresh basil pesto dropped into the bowl, and shavings of aged Parmigiano-Reggiano on top of that. My kitchen might be all modern minimalism, but my soups can be baroque.

Many garnishes do double duty as spreads for crostini. The simple pesto you stir into soup can be elaborated with pine nuts and Parmesan to become a topping for bruschetta or a sauce for pasta; chile salsas can be dabbed onto a piece of lavash with hummus or cheese. Flexibility is the name of this game.

Here's my top ten! This is the list of my favorite soup garnishes, and after the first one they are not in any order of preference:

1. Fruity extra-virgin olive oil
2. Simple Basil Pesto (p. 436)
3. Crumbled, moist feta cheese, Cotija cheese, or *queso fresco*
4. Homemade Croutons (p. 446)
5. Simple Chipotle Sauce (p. 439) or Ancho and Guajillo Chile Puree (p. 440)
6. Chopped fresh cilantro
7. Toasted pine nuts (p. 232)
8. Pumpkinseed oil
9. Harissa (p. 444)
10. Tamari-toasted pecans or walnuts (p. 230)
11. Crème fraîche or Greek-style yogurt (pp. 317 and 502)
12. Sautéed fresh fava beans

Well, there you have it. My top ten runs to a dozen. I like dressing up my soups.

sprouted garbanzo hummus

For this hummus I use the sprouted garbanzo beans I buy at my farmers' market, and I cook them for just a few minutes before processing. Sprouted beans are fresh and alive, so they taste that way—and have the further advantage of not needing any long soaking or cooking. It's the best hummus you'll ever make, and you can have it in a hurry.

· · · MAKES ABOUT 2 CUPS · · ·

½ lb. (225 g) sprouted garbanzo beans
1 scant tsp. sea salt
2 cloves garlic
¼ cup (60 ml) tahini
4–6 Tbs. (60–90 ml) fresh lemon juice
4–6 Tbs. (60–90 ml) fruity green olive oil, plus
    more to taste

½ tsp. toasted sesame oil
Piment d'Espelette (a spicy paprika) or cayenne

· · ·

optional garnish: 2 Tbs. (30 ml) fruity green olive oil

Put the sprouted garbanzos in a stainless steel pot with about 3 cups water and ½ teaspoon salt. Bring the water to a boil, skim the foam off the top, then turn down the heat and simmer for 10 to 15 minutes. The beans should be tender but not mushy. You can cook the beans longer, but it won't make much difference to their texture.

Strain the beans, reserving the liquid, and let them cool slightly. If you like, you can run water over them and rub them gently between your fingers to loosen the skins, which can be discarded, but this is not a necessary step.

Pulse the garlic cloves in a food processor until they are minced, then add the garbanzos, tahini, 4 tablespoons each of lemon juice and olive oil, the sesame oil, a big pinch of salt, and a small pinch of spicy paprika or cayenne. Process briefly and taste. Adjust the flavor with more lemon juice,

recipe continues on next page

olive oil, and salt as needed. Hummus does need some salt for all the flavors to come into focus, but remember that salt needs a few moments to dissolve into the hummus and make itself felt, so wait a bit between additions.

If the hummus seems too thick, add 3 or 4 tablespoons of the reserved bean liquid and process again until very smooth. Texture is a matter of personal preference. Some like their hummus thick and dense, others like it to resemble a sauce. I like mine just thick enough to hold a shape.

To serve, spoon the hummus into a shallow bowl and smooth the top, then drizzle it with some fruity olive oil if you wish. Serve a basket of lightly toasted or warmed pita bread triangles with it, or any crisp or chewy bread you like. (Avoid crumbly breads!) I like to serve a platter of snap peas, endive leaves, and red bell pepper strips as well.

A few other ways . . .

Hummus seems to cry out for variations. For a while I was making a different hummus or two every week. Then I went into a classic phase: I wanted only the plain, original hummus—until I couldn't resist throwing a few chopped herbs on top, and then off I went again.

spicy paprika hummus: To the basic hummus, add a teaspoon of Pimentón de la Vera and a teaspoon of toasted ground cumin seeds. The pimentón is a spicy smoked paprika from Spain that is absolutely delicious and can now be easily ordered online.

chipotle hummus: If you have your own simple chipotle salsa on hand, the easiest way is to add a spoonful of that to the hummus. Blend it in, taste, add more if you want it spicier. But you can also open a can of chipotles in adobo, add one chile, process, taste . . . and so on.

hummus with fire-roasted red peppers: You can use red bell peppers you char and peel yourself or fire-roasted peppers from a jar; good roasted and peeled red peppers are available in most markets. Chop one or two peppers coarsely, add them to the hummus while it is still in the food processor, and pulse briefly, until you have the texture you like. I like to see small pieces of red pepper in the rosy hummus.

hummus with olives: Chopped or sliced olives go beautifully with hummus. You can use Greek Kalamata olives, Niçoise olives, or almost any kind of oil-cured olives you like. Slice about 20 medium-sized olives off their pits and stir them into the finished hummus.

hummus with fresh herbs: Fresh marjoram and oregano are both good matches for hummus, and fresh thyme is also lovely. All of these herbs marry well with the raw garlic in the hummus. Another nice combination is a lot of chopped cilantro with a tiny bit of minced jalapeño. Chop whatever herbs you are using and stir in 1 teaspoon or so. Wait a few minutes, taste, and add more until you like it, but remember that the herbal taste will become more apparent after an hour or so, as the hummus becomes infused with it.

tapenade with figs and citrus

This is one of the most delicious things I can think of to have with an aperitif on a warm summer evening. A glass of Prosecco or a chilled rosé from Tavel, a basket of breads, a bowl of tapenade—I could wait a long time for dinner.

Tapenade is also your secret weapon for making spectacular sandwiches: goat cheese and tapenade, tomato slices and tapenade, cucumber and hummus and tapenade . . .

· · · MAKES ABOUT 1 2/3 CUPS · · ·

3 oz. (90 g) dried black figs
1 cup pitted Kalamata olives (6 oz.; 180 g)
1 Tbs. drained capers
1 tsp. minced garlic
1 tsp. chopped fresh or dried rosemary
½ tsp. chopped fresh or dried thyme

¼ cup (60 ml) fruity green olive oil
2 tsp. (10 ml) fresh lemon juice
1 tsp. grated orange zest
freshly ground black pepper
sea salt, if needed

If the figs are large, cut them into halves or quarters, then put them in a small pot with about ¾ cup water. Bring the water to a boil, then turn the heat down to low, cover the pot, and leave the figs to simmer and soften for about 20 minutes. Drain the figs and reserve the liquid.

Combine all the ingredients in a food processor and pulse briefly, just enough to get a thick, chunky paste. If it seems too thick, add a few spoonfuls of the reserved fig liquid and pulse again, very briefly. The tapenade should be thick but not stiff, and full of distinct little bits of olive and fig.

It is very unlikely that the tapenade will need salt, as the olives and capers are both salty, but taste it to be sure, and add a tiny pinch of sea salt if it's needed.

Serve the tapenade with plain crostini, plain crackers, or triangles of toasted pita bread.

persian spinach spread

This is a simple and appetizing spread made mainly of spinach, in which the sweetness of caramelized onions is balanced by a touch of lemon juice and some tangy yogurt. You can use nonfat, low-fat, or whole yogurt, but be sure that it has no added starches or emulsifiers.

· · · MAKES ABOUT 3 CUPS · · ·

1½ cups (360 ml) plain yogurt

1 lb. (450 g) spinach

2 Tbs. (28 g) unsalted butter

1 large yellow onion, finely chopped (300 g)

1 tsp. sea salt, plus more to taste

2 Tbs. (30 ml) olive oil

1 clove garlic, minced

2–3 tsp. (10–15 ml) lemon juice, plus more to taste

1–2 tsp. chopped fresh oregano

freshly ground black pepper to taste

Line a sieve or a small colander with a triple layer of cheesecloth and put the yogurt in it. Let the yogurt drain over a measuring cup for an hour or so, until it is reduced by at least a third; discard the liquid. Wash the spinach and chop it coarsely; you should have 2 ½ cups.

Meanwhile, melt the butter in a nonstick skillet and cook the chopped onion with a big pinch of salt over low heat, stirring often, for at least half an hour, until it is soft and golden brown. You cannot hurry this part, or you will not get the rich sweetness you need from the onion. When the onion is caramelized, remove it from the pan and set it aside.

Add 1 tablespoon olive oil to the pan and sauté the garlic in it for 1 to 2 minutes, until it sizzles. Add the spinach and half a teaspoon salt and sauté the spinach until all the excess water has cooked

recipe continues on next page

away. Scoop the spinach out onto a board and chop it quite finely, but do not put it in a food processor—you don't want a puree.

Combine in a bowl and stir together the caramelized onion, spinach, 2 teaspoons lemon juice, 1 teaspoon oregano, the drained yogurt, the remaining tablespoon of olive oil, and black pepper to taste. Taste, and season with additional salt, pepper, lemon juice, and oregano as needed. Chill the spread for an hour or two, and serve with crackers or flatbread as an appetizer.

marbled cannellini dip with roasted tomatoes

This is a seductive combination of creamy, slightly garlicky white beans and dark, slow-roasted tomatoes. There's not much work to it, but it takes some time while the tomatoes slowly caramelize in the oven and the beans simmer on the stove.

I always start with dried cannellini and simmer them until tender. There's no work involved after you put the beans in the pot with the water, and it seems worth it to have the best flavor. In a pinch, a good can of cannellini can be called into service, as long as you rinse the beans well in several changes of water.

· · · MAKES ABOUT 2 CUPS · · ·

1 cup (200 g) dried cannellini, to make 1½ cups (350 g) cooked cannellini
4–5 large fresh sage leaves or 1 Tbs. dried sage
4 cloves garlic, peeled
1½ tsp. sea salt, plus more to taste
2 lbs. (900 g) ripe red tomatoes

4 Tbs. (60 ml) olive oil
1½ Tbs. (22 ml) fresh lemon juice, plus more to taste
1½ tsp. chopped fresh oregano
10 Kalamata olives, slivered
freshly ground black pepper

Put the dried cannellini in a medium pot with 6 cups water, the sage, and 3 whole peeled garlic cloves. Bring the water to a boil, lower the heat, and simmer the beans for an hour or two, until they are completely soft. In the last 10 minutes, add 1 teaspoon salt. Drain the beans and discard the sage leaves and garlic.

While the beans cook, preheat the oven to 275°.

Wash the tomatoes and cut them in halves or quarters. Place them skin side down on a non-stick baking sheet, drizzle them with a tablespoon of olive oil, and sprinkle them lightly with salt.

recipe continues on next page

Roast the tomatoes slowly for 2 to 2 ½ hours. They will be reduced in size, and the caramelized juices will be dark, perhaps even charred.

Allow the tomatoes to cool until you can handle them, then scrape the pulp gently off the skins into a bowl. Discard the skins. You will have about ⅔ cup of dark, concentrated tomato pulp; chop it coarsely if you see big pieces.

Meanwhile, mince the remaining clove of garlic. Combine the cooked cannellini, the remaining 3 tablespoons olive oil, the minced garlic, the lemon juice, the oregano, and a pinch of salt in the food processor and process until fairly smooth. Add the olives and process for a few seconds only, to chop a few of the olives coarsely. Taste, and correct the seasoning with more salt, a dash of pepper, or a little more lemon juice if needed.

Pour the bean mixture into a shallow bowl, and spoon all or some of the roasted tomatoes in the center, to your taste. Serve with plain crostini, crackers, focaccia, or toasted pita triangles.

Another way . . .

You can skip the step of cooking dried beans if you like and open a 15 oz. can of cooked cannellini. Drain the beans and rinse them well in running water to get all the salty liquid off them, then proceed as you would with freshly cooked beans.

lima bean spread

This is the easiest little dip in the world, good plain or dressed up. Start with dried lima beans that you have cooked yourself if possible, but you can use canned limas, well drained and rinsed, in an emergency.

· · · MAKES ABOUT 1½ CUPS · · ·

1½ cups (350 g) cooked lima beans, drained
2 small cloves garlic, minced
2 Tbs. (30 ml) olive oil
2 Tbs. (30 ml) fresh lemon juice

1 Tbs. chopped fresh oregano or 1½ tsp. dried oregano
½ tsp. sea salt, or to taste
freshly ground black pepper

Combine everything except the salt and pepper in the container of a food processor and pulse for a few seconds.

Add the salt a pinch at a time, pulsing briefly each time, until you have enough. Go slowly and taste. This is especially important if you are using canned lima beans, as they may be salty to begin with.

Grind in a lot of black pepper. Taste, and correct the flavors by adjusting quantities slightly if you like.

Serve the bean spread with crackers, toasted pita triangles, crostini, or raw vegetables for dipping. Cucumber slices and strips of red bell pepper are a good pairing with this spread.

Another way . . .

For a more herbal spread, add a big handful of chopped fresh flat-leaf parsley and add a little more lemon juice. For something with more texture, add chopped cured black olives or roasted red peppers.

eggplant and roasted garlic pesto

The rich taste and fragrance of oven-roasted garlic permeates this spread and marries beautifully with the roasted eggplant. Have this pesto as an appetizer, drop a spoonful of it on top of a salad, or make your sandwich much more interesting by spreading some of this on the bread.

· · · MAKES ABOUT 1½ CUPS · · ·

2 medium globe eggplants (2 lbs.; 900 g)
1 small head garlic
1½ tsp. chopped fresh thyme
1 teaspoon cumin seeds, toasted and ground
½ tsp. sea salt, plus more to taste

freshly ground black pepper to taste
1 Tbs. (15 ml) fresh lemon juice, plus more to taste
1 tsp. (5 ml) balsamic vinegar
1 Tbs. (15 ml) olive oil

Preheat the oven to 400°.

Pierce the eggplants in a few places with a fork, place them on a baking sheet, and roast them for about 1 hour, or until they are soft and their skins are dark. The roasting time will vary with the size and shape of the eggplants.

At the same time, roast the garlic: slice the top off the head with a very sharp knife, place the head on a square of aluminum foil, and drizzle a little olive oil on the cut surface. Wrap the foil up around the garlic, crimping the top to seal. Roast it for 30 to 45 minutes, or until the garlic is soft. Allow it to cool, then pull apart the cloves and squeeze out as much of the soft garlic as you need.

When the eggplants are done, allow them to cool until you can handle them, then slice them open and scoop the flesh out of the skins. If you find pockets of very dark seeds, remove and discard them, as they could be bitter; younger eggplants will have lighter seeds, which are fine.

Allow the roasted eggplant to drain in a colander or sieve for a few minutes, then chop the flesh coarsely. Add the soft roasted garlic to the eggplant, chopping again to incorporate. Stir in all the remaining ingredients, taste, and correct the seasoning with more salt, pepper, or lemon juice as needed.

Serve cool, with plain crackers or crostini and a bowl of olives.

simple basil pesto

When we hear *pesto*, we think immediately of basil, lots of it, with olive oil, garlic, pine nuts, and Parmesan cheese. That is the classic pesto Genovese, which has become a staple of our kitchens. But in fact pesto is simply anything that is ground up with a mortar and pestle, and these days more often in a blender or food processor.

Pesto can be made with parsley and walnuts; it can be made with roasted red peppers or with sun-dried tomatoes; and all are good. A savory, intensely flavored pesto is lovely to have on hand, as it turns plain crostini or crackers into an appetizing nibble to serve with an aperitif or to have alongside a soup. A pesto can elevate a plain goat cheese or a home-made yogurt cheese to something special. And it can be the perfect condiment for certain vegetable soups.

The pesto I like to spoon into a minestrone is an ultra-simple version. I combine some good olive oil in a blender with lots of fresh basil leaves, a spoonful of chopped garlic, and a bit of sea salt and blend it for less than a minute. Here is the formula for my stripped-down pesto. The classic version follows.

· · · MAKES ABOUT ½ CUP · · ·

1 bunch fresh basil leaves (2 oz; 60 g)

2 medium cloves garlic, coarsely chopped

½ cup (120 ml) fruity green olive oil

½ tsp. sea salt, plus more to taste

Strip the basil leaves off their stems, wash them, and dry them in a salad spinner or tea towels. You should have about 2 cups dry leaves, loosely packed.

Drop the garlic into the blender or food processor and give it a spin, then add the olive oil and process again, briefly. The garlic should be pretty well minced. Add the basil leaves and salt, and process until the basil is either finely minced or pureed into the oil. Taste and correct the salt if you want a bit more.

This pesto is thinner than the traditional one. It becomes thicker in the refrigerator, but at room temperature it will pour from a spoon in a thick stream. It is just the right consistency to garnish a soup.

The traditional way . . .

In a food processor, combine the ingredients above with ½ cup freshly grated Parmesan cheese and ½ cup lightly toasted pine nuts (technique on p. 232), and pulse until the pesto has a thick, even consistency, with just a bit of texture. This version makes about 1 cup.

parsley and walnut pesto

Spread this pesto on baguette slices or bruschetta, drop a spoonful into a bowl of soup, toss it with angel hair pasta, or slather it between ripe tomatoes in a spectacular sandwich.

· · · MAKES ABOUT 1⅓ CUPS · · ·

1 bunch fresh flat-leaf parsley (3 oz; 90 g)

2 cloves garlic

1 cup (90 g) walnut pieces

½ cup (120 ml) fruity or peppery olive oil, plus more if needed

2 tsp. (10 ml) fresh lemon juice

¾ tsp. sea salt, plus more to taste

· · ·

garnish: fruity or peppery olive oil

Wash the parsley, dry it in a salad spinner or paper towels, and remove any tough stems. When the leaves are trimmed and clean, pack them well in a measuring cup to be sure you have about 2 cups.

Combine the garlic and walnuts in the bowl of a food processor and pulse briefly, just to chop. Add the parsley, olive oil, lemon juice, and sea salt, and pulse again until everything is combined but not pureed.

Taste the pesto and add more salt, a pinch at a time, as you pulse again. Stop as soon as you have the flavor and texture you like. I prefer to leave the pesto somewhat coarse. If you want a smoother pesto, process a little more; if you want it thinner, add a little more olive oil.

Mound the pesto in a shallow bowl and, just before serving, drizzle with a bit more oil.

Another way . . .

Add ½ cup (10 g) chopped fresh mint leaves to the parsley leaves for an even more vibrant flavor. The mint will not announce itself; it will just make the parsley seem more interesting.

simple chipotle sauce

It's a simple sauce to make, but there is nothing simple about the flavor of chipotle chiles—spicy and smoky, with a memory of the ripe, fresh chile behind it all.

··· MAKES 1–1¼ CUPS ···

2–3 dried chipotle chiles (½ oz.; 13 g)
1 medium tomato (4 oz.; 120 g)
½ yellow onion (4 oz.; 120 g)
2 cloves garlic

½ tsp. sea salt, plus more to taste
1 tsp. cumin seeds, toasted and ground
 (optional)

Put the chipotle chiles in a small saucepan with about a cup of water, at least enough to cover them, and simmer for 5 minutes. Turn off the heat and leave the chiles to soak, covered, for 20 minutes. Take out the chiles and pull out and discard their stems and seeds. Reserve the liquid.

Peel and chop the tomato, chop the onion, and peel the garlic cloves.

Return the torn chiles to the liquid in the pot and add the tomato, onion, garlic, and salt. There should be enough water just to cover everything; if not, add a little. Simmer the vegetables, covered, for 20 to 30 minutes, or until everything is soft.

Transfer the vegetables and liquid to the blender. Allow the mixture to cool slightly, then puree it until it's fairly smooth. If you have an excessive amount of liquid, use only as much as you need to make a sauce the consistency of thin applesauce.

Taste the sauce, and add more salt as needed and the cumin, if you like. Remember, chiles need salt to bring out their flavor. Although it has heat, a cooked salsa of this type will taste bland until the salt is at the right level.

ancho and guajillo chile puree

A good, basic chile puree is a useful thing to have on hand and easy to make. It is one of the simplest ways to add a little heat or chile flavor to a soup. And if you add some chopped cilantro and green onion, you've instantly got a table salsa of top quality.

Why make your own? There are good reasons. Commercial salsas vary tremendously in style, content, and heat. Even if they are tasty, they blend many ingredients and can introduce flavors that you might not want when adding chiles to a soup. Bottled hot sauces, such as Tabasco, are all about heat, and you generally can't use more than a few drops—not enough to get the rich and interesting flavor of the chile itself. But if you make a simple puree of dried chiles and garlic, you can moderate the heat level and have a great-tasting puree to use as an ingredient in soups, as a condiment, or as a base for your homemade salsa.

Many varieties of chiles are commonly available dried. For my basic puree, I use ancho chiles for their mild and fruity flavor and a little guajillo chile for more intense flavor and some heat. For more heat, add more guajillo to the mix. And remember, this takes just a little longer than making a smoothie.

· · · MAKES 1½ CUPS · · ·

4–5 dried ancho chiles (2 oz.; 60 g)
1–2 dried guajillo chiles (1 oz.; 30 g)
3–4 cloves garlic, peeled and sliced

½ tsp. sea salt, plus more to taste
2 tsp. cumin seeds, toasted and ground
  (optional)

Pull the stems out of the dried chiles, tear open the pods, and remove the seeds. Combine the torn chiles, garlic, and salt in a small pot with about 1 ½ cups of water and bring the water to a boil. Lower the heat and let the chiles simmer, covered, for about half an hour, or until both chiles and garlic are soft. Check them near the end of that time to make sure the water has not cooked away, and add a bit more water if needed.

Allow the mixture to cool to lukewarm, then put it in a blender, with the cumin if you like, and enough of the liquid to make a sauce that is thick but not stiff. Puree until smooth, adding a few teaspoons of water if needed. Taste the puree on a cracker or a piece of plain bread, and add salt if needed.

Use this basic puree for stirring into soups, scrambled eggs, or a pot of beans. It can be stored in a jar in the refrigerator for a couple of weeks, and can be made into a table salsa with the addition of a few oven-roasted tomatillos or some chopped cilantro, or both.

Many other ways . . .

increase the amount of guajillo chiles for a hotter, stronger puree.

add one or two chipotle chiles for a smoky flavor.

vary the formula with Santa Fe chiles, chiles negros, poblanos, or even some dried red serranos if you want a really fiery puree.

table salsa

This salsa represents the most basic type of cooked salsa, the delicious everyday condiment found on thousands of kitchen tables throughout Mexico and the American Southwest. The ingredients and the technique are perfectly simple: roasted tomatillos, simmered chiles, blender. The same formula can be applied to any combination of chiles you like.

If you are not familiar with chiles and have not made your own salsa before, begin here: walk before you run.

This particular combination of chiles makes a mild but flavorful salsa. I like to drop it by the spoonful into squash soup, corn soup, potato soup . . . or on scrambled eggs or a quesadilla. If you want a hotter salsa, add guajillos, take away anchos. If you want a really hot salsa, move up to serrano chiles or habaneros.

· · · MAKES ABOUT 2½ CUPS · · ·

12 oz. (350 g) tomatillos
3 dried ancho chiles (40 g)
2 dried guajillo chiles (30 g)
2 dried chiles negros (15 g)
3 whole cloves garlic, peeled
1 tsp. sea salt, plus more to taste

2–3 tsp. cumin seeds, toasted and ground
· · ·

to add before serving:
chopped cilantro
chopped green onion

Preheat the oven to 425°.

Take the tomatillos out of their dry husks and wash them. If they are very large—that is, larger than a walnut—cut them in half or in quarters. Spread them in one layer on a foil-lined baking pan and roast them until their skins are blackened, 15 to 20 minutes. Turn them over and blacken the other side, another 10 to 15 minutes. When they are mushy and charred, scrape them into a bowl—and remember, the blackened bits are good!

Meanwhile, rinse the chile pods, pull out their stems, tear them into pieces, and shake out the seeds. Combine the torn chiles, 2 cups water, the garlic cloves, and 1 teaspoon salt in a stainless steel pot and simmer, covered, for about half an hour, or until all the chiles are completely soft.

Add the tomatillos to the cooked chiles and puree the mixture in a blender, working in batches. Stir in the cumin and taste for salt, adding more if needed. Chiles need salt; they are flat without it, so use your taste buds here.

Now you have a salsa that can be used for quesadillas, as a condiment in many soups, or as a dip with tortilla chips—and it will keep for a couple of weeks in a jar in your refrigerator. If you want to make your salsa more fabulous, add anywhere from ½ cup to 1 cup roughly chopped fresh cilantro and ½ cup or so of chopped green onions. But once you've added fresh herbs, the salsa will last for only a few days and is really best the first day, so add these greens when you plan to use the salsa, not before.

harissa

Harissa is a delightfully fiery North African condiment. This thick, deep red sauce has complexity with its heat and an undercurrent of sweet spice. It's bound together with olive oil, which gives it a subtle richness. In Morocco and Tunisia it is made with peppers common to that region, but I make a delicious harissa with three easily available Mexican chiles. It is hot enough to make an impact, but not so hot that the fruitiness of the chiles is lost.

Use this as a finishing touch for winter squash soups, lentil soups, and black bean soups. It's also fabulous to have a little bowl of this alongside a bigger bowl of hummus, or to put a dab of harissa on top of the goat cheese on your crostini.

$\cdots$ MAKES 1½ CUPS $\cdots$

4 dried chiles negros (1 oz.; 28 g)
5–6 dried guajillo chiles (1 oz.; 28g)
6–7 dried chipotle chiles (¾ oz.; 21 g)
1 Tbs. caraway seeds

1 Tbs. coriander seeds
4–5 cloves garlic, peeled
2 tsp. sea salt
3 Tbs. (45 ml) olive oil

Pull the stems out of the chile pods, tear them open, and pull out and discard the seeds. Rinse the torn pods and put them in a small pot with about 2 cups water, enough to cover them. Simmer the chiles, covered, for 5 minutes, then turn off the heat and leave them to soak in the hot water for at least half an hour, but preferably until they have cooled to room temperature. They will absorb a lot of the water.

Transfer the softened chiles to a blender with ⅔ cup of the remaining liquid and process until you have a puree. If you don't have that much liquid left, add a little more water, just enough to enable the blender to do its work.

Press the thick puree through a medium sieve and discard the skins and seeds that remain.

Combine the caraway and coriander seeds in a small dry skillet and toast them over medium heat, stirring almost constantly, for a few minutes—just until they release their toasty, spicy fragrance. Grind the toasted seeds finely in a mortar or a spice grinder.

Mince the garlic cloves in a food processor. Add the strained chile puree, ground spices, salt, and olive oil, and process briefly to combine. You should have a puree about the consistency of thick ketchup.

This makes quite a lot of harissa, which is an intense condiment. But harissa can be kept in the refrigerator in a sealed jar for several weeks, and longer if a thin layer of olive oil is poured over the top.

Another way . . .

For a sweeter and somewhat milder condiment, soak an ounce or two of sliced sun-dried tomatoes in hot water while you are soaking the chiles, and add them to the mix in the food processor.

a note about handling chiles: After handling chiles, be sure to wash all your bowls and utensils very thoroughly. Even more important, wash your hands properly. I find that the only way to get the chile off my fingers is first to rub my hands down very well with oil—any kind will do—and then to wash the oil off with soap and hot water.

croutons

Making homemade croutons is just an *utz* harder than falling off a log.

Croutons can be made from almost any yeast bread—baguettes, sourdough loaves, whole-grain loaves, rye bread, pumpernickel, ciabatta, olive bread . . . whatever you have on hand.

HERE'S HOW TO MAKE BASIC CROUTONS . . .

Take day-old or several-days-old bread and cut it up into cubes, any size up to 1 inch square. Spray the bread cubes with olive oil or drizzle olive oil over them in a large bowl and quickly toss them until all are slightly moistened. For half a baguette (about 200 g) you might need 2 or 3 tablespoons (30–45 ml) of oil, but the exact amount will depend on your taste; more oil means richer and crispier croutons. Sprinkle on some crushed sea salt and toss again.

Spread the bread cubes on a baking sheet and bake them in a moderate oven (about 350°) until they are light golden brown and crisp. The time will vary with the density of the bread and the size of the cubes, but figure on 10 to 20 minutes. Keep an eye on them, as they can burn quickly once they are dry.

Voila! Homemade croutons for your next bowl of soup.

Other ways . . .

garlic croutons: Heat a few spoonfuls of olive oil in a large sauté pan and add a tablespoon of minced garlic, more if you're a garlic fiend. Warm the garlic in the oil for about a minute, stirring constantly, then throw in about 4 cups (200 g) of soft bread cubes and immediately toss, toss, toss. Sprinkle on a liberal amount of salt and toss again. All the bread cubes should be touched by oil and garlic. Spread the bread cubes on a baking sheet and bake in a moderate oven until they are golden brown and crisp.

herbed croutons: I am especially fond of these. I warm 2 or 3 tablespoons (30–45 ml) olive oil in the big pan and throw in a couple of teaspoons of herbes de Provence, or I add minced fresh thyme, rosemary, sage, or other herbs to the oil. I stir the herbs around in the warm oil for a minute or so, then add 4 cups of bread cubes and toss, toss, toss until all the bread is coated with oil and herbs. Add salt, toss again, and bake as above.

note: Croutons become even more crisp as they cool off, which happens quickly. They keep very well for days or weeks in a tightly sealed jar or canister.

jeri's spiced nuts

For years my friend Jeri Oshima has made this simple version of the always popular spiced nuts. I persuaded her to tell me exactly what she did, and now I'm going public with it. Sorry, Jeri—too good not to share!

The technique is straightforward; it's all done in a big pan on top of the stove, and it only takes about 20 minutes from start to finish. You can use either butter or olive oil. I find that the olive oil slightly lifts the savory-spicy side, while the butter tends to underline the caramelized sugar, but both are delicious—and honestly, could I tell in a blind tasting? I'm not sure.

Serve these nuts with a glass of champagne or any aperitif and watch them vanish.

· · · MAKES 2 CUPS · · ·

2 cups (240 g) shelled pecans or almonds, or a
 combination
1½ Tbs. butter or olive oil

3½ Tbs. (40 g) sugar
½ tsp. cayenne
½–¾ tsp. sea salt

Line a large baking sheet with a piece of parchment.

Combine the nuts and the butter or oil in a very large, heavy-bottomed sauté pan. The size of the pan matters, as maximum contact between nuts and pan is needed for even heating and melting; too small a pan will make the job harder. Stir the nuts over medium heat for about 4 minutes.

Mix together the sugar, cayenne, and salt and sprinkle them over the nuts in the pan. Stir gently over medium heat for another 8 to 10 minutes, or until all the sugar has caramelized and coated the nuts. You can raise the heat at the very end if you see bits of sugar that still have not fully melted, but remove the pan from the heat the moment the fat begins to smoke.

Spread the nuts immediately on the baking sheet and allow them to cool. They will crisp up as they cool. When the nuts have cooled, break them apart. If you find any big lumps of hardened caramel, simply discard them. Don't worry, you'll have plenty of flavor.

Store the nuts in an airtight container. They will keep well for a few weeks, but I rarely can keep them around that long.

grilled goat cheese sandwich

This is the best grilled cheese sandwich I've tasted. It's full of sunny summer flavor, but I first made it one rainy day, when comfort food seemed in order. Eating it alongside a bowl of garbanzo bean soup, my friend and I experienced one of those unexpected moments of culinary ecstasy. So simple, so perfect.

The semi-sun-dried tomatoes are a Sicilian wonder, recently discovered by a good friend who earned many gourmet points when she brought them over to my house. The tomatoes are dried in the sun, but not all the way, so they don't become leathery. Then the semisoft tomatoes are marinated in olive oil and herbs. If you can find a jar of these, snap them up—they're worth the price. Otherwise, take your favorite marinated sun-dried tomatoes and cut them into very thin strips.

· · · MAKES 1 SANDWICH · · ·

for each sandwich

2 smallish slices French or sourdough bread
(1½ oz.; 45 g)
1 rounded tsp. basil pesto
1 oz. (30 g) Montrachet cheese or other fresh
white goat cheese

1–2 marinated semi-sun-dried tomato halves,
cut in strips
olive oil for the pan

If you are cutting slices from a baguette, cut on a slant. You want medium to small pieces of bread, no more than ½-inch thick.

Spread one slice of bread with the pesto, the other with the goat cheese. Arrange the slices of marinated tomatoes on top of the cheese and cover with the pesto-smeared slice.

Heat a teaspoon or two of olive oil in a pan or on a griddle and cook the sandwich on one side, pressing down occasionally with a spatula, until the bread is golden brown and crusty. Add another teaspoon of oil to the pan and turn the sandwich over, repeating the process until the other side is golden brown as well. The cooking time will probably be about 4 minutes on a side, but will vary with the specific heat of the pan or griddle.

I like to place a small cast-iron lid, smaller than the pan, on top of the sandwich as it cooks. The lid acts as a weight, keeping the sandwich pressed down so it grills evenly. Gentle pressing with a spatula is also fine but takes more attention.

Serve immediately!

sara's spinach pie

I call this Sara's Spinach Pie because my friend Sara showed me how to make it. She calls it Andy's Spinach Pie, because she learned it from her husband, Andy. He calls it Grandma Anna's Spinach Pie. His Grandma Anna learned it somewhere in Turkey, but I don't go back more than three steps in the provenance of recipes. Further back than that, all is one in the mist of time.

Basically, this pie is a spanakopita without the crust, or the part of the quiche that you really want: the inside. It keeps well for several days in the fridge, and it's good cold as well as warm.

· · · SERVES 6—8 · · ·

12 oz. (350 g) ricotta cheese, drained
2 large yellow onions (about 1¼ lbs.; 550 g)
5 Tbs. (75 ml) olive oil, plus more if needed
sea salt
2 lbs. (900 g) fresh spinach
1 lb. (450 g) feta cheese

5 oz. (150 g) Parmigiano-Reggiano cheese,
    grated
5 large eggs, lightly beaten
freshly ground black pepper
chopped fresh dill to taste or 1 teaspoon
    chopped fresh oregano (optional)

Put the ricotta cheese into a colander lined with cheesecloth and set it over a bowl to drain.

Finely chop the onions. Heat 3 tablespoons olive oil in a large nonstick pan and cook the onions with a pinch of salt over low heat, stirring fairly often, until they are soft and beginning to turn golden, 30 to 40 minutes. While the onions are cooking, wash the spinach in several changes of water, getting rid of all the grit.

When the onions are caramelized, remove them from the pan into a large mixing bowl. Add another 1 tablespoon oil to the pan and as much spinach as the pan will hold. Sauté the spinach over medium heat until it wilts completely and all the excess liquid cooks away, then remove it to another bowl. Continue sautéing spinach this way in batches, adding the remaining tablespoon of oil by drops as needed, until all of the spinach is cooked. Coarsely chop the cooked spinach and add it to the onions.

Preheat the oven to 325°.

Rinse the feta cheese briefly in a bowl of cool water, then drain it well on paper towels and crumble it into small pieces. Mix together the crumbled feta, drained ricotta, and grated Parmigiano-Reggiano (you should have 2 cups of Parmigiano) and stir in the beaten eggs, along with a pinch of salt and a generous amount of freshly ground pepper.

Combine the cheese mixture with the spinach and onions and mix everything very thoroughly; your clean hands are the best tool for this. Taste and add salt only if needed, remembering that feta cheese and Parmigiano-Reggiano both are quite salty. Mix in the dill or oregano if you like.

Spoon the mixture into a lightly oiled shallow casserole or gratin dish, about 9 inches by 13 inches. Drizzle with a few drops of olive oil if you like. Bake the pie for about half an hour, then raise the heat to 350° and bake for another 20 minutes. Check the top, and if it is becoming very dark, cover loosely with a sheet of aluminum foil. Continue baking for another 10 to 15 minutes, until the center of the pie feels firm. Total baking time is about an hour or a bit more.

Allow the pie to cool for at least half an hour before cutting it into squares to serve. This is delicious warm or cool, and goes well with all sorts of Mediterranean foods. Add a tomato soup, some black olives, and a good piece of bread and you'll have a perfect meal.

tortilla española with charred red peppers

Tortilla española is ubiquitous in Spain, and one of the great examples of how a few simple ingredients can combine to make a dish of enduring appeal. It is a flat omelet made of potatoes, onions, and eggs, cooked to a savory golden brown in olive oil. That's all. But when those eggs and potatoes are good, when that olive oil is flavorful, there is nothing I'd rather eat with a glass of red wine at a tapa bar, or with my café con leche in the morning for breakfast.

This variation adds charred sweet red peppers to the classic mix of potatoes and onions. You can use green bell peppers if you don't have the red ones, or use roasted and peeled red peppers from a jar. As for the potatoes, I always use Yukon Gold potatoes for this tortilla now. I've tried many varieties, and these are just the best.

· · · SERVES 6, MORE IF SERVED AS AN APPETIZER WITH OTHER FOODS · · ·

1½ lbs. (700 g) Yukon Gold potatoes
2½ Tbs. (40 ml) olive oil
2 large yellow onions, chopped (500 g)
1½ tsp. sea salt, plus more to taste

freshly ground black pepper
2 large red bell peppers (400 g) or ¾ cup (200 g) roasted and peeled peppers
8 large eggs

Scrub the potatoes well and cut them into ½-inch dice. Heat 2 tablespoons oil in a large nonstick pan. Add the potatoes and the chopped onions, along with a teaspoon of salt and some freshly ground pepper. Cook over medium heat, stirring often, until the potatoes and onions are tender and browning, at least 25 to 30 minutes. Taste, and add more salt if it's needed.

Meanwhile, char the peppers under a broiler until their skins are blistered and blackened all over. Put the charred peppers in a paper bag for a few minutes to let them sweat, then peel, stem, and seed them. Cut the peppers into ½-inch pieces and add them to the potatoes and onions. If you are using peppers from a jar, drain them, rinse them, and pat them dry, then proceed as above.

Beat the eggs, adding about ½ teaspoon salt and pepper to taste, and stir the cooked vegetables into the eggs.

Wipe the pan clean and add the remaining ½ tablespoon olive oil. Heat the oil, then pour in the egg and vegetable mixture. Turn the heat very low, cover the pan, and cook until the eggs are completely set, about 10 minutes.

Loosen the edges of the tortilla with a thin spatula, making sure it slides freely in the pan. Cover the pan with a flat lid, grasp the pan and lid firmly with pot holders, pressing them together, and invert the pan, letting the tortilla drop onto the lid. Slide the tortilla back into the pan and cook it on the other side for another 4 to 5 minutes, enough to brown that side lightly as well, then slide it out or invert it onto a serving platter.

The tortilla can be served hot, warm, at room temperature, or cool. Cut it in thick wedges or in thin ones, depending on how much other food is being served.

black bean quesadillas

Quesadillas are the food my kids lived on through most of grade school, the one thing they were always willing to eat. It is the easy, infinitely adaptable tortilla version of the grilled cheese sandwich. The most basic quesadilla is a flour tortilla folded over some melted cheese and toasted lightly on both sides. From there, the variations are endless.

This quesadilla is the basic version with delicious refried black beans added, along with a little salsa, the most frequent addition to any quesadilla.

· · · SERVES 6 · · ·

for the refried beans

2 cups (400 g) cooked black beans
1 medium yellow onion (250 g)
2 Tbs. (30 ml) olive oil
sea salt
2 cloves garlic, minced

½ cup (25 g) chopped cilantro
½ tsp. cumin seeds, toasted and ground
¼ tsp. spicy smoked paprika
2–3 Tbs. (30–45 ml) Table Salsa (p. 442) or
    Simple Chipotle Sauce (p. 439) (optional)

for the quesadillas

6 whole-wheat tortillas (180 g)
6 oz. (180 g) grated jack cheese or crumbled
    queso fresco

Simple Chipotle Sauce or other salsa

To make the refried beans, it is ideal to start with black beans you have cooked yourself—they taste much better than canned beans and are no trouble to cook as long as you allow the time for them to simmer. But in a pinch you can use canned beans.

Finely chop the onion and sauté it in the olive oil with a pinch of salt, stirring over medium heat, for about 5 minutes. Add the minced garlic, lower the heat, and continue cooking, stirring occasionally, for another 8 to 10 minutes.

Add the cooked black beans with about ¾ cup of their cooking liquid (if you are using canned beans, add some vegetable broth or water), the cilantro, cumin, and paprika. Cook the beans for 10 to 12 minutes, mashing them a little with a potato masher. They should have the consistency of a soft paste, with some of the beans smashed and others whole. Add salt to taste (this depends on how salty the beans are to start with) and, if you like, a few tablespoons of salsa.

To assemble your quesadillas, first lightly heat the tortillas on a griddle or in a pan to soften them. Spread about 2 heaping tablespoons of the beans over half of each tortilla and sprinkle an ounce of cheese over that. Spoon on as much salsa as you like.

Fold the tortilla over the filling and cook the quesadillas in batches in a hot pan or on a griddle, about 1 ½ minutes on a side, or until they are nicely browned and hot through. A large pan should hold 2 or 3 quesadillas at a time, and if you cover the pan, the cheese will melt a little faster.

Serve the quesadillas hot, with additional salsa. Cut them into wedges if you like.

salads for summer and winter

Salad of Baby Arugula, Aged Jack Cheese, and Asian Pears

Barley Salad with Corn and Zucchini • **V**

Chopped Salad with French Green Lentils

Cucumber, Rice, and Fresh Herb Salad

Summer Chopped Salad with Grilled Halloumi

Heirloom Tomato Salad

Kale Salad with Cranberries and Walnuts • **V**

Red Cabbage and Apple Salad • **V**

Brown Rice and Chinese Cabbage Salad • **V**

Lentil and Spinach Salad • **V**

Napa Cabbage Slaw • **V**

a salad of mixed greens

A plate of fresh mixed greens thoughtfully put together with the freshest seasonal ingredients can be a delight, and is endlessly variable.

Start by considering the balance of spicy to mild. Peppery arugula and watercress, pleasantly bitter radicchio, and baby mustard greens are all assertive flavors. I sometimes make a salad of only arugula, or arugula with shreds of radicchio. I dress it with a fruity olive oil and add slices of crisp Fuyu persimmon, Asian pear, or tangerine sections.

More often, I combine strong flavors with mild. Sweet butter lettuces, Belgian endive, hearts of romaine, red oak-leaf lettuce—the list varies with the season. Baby spinach leaves are always tasty, and don't overlook the loopy, tender shoots of sweet pea vines.

Greens that we think of as cooking vegetables can be excellent in raw salads when they are babies. Tiny bok choy and young kale or chard, cut into strips, add body and interest to the mix. And consider raw, bright green asparagus sliced into thin ribbons, or first-of-season turnips cut into thin white discs, or whole sugar snap peas.

Radishes, paper-thin shavings of fennel bulb, cherry tomatoes, and avocados are regular players. And fresh herbs—basil leaves, fennel tops, dill, mint leaves, and cilantro sprigs—all bring explosively bright flavor to salads.

Remember that salads love accessories. Mix in some fruit. Make a delicious slaw of endive and radicchio with Fuji apples, or mix thin-sliced dried pears with pecans and watercress. Nuts provide crunch and richness: walnuts, plain or caramelized; chopped almonds; toasted pine nuts. I also like tamari-toasted pumpkin seeds.

And glorious cheese: crumbles of Roquefort and curls of Parmigiano-Reggiano are old friends, but try shredding in some aged jack cheese or a very sharp cheddar, or pull apart a soft burrata and lay it gently over the top of your glistening, leafy mix.

A salad made with flavorful ingredients needs only a subtle touch of oil and vinegar, and a dusting of sea salt. My most frequent choice is fruity extra-virgin olive oil from California or Italy, and a discreet splash of good wine vinegar. But for a salad of mild-flavored greens, such as spinach, a peppery olive oil might be just the thing. I also love pumpkinseed oil from Austria, and in certain salads I like to add a few drops of toasted sesame seed oil.

AND THE SUBSTANTIAL SALAD . . .

Sometimes mixed greens become a bed for an interesting topping, and thus make the leap to a dish of substance. Tuscan white beans that have been simmered with sage and garlic are excellent on a salad of spicy-bitter greens. Black beans spiked with salsa are marvelous ladled over crisp romaine, cilantro, and sweet onion. Roasted or grilled vegetables are good with all greens, as are cooked grains such as wheat berries, farro, rice, and quinoa.

In hot weather, a heftier salad can be partnered with a lighter soup to make an interesting meal. With that idea in mind, in this chapter I share four of my favorite chopped salads for the summer season, as well as a ravishing arrangement of heirloom tomatoes.

In fall and winter we make salads of earthier, hardier ingredients, those vegetables and fruits that shine in cold weather. Cabbages come into their own, apples are crisp and juicy, and freshly harvested walnuts are sweet. The salads and slaws in this group are nourishing and hearty, and bring welcome refreshment into the dark season.

salad of baby arugula, aged jack cheese, and asian pears

Here is a perennial favorite of mine, the irresistible combination of arugula, sharp cheese, and sweet Asian pears. Other fruits can be used in place of the Asian pears; apples and Fuyu persimmons immediately come to mind. Asparagus can be deleted in the winter, and avocado added. It's a green salad that works all year round.

Asian pears are one of the few fruits I know that taste best when chilled, so keep them in the refrigerator until you're ready to use them.

· · · SERVES 6 · · ·

8–10 cups (450 g) lightly packed very tender young arugula

1 medium fennel bulb

1 small bunch asparagus

2 medium Asian pears, chilled (350 g)

⅔ cup (75 g) coarsely grated or shaved dry Monterey jack cheese

fruity green olive oil or walnut oil

sherry vinegar

sea salt if needed

· · ·

optional garnish: chopped, lightly toasted walnuts or Jeri's Spiced Nuts (p. 448)

Trim any long stems from the arugula, wash it, and spin it in a salad spinner. If the leaves are tiny, leave them whole. If longer, take them in bunches and cut them in half.

Trim the fennel bulb and quarter it lengthwise, cutting out the core, then slice it crosswise into paper-thin slivers. Trim the asparagus and cut it on a radical slant into very thin slices. Quarter and core the Asian pears and cut them crosswise into thin slices.

In an ample bowl, toss together the arugula, fennel, asparagus, sliced pears, and grated cheese.

Drizzle on a small amount of olive or walnut oil and toss again. Add a few drops of a good sherry vinegar. Toss again and taste. Add salt only if it is needed—the cheese may provide enough.

Adjust the amounts of oil and vinegar to your taste; the leaves should be shiny, but there should be no residue of oil in the bottom of the bowl. Toss the salad one more time and serve. You can sprinkle nuts on top of each serving if you like.

barley salad with corn and zucchini

Barley provides the sturdy, chewy foundation for all the exuberant flavors of summer in this chopped salad. Pair this savory melange with an easy fruit soup for a beautiful hot-day meal.

· · · SERVES 6 · · ·

1 cup (200 g) pearl barley, uncooked

2 tsp. salt, plus more to taste

12 oz. (350 g) tomatoes

12 oz. (350 g) zucchini

3 Tbs. (45 ml) olive oil

3 cloves garlic, minced

4 Tbs. (60 ml) fresh lemon juice

2 ears fresh sweet corn (200 g)

1–2 Tbs. minced red onion

a small handful of fresh basil leaves

¼ cup (45 g) coarsely chopped oil-cured olives

1 Tbs. (15 ml) balsamic vinegar

freshly ground black pepper

Wash the barley in several changes of water, until the water is no longer cloudy. Cook the barley in 8 cups boiling water with 2 teaspoons salt for 30 to 40 minutes; it should be pleasantly chewy but tender. Drain it in a colander and run cold water over it.

Cut the tomatoes into ½-inch dice, salt them lightly, and leave them in a coarse sieve to drain for about 20 minutes. You should have 1 ½ cups.

While the barley is cooking and the tomatoes are draining, wash and trim the zucchini and cut it into ½-inch dice; you should have 2 ½ cups. Heat 2 tablespoons olive oil in a large sauté pan and sauté the zucchini with a generous pinch of salt over medium-high heat, tossing frequently. After 3 minutes, add the minced garlic and continue tossing over high heat for another 3 to 4 minutes, or until the zucchini is beginning to develop golden brown spots. Don't let it get mushy.

Remove the zucchini from the heat, sprinkle it with 2 tablespoons lemon juice, and leave it to cool.

Husk and clean the corn, check it to be sure it is perfectly fresh and sweet, and cook it 5 minutes in boiling, salted water. Slice the kernels off the cobs with a sharp knife and rub them between your hands a bit to separate them. You should have 1 ½ cups.

In a large bowl, combine the cooled barley, sautéed zucchini, corn kernels, and minced red onion to taste. Cut your basil leaves into a chiffonade: remove the leaves from their stems, stack them together, roll them tightly into a little green cigar, then slice very thinly crosswise. You will have a mound of basil shreds: a chiffonade. Add it to the salad, along with the drained tomatoes and the olives.

Whisk together the remaining 1 tablespoon olive oil, 2 tablespoons lemon juice, and the vinegar and pour the mixture over the salad. Toss everything together and taste. Add some freshly ground black pepper and a dash more salt if needed.

Chill the salad for an hour or so, then try it again. Correct the seasoning if needed, and serve.

chopped salad with french green lentils

Dark green French lentils, sometimes called Le Puy lentils, look like beautiful, tiny pebbles and hold their shape well when cooked, making them perfect for this end-of-summer salad.

Corn and peppers give the salad its summer color and sweetness, and crisp new apples, walnuts, and a bit of sharp cheddar cheese herald the coming of fall. Somehow it all goes together splendidly to make a dish that matches with a lighter soup for an ideal warm-weather meal. Make this salad ahead of time—it will only improve over the course of the day.

Other vegetables could be added to this, such as slivers of snow peas, parboiled green beans, or diced zucchini. Balance the combination of sweet and savory tastes with the tart dressing.

This looks like a lot when you are mixing it up, but it goes fast. And since it is a salad that keeps well and is perfect for a packed lunch or a picnic, it seems worthwhile to make enough for a couple of meals.

· · · SERVES 8 · · ·

1½ cups (300 g) dried French green lentils

1 tsp. sea salt, plus more to taste

1 cup (130 g) diced parboiled carrots

1½ cups (240 g) cooked corn kernels

1 cup (120 g) diced celery

1 cup (120 g) diced red bell pepper

½ cup (40 g) sliced green onions, white and green parts

1 cup (40 g) coarsely chopped fresh flat-leaf parsley

2 cups (220 g) diced apple

4–5 Tbs. (60–75 ml) olive oil

2 cloves garlic, chopped

hot paprika, pimentón de la Vera if possible

½ cup (75 g) crumbled sharp cheddar cheese

½ cup (45 g) coarsely chopped walnuts

6 Tbs. (90 ml) fresh lemon juice

freshly ground black pepper

Bring 3 cups water to a boil, add the lentils and a scant teaspoon salt, lower the heat to medium-low, and simmer the lentils, loosely covered, for about 35 minutes, or until they are just tender. Do not overcook them—they should be tender to the bite but still holding their shape. Drain the lentils and allow them to cool.

While the lentils are cooking, prepare the other ingredients. Your goal in a chopped salad is to have everything in pieces of similar size, somewhere between a corn kernel and a ½-inch dice.

I've listed the ingredients in cup amounts because the balance of all these ingredients is essential to the taste and texture of this salad. You'll need 2 or 3 medium carrots to get a cup; they should be peeled and dropped into boiling water for about 3 minutes, just until they are tender-crisp, then diced. The corn—3 ears should be enough—must be husked and boiled for about 3 minutes, then drained and the kernels sliced off. Cut the celery and bell peppers into ½-inch dice. Thinly slice the green onions. Remove the stems from the parsley and coarsely chop enough leaves to fill a cup. Quarter and core a large apple (no need to peel) and cut it into ½-inch dice. Combine all these ingredients in a large bowl.

When the lentils are ready, heat a tablespoon of olive oil in a large nonstick pan and add the garlic. Stir it over medium heat for about 2 minutes, then remove it from the heat and stir in a pinch of paprika and the drained lentils. Stir the lentils gently in the hot pan for another couple of minutes, until they are all evenly coated with the garlic-infused oil.

Add the lentils to the vegetables in the bowl, along with the crumbled cheese, the walnuts, 3 or 4 tablespoons more olive oil, the lemon juice, and pepper to taste, and mix the salad together gently. Wait a few minutes, then taste and adjust the salt and lemon juice as needed.

The salad can be served at room temperature or chilled, alone or over mixed greens. I like to put it away in the refrigerator for a few hours to allow the flavors to develop and marry, then serve it over a few lightly dressed mixed lettuce leaves.

cucumber, rice, and fresh herb salad

This is such a refreshing, bright-tasting salad that I always try to make more than I think I need. Everyone wants seconds.

Crisp, lightly salted cucumbers and chopped walnuts provide its crunchy texture, while lavish amounts of fresh mint and cilantro and a dusting of cumin give it brilliant flavor. Serve this cool rice salad on its own or as part of a buffet. And here's a bonus: it's a good traveler, so take it to a picnic.

I use thin-skinned cucumbers that do not need peeling or seeding. You can use Middle Eastern, Persian, Japanese, or European greenhouse cucumbers—all of them have tender, edible skin and are generally crisp and flavorful. But as always, check your cucumbers for possible bitterness in the ends.

· · · SERVES 6—8 · · ·

1 cup (180 g) jasmine rice or other long-grain white rice

2 tsp. sea salt, plus more to taste

1½ lbs. (700 g) Persian or Japanese cucumbers

2 Tbs. whole cumin seeds

1 cup (240 ml) plain low-fat yogurt

3 Tbs. (45 ml) olive oil

3 Tbs. (45 ml) white wine vinegar, plus more to taste

¼ cup (60 g) finely chopped Texas or other sweet onion

½ cup (40 g) chopped cilantro

¼ cup (30 g) chopped fresh mint

¼ cup (20 g) chopped fresh parsley

½ cup (80 g) chopped walnuts

freshly ground black pepper

Bring 6 cups water to a boil with a teaspoon of salt, add the rice, lower the heat to a simmer, and cook the rice for about 15 minutes, or just until it is tender but still firm. Different kinds of rice require different cooking times, so you can know when you've reached the right moment only by tasting it, starting at 14 or 15 minutes. When the rice is ready, drain it in a fine colander, then give it a quick rinse with cold water and drain again thoroughly. You should have about 3 cups cooked rice.

While the rice cooks, trim the cucumbers, taste the ends, and trim away any bitter parts. You do not need to peel these soft-skinned cucumbers; simply cut them into ½-inch dice. You should have 3 to 4 cups. Toss the cucumbers in a bowl with about 1 teaspoon salt, leave them there for half an hour, then drain away the water they have released and taste them. If they seem too salty, give them a rinse and press all excess liquid out; but most of the salt will probably wash away with the liquid they release.

Toast the cumin seeds in a pan over medium heat, stirring and watching, until they release their perfume and barely begin to color. Grind the toasted seeds roughly in a mortar or a spice grinder.

Whisk together the yogurt, olive oil, vinegar, and cumin and stir in the chopped onion and all the chopped herbs.

Combine the cooked rice with the well-drained cucumbers, the yogurt mixture, and the walnuts in a large bowl and toss everything together lightly until it is well combined. Don't go too far—you don't want the rice to turn mushy.

Taste for salt and sufficient vinegar, and correct the seasoning if you need to. Add pepper to taste, toss once more, and serve at room temperature or cold. You can serve this alone, on a bed of watercress or lettuce leaves, or as part of an appetizer assortment.

summer chopped salad with grilled halloumi

Halloumi is an interesting cheese from Cyprus. It is preserved in a brine, and it can be grilled on an open grill or in an ungreased pan without losing its shape. Instead of melting, it develops a toasty crust. Its briny taste and that golden crust make a wonderful contrast with the sweet summer vegetables in this salad.

· · · SERVES 6—7 · · ·

2 cups (300 g) chopped cucumbers

1½ cups (180 g) chopped bell peppers

1 cup (150 g) thinly sliced raw asparagus

1½ cups (300 g) diced tomatoes

2 cups (300 g) fresh sweet corn kernels

½ cup (30 g) chopped chives

3 Tbs. (45 ml) olive oil

3 Tbs. (45 ml) wine vinegar

1½ tsp. sea salt, or to taste

freshly ground black pepper

2–3 Tbs. (15 g) slivered fresh basil leaves

8 oz. (225 g) halloumi

The cucumbers, bell peppers, asparagus, and tomatoes should all be cut into ½-inch dice; try for as uniform a size as possible without going crazy. Parboil the corn: drop it into a pot of boiling salted water for 3 minutes only, then run cool water over it and slice the kernels off the cobs to get about 2 cups.

Combine all the ingredients except the cheese in a large bowl and mix gently.

Slice the cheese in ¼-inch-thick pieces and place the slices in a hot nonstick pan or on a grill pan. The slices should not be touching each other. Cook the halloumi over medium-high heat for 2 to 3 minutes, or until golden brown on the bottom. Flip the slices over and lightly brown the other side, which should take only a couple of minutes. Remove the cheese from the pan, let it cool slightly, and cut it into thin strips.

Serve the salad on its own or over a few tender lettuce leaves and scatter the grilled halloumi strips over each serving.

heirloom tomato salad

When heirloom tomatoes began making their comeback, they were a revelation for tomato lovers. For me, it marked the moment when I genuinely understood what I had learned academically about the loss of biodiversity—the rich and marvelous array of edible plants that were already gone or were on the verge of vanishing forever. What if Purple Cherokees had slipped over that edge? What if there were no more Yellow Germans or Green Zebras, ever?

I won't give up Early Girls or Premiums, or the other excellent varieties of tomatoes that are widely distributed. But I consider it a blessing that I can now go to a farmers' market and buy six or seven kinds of tomatoes that I hadn't tasted until a few years ago, each with its distinct flavor and look. And I know if I went to a different part of the country, I'd find six or seven other varieties, and so on.

This salad is a celebration of the flavor and beauty of summer tomatoes at their peak. I use Purple Cherokees, my favorite, along with one of the golden varieties and some bright red ones. Small cherry or grape tomatoes can be added as well. I mix them up for taste and for sheer visual splendor.

· · · SERVES 4 · · ·

1½ lbs. (700 g) mixed heirloom tomatoes
½ cup packed fresh basil leaves (½ oz.; 15 g)
a few thin slices red onion
3 Tbs. (45 ml) olive oil
1 Tbs. (15 ml) red wine vinegar
½ tsp. sea salt, plus more to taste

freshly ground black pepper
large shavings of Parmigiano-Reggiano cheese, thin slices of ricotta salata, or thick slices of fresh mozzarella
cured black olives (optional)

recipe continues on next page

Wash and trim all the tomatoes and cut them in wedges. Small cherry tomatoes can be left whole.

Tear the basil leaves into large pieces or cut them in a chiffonade, as you prefer. To make a chiffonade, roll the large leaves into a tight cylinder and then cut into very thin strips. If your basil leaves are too small to do this, don't cut them at all!

Combine half the basil with the tomatoes, onions, oil, vinegar, salt, and pepper to taste, and mix very gently. The best way to do this is with your hands, so that the tomatoes do not get bruised or beat up. Arrange the salad on a platter or in a shallow serving bowl, and scatter the rest of the basil over the top, along with the shavings of Parmigiano or slices of ricotta salata or mozzarella, and the olives.

kale salad with cranberries and walnuts

I love kale and have used it for years in soups, frittatas, and other dishes. But I always cooked it, until a friend brought over a shredded kale salad one day—young kale cut in thin strips, tossed with cranberries and walnuts in some olive oil and lemon juice. I remember the happy surprise of that raw, crunchy, earthy-flavored kale. And why not?

My version is mostly kale, with some arugula or mizuna for a peppery bite, tossed with cranberries, nuts, and a few slivered olives. But this salad begs for a new variation every time I make it, so I've given a few alternatives, and you will undoubtedly find your own version.

Dinosaur kale is the one that has long oval leaves with a bumpy texture—the look of a dinosaur's hide as we imagined it in fourth grade. Any young kale will taste fine in this salad, though.

· · · SERVES 4–6 · · ·

8–9 oz. (250 g) young dinosaur kale (also called Tuscan kale) or any young kale
3 oz. (100 g) arugula or baby mizuna
½ cup (75 g) dried cranberries
⅓ cup (50 g) Kalamata or other cured olives
½ cup (60 g) chopped walnuts, or pine nuts
1 small sweet red bell pepper (100 g)
1 Tbs. (15 ml) olive oil

1 Tbs. (15 ml) walnut oil
2 Tbs. (30 ml) aged balsamic vinegar, plus more to taste
½ tsp. sea salt, plus more to taste
freshly ground black pepper to taste

· · ·

optional garnish: 4 oz. (125 g) crumbled blue cheese, feta cheese, or sharp cheddar cheese

recipe continues on next page

Wash the kale, slice away the stems, and discard them. Stack the greens and roll them into tight bundles, then slice very thinly with a sharp knife—you're aiming for a shredded look. You should have about 6 cups of shredded kale, which will shrink quite a bit the moment it is tossed with oil and vinegar. Wash and dry the arugula, cut off any tough-looking stems, and cut it in short pieces.

Pour about ½ cup boiling water over the cranberries and leave them to soften until you are ready to toss the salad, at least 15 minutes.

Slice the olives off their stones and cut them in slivers. If using pine nuts, toast them lightly in a dry pan over low heat, stirring until they begin to turn golden and release their toasty fragrance. Core and seed the red pepper, quarter it lengthwise, and cut it in matchsticks.

Drain the cranberries, then toss together all the ingredients. Taste the salad, and correct the seasoning with a touch more salt or a drop of vinegar if it's needed; how much salt you need will depend on how salty the olives are. Just before serving, add the crumbled cheese if you like.

This salad keeps well for a day or so, though it will become softer as it sits. Because it is sturdy, it can travel to a picnic or a potluck.

Fall variation: Kale Salad with Roasted Kabocha

My favorite! In fall or winter, when kabocha squash is easily available, I skip the red pepper, add squash, a bit more olive oil, and a touch of lemon—and fall in love.

Cut a small kabocha squash (2 lbs.; 1 kg) in half, scrape out the seeds, and trim off all the hard skin. Cut the squash into 1-inch cubes, toss them with a tablespoon of olive oil and a big pinch of sea salt, and spread the cubes on a baking sheet. Roast the squash at 400° for about half an hour, maybe a little longer, turning once or twice, or until all the pieces are tender and some have brown spots. Let the squash cool. Make the salad as above, and toss the squash in very gently at the last minute.

Summer variation: Kale Salad with Tomatoes and Corn

In the summer, when tomatoes are vine-ripe, they provide a marvelous blast of sweetness and acid against the earthy kale. Skip the cranberries for this one; the tomatoes will have plenty of natural sugar. And use feta cheese.

Cut up 2 or 3 ripe tomatoes of your favorite variety (mine is Purple Cherokee), very finely chop 1 clove garlic, and chop or slice a few large basil leaves. Toss in the tomatoes, garlic, and basil when the salad is ready to serve, along with a little extra olive oil, and sprinkle crumbled feta cheese and toasted pine nuts on top.

This version of kale salad is not going to keep as well as the others, because tomatoes give up a lot of juice as soon as they are in contact with salt.

red cabbage and apple salad

This versatile concoction started as a hot cabbage dish, but as I kept eating it, warm, cool, and then cold from the fridge, I realized it was really meant to be a salad. It's an easy, bright-tasting dish that can be served at any temperature.

· · · MAKES ABOUT 8 CUPS, OR 6—8 SERVINGS · · ·

1 large head red cabbage (3 lbs.; 1.4 kg)
3 crisp Fuji apples (500 g)
2 Tbs. (30 ml) grapeseed oil or olive oil
2½ tsp. salt, plus more to taste

1 tsp. fennel seeds
freshly ground black pepper
4–5 Tbs. (60–75 ml) cider vinegar

Shred the cabbage. Peel and core the apples, cut them into wedges, and slice the wedges crosswise, thinly.

In a large nonstick pan, heat the oil. Add the cabbage, along with 2 teaspoons salt and the fennel seeds, and cook over medium heat, stirring often, for about 15 minutes. Add the apples, lots of freshly ground black pepper, and 4 tablespoons cider vinegar. Continue cooking, stirring now and then, for another 20 minutes, or until the cabbage is soft and juicy and reduced by almost half.

Taste the cabbage, and correct the seasoning with more salt and vinegar, as needed. The apples should provide just the right touch of sweetness, and the pepper some real bite. Serve hot, warm, or cold.

brown rice and chinese cabbage salad

I first encountered this salad on the buffet table at a friend's party. My friend is a personal chef to the rich and famous; she cooks fancy meals on private jets, but at home she likes to eat only the healthiest food, like this robust and delicious mix of shredded cabbage, brown rice, and a savory, Asian-inspired dressing.

· · · SERVES 6—8 AS A MAIN SALAD, MORE IF PART OF A LARGER SPREAD · · ·

1 small head Napa cabbage (1 lb.; 450 g)

2 cups cooked brown rice (12 oz.; 350 g)

2 small carrots, grated (90 g)

½ cup (75 g) very finely sliced green onions

½ cup (75 g) chopped roasted peanuts

1 cup (30 g) cilantro leaves

for the dressing

1 clove garlic, minced

1½ Tbs. minced fresh ginger

1 Tbs. (15 ml) dark sesame oil

2 Tbs. (30 ml) soy sauce

2 Tbs. (30 ml) rice vinegar

2 Tbs. (30 ml) honey or agave nectar

2 Tbs. (30 ml) fresh lemon juice

½ tsp. sea salt

· · ·

garnish: chopped roasted peanuts

Wash and thinly slice the cabbage. Combine it in a large bowl with the cooked brown rice, grated carrots, green onions, peanuts, and most of the cilantro.

Whisk together all the ingredients for the dressing, or pulse them briefly in a blender. Pour about half the dressing over the salad and toss for at least a minute, letting everything get well and evenly coated. Wait a minute or two, then taste, and if you decide you'd like more dressing, add just 1 teaspoon at a time.

recipe continues on next page

The salad will look big when you first mix it up, but it will soften and shrink down as the salt and vinegar affect the cabbage, just as coleslaw shrinks.

Scatter the rest of the cilantro leaves over the top of the salad when you serve it, and pass the remaining dressing at the table for anyone who'd like more. You can serve this salad by itself, over some mixed greens, or with slices of grilled tofu.

lentil and spinach salad

Lentils, sautéed leeks, and wilted spinach combine in a salad that looks much more attractive than you might predict for wilted spinach and tastes divine. It's also practical: it can be made ahead of time and travels well in a brown bag lunch to the office, right next to your thermos of soup.

Serve this salad alone or over mixed greens lightly dressed with oil and vinegar. A mix of Asian greens with mizuna and baby bok choy were a great success with this salad.

··· SERVES 6 ···

1¼ lb. (225 g) dried brown lentils

2 cups (200 g) chopped leeks, white part

2 Tbs. (30 ml) olive oil, plus more to taste

⅓ cup (70 g) raisins

½ cup (30 g) chopped fresh flat-leaf parsley

¼ cup (15 g) chopped cilantro

1 large stalk celery, thinly sliced (30 g)

2 Tbs. (30 ml) rice wine vinegar, plus more to taste

sea salt

½ lb. (225 g) fresh spinach

1 clove garlic, minced

fresh lemon juice

freshly ground black pepper

Bring to a boil 4 cups water with a teaspoon of salt, add the lentils, lower the heat, and simmer the lentils, covered, until tender, 20 to 22 minutes. Taste them as you near the end of that time; brown lentils cook quickly, and you want to drain them at the moment when they are tender but before they turn mushy. Allow the lentils to cool. You should have 3 ½ cups.

Sauté the chopped leeks in 1 tablespoon olive oil over medium heat until they are soft and beginning to turn golden, about 15 minutes. Meanwhile, plump the raisins in a cup of scalding water for at least 10 minutes, then drain well.

recipe continues on next page

Combine the cooked lentils, the sautéed leeks, and the raisins in a large bowl. Add the parsley, cilantro, sliced celery, 2 tablespoons rice vinegar, and ½ teaspoon salt and toss gently but thoroughly.

Wash the spinach, spin it dry, and cut it into 1-inch strips, or leave it whole if you are using baby spinach. Add the remaining tablespoon of olive oil to the pan in which you sautéed the leeks and stir the minced garlic in it for about a minute. Add the spinach and toss over high heat just until the spinach is wilted and the excess water cooks away, 3 to 4 minutes. Squirt a little fresh lemon juice on the spinach, toss again, and add it to the salad.

Toss the salad gently—you don't want to destroy the integrity of the lentils—and taste it. Season with salt, freshly ground black pepper, and more rice vinegar or lemon juice, to your taste. Then let the salad marinate for half an hour or so and taste it again. If you're not worried about your fat intake, drizzle on a little more fruity green olive oil.

napa cabbage slaw

D o not be alarmed by the word *slaw*. This is nothing like the soupy white side dish you can encounter in a roadside diner. It is a crisp, vibrant, and sophisticated salad: cabbage and cool-weather greens, toasted nuts, a flash of heat from chiles and ginger, and a delight of sweetness from raisins and snap peas. You will come back for more.

· · · SERVES 6—8 · · ·

⅓ cup (60 g) raisins

1 medium head Napa cabbage (1 lb.; 450 g)

1 small head radicchio or 1 small bunch mizuna (90 g)

6 oz. (180 g) sugar snap peas

½ cup (60 g) pine nuts

½ cup (45 g) sliced green onions

2–3 small red jalapeño peppers (30–45 g)

3 Tbs. (45 ml) olive oil

2 Tbs. (30 ml) rice vinegar

1 Tbs. (15 ml) fresh lime or lemon juice, plus more to taste

¾ tsp. sea salt, plus more to taste

2 Tbs. (40 g) minced fresh ginger

a few drops of good soy sauce (optional)

1 cup (30 g) cilantro leaves

Put the raisins in a small bowl and pour a little boiling water over them, just enough to cover them and allow them to plump up while you prepare the salad.

Peel away any soft or damaged leaves of cabbage, then wash and dry all the crisp leaves and slice them crosswise into ¼-inch strips. Quarter and shred the radicchio, or cut the mizuna into 1-inch pieces. String the snap peas and cut them into 1-inch pieces or thin slivers.

Toast the pine nuts in a small dry skillet over medium heat, stirring them the whole time, just until they begin to turn a warm golden brown, 6 or 7 minutes.

Thinly slice the jalapeño peppers and taste one. I like to add a couple of tablespoons of paper-thin slices to the salad, but if the peppers are very hot and you don't want an overly spicy salad, then mince them and add little bits at a time, to your taste.

recipe continues on next page

Drain the raisins, and combine all the ingredients except the cilantro in a large bowl. Toss everything together thoroughly, then wait a few minutes for the flavors to integrate and taste. Add a little more salt if needed, or a touch more lime juice, and toss again. Just before serving, stir in the cilantro.

This salad is great when just made, gets even better over the next couple of hours, and keeps well in the refrigerator, tightly covered, for at least another 2 days. I haven't been able to keep it around longer than that.

Another way . . .

In deep winter, I sometimes add one or two Fuyu persimmons, cut into 1/2-inch dice, and I use dried cranberries instead of raisins. Excellent!

CHAPTER 17

a few easy sweets

Butter Cake with Summer Fruits

Octavia's Gingerbread

Olive Oil and Lemon Cake

Angel Cookies

Lauren's Badass Trailmix Cookies

Bittersweet Chocolate Brownies

Farmhouse Apple Crumble

Rice Pudding with Dried Cranberries

Greek Yogurt with Honey and Walnuts

Melons in Orange and Mint Syrup • **V**

Tangerine and Strawberry Compote • **V**

what's for dessert?

Even in a book about soup, there must be room for dessert. Soups that can in themselves be dessert have already been included and discussed; a chilled fruit soup, for instance, can go either way, start a meal or finish it. But for all those other soups and the relaxed meals they inspire, the question remains, what's for dessert?

Fruit, or a fruit-based dessert, is the most frequent answer. There are few things better in the world than a juicy piece of fruit in its season, perfectly ripe. I once heard Julia Child remark, "A perfect peach—you give that to the queen." But perhaps the queen would like an almond cookie with her peach, or to have it sliced and arranged around a piece of butter cake, or to have it baked under a crumble topping.

So here are a few sweets.

In the spirit of home cooking and easy soup meals, none of these desserts are elaborate or difficult to make. Mainly they are old friends, familiar, always welcome. A few might be twists on old favorites. None will strain a basic kitchen, and all will delight you at the end of a meal.

THREE CAKES

First there are three lovely cakes: one for summer, one for winter, and one for every single day of the year. The Butter Cake (p. 488) is delicate, slightly crumbly, and a matchless companion for soft summer fruits or a compote. Octavia's Gingerbread (p. 490) is dark and sticky, tangy with molasses and spice, and recalls the best winter days of childhood. And the Olive Oil and Lemon Cake (p. 492) is quietly elegant, dense, excellent on its own but ready to be elaborated with sliced fruit, crème fraîche, sorbet, or lemon curd.

All of them are really cakes for all seasons, and they have this in common: they're easy. No frosting, no fillings, nothing that takes pastry-making skill—just three utterly delicious cakes that anybody can make and that will finish your meals gloriously.

COOKIES, CRUMBLES, COMPOTES

The right cookie can turn a dish of sliced fruit or a bowl of berries into a real dessert. Representing the big and wonderful world of cookies (after diligent testing—yes, someone has to do it!), I include two cookies from opposite ends of the spectrum and one spectacular brownie.

The first cookie is a delicate almond wafer, near cousin to a macaroon but thinner, crisper, lighter; it's the crunchy sweet something you want with a compote or sorbet. The second is packed with nuts, raisins, seeds, bananas, and chocolate chips; Lauren's Badass Trailmix Cookies (p. 495) was a gift from a college student and packs some nourishment into dessert. And because chocolate is one of the principal food groups, there must be one superb dark chocolate brownie.

And finally, a handful of other ideas: a crumble stripped back to its unfussy perfection, a pudding that a child can make and everyone will eat, and a few exquisitely simple compositions of fruits, syrups, yogurt cheese, walnuts, honey. . . . Every answer is a good one.

butter cake with summer fruits

Fancy enough for company, easy enough for anytime: you can have this cake in the oven in about fifteen minutes and be eating it not much more than an hour later.

The fruit can be varied. I've made this cake with cherries, blackberries, and diced nectarines. You might also use blueberries, or peaches, or apricots. But remember to adjust the sugar to the sweetness or tartness of the fruit, and don't use something overly juicy, like most plums, or it will turn the cake into a pudding.

··· SERVES 6—8 ···

1 cup (150 g) unbleached white flour
1 tsp. baking powder
sea salt
1 tsp. ground cinnamon
½ cup (120 g) butter, softened
1 cup plus 2 Tbs. (225 g) sugar
2 large eggs
½ tsp. almond extract

½ cup (75 g) finely chopped almonds (optional)
1 generous cup (150–200 g) fresh pitted
    cherries, blackberries, or other summer fruit
powdered sugar

···

garnish: vanilla ice cream, whipped cream,
    cherries or other fruit

Prepare a 9- or 10-inch springform cake pan by buttering it and dusting it with flour. Alternately, you can butter the sides and line the bottom with a circle of buttered parchment. Preheat the oven to 350°.

Sift together the flour, baking powder, a pinch of salt, and the cinnamon and set aside. Beat the softened butter with 1 cup sugar until it is smooth and fluffy, 4 to 5 minutes. Beat in the eggs, then lightly whisk the dry mixture into the wet one and stir in the almond extract, and the chopped almonds if you like.

Spoon the batter into the prepared cake pan and spread it gently until it is fairly smooth. Place the cherries here and there over the top, distributing them evenly. Sprinkle the top with the remaining sugar—as little as 1 tablespoon or as much as 2, depending on the sweetness of the fruit.

Bake the cake for about 50 minutes. The sides should be pulling away from the pan and the top should be light golden brown. Let the cake cool a bit, then carefully remove it from the pan and dust it with sieved powdered sugar.

Serve the cake warm or at room temperature, with ice cream or whipped cream and few more berries or some sliced summer fruit on the side.

octavia's gingerbread

I've had side-by-side tastings of this gingerbread with others and this one wins. Here is how I happened to get the recipe.

I was involved with a film about the architect John Lautner, and the production involved filming many Lautner houses. Normally when a film crew shows up on a location, the producers are met with a list of warnings about what not to touch, reminders of liability issues, and various prohibitions. But when we went to shoot at the Walstrom residence, a lovely house in which the original owners still resided, we were met with . . . gingerbread!

Octavia Walstrom had made it for us, and when we finally took a coffee break in the afternoon, we simply could not stop eating it. I asked for the recipe, and she kindly obliged. I altered her formula only slightly, adding some fresh ginger along with the ground ginger. Thank you, Octavia!

· · · SERVES 12 · · ·

1 cup (215 g) turbinado sugar
¾ cup (180 ml) canola oil
1 cup (240 ml) dark molasses
2 tsp. baking soda
2¾ cups (410 g) unbleached flour
½ tsp. sea salt

1 tsp. ground ginger
½ tsp. ground cinnamon
½ tsp. ground cloves
2 large eggs, beaten
1½ Tbs. minced fresh ginger

Oil a 9- by 12-inch baking pan, line the bottom with a piece of parchment paper, and oil the parchment. Preheat the oven to 350°.

Combine the sugar, oil, and molasses in a large mixing bowl. Dissolve the baking soda in 1 cup boiling water and stir it into the sugar mixture. Sift together the flour, salt, and spices and stir the dry mixture into the wet one. Gently beat in the eggs and the fresh ginger, using a whisk or a low setting on an electric mixer, just until everything is combined and there are no lumps of flour left.

Pour the batter into the prepared baking pan. Bake for about 45 minutes, or until a toothpick inserted near the center comes out clean.

Allow the gingerbread to cool before cutting. This is a treat by itself, and a wonderful dessert served with a mound of whipped cream or a scoop of vanilla ice cream.

olive oil and lemon cake

There are many olive oil cakes, dense ones made with semolina, lighter ones, sweet and less sweet.... This is my favorite, full of lemon zest and fresh juice from the fruit in my backyard. The citrus marries so well with the fruitiness of the olive oil, and the cake is just sweet enough to be dessert but not so sweet that it can't be breakfast the next day.

Since the taste of this cake depends on the olive oil, it should go without saying that you must use an excellent one (I'll say it anyway). Use a fresh, fruity olive oil, but one that is not too peppery, and make sure the lemons are absolutely fresh.

· · · SERVES 8 · · ·

1 cup (200 g) superfine sugar

5 large egg yolks, at room temperature

¾ cup (180 ml) fruity extra-virgin olive oil, plus a
   little more for the pan

1½ Tbs. finely grated lemon zest

2 Tbs. (30 ml) fresh lemon juice

1 cup (160 g) white flour, preferably cake flour

4 large egg whites, at room temperature

sea salt

· · ·

optional garnishes:

powdered sugar

fresh fruit

fruit compote

Oil a 9- or 10-inch springform pan with a little olive oil, cut a circle of parchment paper to fit the bottom, line the pan with it, and then oil the parchment. Preheat the oven to 350°.

Reserve 2 tablespoons sugar and beat the rest of it into the egg yolks until they are thick and pale. Gently beat in the olive oil and lemon zest and juice. Mix in the flour, using a spoon.

Beat the egg whites with a pinch of salt in another bowl until they are thick and hold soft peaks. Do not overbeat. Fold some of the beaten egg whites thoroughly into the batter, then lightly fold in the rest, just until everything seems well combined and no more.

Scrape the batter into the prepared pan and smooth it with a spatula. Sprinkle the reserved 2 tablespoons sugar over the top. Bake the cake for 45 to 50 minutes, or until a toothpick inserted near the center comes out clean. Let the cake cool in its pan for 15 minutes or so, then slip a thin knife blade around the edge and release the side of the springform. Allow the cake to cool completely before slicing.

To serve, gently turn the cake over, remove the pan bottom and peel away the parchment, then place the cake on a platter. You can dust it with a little powdered sugar if you like, and arrange some fresh fruit around the edges—strawberries, blackberries, orange or tangerine slices, or a big spoonful of any fresh fruit compote.

angel cookies

Any plate of sliced fruit, any compote, any scoop of ice cream, is elevated to a fine dessert when paired with one of these almond crisps.

··· MAKES 12 LARGE COOKIES OR 24 SMALL ONES ···

2 cups (250 g) unblanched almonds

2 large egg whites, at room temperature

1 cup (200 g) sugar

cream of tartar

¾ tsp. almond extract

¾ tsp. vanilla extract

Preheat the oven to 375°. Line 2 baking sheets with parchment paper.

Grind the almonds in a food processor, pulsing them until they have the texture of coarse cornmeal.

Beat the egg whites and sugar together with a pinch of cream of tartar until the whites are glossy and hold soft peaks. Beat in the ground almonds and the almond and vanilla extracts.

Scoop out either rounded tablespoons or rounded teaspoons of the batter, depending what size cookies you want, and drop them on the parchment-lined baking sheets, leaving at least 2 inches between cookies. The batter will be sticky, and it is easiest to do this with two spoons, using one to push the batter from the other. Flatten the cookies slightly with the back of a damp spoon.

Bake the cookies just until their tops are brown, 12 to 14 minutes for the larger size and 10 to 12 minutes for smaller ones. Remove them from the oven and cool them on a wire rack for about 10 minutes. They will crisp up as they cool.

lauren's badass trailmix cookies

Lauren spent a month working with me as an intern when I was finishing this book. We had a lot of fun in the kitchen, testing and retesting, weighing, measuring, taking notes . . . and eating. She had just graduated from college and was about the same age as I was when I wrote my first book. Having a college student in the kitchen brought back a lot of wonderful memories.

It also brought these cookies. Lauren had worked out the recipe over the course of her college career and proudly called them Lauren's Badass Trailmix Cookies. She swears they got her and her friends through finals more than once. "Oatmeal, raisins, chocolate chunks, nuts, combined with a few other things," she said when she first described them. "I like how the brown sugar makes them slightly crispy on top, but they're still chewy inside. I've made them with cranberries, sunflower seeds, pecans, peanuts . . ."

A jar full of these in the cupboard and soup in the fridge: you're set.

· · · MAKES ABOUT 4½ DOZEN COOKIES · · ·

¾ cup (100 g) unbleached white flour

1 cup (130 g) whole-wheat flour

¾ tsp. baking powder

¾ tsp. baking soda

½ tsp. ground cinnamon

½ tsp. ground nutmeg

½ tsp. sea salt

1 cup (225 g) unsalted butter, softened

¼ cup (50 g) white sugar

1½ cups (250 g) packed brown sugar

2 large eggs

1 ripe medium banana, mashed (120 g)

2½ tsp. (38 ml) vanilla extract

3½ cups (330 g) rolled oats

1 cup (130 g) raisins

¾ cup (80 g) chopped walnuts

¾ cup (125 g) bittersweet or semisweet
   chocolate chunks

recipe continues on next page

Preheat the oven to 350°. Line 2 or 3 large baking sheets with parchment.

Whisk together the flours, baking powder, baking soda, cinnamon, nutmeg, and salt in a small bowl.

In a large bowl, beat the softened butter with the white and brown sugars until it looks fluffy, then beat in the eggs, mashed banana (you should have at least ½ cup), and vanilla extract.

Stir or beat the flour mixture into the butter mixture until well combined, but do not overbeat. Stir in the oats, raisins, chopped walnuts, and chocolate, until everything is well mixed.

Scoop up rounded tablespoons of the dough and use a second spoon to push them off onto the parchment-lined baking sheets. Another way to do this is to scoop up a rounded tablespoon of dough and shape it into a ball with damp fingers, then place it on the parchment. Leave at least 2 inches space between cookies. Bake the cookies for 16 to 18 minutes, or until lightly browned around the edges, and reverse the position of the pans halfway through.

Transfer the cookies to a rack while they are still warm and allow them to cool.

The other ways . . .

. . . are innumerable. Dried cranberries can be substituted for raisins. Coarsely chopped dried apricots or dried cherries also work. Pecans can be used instead of walnuts. A few tablespoons of plain hulled sunflower seeds or pumpkin seeds can be added. Or sesame seeds. And so on. Let your favorite trail mix be your guide.

bittersweet chocolate brownies

These are brownies for grown-ups, although the children who've been around them have had no trouble stepping up and eating their share. They are simple, dense, almost fudgelike, and depend on the best chocolate for their flavor. I generally use Valrhona, Scharffen Berger, or Callebaut, but there are many excellent chocolates available now.

· · · MAKES 25 SMALL BROWNIES · · ·

½ lb. (227 g) bittersweet chocolate, about 65% cacao

½ lb. (227 g) unsalted butter

1¼ cups (255 g) superfine sugar

3 Tbs. (28 g) white flour, pastry flour if possible

4 large eggs

½ tsp. vanilla extract

sea salt

Butter a square baking pan, line the bottom with a piece of parchment paper, and butter the parchment.

Coarsely chop the chocolate, cut the butter in pieces, and melt them together in the top of a double boiler or in a bowl set over a pot of simmering water. When both are completely melted, stir and remove the bowl from the heat.

Sift together the sugar and flour. Beat the eggs with the vanilla and a pinch of salt.

Gently whisk the sugar mixture into the melted chocolate, then whisk in the beaten eggs. Allow the batter to rest for about half an hour. It will become slightly thicker.

Preheat the oven to 325°.

Pour the batter into the prepared baking pan and bake the brownies for 40 to 45 minutes, or slightly longer if the center is still wet. The brownies are done when a toothpick inserted near the center comes out almost clean.

recipe continues on next page

Let the brownies cool (they will fall slightly as they do), then cut them with a sharp knife into 25 small squares. I tried chilling the brownies once so that I could cut them more easily. It worked beautifully, and the texture became denser, somewhere between a brownie and a truffle—not a bad place to be!

Another way . . .

To make sensational mocha brownies, add 2 tablespoons (14 g) of very coarsely ground coffee beans to the batter. Use your favorite beans and pulse them briefly in the coffee grinder until they are broken up into a kind of coffee gravel, but not nearly fine enough to brew. They give a satisfying crunch to the finished brownie.

farmhouse apple crumble

Fruit crisps and crumbles are the most basic of simple desserts: cut up some fruit, mix up a little butter, sugar, and flour in a rough sort of way, drop it on top of the fruit, and bake. There is a reason that this idea persists and flourishes over the decades: it's the combination of ease and deliciousness.

Over the years I've elaborated my apple crumble, adding raisins or nuts, using brown sugar or different spices. This time I decided to strip it down to the basics, and I made this back-to-the-farmhouse version. Wonderful.

You can use any kind of apples, as long as they are fresh and flavorful. The best are those on the tart and crisp side. A mix of tart and sweet apples will also be good. But you can hardly go wrong here—different apples will give their own character to this homey dessert, and it's always a treat.

If you have children, double the recipe and make it in a large gratin or oval baker.

· · · SERVES 5—6 · · ·

for the apples

2 lbs. (900 g) apples
3 Tbs. (45 ml) fresh lemon juice
¼ cup (50 g) sugar

1 tsp. ground cinnamon
¼ tsp. ground nutmeg

for the crumble

½ cup (65 g) unbleached white flour
¾ cup (150 g) sugar
½ cup (50 g) rolled oats

6 Tbs. (90 g) cold unsalted butter, sliced
sea salt

recipe continues on next page

Peel and core the apples, quarter them, and slice them crosswise thickly. Toss them in a bowl with the lemon juice, ¼ cup sugar, cinnamon, and nutmeg. Spread the apples in a 9-inch square baking pan.

Preheat the oven to 375°.

Combine the flour, ¾ cup sugar, oats, sliced butter, and a pinch of salt in the container of the food processor fitted with the steel blade, and pulse for 30 to 40 seconds. Check the mixture: it should look like a coarse meal that is starting to clump together. If you see any large chunks of butter or if the meal is not holding together at all, pulse a few more seconds.

Push the crumble together into a rough mass, then take a little at a time—as much as you can hold in your fingers—and gently break it up into smaller chunks as you drop it on top of the prepared apples. Distribute all the crumble over the apples.

Bake the apple crumble in the hot oven for 45 to 55 minutes, or until the topping is light golden brown and the juice of the apples is bubbling up around the edges. Serve the crumble warm or cool, by itself or with a scoop of vanilla ice cream.

rice pudding with dried cranberries

Nothing is more comforting or easier to do than a simple stovetop rice pudding. In England this would be called a nursery sweet, but I find that adults eat it down to the bottom of their bowls.

Dried cranberries, in place of the usual raisins, make a slightly tart contrast to the sweet rice, but you can use raisins if that's what you have around, and they will be fine.

··· SERVES 6 ···

4 cups (1 liter) whole milk, plus a bit more if
   needed
¾ cup (150 g) Arborio rice
⅓ cup (65 g) sugar
¼ tsp. vanilla extract

¼ tsp. sea salt
ground nutmeg
ground cinnamon
½ cup (75 g) dried cranberries

Combine the milk, rice, sugar, vanilla, salt, a pinch each of nutmeg and cinnamon, and the cranberries in a medium-sized heavy-bottomed saucepan and bring to a boil, stirring. Lower the heat and let the mixture simmer, stirring often, for 35 to 40 minutes, or until the rice is tender-firm and the liquid around it is thickening.

I like to serve this hot, freshly made, just thick enough to hold a soft shape. You can also chill it, but it will thicken more as it cools, so stir in some additional milk or cream before serving to regain the moist texture.

greek yogurt with honey and walnuts

When I was traveling in Greece I tasted exceptional yogurt, and I fell in love with it. It became my daily dessert: a bowl of creamy, thick yogurt with dark amber honey poured over it and walnuts scattered on top.

Greek-style yogurt is yogurt that has been drained until it is thicker and creamier in texture than regular yogurt. This is done by leaving it in a cheesecloth-lined sieve for a while—that's all. It's an intermediate step on the way to yogurt cheese.

· · · SERVES 6 · · ·

8 cups (2 liters) plain whole yogurt
½–¾ cup (180 ml) wildflower honey

1 cup (160 g) halved or coarsely chopped very fresh walnuts

To make your Greek-style yogurt, begin with yogurt that has no starch or added gums.

Line a large sieve or a colander with a triple thickness of cheesecloth and pour the yogurt into it. Set the sieve over a bowl and leave the yogurt to drain for 1 ½ to 2 hours. There should be several cups of liquid in the bowl. Your two quarts of yogurt will yield a little over 4 cups of much thicker Greek-style yogurt; the exact amount will depend on how long you leave it to drain.

Keep the thickened yogurt in a bowl in the refrigerator, covered, until you are ready to use it, and stir it up again before serving.

Spoon a little less than a cup of yogurt into each dessert bowl. Drizzle about 2 tablespoons honey over the yogurt and scatter a few walnut halves or some chopped walnuts on top. Serve at once.

Another way . . .
In the summer, when soft fruits are in season, add sliced white nectarines, quartered fresh figs, blackberries, or apricot halves.

melons in orange and mint syrup

For this cooling, fragrant dessert, the flavor of the melons is the most important thing. In midsummer, many varieties of melon are available, and they vary from place to place. You can use Canary, Sugar Queen, honeydew, Sharlyn, cantaloupe, or whatever melon you like, but it must be sweet and perfectly ripe, juicy without being mushy.

· · · SERVES 6—8 · · ·

2 medium melons, preferably 2 different kinds (6 lbs ; 3 kg)

2–3 cups Orange and Mint Syrup (recipe follows)
¼ cup fresh mint leaves

Halve the melons and clean out the seeds. Use a melon baller to scoop out the flesh, or cut the melon into 1-inch wedges, slice off the rind, and cut the flesh into cubes.

In a large bowl, combine the melon pieces with enough syrup to cover them. Cut the mint leaves into thin strips and stir them into the compote, then cover the bowl with plastic wrap and chill the compote in the refrigerator for at least 4 hours.

Serve this in dessert bowls or in compote glasses, with ginger biscotti or angel cookies on the side.

orange and mint syrup

This delicate syrup is ideal for a compote of melons (p. 503) or white peaches. The clear, pale orange color and the flowery, minty perfume are subtle and refreshing. Leave the orange zest and mint leaves to steep in the liquid longer for a more pronounced flavor.

· · · MAKES 3 CUPS · · ·

2 cups (500 ml) water
1 cup (250 ml) fresh orange juice, strained
½ cup (100 g) sugar

zest of ½ orange
½ cup loosely packed fresh mint leaves

Combine the water, orange juice, and sugar in a stainless steel pot and heat it, stirring a little, until the sugar is dissolved. Add the orange zest and the mint leaves to the liquid, bring it to a boil, and let it boil for 2 minutes. Turn off the heat and allow the syrup to cool to room temperature.

Strain out the orange zest and mint leaves and chill the syrup well. For a stronger flavor, leave the zest and mint leaves to steep in the syrup overnight before removing them.

tangerine and strawberry compote

This simple fruit compote is like an Ojai spring in a bowl. I made it with Gaviota strawberries, local Tahoe Gold tangerines, lemons from the backyard, fresh mint, and the surprise taste of the first basil. You should use whichever strawberries are best in your area, and if you can't get sweet tangerines, substitute blood oranges or sweet navel oranges.

· · · SERVES 6—8 · · ·

6 cups (1 kg) Gaviota strawberries

1 lb. (450 g) large, sweet seedless tangerines

2 Tbs. (30 ml) fresh lemon juice, plus more to taste

2 Tbs. superfine sugar, plus more to taste

a pinch of sea salt

¼ cup finely sliced fresh basil leaves

2 Tbs. finely chopped fresh mint

Trim and rinse the strawberries and cut larger ones in half. Peel the tangerines, section them, and remove any pith from the sections.

Combine all the ingredients in a bowl and mix gently, trying not to bruise or break up the fruit. Leave the fruit to macerate for about half an hour, but after the first 15 minutes taste and adjust the lemon juice and sugar slightly, if needed. The acidity of these fruits will vary considerably with variety and with weather, so you will need to use your taste buds to find the exact balance.

Spoon this compote over ice cream, top it with whipped cream, pour it around Butter Cake (p. 488) or Olive Oil and Lemon Cake (p. 492), or have it all by itself.

sincere thanks

I do love soup, and writing this book was a joy, but it did not happen in solitude or without effort; and it certainly didn't happen without a whole lot of help from some wonderful people.

And so, my sincere thanks go to . . .

Maria Guarnaschelli, my extraordinary editor, for her immediate and never-wavering enthusiasm, her brains, and her heart. She saw the book with me from the start, and without her it would not have been realized. Thank you, Maria!

And to the team at W. W. Norton, in particular to Susan Sanfrey, the project editor, Melanie Tortoroli, who chased down every detail, and the patient and meticulous copy editor Liz Duvall, who combed through every word and comma and fraction.

And to the wonderful Kris Dahl, my supportive and encouraging agent, who thought this was a good idea and knew how to run with it.

In the beautiful Ojai valley where I live and cook, I am surrounded by talented farmers who grow our food in their orchards, farms, fields, and backyards. It is their hard work that makes me look good in the kitchen.

Thanks especially to . . .

Peter Wilsrud—I think of him as my personal farmer—for his weekly produce basket filled with fresh vegetables, surprises, and an education.

Larry Yee, for so many wonderful times in the kitchen, for leaving piles of exotic squashes on my doorstep, for the sublime persimmons, for stone soup every year, and most of all for working tirelessly to save family farms.

Steve Fields and Sims Brannon, a passionate gardener and a marvelous cook, for the heirloom tomatoes, the ambrosial white peaches, the spectacular pumpkins, the freshly dried cranberry beans, and all the potlucks.

Bruce and Marie Botnick, for planting an olive orchard across the road so I could have really, truly local olive oil.

Phil McGrath, B. D. Dautch, Jim and Lisa Churchill, Steve Sprinkel, and the many other farmers who bring their delicious fruits and vegetables to our farmers' market, for showing up every Sunday morning.

I am blessed also with a local tribe of fellow cooks who join me in the kitchen and at the table, share ideas and enthusiasms, eat, drink, laugh, keep the party going, and generally make life here an ongoing pleasure.

A big and happy thank you to . . .

Tracey Ryder and Carole Topalian, for starting their little magazine, *Edible Ojai*, for promoting the cause of local cuisine, for being part of my cook's progress, and for tasting, encouraging, and always sharing.

Lisa Robertson, for bringing books and ideas, for testing recipes, for coming over to try something at the drop of an e-mail, and for leading the cheering section at the kitchen bar.

The many friends who shared delicious ideas, advice, and encouragement, first among them Sara Sackner, Holly Mitchem, Carol Hogel, Claud Mann, Jeri Oshima, Jane Handel, Maria Nation, and Mary Goldberg.

My sister Eve Lowry, whose freezer bulged with soups as I kept sending her recipes to try out, and whose comments were always so useful.

Lauren Smith, the freshly minted college graduate who came into the kitchen as an intern, cooked with me like a wild dynamo for a solid month, learned to take notes in metric, and shared her badass cookies!

And a special thank you to Kathy Yee, for taking big pots of my soup to the people who needed it most.

And a warm hug to my two sons, my favorite mouths to feed—Chris Nava, whose energy and creativity in the kitchen are infectious, and Teddy Nava, who struck out on the vegan trail ahead of us all and always inspires new recipes.

And a cheery shout to everyone who dropped by all those times when, late some afternoon, they got this e-mail:

THE SOUP KITCHEN IS OPEN!

index

Note: Page numbers in **boldface** refer to recipes themselves.

almonds
    Angel Cookies, 364–65, **494**
    Butter Cake with Summer Fruits, 318–19, 486, **488–89**
    Jeri's Spiced Nuts, 220–21, **448–49,** 462
Ancho and Guajillo Chile Puree, 78, 117, 142, 183, 188, 338,
    440–41
Angel Cookies, **494**
    menu using, 364–65
apples
    Arugula and Apple Soup with Toasted Walnuts, **98–99**
    Carol's Finnish Pea Soup with Apples, **117–18**
    Chopped Salad with French Green Lentils, 64–65,
    466–67
    Farmhouse Apple Crumble, **499–500**
    Red Cabbage and Apple Salad, 138–39, 181, **476**
artichokes
    Creamy Artichoke Soup, **266–68**
    Potato Pizza, 277, **402–4**
    Rustic Artichoke and Potato Stew, **262–65**
arugula
    Arugula and Apple Soup with Toasted Walnuts, **98–99**
    Salad of Baby Arugula, Aged Jack Cheese, and Asian
        Pears, 220–21, **462–63**
Arugula and Apple Soup with Toasted Walnuts, **98–99**
asparagus
    Asparagus Bisque with Fresh Dill, 243–44, **245–46**
    Cold Asparagus Soup, 362, **371–72**
    Salad of Baby Arugula, Aged Jack Cheese, and Asian
        Pears, 220–21, **462–63**
    Snap Pea, Asparagus, and Fennel Soup with Fresh Herbs,
        274, **280–81**
    Sorrel Soup with Mint and Spring Vegetables, 244,
        247–48, 277
    Springtime Barley and Mushroom Soup, 256–57, **258–59**
    Summer Chopped Salad with Grilled Halloumi, **470**
Asparagus Bisque with Fresh Dill, **245–46**
    menu using, 243–44

avocados
    Cold Cucumber and Avocado Soup, **369–70**
    Tortilla Soup, 332, **338–40**
bananas
    Lauren's Badass Trailmix Cookies, 487, **495–96**
barley
    Barley, Mushroom, and Vegetable Soup, 20, 26, **185–87**
    Barley Salad with Corn and Zucchini, **464–65**
    Mushroom-Barley Soup with Cabbage, **162–63**
    Pickle Soup, 20, 26, **185–87**
    Roasted Root Vegetable Soup, 25, **166–68**
    Springtime Barley and Mushroom Soup, 256–57, **258–59**
Barley, Mushroom, and Vegetable Soup, 20, 26, **185–87**
Barley Salad with Corn and Zucchini, **464–65**
Basic Croutons, 446
Basic Dark Vegetable Broth, 45, **50–51**
    big soups and stews using, 206–9
    summer soups using, 338–40
    winter soups using, 160–61
Basic Light Vegetable Broth, **47–48**
    bean soups using, 132–37, 145–48
    big soups and stews using, 198–202, 210–11
    cold soups using, 371–72, 375–76
    fall soups using, 66–69, 70–71, 74–75, 78–79
    green soups using, 94–99, 102–3, 278–81, 284–91
    holiday soups using, 226–34
    spring soups using, 245–55, 258–59, 262–70
    summer soups using, 302–8, 311–17, 320–27, 336–37,
        341–46, 350–59
    winter soups using, 158–59, 164–65, 169–75
    winter squash soups using, 111–19, 122–23
Basic Root Vegetable Broth, 45, **49**
    bean soups using, 147–48
    big soups and stews using, 200–202
    fall soups using, 66–67, 68–69
    green soups using, 94–95, 102–3

Basic Root Vegetable Broth (*continued*)
   holiday soups using, 231–34
   summer soups using, 338–40
   winter soups using, 160–61, 164–65, 169–75
   winter squash soups using, 111–13, 116–17, 122–23
basil
   Butter Bean and Summer Vegetable Soup, 298–99,
      300–301
   Cold Peach and Nectarine Soup with Strawberry Sauce,
      381–82
   Curried Spinach and Sorrel Soup, **269–70**
   Heirloom Tomato Salad, 309–10, 334–35, **471–72**
   Kale and Tomato Soup, **345–46**
   Minestrone for a Crowd, **193–95**
   Simple Basil Pesto, 191, 334–35, 345, **436–37**
   Summer Minestrone, 332, **358–59**
   Summer Tomato and Basil Soup, 23, 318–19, **320–21**
   Tangerine and Strawberry Compote, 276–77, **505**
   Tomato and Zucchini Soup with Summer Herbs, **326–27**
   Vegetable Soup Pistou, 332, **352–54**
   Zucchini and Basil Soup, 25, 309–10, **311–12**
   Zucchini and Potato Soup, **313–14**
beans. *See* black bean(s); cannellini beans; cranberry beans;
     dried beans; fava beans; garbanzo beans; Great
     Northern beans; green beans; kidney beans; lima
     beans; pinto beans; white beans
beets/beet greens
   Beet Soup with Ginger, 218, **226–27**
   Potage of Baby Spring Greens, 274, **288–89**
   Roasted Golden Beet Soup, **74–75**
Beet Soup with Ginger, 218, **226–27**
bell peppers
   about, 52
   Barley, Mushroom, and Vegetable Soup, 20, 26, **185–87**
   Butter Bean and Summer Vegetable Soup, 298–99,
      300–301
   Chopped Salad with French Green Lentils, 64–65,
      466–67
   Corn and Pepper Soup, **343–44**
   Gazpacho Andaluz, 362–63, 364–65, **366–67**
   Hummus with Fire Roasted Red Peppers, **426–27**
   Mung Bean Soup with Spinach and Tomatoes, 332,
      341–42
   Pickle Soup, 20, 26, **185–87**

Roasted Eggplant and Garbanzo Bean Soup, **355–57**
Spicy Black Bean Soup with Sweet Peppers, 43, **142–44**
Summer Chopped Salad with Grilled Halloumi, **470**
Summer Minestrone, 332, **358–59**
Ten-Vegetable Soup with Cranberry Beans, **190–92**
Three-Bean and Vegetable Chili, 178, **212–15**
Tortilla Española with Charred Red Peppers, 364–65,
     422, **454–55**
berries. *See* blackberries; dried cranberries; strawberries
biscotti
   Parmesan and Fennel Biscotti, 220–21, **418–19**
bisques
   Asparagus Bisque with Fresh Dill, 243–44, **245–46**
   Cauliflower Bisque with Buttered Breadcrumbs, **169–71**
   Sweet Potato Bisque, 218, **231–32**
Bittersweet Chocolate Brownies, **497–98**
black bean(s)
   Black Bean and Squash Soup, 138–39, **140–41**
   Black Bean Quesadillas, **456–57**
   Spicy Black Bean Soup with Sweet Peppers, 43, **142–44**
Black Bean and Squash Soup, **140–41**
   menu using, 138–39
Black Bean Quesadillas, **456–57**
blackberries
   Butter Cake with Summer Fruits, 318–19, 486, **488–89**
blenders, 34–35
Borlotti beans
   Kabocha Squash and Cranberry Bean Stew, 178, **203–5**
brassicas, about, 242
bread, 387–419
   Buttered Breadcrumbs, **170**
   Crostini, **415–16**
   Croutons, 136, **446–47**
   doubling recipes for, 391, 393, 396, 401
   Fresh Corn and Cheddar Cheese Cornbread, 180–81, 358,
      407
   Garlic Soup, 49, 154–55, **156–57**
   Gazpacho Andaluz, 362–63, 364–65, **366–67**
   Grandma's Dinner Rolls, **397–99**
   Greek Pizza, **404**
   Green Pizza, **404**
   Grilled Goat Cheese Sandwich, 243–44, **450–51**
   Irish Soda Bread with Fennel and Orange, 256–57,
      405–6

Multigrain Scones with Fennel and Orange, **411–12**
Mushroom Pizza, **404**
Oatmeal Molasses Bread, 138–39, 337, **394–96**
Olive and Rosemary Focaccia, 128–29, 318–19, **400–401**
Pappa al Pomodoro, **328–29**
Parmesan and Fennel Biscotti, 220–21, **418–19**
Parmesan Crostini, 81, **417**
Popovers, 276–77, **409–10**
Potato Pizza, 277, **402–4**
quick, 389
Quick Whole-Wheat Oatmeal Bread, **408**
Savory Walnut and Herb Biscuits, **413–14**
Sopa de Ajo, 49, 154–55, **156–57**
Three-Grain Bread, **390–91**
Vegetarian Onion Soup Gratin, 50, **160–61**
Whole-Wheat Walnut Bread, 109–10, 309–10, **392–93**
broccoli
  Green Soup with Broccoli, Fennel, and Sorrel, **290–91**
broth, 41–57. *See also* Basic Dark Vegetable Broth; Basic Light Vegetable Broth; Basic Root Vegetable Broth; Mushroom Stock; Pea Pod Broth; Vegetable and Ginger Broth; Vegetable Broth with No Onions
  canned, 43, 46
  freezing, 44
  making, 43–44
brownies
  Bittersweet Chocolate Brownies, **497–98**
Brown Rice and Chinese Cabbage Salad, **477–78**
Butter Bean and Summer Vegetable Soup, **300–301**
  menu using, 298–99
Butter Cake with Summer Fruits, 486, **488–89**
  menu using, 318–19
Buttered Breadcrumbs, **170**
buttermilk
  Fresh Corn and Cheddar Cheese Cornbread, 180–81, 358, **407**
  Irish Soda Bread with Fennel and Orange, 256–57, **405–6**
  Multigrain Scones with Fennel and Orange, **411–12**
  Parmesan and Fennel Biscotti, 220–21, **418–19**
  Quick Whole-Wheat Oatmeal Bread, **408**
  Savory Walnut and Herb Biscuits, **413–14**
butternut squash
  Black Bean and Squash Soup, 138–39, **140–41**

Red Lentil and Squash Soup, 52, **118–19**
Roasted Turnip and Winter Squash Soup, **116–17**
Stewed Root Vegetables with Moroccan Spices, 179, **200–202**
Tomatillo, Squash, and Mustard Greens Soup, **122–23**
Winter Squash and Yam Soup with Poblano Peppers, 43, **120–21**

cabbage. *See* green cabbage; Napa cabbage; savoy cabbage
  Red Cabbage and Apple Salad, 138–39, 181, **476**
cakes
  Butter Cake with Summer Fruits, 318–19, 486, **488–89**
  Octavia's Gingerbread, 109–10, 486, **490–91**
  Olive Oil and Lemon Cake, 220–21, 487, **492–93**
canned broth, 43, 46
Cannellini and Golden Tomato Soup, **324–25**
cannellini beans
  Cannellini and Golden Tomato Soup, **324–25**
  The Great Pumpkin Soup, 180–81, **182–84**
  in Kale and Tomato Soup, 346
  Marbled Cannellini Dip with Roasted Tomatoes, 220–21, **431–32**
  Minestrone for a Crowd, **193–95**
  Vegetable Soup Pistou, 332, **352–54**
  White Bean and Garlic Soup with Greens, 26, 128–29, **130–31**
Caramelized Cabbage Soup, **174–75**
Carol's Finnish Pea Soup with Apples, **147–48**
carrot(s)
  Barley, Mushroom, and Vegetable Soup, 20, 26, **185–87**
  Basic Dark Vegetable Broth, 45, **50–51**
  Basic Light Vegetable Broth, **47–48**
  Basic Root Vegetable Broth, 45, **49**
  Carrot, Orange, and Ginger Soup, 53, **254–55**
  Chopped Salad with French Green Lentils, 64–65, **466–67**
  Farro with Stewed and Roasted Winter Vegetables, 178, **206–9**
  French Lentil Stew with Roasted Carrots and Mint, 196–97, **198–99**
  Hearty Brown Lentil Soup, **188–89**
  Mushroom Stock, 46, **56–57, 224–25**
  Pea Pod Broth, 46, **55**
  Pickle Soup, 20, 26, **185–87**

carrot(s) (*continued*)

Puree of Carrot and Yam with Citrus and Spices, 52, **78–79**

Roasted Root Vegetable Soup, 25, **166–68**

Rustic Artichoke and Potato Stew, **262–65**

Spicy Black Bean Soup with Sweet Peppers, 43, **142–44**

Spicy Indonesian Yam and Peanut Soup, **164–65**

Stewed Root Vegetables with Moroccan Spices, 179, **200–202**

Ten-Vegetable Soup with Cranberry Beans, **190–92**

Three-Bean and Vegetable Chili, 178, **212–15**

Vegetable and Ginger Broth, 45, **52**

Vegetable Broth with No Onions, 45, **53–54**

Vegetable Soup Pistou, 332, **352–54**

Carrot, Orange, and Ginger Soup, 53, **254–55**

Cauliflower Bisque with Buttered Breadcrumbs, **169–71**

cavalo nero

Kale and Sweet Potato Soup with Cumin and Lemon, 52, **100–101**

celery

Barley, Mushroom, and Vegetable Soup, 20, 26, **185–87**

Basic Dark Vegetable Broth, 45, **50–51**

Basic Light Vegetable Broth, **47–48**

Basic Root Vegetable Broth, 45, **49**

Chopped Salad with French Green Lentils, 64–65, **466–67**

Pea Pod Broth, 46, **55**

Pickle Soup, 20, 26, **185–87**

Ten-Vegetable Soup with Cranberry Beans, **190–92**

Vegetable and Ginger Broth, 45, **52**

Vegetable Broth with No Onions, 45, **53–54**

celery root

Basic Root Vegetable Broth, 45, **49**

Puree of Carrot and Yam with Citrus and Spices, 52, **78–79**

Roasted Golden Beet Soup, **74–75**

Roasted Kabocha Squash and Celery Root Soup, 24, 109–10, **111–13**

Sweet Potato Bisque, 218, **231–32**

chard

Barley, Mushroom, and Vegetable Soup, 20, 26, **185–87**

Chard and Yam Soup, 49, **72–73**

The Great Pumpkin Soup, 180–81, **182–84**

Green Lentil Soup with Cumin and Lemon, **134–35**

Green Soup, 19, 20, 22, 30, **90–91**

Green Soup with Ginger, 52, **96–97**

Green Soup with Mushrooms, **92–93**

Green Soup with Sweet Potatoes and Sage, **94–95**

Pickle Soup, 20, 26, **185–87**

Quinoa Stew with Potatoes, Spinach, and Chard, **210–11**

Three-Bean and Vegetable Chili, 178, **212–15**

Vegetable Broth with No Onions, 45, **53–54**

White Bean and Garlic Soup with Greens, 26, 128–29, **130–31**

Chard and Yam Soup, 49, **72–73**

Charred Zucchini Soup with Yogurt and Pine Nuts, **315–17**

cheddar cheese

Chopped Salad with French Green Lentils, 64–65, **466–67**

Corn and Cheese Chowder, 332, 334–35, **336–37**

Fresh Corn and Cheddar Cheese Cornbread, 180–81, 358, **407**

cheese. *See* cheddar cheese; feta cheese; goat cheese; Gruyère cheese; halloumi; jack cheese; Montrachet cheese; mozzarella cheese; panella cheese; Parmesan cheese; provolone cheese; *queso fresco*; ricotta cheese; white farmer cheese; yogurt cheese

cherries

Butter Cake with Summer Fruits, 318–19, 486, **488–89**

Cold Cherry-Lemon Soup, 297, 363, **377–78**

chestnuts

Chestnut Soup, 218, **233–34**

roasting, 234

Chestnut Soup, 218, **233–34**

chickpeas. *See* garbanzo beans

chiles

about, 62–63

Ancho and Guajillo Chile Puree, 78, 117, 142, 183, 188, 338, **440–41**

Black Bean and Squash Soup, 138–39, **140–41**

Chipotle Hummus, **426**

Cold Cream of Poblano Peppers with Red Grapes, 362, **375–76**

Cold Cucumber and Avocado Soup, **369–70**

Cold Cucumber-Cilantro Soup with Goat Yogurt, **368**

Corn and Pepper Soup, **343–44**

Deconstructed Hummus Soup, 26, 347–49, **350–51**

Farro with Stewed and Roasted Winter Vegetables, 178, **206–9**

handling, 445

Harissa, 196–97, 198, 210, **444–45**

Kabocha Squash and Cranberry Bean Stew, 178, **203–5**

Napa Cabbage Slaw, **481–82**

Roasted Eggplant and Garbanzo Bean Soup, **355–57**

Roasted Poblano Chile Soup, **70–71**

Simple Chipotle Sauce, 72, 117, 180–81, 183, 198, **439,** 456

Sopa de Poblanos, **70–71**

Stewed Root Vegetables with Moroccan Spices, 179, **200–202**

Table Salsa, 188, 210, **442–43,** 456

Three-Bean and Vegetable Chili, 178, **212–15**

Tomatillo, Squash, and Mustard Greens Soup, **122–23**

Tortilla Soup, 332, **338–40**

Vegetable Soup Pistou, 332, **352–54**

Winter Squash and Yam Soup with Poblano Peppers, 43, **120–21**

Chilled Melon Soup with Mint, **379–80**

chilled soups. See cold soups

Chipotle Hummus, **426**

chives

    Savory Walnut and Herb Biscuits, **413–14**

    Summer Chopped Salad with Grilled Halloumi, **470**

chocolate

    Bittersweet Chocolate Brownies, **497–98**

    Lauren's Badass Trailmix Cookies, 487, **495–96**

Chopped Salad with French Green Lentils, **466–67**

    menu using, 64–65

chowder

    Corn and Cheese Chowder, 332, 335–36, **336–37**

Christmas Eve Porcini Soup, 23, 43, 218, **222–23,** 224

    menu using, 220–21

cilantro

    Basic Dark Vegetable Broth, 45, **50–51**

    Black Bean Quesadillas, **456–57**

    Cold Cucumber-Cilantro Soup with Goat Yogurt, **368**

    Cucumber, Rice, and Fresh Herb Salad, 347–49, **468–69**

    The Great Pumpkin Soup, 180–81, **182–84**

    Green Lentil Soup with Cumin and Lemon, **134–35**

    Green Soup, 19, 20, 22, 30, **90–91**

    Hearty Brown Lentil Soup, **188–89**

    Kabocha Squash and Cranberry Bean Stew, 178, **203–5**

Kale and Sweet Potato Soup with Cumin and Lemon, 52, **100–101**

Lentil and Spinach Salad, **479–80**

Mung Bean Soup with Spinach and Tomatoes, 332, **341–42**

Mushroom Stock, 46, **56–57, 224–25**

Napa Cabbage Slaw, **481–82**

Quinoa Stew with Potatoes, Spinach, and Chard, **210–11**

Roasted Poblano Chile Soup, **70–71**

Sopa de Poblanos, **70–71**

Spicy Butternut Ginger Soup, 24, 30, 52, **114–15**

Stewed Root Vegetables with Moroccan Spices, 179, **200–202**

Three-Bean and Vegetable Chili, 178, **212–15**

Tomatillo, Squash, and Mustard Greens Soup, **122–23**

Tortilla Soup, 332, **338–40**

Vegetable and Ginger Broth, 45, **52**

Winter Squash and Yam Soup with Poblano Peppers, 43, **120–21**

coffee in Bittersweet Chocolate Brownies, 498

Cold Asparagus Soup, 362, **371–72**

Cold Cherry-Lemon Soup, 297, 363, **377–78**

Cold Cream of Poblano Peppers with Red Grapes, 362, **375–76**

Cold Cucumber and Avocado Soup, **369–70**

Cold Cucumber and Mint Soup with Radishes, **373–74**

Cold Cucumber-Cilantro Soup with Goat Yogurt, **368**

Cold Peach and Nectarine Soup with Strawberry Sauce, **381–82**

cold soups

    Beet Soup with Ginger, 227

    Chilled Melon Soup with Mint, **379–80**

    Cold Asparagus Soup, 362, **371–72**

    Cold Cherry-Lemon Soup, 297, 363, **377–78**

    Cold Cream of Poblano Peppers with Red Grapes, 362, **375–76**

    Cold Cucumber and Avocado Soup, **369–70**

    Cold Cucumber and Mint Soup with Radishes, **373–74**

    Cold Cucumber-Cilantro Soup with Goat Yogurt, **368**

    Cold Peach and Nectarine Soup with Strawberry Sauce, **381–82**

    Gazpacho Andaluz, 362–63, 364–65, **366–67**

    Rustic Leek and Potato Soup, 159

cookies
    Angel Cookies, 364–65, **494**
    Bittersweet Chocolate Brownies, **497–98**
    Lauren's Badass Trailmix Cookies, 487, **495–96**
corn
    Barley Salad with Corn and Zucchini, **464–65**
    Chopped Salad with French Green Lentils, 64–65,
        466–67
    Corn and Cheese Chowder, 332, 334–35, **336–37**
    Corn and Pepper Soup, **343–44**
    Fresh Corn and Cheddar Cheese Cornbread, 180–81, 358,
        407
    Kale Salad with Tomatoes and Corn, **475**
    Summer Chopped Salad with Grilled Halloumi, **470**
    Sweet Corn Soup, 26, **302–3**
Corn and Cheese Chowder, 332, **336–37**
    menus using, 334–35
Corn and Pepper Soup, **343–44**
cranberries. *See* dried cranberries
cranberry beans
    Kabocha Squash and Cranberry Bean Stew, 178, **203–5**
    Ten-Vegetable Soup with Cranberry Beans, **190–92**
cream
    Chilled Melon Soup with Mint, **379–80**
    Mint Cream, **251**
cream cheese
    Cauliflower Bisque with Buttered Breadcrumbs, **169–71**
Cream of Baby Spring Greens, **289**
Creamy Artichoke Soup, **266–68**
Creamy Potato and Roasted Garlic Soup, **80–82**
crème fraîche
    Cold Cherry-Lemon Soup, 297, 363, **377–78**
crostini
    Crostini, **415–16**
    Parmesan Crostini, 81, **417**
croutons, 446–47
    Basic Croutons, 446
    Croutons, **446–47**
    Garlic Croutons, **446**
    Herbed Croutons, 136, **447**
    storing, 447
cucumber(s)
    Cold Cucumber and Avocado Soup, **369–70**
    Cold Cucumber and Mint Soup with Radishes, **373–74**
    Cold Cucumber-Cilantro Soup with Goat Yogurt, **368**
    Cucumber, Rice, and Fresh Herb Salad, 347–49, **468–69**
    Gazpacho Andaluz, 362–63, 364–65, **366–67**
    Summer Chopped Salad with Grilled Halloumi, **470**
Cucumber, Rice, and Fresh Herb Salad, **468–69**
    menu using, 347–49
cumin
    Kale and Sweet Potato Soup with Cumin and Lemon, 52,
        100–101
Curried Spinach and Sorrel Soup, **269–70**
cutting boards, 34

dandelion greens
    Rustic Artichoke and Potato Stew, **262–65**
Deconstructed Hummus Soup, 26, **350–51**
    menu using, 347–49
defrosting soups, 38
desserts. *See* sweet(s)
dill
    Asparagus Bisque with Fresh Dill, 243–44, **245–46**
    Cold Asparagus Soup, 362, **371–72**
    Mushroom Stock, 46, **56–57, 224–25**
    Snap Pea, Asparagus, and Fennel Soup with Fresh Herbs,
        274, **280–81**
    Springtime Barley and Mushroom Soup, 256–57,
        258–59
dill pickles
    Barley, Mushroom, and Vegetable Soup, 20, 26, **185–87**
    Pickle Soup, 20, 26, **185–87**
dip
    Marbled Cannellini Dip with Roasted Tomatoes, 220–21,
        431–32
doubling recipes
    for bread, 391, 393, 396, 401
    for soup, 38
Drained Yogurt, **317**
dried beans. *See also* black beans; cannellini beans; cran-
        berry beans; garbanzo beans; kidney beans; white
        beans; *specific types of beans*
    cooking, 126–27
dried cranberries
    Kale Salad with Cranberries and Walnuts, **473–74**
    Rice Pudding with Dried Cranberries, **501**
dried herbs, 36–37

dried split peas
    Carol's Finnish Pea Soup with Apples, **147–48**
    Old-Fashioned Split Pea Soup, 23, **145–46**

egg(s)
    Olive Oil and Lemon Cake, 220–21, 487, **492–93**
    Sara's Spinach Pie, 422, **452–53**
    Tortilla Española with Charred Red Peppers, 364–65, 422, **454–55**
eggplant
    Eggplant and Roasted Garlic Pesto, **434–35**
    Roasted Eggplant and Garbanzo Bean Soup, **355–57**
    Smoky Eggplant Soup with Mint and Pine Nuts, **304–6**
Eggplant and Roasted Garlic Pesto, **434–35**
epazote
    about, 127
    Black Bean and Squash Soup, 138–39, **140–41**
    Kabocha Squash and Cranberry Bean Stew, 178, **203–5**
    Roasted Poblano Chile Soup, **70–71**
    Sopa de Poblanos, **70–71**
    Spicy Black Bean Soup with Sweet Peppers, 43, **142–44**
    Three-Bean and Vegetable Chili, 178, **212–15**
    Vegetable Soup Pistou, 332, **352–54**
equipment, 33–35
Escarole and Potato Soup, **307–8**

farmers' markets, 28–32
    in harvest season, 62–63
    in spring, 240–42
    in summer, 332–33
    in winter, 152–53
Farmhouse Apple Crumble, **499–500**
    menu using, 88–89
farro
    cooking, 208
Farro with Stewed and Roasted Winter Vegetables, 178, **206–9**
Fasolia Gigante Soup with Spinach, **132–33**
fava beans
    about, 241–42
    Fresh Fava Bean and Sweet Pea Soup, **260–61,** 277
Fennel and Onion Soup, 49, **68–69**
fennel/fennel greens
    about, 241

Asparagus Bisque with Fresh Dill, 243–44, **245–46**
Basic Light Vegetable Broth, **47–48**
Beet Soup with Ginger, 218, **226–27**
Escarole and Potato Soup, **307–8**
Fennel and Onion Soup, 49, **68–69**
Green Soup with Broccoli, Fennel, and Sorrel, **290–91**
Irish Soda Bread with Fennel and Orange, 256–57, **405–6**
Minestrone for a Crowd, **193–95**
Multigrain Scones with Fennel and Orange, **411–12**
Nettle Soup with Fennel and Leeks, 25, **285–86**
Parmesan and Fennel Biscotti, 220–21, **418–19**
Potage of Baby Spring Greens, 274, **288–89**
Roasted Root Vegetable Soup, 25, **166–68**
Rustic Artichoke and Potato Stew, **262–65**
Salad of Baby Arugula, Aged Jack Cheese, and Asian Pears, 220–21, **418–19**
Snap Pea, Asparagus, and Fennel Soup with Fresh Herbs, 274, **280–81**
Sorrel Soup with Mint and Spring Vegetables, 244, **247–48**, 277
Springtime Barley and Mushroom Soup, 256–57, **258–59**
Stewed Root Vegetables with Moroccan Spices, 179, **200–202**
Tomato and Fennel Soup with Blood Orange, **322–23**
Tomato and Zucchini Soup with Summer Herbs, **326–27**
Vegetable and Ginger Broth, 45, **52**
Vegetable Broth with No Onions, 45, **53–54**
Vegetable Soup Pistou, 332, **352–54**
feta cheese
    Quinoa Stew with Potatoes, Spinach, and Chard, **210–11**
    Sara's Spinach Pie, 422, **452–53**
figs
    Tapenade with Figs and Citrus, 220–21, 298–99, **428**
focaccia
    Olive and Rosemary Focaccia, 128–29, 318–19, **400–401**
freezing
    broth, 44
    soups, 37–38
French Lentil Stew with Roasted Carrots and Mint, **198–99**
    menu using, 196–97

Fresh Corn and Cheddar Cheese Cornbread, 180–81, 358, **407**
  menu using, 180–81
Fresh Fava Bean and Sweet Pea Soup, **260–61,** 277
fresh herbs, 36. *See also specific herbs*
Fresh Pea Soup with Mint Cream, 26, 43, **249–51**
fruit
  about, 242
  Butter Cake with Summer Fruits, 318–19, 486, **488–89**

garbanzo beans
  Deconstructed Hummus Soup, 26, 347–49, **350–51**
  dried vs. canned, 359
  Roasted Eggplant and Garbanzo Bean Soup, **355–57**
  Sprouted Garbanzo Hummus, **425–27**
  Summer Minestrone, 332, **358–59**
  Three-Bean and Vegetable Chili, 178, **212–15**
garlic
  Ancho and Guajillo Chile Puree, 78, 117, 142, 183, 188, 338, **440–41**
  Creamy Potato and Roasted Garlic Soup, **80–82**
  Eggplant and Roasted Garlic Pesto, **434–35**
  Garlic Soup, 49, 154–55, **156–57**
  Harissa, 196–97, 198, 210, **444–45**
  Sopa de Ajo, 49, 154–55, **156–57**
  Table Salsa, 188, 210, **442–43,** 456
Garlic Croutons, **446**
Garlic Soup, 49, **156–57**
  menu using, 154–55
Gazpacho Andaluz, 362–63, **366–67**
  menu using, 364–65
ginger
  Beet Soup with Ginger, 218, **226–27**
  Carrot, Orange, and Ginger Soup, 53, **254–55**
  Green Soup with Ginger, 52, **96–97**
  Mung Bean Soup with Spinach and Tomatoes, 332, **341–42**
  Napa Cabbage Slaw, **481–82**
  Octavia's Gingerbread, 109–10, 486, **490–91**
  Persimmon Soup with Tamari-Toasted Walnuts, 25, 219, **228–30**
  Spicy Butternut Ginger Soup, 24, 30, 52, **114–15**
  Spicy Indonesian Yam and Peanut Soup, **164–65**
  Vegetable and Ginger Broth, 45, **52**

goat cheese
  Cauliflower Bisque with Buttered Breadcrumbs, **169–71**
  Cold Asparagus Soup, 362, **371–72**
  Curried Spinach and Sorrel Soup, **269–70**
  Grilled Goat Cheese Sandwich, 243–44, **450–51**
  Roasted Poblano Chile Soup, **70–71**
  Sopa de Poblanos, **70–71**
Grandma's Dinner Rolls, **397–99**
grapes
  Cold Cream of Poblano Peppers with Red Grapes, 362, **375–76**
Great Northern beans
  White Bean and Garlic Soup with Greens, 26, 128–29, **130–31**
The Great Pumpkin Soup, **182–84**
  menu using, 180–81
Greek Pizza, **404**
Greek Yogurt with Honey and Walnuts, **502**
  menu using, 138–39
green beans
  Butter Bean and Summer Vegetable Soup, 298–99, **300–301**
  Summer Minestrone, 332, **358–59**
  Vegetable Soup Pistou, 332, **352–54**
green cabbage
  Caramelized Cabbage Soup, **174–75**
  Roasted Golden Beet Soup, **74–75**
  Ten-Vegetable Soup with Cranberry Beans, **190–92**
Green Lentil Soup with Cumin and Lemon, **134–35**
green onions
  Arugula and Apple Soup with Toasted Walnuts, **98–99**
  Chard and Yam Soup, 49, **72–73**
  Chopped Salad with French Green Lentils, 64–65, **466–67**
  Curried Spinach and Sorrel Soup, **269–70**
  Fresh Corn and Cheddar Cheese Cornbread, 180–81, 358, **407**
  Green Soup, 19, 20, 22, 30, **90–91**
  Kale and Sweet Potato Soup with Cumin and Lemon, 52, **100–101**
  Mushroom-Barley Soup with Cabbage, **162–63**
  Napa Cabbage Slaw, **481–82**
  Quinoa Stew with Potatoes, Spinach, and Chard, **210–11**

Snap Pea, Asparagus, and Fennel Soup with Fresh Herbs, 274, **280–81**

Sorrel Soup with Mint and Spring Vegetables, 244, **247–48**, 277

green peas

Carol's Finnish Pea Soup with Apples, **147–48**

Fresh Pea Soup with Mint Cream, 26, 43, **249–51**

Rustic Artichoke and Potato Stew, **262–65**

Green Pizza, **404**

greens. *See also* arugula; beets/beet greens; chard; dandelion greens; fennel/fennel greens; kale; lettuce; spinach; turnip greens; watercress

about, 241

Green Soup, 19, 20, 22, 30, **90–91**

Green Soup with Broccoli, Fennel, and Sorrel, **290–91**

Green Soup with Ginger, 52, **96–97**

Green Soup with Mushrooms, **92–93**

Green Soup with Sweet Potatoes and Sage, **94–95**

green tomatoes

Stewed Root Vegetables with Moroccan Spices, 179, **200–202**

Grilled Goat Cheese Sandwich, **450–51**

menu using, 243–44

Gruyère cheese

Vegetarian Onion Soup Gratin, 50, **160–61**

halloumi

Summer Chopped Salad with Grilled Halloumi, **470**

Harissa, 198, 210, **444–45**

menu using, 196–97

Hearty Brown Lentil Soup, **188–89**

Heirloom Tomato Salad, **471–72**

menus using, 309–10, 334–35

herb(s). *See also specific herbs*

about, 36–37, 241

crostini with, 416

Herbed Croutons, 136, **447**

Hummus with Fresh Herbs, 427

Herbed Croutons, 136, **447**

honey

Greek Yogurt with Honey and Walnuts, 138–39, **502**

hummus

Chipotle Hummus, **426**

Hummus with Fire Roasted Red Peppers, **426–27**

Hummus with Fresh Herbs, 427

Hummus with Olives, 427

Spicy Paprika Hummus, **426**

Sprouted Garbanzo Hummus, **425–27**

Hummus with Fire Roasted Red Peppers, **426–27**

Hummus with Fresh Herbs, 427

Hummus with Olives, 427

immersion blenders, 34, 35

ingredients. *See also specific ingredients*

basic, for pantry, 31–32

shopping for. *See* farmers' markets

Irish Soda Bread with Fennel and Orange, **405–6**

menu using, 256–57

jack cheese

Black Bean Quesadillas, **456–57**

Salad of Baby Arugula, Aged Jack Cheese, and Asian Pears, 220–21, **462–63**

Jeri's Spiced Nuts, **448–49,** 462

menu using, 221–22

kabocha squash

Black Bean and Squash Soup, 138–39, **140–41**

Farro with Stewed and Roasted Winter Vegetables, 178, **206–9**

Kabocha Squash and Cranberry Bean Stew, 178, **203–5**

Kale Salad with Roasted Kabocha, **474**

Roasted Kabocha Squash and Celery Root Soup, 24, 109–10, **111–13**

Stewed Root Vegetables with Moroccan Spices, 179, **200–202**

Winter Squash and Yam Soup with Poblano Peppers, 43, **120–21**

Kabocha Squash and Cranberry Bean Stew, 178, **203–5**

kale

about, 52

Farro with Stewed and Roasted Winter Vegetables, 178, **206–9**

Green Soup, 19, 20, 22, 30, **90–91**

Green Soup with Sweet Potatoes and Sage, **94–95**

Kale and Sweet Potato Soup with Cumin and Lemon, 52, **100–101**

kale (*continued*)
 Kale and Tomato Soup, **345–46**
 Kale Salad with Cranberries and Walnuts, **473–74**
 Kale Salad with Roasted Kabocha, **474**
 Kale Salad with Tomatoes and Corn, **475**
 Nettle and Kale Soup, **284–85**
 Ten-Vegetable Soup with Cranberry Beans, **190–92**
 Vegetable Broth with No Onions, 45, **53–54**
 Vegetable Soup Pistou, 332, **352–54**
Kale and Sweet Potato Soup with Cumin and Lemon, 52,
 100–101
Kale and Tomato Soup, **345–46**
Kale Salad with Cranberries and Pine Nuts
 menu using, 109–10
Kale Salad with Cranberries and Walnuts, **473–74**
Kale Salad with Roasted Kabocha, **474**
Kale Salad with Tomatoes and Corn, **475**
kidney beans
 Ten-Vegetable Soup with Cranberry Beans, **190–92**
 Three-Bean and Vegetable Chili, 178, **212–15**
knives, 33–34

ladles, 34
Lauren's Badass Trailmix Cookies, 487, **495–96**
lavender
 Olive and Rosemary Focaccia, 128–29, 318–19, **400–401**
leeks
 Asparagus Bisque with Fresh Dill, 243–44, **245–46**
 Barley, Mushroom, and Vegetable Soup, 20, 26, **185–87**
 Basic Dark Vegetable Broth, 45, **50–51**
 Basic Light Vegetable Broth, **47–48**
 Basic Root Vegetable Broth, 45, **49**
 Beet Soup with Ginger, 218, **226–27**
 Caramelized Cabbage Soup, **174–75**
 Chestnut Soup, 218, **233–34**
 Creamy Artichoke Soup, **266–68**
 Escarole and Potato Soup, **307–8**
 The Great Pumpkin Soup, 180–81, **182–84**
 Green Lentil Soup with Cumin and Lemon, **134–35**
 Green Soup with Ginger, 52, **96–97**
 Green Soup with Mushrooms, **92–93**
 Kale and Sweet Potato Soup with Cumin and Lemon, 52,
 100–101
 Kale and Tomato Soup, **345–46**
 Lentil and Spinach Salad, **479–80**

Mushroom Stock, 46, **56–57, 224–25**
Neeps and Tatties Soup, 49, **172–73**
Nettle and Kale Soup, **284–85**
Nettle Soup with Fennel and Leeks, 25, **285–86**
Parsley Soup, **102–3**
Persimmon Soup with Tamari-Toasted Walnuts, 25, 219,
 228–30
Pickle Soup, 20, 26, **185–87**
Potage of Baby Spring Greens, 274, **288–89**
Purple Cauliflower Soup, **252–53**
Roasted Kabocha Squash and Celery Root Soup, 24,
 109–10, **111–13**
Roasted Turnip and Winter Squash Soup, **116–17**
Rustic Leek and Potato Soup, **158–59**
Snap Pea, Asparagus, and Fennel Soup with Fresh Herbs,
 274, **280–81**
Spring Green Soup, 53, 274, 276–77, **278–79,** 423
Springtime Barley and Mushroom Soup, 256–57,
 258–59
Ten-Vegetable Soup with Cranberry Beans, **190–92**
Turnip and Potato Soup, **172–73**
Vegetable and Ginger Broth, 45, **52**
Vegetable Soup Pistou, 332, **352–54**
lemons/lemon juice
 Chilled Melon Soup with Mint, **379–80**
 Chopped Salad with French Green Lentils, 64–65,
 466–67
 Cold Cherry-Lemon Soup, 297, 363, **377–78**
 Cold Cucumber and Avocado Soup, **369–70**
 Cold Cucumber and Mint Soup with Radishes, **373–74**
 Cold Peach and Nectarine Soup with Strawberry Sauce,
 381–82
 Deconstructed Hummus Soup, 26, 347–49, **350–51**
 Green Lentil Soup with Cumin and Lemon, **134–35**
 Kale and Sweet Potato Soup with Cumin and Lemon, 52,
 100–101
 Olive Oil and Lemon Cake, 220–21, 487, **492–93**
 Rustic Artichoke and Potato Stew, **262–65**
 Sprouted Garbanzo Hummus, **425–27**
lentil(s)
 Chopped Salad with French Green Lentils, 64–65,
 466–67
 French Lentil Stew with Roasted Carrots and Mint,
 196–97, **198–99**
 Green Lentil Soup with Cumin and Lemon, **134–35**

Hearty Brown Lentil Soup, **188–89**
Lentil and Spinach Salad, **479–80**
Red Lentil and Squash Soup, 52, **118–19**
Lentil and Spinach Salad, **479–80**
lettuce
   Fresh Pea Soup with Mint Cream, 26, 43, **249–51**
lima beans
   Butter Bean and Summer Vegetable Soup, 298–99,
      300–301
   Fasolia Gigante Soup with Spinach, **132–33**
Lima Bean Soup, **136–37**
Lima Bean Spread, **433**
limes/lime juice
   Tortilla Soup, 332, **338–40**

Marbled Cannellini Dip with Roasted Tomatoes, **431–32**
   menu using, 220–21
marjoram
   Savory Walnut and Herb Biscuits, **413–14**
measurements, 39
   scales and, 34
melons
   Chilled Melon Soup with Mint, **379–80**
   Melons in Orange and Mint Syrup, 298–99, **503**
Melons in Orange and Mint Syrup, **503**
   menu using, 298–99
menus
   with Angel Cookies, 364–65
   with Asparagus Bisque with Fresh Dill, 243–44
   with Black Bean and Squash Soup, 138–39
   with Butter Bean and Summer Vegetable Soup, 298–99
   with Butter Cake with Summer Fruits, 318–19
   with Chopped Salad with French Green Lentils, 64–65
   with Christmas Eve Porcini Soup, 220–21
   with Corn and Cheese Chowder, 334–35
   with Cucumber, Rice, and Fresh Herb Salad, 347–49
   with Deconstructed Hummus Soup, 347–49
   with Farmhouse Apple Crumble, 88–89
   with French Lentil Stew with Roasted Carrots and Mint,
      196–97
   with Fresh Corn and Cheddar Cheese Cornbread, 180–81
   with Garlic Soup, 154–55
   with Gazpacho Andaluz, 364–65
   with The Great Pumpkin Soup, 180–81
   with Greek Yogurt with Honey and Walnuts, 138–39
   with Grilled Goat Cheese Sandwich, 243–44
   with Harissa, 196–97
   with Heirloom Tomato Salad, 309–10, 334–35
   with Irish Soda Bread with Fennel and Orange, 256–57
   with Jeri's Spiced Nuts, 221–22
   with Kale Salad with Cranberries and Pine Nuts, 109–10
   with Marbled Cannellini Dip with Roasted Tomatoes,
      220–21
   with Melons in Orange and Mint Syrup, 298–99
   with Oatmeal Molasses Bread, 138–39
   with Octavia's Gingerbread, 109–10
   with Olive and Rosemary Focaccia, 128–29, 318–19
   with Olive Oil and Lemon Cake, 220–21
   with Orange and Mint Syrup, 243–44
   with Parmesan and Fennel Biscotti, 220–21
   with Popovers, 276–77
   with Potato and Tomato Soup with Sage, 64–65
   with Red Cabbage and Apple Salad, 138–39
   with Roasted Kabocha Squash and Celery Root Soup,
      109–10
   with Salad of Baby Arugula, Aged Jack Cheese, and Asian
      Pears, 220–21
   with Simple Basil Pesto, 334–35
   with Simple Chipotle Sauce, 180–81
   with Sopa de Ajo, 154–55
   with Spring Green Soup, 276–77
   with Springtime Barley and Mushroom Soup, 256–57
   with Sprouted Garbanzo Hummus, 88–89
   with Summer Tomato and Basil Soup, 318–19
   with Tangerine and Strawberry Compote, 276–77
   with Tapenade with Figs and Citrus, 220–21, 298–99
   with Three-Grain Bread, 88–89
   with Tortilla Española with Charred Red Peppers,
      364–65
   with White Bean and Garlic Soup with Greens, 128–29
   with Whole-Wheat Walnut Bread, 309–10
   with Zucchini and Basil Soup, 309–10
milk
   Caramelized Cabbage Soup, **174–75**
   Cold Cream of Poblano Peppers with Red Grapes, 362,
      375–76
   Corn and Cheese Chowder, 332, 334–35, **336–37**
   Creamy Artichoke Soup, **266–68**
   Curried Spinach and Sorrel Soup, **269–70**
   Rice Pudding with Dried Cranberries, **501**

milk (*continued*)

    Sweet Corn Soup, 26, **302–3**

Minestrone for a Crowd, **193–95**

mint

    Charred Zucchini Soup with Yogurt and Pine Nuts, **315–17**

    Chilled Melon Soup with Mint, **379–80**

    Cold Cucumber and Mint Soup with Radishes, **373–74**

    Cold Cucumber-Cilantro Soup with Goat Yogurt, **368**

    Cold Peach and Nectarine Soup with Strawberry Sauce, **381–82**

    Cucumber, Rice, and Fresh Herb Salad, 347–49, **468–69**

    French Lentil Stew with Roasted Carrots and Mint, 196–97, **198–99**

    Fresh Fava Bean and Sweet Pea Soup, **260–61,** 277

    Melons in Orange and Mint Syrup, 298–99, **503**

    Mint Cream, **251**

    Mung Bean Soup with Spinach and Tomatoes, 332, **341–42**

    Orange and Mint Syrup, 243–44, 503, **504**

    in Parsley and Walnut Pesto, **438**

    Roasted Eggplant and Garbanzo Bean Soup, **355–57**

    Smoky Eggplant Soup with Mint and Pine Nuts, **304–6**

    Snap Pea, Asparagus, and Fennel Soup with Fresh Herbs, 274, **280–81**

    Sorrel Soup with Mint and Spring Vegetables, 244, **247–48**, 277

    Spring Green Soup, 53, 274, 276–77, **278–79,** 423

    Tomato and Zucchini Soup with Summer Herbs, **326–27**

Mint Cream, **251**

mizuna

    Kale Salad with Cranberries and Walnuts, **473–74**

    Napa Cabbage Slaw, **481–82**

molasses

    Oatmeal Molasses Bread, 138–39, 337, **394–96**

molcahetes, 35

Monterey jack cheese. *See* jack cheese

Montrachet cheese

    Grilled Goat Cheese Sandwich, 243–44, **450–51**

morels in Springtime Barley and Mushroom Soup, 259

mortars, 35

mozzarella cheese

    Heirloom Tomato Salad, 309–10, 334–35, **471–72**

Multigrain Scones with Fennel and Orange, **411–12**

Mung Bean Soup with Spinach and Tomatoes, 332, **341–42**

mushroom(s)

    about, 63

    Barley, Mushroom, and Vegetable Soup, 20, 26, **185–87**

    Basic Dark Vegetable Broth, 45, **50–51**

    Christmas Eve Porcini Soup, 23, 43, 218, 220–21, **222–23,** 224

    Green Soup with Mushrooms, **92–93**

    Mushroom-Barley Soup with Cabbage, **162–63**

    Mushroom Stock, 46, **56–57, 224–25**

    Old-Fashioned Cream of Mushroom Soup, **76–77**

    Pickle Soup, 20, 26, **185–87**

    Springtime Barley and Mushroom Soup, 256–57, **258–59**

Mushroom-Barley Soup with Cabbage, **162–63**

Mushroom Pizza, **404**

Mushroom Stock, 46, **56–57, 224–25**

    holiday soup using, 222–23

mustard greens

    Tomatillo, Squash, and Mustard Greens Soup, **122–23**

Napa cabbage

    Beet Soup with Ginger, 218, **226–27**

    Brown Rice and Chinese Cabbage Salad, **477–78**

Napa Cabbage Slaw, **481–82**

nectarines

    Cold Peach and Nectarine Soup with Strawberry Sauce, **381–82**

Neeps and Tatties Soup, 49, **172–73**

nettle(s)

    about, 241, 282

    handling, 282–83

Nettle and Kale Soup, **284–85**

Nettle Soup with Fennel and Leeks, 25, **285–86**

nuts. *See also* chestnuts; peanut butter; pecans; pine nuts; walnuts

    Jeri's Spiced Nuts, 221–22, **448–49,** 462

oat(s)

    Farmhouse Apple Crumble, **499–500**

    Lauren's Badass Trailmix Cookies, 487, **495–96**

    Multigrain Scones with Fennel and Orange, **411–12**

    Oatmeal Molasses Bread, 138–39, 337, **394–96**

    Quick Whole-Wheat Oatmeal Bread, **408**

Oatmeal Molasses Bread, **394–96**
    menu using, 138–39
Octavia's Gingerbread, 486, **490–91**
    menu using, 109–10
Old-Fashioned Cream of Mushroom Soup, **76–77**
Old-Fashioned Split Pea Soup, 23, **145–46**
olive(s)
    Barley Salad with Corn and Zucchini, **464–65**
    Hummus with Olives, 427
    Kale Salad with Cranberries and Walnuts, **473–74**
    Marbled Cannellini Dip with Roasted Tomatoes, 220–21,
        431–32
    Olive and Rosemary Focaccia, 128–29, 318–19, **400–401**
    Potato Pizza, 277, **402–4**
    Tapenade with Figs and Citrus, 220–21, 298–99, **428**
Olive and Rosemary Focaccia, **400–401**
    menus using, 128–29, 318–19
Olive Oil and Lemon Cake, 487, **492–93**
    menu using, 220–21
omelet
    Tortilla Española with Charred Red Peppers, 364–65,
        422, **454–55**
onions. *See also* green onions
    Basic Dark Vegetable Broth, 45, **50–51**
    Basic Light Vegetable Broth, **47–48**
    Basic Root Vegetable Broth, 45, **49**
    Butter Bean and Summer Vegetable Soup, 298–99,
        300–301
    Cannellini and Golden Tomato Soup, **324–25**
    Carrot, Orange, and Ginger Soup, 53, **254–55**
    Charred Zucchini Soup with Yogurt and Pine Nuts,
        315–17
    Christmas Eve Porcini Soup, 23, 43, 218, 220–21,
        222–23, 224
    Corn and Pepper Soup, **343–44**
    Escarole and Potato Soup, **307–8**
    Farro with Stewed and Roasted Winter Vegetables, 178,
        206–9
    Fennel and Onion Soup, 49, **68–69**
    French Lentil Stew with Roasted Carrots and Mint,
        196–97, **198–99**
    Green Soup with Broccoli, Fennel, and Sorrel, **290–91**
    Green Soup with Mushrooms, **92–93**
    Green Soup with Sweet Potatoes and Sage, **94–95**

Kabocha Squash and Cranberry Bean Stew, 178, **203–5**
Mushroom-Barley Soup with Cabbage, **162–63**
Nettle and Kale Soup, **284–85**
Old-Fashioned Cream of Mushroom Soup, **76–77**
Persimmon Soup with Tamari-Toasted Walnuts, 25, 219,
    228–30
Potato and Tomato Soup with Sage, 64–65, **66–67**
Potato Pizza, 277, **402–4**
Red Lentil and Squash Soup, 52, **118–19**
Roasted Eggplant and Garbanzo Bean Soup, **355–57**
Roasted Golden Beet Soup, **74–75**
Roasted Poblano Chile Soup, **70–71**
Roasted Root Vegetable Soup, 25, **166–68**
Sara's Spinach Pie, 422, **452–53**
Smoky Eggplant Soup with Mint and Pine Nuts, **304–6**
Sopa de Poblanos, **70–71**
Sorrel Soup with Mint and Spring Vegetables, 244, **247–
    48,** 277
Spicy Butternut Ginger Soup, 24, 30, 52, **114–15**
Spicy Indonesian Yam and Peanut Soup, **164–65**
Stewed Root Vegetables with Moroccan Spices, 179,
    200–202
Sweet Corn Soup, 26, **302–3**
Sweet Potato Bisque, 218, **231–32**
Ten-Vegetable Soup with Cranberry Beans, **190–92**
Three-Bean and Vegetable Chili, 178, **212–15**
Tomatillo, Squash, and Mustard Greens Soup, **122–23**
Tomato and Zucchini Soup with Summer Herbs,
    326–27
Tortilla Española with Charred Red Peppers, 364–65,
    422, **454–55**
Vegetable Soup Pistou, 332, **352–54**
Vegetarian Onion Soup Gratin, 50, **160–61**
Winter Squash and Yam Soup with Poblano Peppers, 43,
    120–21
Zucchini and Basil Soup, 25, 309–10, **311–12**
Zucchini and Potato Soup, **313–14**
Orange and Mint Syrup, 503, **504**
    menu using, 243–44
oranges/orange juice
    Carrot, Orange, and Ginger Soup, 53, **254–55**
    Irish Soda Bread with Fennel and Orange, 256–57, **405–6**
    Melons in Orange and Mint Syrup, 298–99, **503**
    Multigrain Scones with Fennel and Orange, **411–12**

oranges/orange juice (*continued*)

  Orange and Mint Syrup, 243–44, 503, **504**

  Puree of Carrot and Yam with Citrus and Spices, 52, **78–79**

  Tomato and Fennel Soup with Blood Orange, **322–23**

panella cheese

  Tortilla Soup, 332, **338–40**

Pappa al Pomodoro, **328–29**

Parmesan and Fennel Biscotti, **418–19**

  menu using, 220–21

Parmesan cheese

  Heirloom Tomato Salad, 309–10, 334–35, **471–72**

  Parmesan and Fennel Biscotti, 220–21, **418–19**

  Parmesan Crostini, 81, **417**

  Sara's Spinach Pie, 422, **452–53**

  Summer Minestrone, 332, **358–59**

Parmesan Crostini, 81, **417**

Parmigiano-Reggiano cheese. *See* Parmesan cheese

parsley

  Basic Dark Vegetable Broth, 45, **50–51**

  Cannellini and Golden Tomato Soup, **324–25**

  Chopped Salad with French Green Lentils, 64–65, **466–67**

  Cucumber, Rice, and Fresh Herb Salad, 347–49, **468–69**

  Deconstructed Hummus Soup, 26, 347–49, **350–51**

  Farro with Stewed and Roasted Winter Vegetables, 178, **206–9**

  The Great Pumpkin Soup, 180–81, **182–84**

  Hearty Brown Lentil Soup, **188–89**

  Kale and Tomato Soup, **345–46**

  Lentil and Spinach Salad, **479–80**

  Minestrone for a Crowd, **193–95**

  Mushroom-Barley Soup with Cabbage, **162–63**

  Mushroom Stock, 46, **56–57, 224–25**

  Parsley and Walnut Pesto, **438**

  Parsley Soup, **102–3**

  Summer Minestrone, 332, **358–59**

  Ten-Vegetable Soup with Cranberry Beans, **190–92**

  Vegetable and Ginger Broth, 45, **52**

  Vegetable Broth with No Onions, 45, **53–54**

  Vegetable Soup Pistou, 332, **352–54**

  Zucchini and Potato Soup, **313–14**

Parsley and Walnut Pesto, **438**

Parsley Soup, **102–3**

parsnips

  Basic Dark Vegetable Broth, 45, **50–51**

  Basic Light Vegetable Broth, **47–48**

  Basic Root Vegetable Broth, 45, **49**

  Beet Soup with Ginger, 218, **226–27**

  Chestnut Soup, 218, **233–34**

  Farro with Stewed and Roasted Winter Vegetables, 178, **206–9**

  Mushroom Stock, 46, **56–57, 224–25**

  Persimmon Soup with Tamari-Toasted Walnuts, 25, 219, **228–30**

  Puree of Carrot and Yam with Citrus and Spices, 52, **78–79**

  Spicy Indonesian Yam and Peanut Soup, **164–65**

  Stewed Root Vegetables with Moroccan Spices, 179, **200–202**

  Vegetable and Ginger Broth, 45, **52**

  Vegetable Broth with No Onions, 45, **53–54**

pasta

  reheating soup with, 321

  in Ten-Vegetable Soup with Cranberry Beans, 192

pea(s). *See* dried split peas; green peas; shelling peas; sugar snap peas

peaches

  Cold Peach and Nectarine Soup with Strawberry Sauce, **381–82**

peanut butter

  Spicy Indonesian Yam and Peanut Soup, **164–65**

pea pod(s)

  Fresh Pea Soup with Mint Cream, 26, 43, **249–51**

Pea Pod Broth, 46, **55**

  cold soups using, 371–72

  green soups using, 278–79, 280–81

  spring soups using, 245–46, 258–59, 260–61

pears

  Salad of Baby Arugula, Aged Jack Cheese, and Asian Pears, 220–21, **462–63**

pecans

  Jeri's Spiced Nuts, 221–22, **448–49,** 462

peppers. *See* bell peppers; chiles; pimiento peppers

Persian Spinach Spread, 181, **429–30**

persimmons
    in Napa Cabbage Slaw, **482**
Persimmon Soup with Tamari-Toasted Walnuts, 25, 219,
    228–30
pesto
    Eggplant and Roasted Garlic Pesto, **434–35**
    Parsley and Walnut Pesto, **438**
pickle(s). *See* dill pickles
Pickle Soup, 20, 26, **185–87**
pimiento peppers
    Minestrone for a Crowd, **193–95**
pine nuts
    Charred Zucchini Soup with Yogurt and Pine Nuts,
        315–17
    Napa Cabbage Slaw, **481–82**
    Parmesan and Fennel Biscotti, 220–21, **418–19**
    Smoky Eggplant Soup with Mint and Pine Nuts, **304–6**
    toasting, 232
    Vegetable Soup Pistou, 332, **352–54**
pinto beans
    Three-Bean and Vegetable Chili, 178, **212–15**
pizza
    Greek Pizza, **404**
    Green Pizza, **404**
    Mushroom Pizza, **404**
    Potato Pizza, 277, **402–4**
Popovers, **409–10**
    menu using, 276–77
Potage of Baby Spring Greens, 274, **288–89**
potato(es)
    Arugula and Apple Soup with Toasted Walnuts, **98–99**
    Barley, Mushroom, and Vegetable Soup, 20, 26, **185–87**
    Basic Root Vegetable Broth, 45, **49**
    Corn and Cheese Chowder, 332, 334–35, **336–37**
    Corn and Pepper Soup, **343–44**
    Creamy Artichoke Soup, **266–68**
    Creamy Potato and Roasted Garlic Soup, **80–82**
    Curried Spinach and Sorrel Soup, **269–70**
    Escarole and Potato Soup, **307–8**
    Farro with Stewed and Roasted Winter Vegetables, 178,
        206–9
    The Great Pumpkin Soup, 180–81, **182–84**
    Green Soup, 19, 20, 22, 30, **90–91**
    Hearty Brown Lentil Soup, **188–89**

Kale and Sweet Potato Soup with Cumin and Lemon, 52,
    100–101
Kale and Tomato Soup, **345–46**
Neeps and Tatties Soup, 49, **172–73**
Nettle and Kale Soup, **284–85**
Parsley Soup, **102–3**
Pickle Soup, 20, 26, **185–87**
Potage of Baby Spring Greens, 274, **288–89**
Potato and Tomato Soup with Sage, 64–65, **66–67**
Potato Pizza, 277, **402–4**
Purple Cauliflower Soup, **252–53**
Quinoa Stew with Potatoes, Spinach, and Chard, **210–11**
Roasted Golden Beet Soup, **74–75**
Roasted Turnip and Winter Squash Soup, **116–17**
Rustic Artichoke and Potato Stew, **262–65**
Rustic Leek and Potato Soup, **158–59**
Spicy Butternut Ginger Soup, 24, 30, 52, **114–15**
Spring Green Soup, 53, 274, 276–77, **278–79,** 423
Stewed Root Vegetables with Moroccan Spices, 179,
    200–202
Ten-Vegetable Soup with Cranberry Beans, **190–92**
Tortilla Española with Charred Red Peppers, 364–65,
    422, **454–55**
Turnip and Potato Soup, **172–73**
Vegetable Broth with No Onions, 45, **53–54**
Zucchini and Potato Soup, **313–14**
Potato and Tomato Soup with Sage, **66–67**
    menu using, 64–65
Potato Pizza, 277, **402–4**
provolone cheese
    Potato Pizza, 277, **402–4**
pudding
    Rice Pudding with Dried Cranberries, **501**
pumpkin
    The Great Pumpkin Soup, 180–81, **182–84**
Puree of Carrot and Yam with Citrus and Spices, 52,
    78–79
Purple Cauliflower Soup, **252–53**

quesadillas
    Black Bean Quesadillas, **456–57**
queso fresco
    Black Bean Quesadillas, **456–57**
    Potato Pizza, 277, **402–4**

quiche
    Sara's Spinach Pie, 422, **452–53**
quick breads, 389
Quick Whole-Wheat Oatmeal Bread, **408**
quinoa
    Kabocha Squash and Cranberry Bean Stew, 178, **203–5**
Quinoa Stew with Potatoes, Spinach, and Chard, **210–11**

raisins
    Lauren's Badass Trailmix Cookies, 487, **495–96**
    Lentil and Spinach Salad, **479–80**
    Multigrain Scones with Fennel and Orange, **411–12**
    Napa Cabbage Slaw, **481–82**
    Stewed Root Vegetables with Moroccan Spices, 179,
        200–202
Red Cabbage and Apple Salad, 181, **476**
    menu using, 138–39
Red Lentil and Squash Soup, 52, **118–19**
reheating soup with pasta, 321
rice
    Brown Rice and Chinese Cabbage Salad, **477–78**
    Cucumber, Rice, and Fresh Herb Salad, 347–49, **468–69**
Rice Pudding with Dried Cranberries, **501**
ricotta cheese
    Heirloom Tomato Salad, 309–10, 334–35, **471–72**
    Sara's Spinach Pie, 422, **452–53**
Roasted Eggplant and Garbanzo Bean Soup, **355–57**
Roasted Golden Beet Soup, **74–75**
Roasted Kabocha Squash and Celery Root Soup, 24, **111–13**
    menu using, 109–10
Roasted Poblano Chile Soup, **70–71**
Roasted Root Vegetable Soup, 25, **166–68**
Roasted Turnip and Winter Squash Soup, **116–17**
roasting
    chestnuts, 234
    vegetables, 167, 209
rolls
    Grandma's Dinner Rolls, **397–99**
root vegetables. *See also specific vegetables*
    about, 63, 242
rosemary
    Olive and Rosemary Focaccia, 128–29, 318–19, **400–401**
    Pappa al Pomodoro, **328–29**
Rustic Artichoke and Potato Stew, **262–65**

Rustic Leek and Potato Soup, **158–59**
rutabagas
    Basic Root Vegetable Broth, 45, **49**
    Roasted Root Vegetable Soup, 25, **166–68**

sage
    Cannellini and Golden Tomato Soup, **324–25**
    Corn and Cheese Chowder, 332, 334–35, **336–37**
    Green Soup with Sweet Potatoes and Sage, **94–95**
    Potato and Tomato Soup with Sage, 64–65, **66–67**
    Vegetable Soup Pistou, 332, **352–54**
salad(s), 459–83
    Barley Salad with Corn and Zucchini, **464–65**
    Brown Rice and Chinese Cabbage Salad, **477–78**
    Chopped Salad with French Green Lentils, 64–65,
        466–67
    Cucumber, Rice, and Fresh Herb Salad, 347–49, **468–69**
    Heirloom Tomato Salad, 309–10, 334–35, **471–72**
    Kale Salad with Cranberries and Walnuts, **473–74**
    Kale Salad with Roasted Kabocha, **474**
    Kale Salad with Tomatoes and Corn, **475**
    Lentil and Spinach Salad, **479–80**
    Napa Cabbage Slaw, **481–82**
    Red Cabbage and Apple Salad, 138–39, 181, **476**
    Salad of Baby Arugula, Aged Jack Cheese, and Asian
        Pears, 220–21, **462–63**
    Summer Chopped Salad with Grilled Halloumi, **470**
Salad of Baby Arugula, Aged Jack Cheese, and Asian Pears,
    462–63
    menu using, 220–21
sandwich
    Grilled Goat Cheese Sandwich, 243–44, **450–51**
Sara's Spinach Pie, 422, **452–53**
sauces
    Harissa, 196–97, 198, 210, **444–45**
    Simple Chipotle Sauce, 72, 117, 180–81, 183, 198, **439,** 456
    Table Salsa, 188, 210, **442–43,** 456
sauté pans, 34
Savory Walnut and Herb Biscuits, **413–14**
savoy cabbage
    Barley, Mushroom, and Vegetable Soup, 20, 26, **185–87**
    Mushroom-Barley Soup with Cabbage, **162–63**
    Pickle Soup, 20, 26, **185–87**
scales, 34

scallions. *See* green onions
shallots
    Chestnut Soup, 218, **233–34**
shelling peas
    about, 240
    Fresh Fava Bean and Sweet Pea Soup, **260–61,** 277
shopping for ingredients. *See* farmers' markets
Simple Basil Pesto, 191, 345, **436–37**
    menu using, 334–35
Simple Chipotle Sauce, 72, 117, 180–81, 183, 198, **439,** 456
    menu using, 180–81
skillets, 34
Smoky Eggplant Soup with Mint and Pine Nuts, **304–6**
Snap Pea, Asparagus, and Fennel Soup with Fresh Herbs,
    274, **280–81**
soaking dried beans, 127
Sopa de Ajo, 49, **156–57**
    menu using, 154–55
Sopa de Poblanos, **70–71**
sorrel
    Curried Spinach and Sorrel Soup, **269–70**
    Green Soup with Broccoli, Fennel, and Sorrel, **290–91**
Sorrel Soup with Mint and Spring Vegetables, 244, **247–48,**
    277
soup pots, 33
sour cream
    Cold Cherry-Lemon Soup, 297, 363, **377–78**
soymilk/soy creamer in soups, 268
soy sauce
    Tamari-Toasted Walnuts, 228, **230**
spice grinders, 35
Spicy Black Bean Soup with Sweet Peppers, 43, **142–44**
Spicy Butternut Ginger Soup, 24, 30, 52, **114–15**
Spicy Indonesian Yam and Peanut Soup, **164–65**
Spicy Paprika Hummus, **426**
spinach
    about, 52
    Butter Bean and Summer Vegetable Soup, 298–99,
        300–301
    Creamy Artichoke Soup, **266–68**
    Curried Spinach and Sorrel Soup, **269–70**
    Fasolia Gigante Soup with Spinach, **132–33**
    Green Soup, 19, 20, 22, 30, **90–91**
    Green Soup with Ginger, 52, **96–97**

Green Soup with Mushrooms, **92–93**
Kabocha Squash and Cranberry Bean Stew, 178, **203–5**
Lentil and Spinach Salad, **479–80**
Mung Bean Soup with Spinach and Tomatoes, 332,
    341–42
Persian Spinach Spread, 181, **429–30**
Potage of Baby Spring Greens, 274, **288–89**
Quinoa Stew with Potatoes, Spinach, and Chard, **210–11**
Sara's Spinach Pie, 422, **452–53**
Snap Pea, Asparagus, and Fennel Soup with Fresh Herbs,
    274, **280–81**
Sorrel Soup with Mint and Spring Vegetables, 244,
    247–48, 277
Spring Green Soup, 53, 274, 276–77, **278–79,** 423
Vegetable Soup Pistou, 332, **352–54**
split peas. *See* dried split peas
spoons, 34
spreads
    Eggplant and Roasted Garlic Pesto, **434–35**
    Lima Bean Spread, **433**
    Parsley and Walnut Pesto, **438**
    Persian Spinach Spread, 181, **429–30**
    Simple Basil Pesto, 191, 334–35, 345, **436–37**
    Tapenade with Figs and Citrus, 220–21, 298–99, **428**
Spring Green Soup, 53, 274, **278–79,** 423
    menu using, 276–77
Springtime Barley and Mushroom Soup, **258–59**
    menu using, 256–57
Sprouted Garbanzo Hummus, **425–27**
    menu using, 88–89
squash. *See* butternut squash; kabocha squash; summer
    squash; zucchini
stew(s)
    Farro with Stewed and Roasted Winter Vegetables, 178,
        206–9
    French Lentil Stew with Roasted Carrots and Mint,
        196–97, **198–99**
    Kabocha Squash and Cranberry Bean Stew, 178, **203–5**
    Quinoa Stew with Potatoes, Spinach, and Chard,
        210–11
    Rustic Artichoke and Potato Stew, **262–65**
Stewed Root Vegetables with Moroccan Spices, 179,
    200–202
stewing vegetables, 207–8

stock
    Mushroom Stock, 46, **56–57,** 222–23, **224–25**
stock pots, 33
strawberries
    Cold Peach and Nectarine Soup with Strawberry Sauce, **381–82**
    Tangerine and Strawberry Compote, 276–77, **505**
sugar snap peas
    about, 240
    Napa Cabbage Slaw, **481–82**
    Snap Pea, Asparagus, and Fennel Soup with Fresh Herbs, 274, **280–81**
Summer Chopped Salad with Grilled Halloumi, **470**
Summer Minestrone, 332, **358–59**
summer squash. *See also* zucchini
    Butter Bean and Summer Vegetable Soup, 298–99, **300–301**
    Tortilla Soup, 332, **338–40**
Summer Tomato and Basil Soup, 23, **320–21**
    menu using, 318–19
sweet(s), 485–505
    Angel Cookies, 364–65, **494**
    Bittersweet Chocolate Brownies, **497–98**
    Butter Cake with Summer Fruits, 318–19, 486, **488–89**
    Farmhouse Apple Crumble, **499–500**
    Greek Yogurt with Honey and Walnuts, 138–39, **502**
    Lauren's Badass Trailmix Cookies, 487, **495–96**
    Melons in Orange and Mint Syrup, 298–99, **503**
    Octavia's Gingerbread, 109–10, 486, **490–91**
    Olive Oil and Lemon Cake, 220–21, 487, **492–93**
    Rice Pudding with Dried Cranberries, **501**
    Tangerine and Strawberry Compote, 276–77, **505**
Sweet Corn Soup, 26, **302–3**
sweet potato(es)
    Creamy Potato and Roasted Garlic Soup, **80–82**
    Green Lentil Soup with Cumin and Lemon, **134–35**
    Green Soup with Ginger, 52, **96–97**
    Green Soup with Sweet Potatoes and Sage, **94–95**
    Kale and Sweet Potato Soup with Cumin and Lemon, 52, **100–101**
    Quinoa Stew with Potatoes, Spinach, and Chard, **210–11**
    Red Lentil and Squash Soup, 52, **118–19**
Sweet Potato Bisque, 218, **231–32**
syrups
    Orange and Mint Syrup, 243–44, 503, **504**

Table Salsa, 188, 210, **442–43,** 456
tahini
    Sprouted Garbanzo Hummus, **425–27**
Tahitian squash
    Roasted Turnip and Winter Squash Soup, **116–17**
    Spicy Butternut Ginger Soup, 24, 30, 52, **114–15**
    Tomatillo, Squash, and Mustard Greens Soup, **122–23**
Tamari-Toasted Walnuts, 228, **230**
Tangerine and Strawberry Compote, **505**
    menu using, 276–77
Tapenade with Figs and Citrus, **428**
    menus using, 220–21, 298–99
tarragon
    Savory Walnut and Herb Biscuits, **413–14**
Ten-Vegetable Soup with Cranberry Beans, **190–92**
Three-Bean and Vegetable Chili, 178, **212–15**
Three-Grain Bread, **390–91**
    menu using, 88–89
thyme
    Olive and Rosemary Focaccia, 128–29, 318–19, **400–401**
toasting pine nuts, 232
tomatillo(s)
    Kabocha Squash and Cranberry Bean Stew, 178, **203–5**
    Stewed Root Vegetables with Moroccan Spices, 179, **200–202**
    Table Salsa, 188, 210, **442–43,** 456
Tomatillo, Squash, and Mustard Greens Soup, **122–23**
tomato(es)
    Barley Salad with Corn and Zucchini, **464–65**
    Butter Bean and Summer Vegetable Soup, 298–99, **300–301**
    Cannellini and Golden Tomato Soup, **324–25**
    Fasolia Gigante Soup with Spinach, **132–33**
    Gazpacho Andaluz, 362–63, 364–65, **366–67**
    Grilled Goat Cheese Sandwich, 243–44, **450–51**
    heirloom, about, 471
    Heirloom Tomato Salad, 309–10, 334–35, **471–72**
    Kale and Tomato Soup, **345–46**
    Kale Salad with Tomatoes and Corn, **475**
    Marbled Cannellini Dip with Roasted Tomatoes, 220–21, **431–32**
    Minestrone for a Crowd, **193–95**
    Mung Bean Soup with Spinach and Tomatoes, 332, **341–42**
    Pappa al Pomodoro, **328–29**

Potato and Tomato Soup with Sage, 64–65, **66–67**
Roasted Eggplant and Garbanzo Bean Soup, **355–57**
Simple Chipotle Sauce, 72, 117, 180–81, 183, 198, **439,** 456
Stewed Root Vegetables with Moroccan Spices, 179, **200–202**
Summer Chopped Salad with Grilled Halloumi, **470**
Summer Minestrone, 332, **358–59**
Summer Tomato and Basil Soup, 23, 318–19, **320–21**
Ten-Vegetable Soup with Cranberry Beans, **190–92**
Three-Bean and Vegetable Chili, 178, **212–15**
Tomato and Fennel Soup with Blood Orange, **322–23**
Tomato and Zucchini Soup with Summer Herbs, **326–27**
Tortilla Soup, 332, **338–40**
Vegetable Soup Pistou, 332, **352–54**
Tomato and Fennel Soup with Blood Orange, **322–23**
Tomato and Zucchini Soup with Summer Herbs, **326–27**
Tortilla Española with Charred Red Peppers, 422, **454–55**
menu using, 364–65
tortillas
Black Bean Quesadillas, **456–57**
Tortilla Soup, 332, **338–40**
turnip(s)
Barley, Mushroom, and Vegetable Soup, 20, 26, **185–87**
Basic Dark Vegetable Broth, 45, **50–51**
Basic Root Vegetable Broth, 45, **49**
Farro with Stewed and Roasted Winter Vegetables, 178, **206–9**
Mushroom Stock, 46, **56–57, 224–25**
Neeps and Tatties Soup, 49, **172–73**
Persimmon Soup with Tamari-Toasted Walnuts, 25, 219, **228–30**
Pickle Soup, 20, 26, **185–87**
Purple Cauliflower Soup, **252–53**
Roasted Kabocha Squash and Celery Root Soup, 24, 109–10, **111–13**
Roasted Root Vegetable Soup, 25, **166–68**
Roasted Turnip and Winter Squash Soup, **116–17**
Stewed Root Vegetables with Moroccan Spices, 179, **200–202**
Ten-Vegetable Soup with Cranberry Beans, **190–92**
Turnip and Potato Soup, **172–73**
Vegetable Broth with No Onions, 45, **53–54**
Turnip and Potato Soup, **172–73**
turnip greens
Potage of Baby Spring Greens, 274, **288–89**

vegan dishes, adapting recipes for, 38–39
Vegetable and Ginger Broth, 45, **52**
fall soups using, 78–79
green soups using, 96–97, 100–101
in holiday soups, 226–27, 228–30
spring soups using, 254–55
summer soups using, 341–42
winter soups using, 164–65
winter squash soups using, 114–15, 118–19
Vegetable Broth with No Onions, 45, **53–54**
fall soups using, 80–82
green soups using, 278–79
spring soups using, 245–46, 254–55
Vegetable Soup Pistou, 332, **352–54**
Vegetarian Onion Soup Gratin, 50, **160–61**

walnuts
Arugula and Apple Soup with Toasted Walnuts, **98–99**
Chopped Salad with French Green Lentils, 64–65, **466–67**
Cucumber, Rice, and Fresh Herb Salad, 347–49, **468–69**
Greek Yogurt with Honey and Walnuts, 138–39, **502**
Kale Salad with Cranberries and Walnuts, **473–74**
Lauren's Badass Trailmix Cookies, 487, **495–96**
Multigrain Scones with Fennel and Orange, **411–12**
Parsley and Walnut Pesto, **438**
Savory Walnut and Herb Biscuits, **413–14**
Tamari-Toasted Walnuts, 228, **230**
Whole-Wheat Walnut Bread, 109–10, 309–10, **392–93**
water
for cooking dried beans, 127
for soups, 37
watercress
Cold Cucumber and Avocado Soup, **369–70**
in Curried Spinach and Sorrel Soup, 271
white bean(s)
Cannellini and Golden Tomato Soup, **324–25**
Fasolia Gigante Soup with Spinach, **132–33**
The Great Pumpkin Soup, 180–81, **182–84**
in Kale and Tomato Soup, 346
Vegetable Soup Pistou, 332, **352–54**
White Bean and Garlic Soup with Greens, 26, **130–31**
menu using, 128–29
white farmer cheese
Potato Pizza, 277, **402–4**

white wine
 Chilled Melon Soup with Mint, **379–80**
 Cold Cherry-Lemon Soup, 297, 363, **377–78**
Whole-Wheat Walnut Bread, 109–10, **392–93**
 menu using, 309–10
wine. *See* white wine
winter squash. *See also* butternut squash; kabocha squash
 about, 63
Winter Squash and Yam Soup with Poblano Peppers, 43,
 120–21

yams
 Chard and Yam Soup, 49, **72–73**
 Green Soup with Broccoli, Fennel, and Sorrel, **290–91**
 Puree of Carrot and Yam with Citrus and Spices, 52,
 78–79
 Red Lentil and Squash Soup, 52, **118–19**
 Roasted Root Vegetable Soup, 25, **166–68**
 Spicy Indonesian Yam and Peanut Soup, **164–65**
 Sweet Potato Bisque, 218, **231–32**
 Winter Squash and Yam Soup with Poblano Peppers, 43,
 120–21
yellow squash. *See* summer squash
yogurt
 Charred Zucchini Soup with Yogurt and Pine Nuts,
 315–17
 Cold Cream of Poblano Peppers with Red Grapes, 362,
 375–76

Cold Cucumber and Mint Soup with Radishes, **373–74**
Cold Cucumber-Cilantro Soup with Goat Yogurt, **368**
Cold Peach and Nectarine Soup with Strawberry Sauce,
 381–82
Cucumber, Rice, and Fresh Herb Salad, 347–49, **468–69**
drained, 317
Drained Yogurt, **317**
Greek Yogurt with Honey and Walnuts, 138–39, **502**
Persian Spinach Spread, 181, **429–30**
Smoky Eggplant Soup with Mint and Pine Nuts, **304–6**
yogurt cheese
 Cold Cherry-Lemon Soup, 297, 363, **377–78**
 making, 317

zucchini
 Barley Salad with Corn and Zucchini, **464–65**
 Charred Zucchini Soup with Yogurt and Pine Nuts,
 315–17
 Minestrone for a Crowd, **193–95**
 Spring Green Soup, 53, 274, 276–77, **278–79**
 Summer Minestrone, 332, **358–59**
 Tomato and Zucchini Soup with Summer Herbs, **326–27**
 Vegetable Soup Pistou, 332, **352–54**
 Zucchini and Basil Soup, 25, 309–10, **311–12**
 Zucchini and Potato Soup, **313–14**
Zucchini and Basil Soup, 25, **311–12**
 menu using, 309–10
Zucchini and Potato Soup, **313–14**